Culture and the Senses

ETHNOGRAPHIC STUDIES IN SUBJECTIVITY

Tanya Luhrmann and Steven Parish, Editors

Culture and the Senses

Bodily Ways of Knowing
in an African Community

Kathryn Linn Geurts

UNIVERSITY OF CALIFORNIA PRESS
Berkeley · *Los Angeles* · *London*

Photographs © 2002 by James E. O'Neal.
Any correspondence regarding the photographs
should be addressed, via the author, to
James E. O'Neal.

Portions of chapters 3 and 4 have previously appeared
in *Ethos: Journal of the Society for Psychological
Anthropology* 30(3).

University of California Press
Berkeley and Los Angeles, California

University of California Press, Ltd.
London, England

Library of Congress Cataloging-in-Publication Data

Geurts, Kathryn Linn, 1960–
   Culture and the senses : bodily ways of knowing in
an African community / Kathryn Linn Geurts.
      p.   cm. (Ethographic studies in subjectivity ; 3)
   Includes bibliographical references and index.
   ISBN 0-520-23455-3(cloth : alk. paper)—
ISBN 0-520-23456-1 (paper : alk. paper)
      1. Anlo (African people)—Psychology.   2. Anlo
(African people)—Socialization.   3. Senses and sensa-
tion—Cross-cultural studies.   I. Title.   II. Series.

DT510.43.A58 G48   2002
155.8′4963374—dc21   2002022585

Manufactured in the United States of America

10   09   08   07   06   05   04   03   02

10   9   8   7   6   5   4   3   2   1

The paper used in this publication meets the minimum
requirements of ANSI/NISO Z39.48-1992(R 1997)
(*Permanence of Paper*). ⊚

*For my husband, James O'Neal,
and our daughter,
Mali Malzetta O'Neal*

Contents

Acknowledgments

Culture and the Senses would not have been possible without the support of a vast network of people in both Ghana and the United States. I would like to thank Matthew Tsikata for tutoring me as I struggled to learn to hear the Anlo-Ewe language and for opening the door to his family, who so graciously assisted my husband and me while we sojourned in Ghana. We are particularly indebted to Victor and Vivian Tsikata. The infrastructural support that Victor provided greatly surpassed anything we had expected when we set off for Ghana; his generosity and trust were overwhelming. Fui and Innocentia Tsikata were very cordial hosts whenever we had occasion to be at the university. Other family members who supported and assisted us in many ways include Wisdom Tsikata and his family; Paulina Dsani Tsikata; Maggie and David Tsikata and their children, especially Florence; Paul Tsikata; Richard Tsikata, his wife, Lena, and their son, Roger; Richard Tsikata the engineer and Richard Tsikata the social scientist, as well as Dona and other members of the Vickata accounting team, and our downstairs neighbor, Mr. Tamakloe.

In Kokomlemle our life was made comfortable and safe with the additional help of Ema Afortudey, his wife, Gladys, and their children, Richmond and Kathryn; Ernest Kobla Tsikata and Aaron Sabla helped in many practical ways and kept us in touch with what interests and concerns youth in Ghana; and Philippine provided my husband with a wonderful introduction to Ghanaian cuisine when he first arrived. My endless gratitude goes to Ema Nyatuame, who taught me so much and provided invaluable insights on Anlo history and culture.

In Osu, we always found Patrick and Fortune energetically ready to assist us in both practical and intellectual ways. At the United States Information Service, Michael and Jan Orlansky, plus Sarpei Nunoo, were incredibly warm and helpful.

In Togbui Tsikata's compound in Srɔgboe, we could not have weathered the daily struggle of rural life without the assistance of Do (Christiana Dartey) and her daughters, Bakhi (Rose Adikah) and Mawusi Baubasa, as well as Grandma (Kofobu Diaba). In addition, we received continual help from the late Kosi Tsikata, his wife, Doris, and their children, Mary, Raphael, Gameli, and Akpene; Edith Tsikata and her daughters, especially Esi; Kosiwo Nyage (now deceased); and Tengey David Atsu and his wife, Patience Enyonam, Rejoice, and her grandma, Gawome Tsikata. During his school break, Elvis Adikah provided welcome assistance as I conducted a census of Srɔgboe, and he has continued to assist me in many ways through his own research and his highly informative letters. We could not have stayed in Srɔgboe without the blessing of various chiefs—Togbui Akrorbortu Akpate, Togbui Kpatamia, and Togbui Tratu.

From Whuti to Kplowotokor, a network of midwives helped me to understand the obstacles to well-being faced by women and children in Anloland. Dali Alegba-Torkornu of Atokor was tireless in teaching me about birth, and Biawose Awudzu Sokpoli also sent for me at all hours when her clients went into labor. I also learned from Abla Zowonu and her husband, Logosu Sabah, as well as from Abla Happy Dunyoe, Adzovi Katahena, and Eyi Atipoh. Among the nurse-midwives who helped in my research, Victoria Togoh was extremely gracious and kind during my pilot study in 1992 and then again in 1993–1995, and was instrumental in introducing me to local birth attendants. Midwife Nancy Harley was an inspiration and arranged some very helpful interviews. Finally, Professor Patrick Twumasi so generously gave of his time and wisdom during the summer of 1992 and briefly in 1994 before he left for Zimbabwe.

In Anloga and Keta, I must thank Dzidzienyo, Reverend F. M. Lawuluvi, the deceased Togbui Adeladze, Queen Ame-Bruce, Charlotte Sabla, Victoria Amegashi, G. Kofi Afetorgbor, Kofi Geraldo, and Raphael Tamakloe. At the Tsikata house in Abutiakofe, I am indebted to Bertha, Suzie, and Emily, who provided a restful place during my hectic summer in 1992.

Edith Vuvor's support and friendship cannot be described. I treasure the times we have shared. In addition, the late Kofi (G. K. Agbe) Ayayee and Regina Abla Ekpatanyo Ayayee befriended and assisted my husband and me in ways we can never repay. It has been a privilege to know these three people. Professor Kofi Anyidoho and Professor G. K. Nukunya at Legon provided initial feedback and guidance on early stages of the research, for which I am grateful. Professor Nukunya's uncle, Mr. Kpodo, graciously gave of his time and deep wisdom before he passed away in 1994. My thanks also extend to those people in Ghana that I have neglected to mention.

Field research was funded by a Fulbright-Hays Doctoral Research Abroad Grant (#P022A30073) with supplementary assistance from the University of Pennsylvania Department of Anthropology, the Explorer's Club, and Sigma Xi Scientific Research Society. I gratefully acknowledge the support of these institutions.

Culture and the Senses was originally a dissertation project for the Department of Anthropology at the University of Pennsylvania. Sandra Barnes has been unflagging in her support and guidance since those early days when I approached her with a half-baked idea about using the senses as my lens for studying childbirth and medical practices in West Africa. Her course Contemporary Approaches to the Study of Culture and Society was a watershed in my graduate studies, laying the groundwork for many of the ideas explored in this book. Everyone deserves a teacher and mentor like Sandra Barnes. I also received encouragement at that stage, and invaluable pre-fieldwork advice, from Marina Roseman and Kris Hardin. Rebecca Huss-Ashmore deserves special thanks for her countless letters and ongoing support of my career.

John Lucy has been instrumental in my efforts to transform the dissertation into a book. He and Richard Shweder invited me to the University of Chicago for a postdoc, and for two years the Committee on Human Development served as a marvelous home for *Culture and the Senses*. Everyone should be so fortunate as to have John Lucy and Rick Shweder critique their work. The Culture, Life Course, and Mental Health Workshop stimulated rethinking and reworking of my material, and in particular I am grateful to my postdoc associates Ben Soares, Stanley Kurtz, and Rebecca Lester. A special thanks to all the HD students—those I had in class and those I did not—for many wonderful conversations and their support of my work. The African Studies Workshop at Chicago provided a second venue in which my project grew, and I am appreciative for the excellent feedback I received there.

Also in Chicago, members of the Ewe Association warmly welcomed us into their circle. Particularly remarkable in this respect were Kafui

Amegashi and his family, as well as George Dzikunoo, Cornelius Kushigbor, and Reverend Ben Quamson, his wife, and their church.

From Chicago we moved further west, and for nine months *Culture and the Senses* was nourished in the luxurious environment of the School of American Research in Santa Fe. I am ever grateful to the anonymous members of the selection committee (and to James Wilce, who revealed himself) for honoring me with their votes, and to Doug Schwartz for awarding me a residential grant. I hope that Nancy Owen-Lewis and all the staff at the School of American Research (SAR) know how deeply we appreciated their tireless efforts on our behalf. My colleagues at SAR—Rebecca Allahyari, James Brooks, Edsel Brown, Gary Gossen, Marnie Sandweiss, Mary Eunice Romero, and Ruth van Dyke—provided wonderful "billiard-house feedback" after my two presentations about the senses in Anlo-Ewe life. Santa Fe was all the more pleasant because of the hospitality of Vicki Davila and Ted Stanley.

I owe a great debt to the pioneering efforts of Constance Classen, Thomas Csordas, Robert Desjarlais, Steven Feld, David Howes, Emiko Ohnuki-Tierney, Marina Roseman, Anthony Seeger, Paul Stoller, Michael Taussig, and others, whose anthropologies attend so richly to sensory matters. I have received personal mentoring from some, while others have nurtured me through the evocative works they have produced. Many conversations, in fact, have influenced my intellectual world in the course of this project. These dialogs have been with people and with their works. But each exchange (however large or small) proved crucial in moving the project along. And so for the inspiration and support that I have derived, I am grateful to Roger Abrahams, Breid and Joseph Amamoo, Felix Ameka, Austin Amegashi, Kodzo (Nelson) Amegashi, Arjun Appadurai, Daniel Avorgbedor, Anne Bailey, Houston Baker, Michelle Bigenho, Phil Bock, Carol Breckenridge, T. David Brent, Karen McCarthy Brown, Brenda Chalfin, John Chernoff, Sheila Cosminsky, Robbie Davis-Floyd, Vivian Dzokoto, Steven Feierman, Farha Ghannam, Sandra Greene, Clare Ignatowski, Barbara Kirshenblatt-Gimblett, Shinobu Kitayama, Kristine Kray, Peshe Kuriloff, Elise Levin, Sabina Magliocco, Achille Mbembe, Margaret Meibohm, Sharon Nagy, Steven Piker, Naomi Quinn, Dan Rose, Judy Rosenthal, Peggy Sanday, Bradd Shore, Gil Stein, Amy Trubek, Peter (Atsu) Tsikata, and Tom Weisner.

Tanya Luhrmann infused a breath of fresh air into *Culture and the Senses* with her masterful editing, suggestions, and advice. Bob Desjarlais introduced me to Stan Holwitz and uttered the magical words that caused Stan's ears to perk up about my book. I am deeply grateful to all three for their efforts on my behalf.

Where I have not gone far or deep enough—in my ethnographic empathies, in my theoretical explanations, in my analysis of language and practices, and in my organization and textual renderings of Anlo (and occasionally Euro-American) ways of life—I hope that these shortcomings will not be judged to reflect on my teachers, mentors, or guides *(mɔfialawo)*. I alone am responsible for flaws and weaknesses present in the book.

At the University of California Press, there are a number of people to gratefully acknowledge for their various roles in ushering this project along: Marian McKenna Olivas, Laura Pasquale, Laura Driussi, Marilyn Schwartz, Diana Feinberg, Sarah Skaggs, and John Connolly. For copyediting and other essentials, I thank the team of people at Impressions Book and Journal Services.

To spend ten to twelve years researching and writing a philosophical and intellectual book requires a great deal of emotional, sensory, spiritual, and material support. For all of that and more, I would like to acknowledge the following individuals: Bob Griffin and Jeanne Gemmil Griffin, Arthur De Leo and Jennifer Nilssen, Bob and Rosina ("George") Bremner and the others at PMG, Jose Casillo, Kristina Klugar and Sasha, Isabel Rachlin, Barbara Rachlin, Elizabeth LaRoche Taylor, Lesley Rimmel, Joan White, Emily Houpt, Linda Lee, Harvey and Carol Finkle, James and Anita Dupree, John and Roseanne Dowell, John Grant and Louann Merkle, Anne O'Neill, Debbie Bintz, Nate Clark, Anne Jaso, J.T. Smith, Gonzalo Santos, Brian McNamara, Merry Pawlowski, and my dear friend, Vandana Kohli. And I would like to acknowledge the role that my siblings, parents, and in-laws played in preparing me for life in a huge extended family in West Africa. Many heartfelt thanks for the "ties that bind" to Don and Betty, Rick and Lynn, Dave and Paula, Mike and Jean, Janna and Polly, Steve and Becky, Mary, Kaari and Dave, Grandma Malzetta, Henny, Marcella, and Nate. My deepest gratitude goes to my husband, James O'Neal, for his companionship, love, and support, plus his devotion to our daughter during the hours that I taught and wrote during the past few years. His remarkable photographs are certain to become an invaluable part of the ethnographic record of Anlo-land. And finally, words cannot express the intense joy that I receive from Mali Malzetta Abla Amegashi O'Neal, who began honoring me with conversations about *seselelame* before she was three years old.

Note on Transliteration and Orthography

The following print symbols are used to represent the major Ewe letters that do not have an equivalent in English.

Symbol	Notes on Pronunciation
ɖ	Retroflex *d* or alveolar flap. Sounds like a Spanish *r*.
Đ	Capitalized retroflex *d* or alveolar flap.
ʤ	Close to the sound *j* in English.
ʤ	Capitalized ʤ.
ɛ	Nasalized *e*, pronounced as eh in bet, but with added nasalization.
ƒ	Bilabial *f* pronounced with both lips as if blowing out a candle.
ɣ	Fricative *g*. To produce this sound, make the air pass through a narrow passage formed by raising the back of the tongue toward the soft palate.
ŋ	The sound *ng* in English sing or singer.
Ŋ	Capitalized *ng*.
ɔ	Open vowel *o*, pronounced as *aw* or the *o* in cost.
ʋ	Corresponding voiced sound of the bilabial *f* previously listed. Sounds like a *v* in English pronounced with both lips.
x	A voiceless velar fricative, pronounced like a voiceless *h*.

Ewe has seven vowel phonemes, and nasalized vowels are very common. Not all of them have been represented in the transliteration. In addition, Ewe is a tonal language, and while a few contemporary English language texts have the tone marks incorporated in the transliteration (such as Agawu's [1995] work on northern Ewe music), it is more common for passages in Ewe not to contain tone marks (see Greene 1996, Meyer 1999, Rosenthal 1998). I have followed the latter convention. Ewe terms and phrases are generally italicized in the text, but proper nouns used frequently (such as Anlo, Anloga, Ewe, etc.) are not typically italicized, and for readability they are usually romanized as is conventional in English language publications about Anlo-Ewe.

Sources used in compiling this guide include Agawu (1995), Bureau of Ghana Languages (1986), Ladzekpo and Pantaleoni (1970), Locke (1978), Pantaleoni (1972b), and Warburton, Kpotufe and Glover (1968).

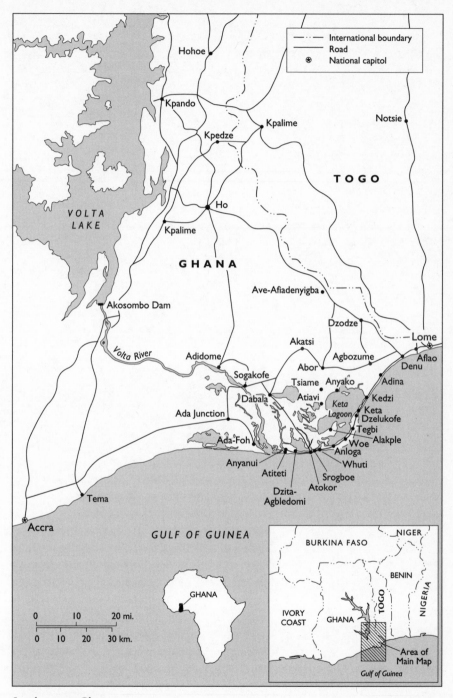

Southeastern Ghana

Cultural Construction of Sensoriums and Sensibilities

CHAPTER I

Is There a Sixth Sense?

In the West, we often treat the domain of <u>sensation</u> and <u>perception</u> as <u>definitively precultural and eminently natural</u>, one of the most basic of the human psychobiological systems. That is the approach in fields of neurology, biology, physiology, psychology, and even philosophy. Research in these disciplines usually compares human sensory perception to the sensory systems of other mammals or to the perceptory abilities of reptiles and birds (e.g., Schone 1984; Baker 1981; Lowenstein 1966).[1] Such research assumes that <u>all humans possess identical sensory capabilities and that any cultural differences we might find would be inconsequential.</u>[2] Perhaps, as a result, we have few ethnographies that document and compare the sensory orders of different societies.[3] The goal of this ethnography is to present a society where the senses are understood quite differently than in our own and, through this comparison, to illustrate that <u>our own approach is only a folk model</u>. Ultimately, this book will argue that *sensing*, which I will define for the moment as "<u>bodily ways of gathering information</u>," is profoundly involved with a society's epistemology, the development of its cultural identity, and its forms of being-in-the-world.[4]

In elementary schools in what we might call mainstream America, students learn (at the beginning of the twenty-first century) that hearing, touch, taste, smell, and sight are senses, but they do not learn to categorize *balance* as a sensation or a sense. Yet balance is clearly treated as a sense in contemporary textbooks from such disciplines as biology, psy-

3

chology, and medicine (e.g., Lowenstein 1966; Aronoff et al. 1970; Barlow and Mollon 1982). A sense of balance even has a corresponding
"organ"—the vestibular organ, or the labyrinth of the inner ear—as the
other five senses (seeing, hearing, touching, tasting, smelling) have theirs.
By the time American students are in college, knowledge of the senses
has not expanded much beyond what they learned in grade school. For
a number of years prior to writing this book, I conducted exercises with
my undergraduate classes, having them first name and describe the various human senses or sensory systems. Typically each group rattled off
the classic five, and then someone inevitably raised the prospect of there
being a sixth sense. By "sixth sense" did they mean balance? In my mind
that would be one possible and somewhat logical extension of our basic
taxonomy of five since we could point to the eye, ear, nose, tongue, skin,
and then the cochlea or the macula (in the inner ear) as the physical organs that form the basis of our classificatory system. However, by "sixth
sense" my students never meant balance. They almost always were referring to something called ESP (extrasensory perception)—some kind
of extrasensory ability that subsequent discussion usually condensed or
transformed into the term *intuition,* once again removing it from our
popular taxonomy of sensations.

By contrast, when I went to Anlo-land in West Africa, the home of
Anlo-Ewe-speaking people (pronounced *AHNG-low EH-vay*), several
individuals emphatically conveyed that—within their own cultural traditions—they were not aware of any clearly delineated taxonomy or system for the senses. Still, I consistently observed practices that signified
cultural valuation of certain subjective and bodily modes. For instance,
I often heard caregivers expressing to infants, *"Do agba! Do agba!"*
which was an imperative statement encouraging the babies to "Balance!
Balance!" They did this when infants were just beginning to hold up their
heads and sit up without support, but the attention to balance continued with toddlers and beyond. "Head-loading" (walking with items balanced on top of one's head) was a common practice among people of all
ages, especially women. Anlo-Ewe people considered balancing (in a
physical and psychological sense, as well as in literal and in metaphorical ways) to be an essential component of what it meant to be human.[5]

Anthropologist Thomas Csordas has suggested that "the answer to the
question of 'what it means to be human' is the same as the answer to the
question of 'how we make ourselves human'" (1994c:vii). How does balance figure into the ways in which we Euro-Americans make ourselves
human? What cultural value do we place on balance, and why does it not

quickly emerge in our ruminations about a possible sixth sense? Balance is clearly important to many Euro-Americans (being upright and balanced is preferable to being off balance and unable to stand [cf. Lakoff and Johnson 1999:291]), and balance undoubtedly forms the basis of moral metaphors that are widespread throughout the world since it is rooted in what is probably a basic human experience of well-being (Lakoff and Johnson 1999:311). But relatively speaking, Anlo-Ewe people seem to give it a discursive and practical priority that Euro-Americans do not. Most Anlo-Ewe people grow up being encouraged to actively balance; they learn to balance their own bodies as infants, they balance small bowls and pans on their heads as toddlers, they carry books and desks on their heads when walking to and from school, and they grow into an adult orientation in which balance is considered a defining characteristic of mature persons and the human species in general (hence an important dimension of their ethos). Balance is "performatively elaborated" (Csordas 1993:146) in many Anlo-Ewe contexts in ways we do not see in either Euro-American discourse or practices.[6]

Why should this matter? I argue that a culture's sensory order is one of the first and most basic elements of *making ourselves human*. I define *sensory order* (or *sensorium*) as a pattern of relative importance and differential elaboration of the various senses, through which children learn to perceive and to experience the world and in which pattern they develop their abilities.[7] I argue that the sensory order—or multiple, sometimes competing sensory orders—of a cultural group forms the basis of the sensibilities that are exhibited by people who have grown up within that tradition. Such sensibilities have been described by anthropologist Robert Desjarlais as "a lasting mood or disposition patterned within the workings of a body" (1992:150). Those moods and dispositions in turn become fundamental to an expectation of what it is to be a person in a given time and place.

If Anlo-Ewe-speaking people think about perception differently than we do and include balance in their sensorium (as well as other so-called interoceptors, or internal senses), this should influence the ways in which their bodies hold and manifest a historical residue of personal and cultural habits (cf. Connerton 1989) and the ways they represent (in language and folkloric motifs) everyday experiences; the sensorial experiences should be encoded and *performatively elaborated* in their rituals and cultural traditions. If we conceive embodiment as a process whereby history is turned into nature (Bourdieu 1977, 1984), their notion of the nature of the person and the nature of health should differ because of their unique repertoire and configuration of senses. In turn, larger abstract cultural ideas can affect the structure of the sensorium. These are some of the issues taken up in this book. My ultimate aim is to fill in the gap between cognitive models of perception and the phenomenal level of sensation, experience, and bodily existence by first examining how culture affects the very basic, fundamental stages of this whole process and by then using the analytic categories of practice, embodiment, sensibility, and identity to trace how these fundamentals affect more abstract processes.

I would like to begin, however, with a brief look at the culturally specific construction of our own sensorium. Why is the most common, popular candidate for a sixth sense something like ESP, or intuition, rather than balance? Americans seem to love the idea of an additional *psychic* sense. Hollywood's *The Sixth Sense* grossed $70 million within ten days of its release in August of 1999. With a plot revolving around an eight-year-old child who is visited by dead people with unresolved problems (he possesses a supernatural ability to interact with ghosts), the movie's popularity suggests a fascination not only with the paranormal and parapsychology but also with the notion that things can be known via channels other than the classic five senses.

Of course, by "sixth sense" not everyone means the ability to receive messages from the dead. A quick search on the Internet generated about six hundred thousand matches for "sixth sense." Most references seemed to have something to do with psychic or occult power. They included the following: a third eye, a gut instinct, intuition, *déjà vu,* moments of just knowing something that defies logic and reason, a religious sense (openness or sensitivity to God), the act of skateboarding, a sense of humor, a classic elegant style of dress that some women possess, an electromagnetic sense (located in the bones and able to detect electrical fields, so that the phrase "I feel it in my bones" is not nonsensical), a voice or The Afflatus, an advertisement for a book entitled *Witchcraft: The Sixth Sense,* an organization called the Sixth Sense Campaign holding the goal of "elevating balance in the public view to the dignity of a sense," and the abilities of remote viewing from a physical distance, predicting the future, and reading thoughts as skills that can be acquired by ordering an audiotape called *Using Your Sixth Sense.*

Another candidate for the sixth sense might be metaphor. Two eminent scholars—linguist George Lakoff and philosopher Mark Johnson—lobby for *metaphor* as an aspect of our functioning that should be regarded as a kind of sense. In *Metaphors We Live By,* they conclude with this reflection:

*handwritten margin notes: idioms/sayings/proverbs : *aphorisms : super imp. in African context*

> We still react with awe when we notice ourselves and those around us liv-
> ing by metaphors like TIME IS MONEY, LOVE IS A JOURNEY, and PROBLEMS
> ARE PUZZLES. We continually find it important to realize that the way we
> have been brought up to perceive our world is not the only way and that it
> is possible to see beyond the "truths" of our culture. But metaphors are not
> merely things to be seen beyond. In fact, one can see beyond them only by
> using other metaphors. It is as though the ability to comprehend experience
> through metaphor were a sense, like seeing or touching or hearing, with
> metaphors providing the only ways to perceive and experience much of the
> world. Metaphor is as much a part of our functioning as our sense of
> touch, and as precious. (Lakoff and Johnson 1980:239)

It is clear that Lakoff and Johnson think metaphor functions in such a
way that it could be included in a class of human experiences that we
usually restrict to the five fields of hearing, touch, taste, smell, and sight.

Why do many Euro-Americans entertain ideas about everything from
witchcraft, remote viewing, and metaphor to electromagnetic sensitivity
as phenomena that could be classified along with our more mundane
abilities to see, hear, touch, taste, and smell? I would suggest that it has
to do with the specific kind of mind-body dichotomy that pervades Western European/Anglo-American philosophy, cultural traditions, and ways
of being-in-the-world. Almost everyone has had some kind of odd, uncanny, intuitive experience that they believe provided them with information outside of the bounds of the kind of "knowing" they have by
virtue of their five senses. All people orient their body with kinesthesia,
but because kinesthetic knowledge tends not to be conscious, it is the
much more conscious psychic phenomenon, or even literary phenomenon, that is identified as a sense—even though the objective grounds for
psychic awareness are not firm. But it seems that many Euro-Americans
opt for something mental rather than somatic when contemplating a
sixth sense.

Despite the belief of many Euro-Americans, the five-senses model is
not a scientific fact, and the enumeration of the senses has been a subject of debate among scholars and philosophers for many centuries (cf.
Classen 1993b; Howes 1991). "The reduction of the sensorium into five
senses was first determined by Aristotle, perhaps for neat numerological
reasons rather than physiological ones; but Galen said there were six,
Erasmus Darwin thought there were 12, and Von Frey reduced them
down to eight" (Synnott 1993:155). From Aristotle to Aquinas and
Descartes, however, cultural traditions have sustained a five-senses model
that privileges mental representations and external modes of knowing.
This construct, I argue, is essentially a folk ideology.

handwritten margin notes: No less powerful/relevant (true?) than science → science as paradigm shifts (comp...)

During the early and mid-nineteenth century a major shift occurred in the Western world's approach to the study of sensation and perception. For several centuries prior to that, the senses were dealt with largely by the empiricist philosophers (or philosopher-psychologists) such as Hobbes, Locke, Berkeley, Hume, and Descartes. But the awakening of science in the nineteenth century was accompanied by the development and improvement of instruments of observation such as the microscope and the telescope and an increase in experimental investigations. According to one historian of the senses, such technological innovations led (in part) to a shift in intellectual climate so that the *measurement of sensation* became "an appropriate and reasonable undertaking" (Boring 1970[1942]:34). To put it simplistically, the study of sensation and perception moved at that point from being not only a philosophical investigation of relations between the external world and the mind but research on the body's role as well—by physiologists, by sensationistic psychologists, and by researchers in a new discipline labeled "psychophysics."

In 1860 Gustav Theodor Fechner (a German physicist and philosopher) established the then new field of psychophysics and wrote that he envisioned it as "an exact theory of the ... relations of body and soul or, more generally, of the material and the mental, of the physical and the psychological worlds" (from his book *Elements of Psychophysics*, quoted in Sekuler and Blake 1994:489). He set out to formalize the methods that others had developed to study perception, and he aspired to *measure the sensations* that physical stimuli evoke in human beings. Such measurement had the potential to demonstrate, it was believed, the precise ways in which the mind, body, and world interrelate. Eventually psychophysics was abandoned and specific disciplines emerged so that *physics* became distinct from *sensory psychology* (which focuses on the response of the human subject to events described in physics) and from *sensory physiology* (which focuses on how the sensory equipment of the human subject transforms physical energy into forms that are useful to our survival) (see Tibbetts 1969:14–16).

Sensory scientists at the end of the twentieth century would probably agree on a taxonomy of approximately nine sensory systems: (1) visual apparatus, responding to luminous and chromatic impressions; (2) auditory apparatus, responding to tonal impressions; (3) olfactory apparatus; (4) gustatory apparatus; (5) tactile apparatus, responding to mechanical impressions; (6) tactile apparatus, responding to thermal impressions; (7) tactile apparatus, responding to kinesthetic impressions;

(8) labyrinthine apparatus, governing balance; and (9) affective apparatus (pleasant and painful), responding to impressions of tickling, itching, voluptuousness, desiccation, burning, distention, pinching, pressure, and so forth (displayed graphically in Pieron 1952:32–33, but compare with Lowenstein 1966:188–197 and with Barlow and Mollon 1982). A second (and complementary) taxonomic scheme divides the sensations into three subcategories: extero-receptors, intero-receptors, and proprio-receptors. The exteroceptive sensations include the classic five, which provide a person with information about external objects. The interoceptive sensations exert action on internal surfaces: esophagus, stomach, and the intestines. Finally, proprioceptive sensations provide a person with information about three conditions: the state of her deep tissue, her own movements and activity, and the effects of her own displacement in space (Pieron 1952:28). Neither the ninefold nor the threefold taxonomy is accepted by all (see Pieron 1952:28–29 for limitations and contradictions, and see Boring 1970[1942]:523–564 on historical developments in acceptance or rejection of various sensory fields), but these two schemes provide a general impression of where conventional science currently stands. One only need look through contemporary textbooks on sensory psychology, perception, and physiology to note that while vision usually receives the greatest amount of space (e.g., Sekuler and Blake [1994] provide seven chapters on vision, two on the auditory system, one on touch, and one that combines the chemical senses of taste and smell), there is almost always information pertaining to proprioception, kinesthesis, and vertigo or a vestibular sense (e.g., Aronoff et al. 1970:287–290; Alpern, Lawrence, and Wolsk 1967; Barlow and Mollon 1982). The point is that while the taxonomies constructed by scientists (nine sensory systems, or perhaps three) differ from the model of sensing accepted by most Euro-Americans (five senses, or possibly six), all of these schemes are culturally embedded. Even within the West, different cultural traditions have treated the senses in varied ways, so that a French scientist named Claude Bernard spent his lifetime going against the grain and trying to understand what he termed the *milieu intérieur*. In 1859 he explained, "The external phenomena which we perceive in the living being are fundamentally very complex; they are the resultant of a host of intimate properties of organic units whose manifestations are linked together with the physiochemical conditions of the internal environment in which they are immersed. *In our explanations we suppress this inner environment and see only the outer environment before our eyes*" (quoted in Alpern, Lawrence, and Wolsk 1967:140, emphasis

added). I have invoked these reflections of Bernard here because he represents a minority voice in the West but articulates what I believe many Anlo-Ewe people would consider eminently reasonable: a concern with the *milieu intérieur*—the internal environment, or what Anlo people refer to as *seselelame* (feeling in the body, flesh, or skin).[8]

INTERPRETIVE FRAMEWORK

This is a study of some of the processes by which history is turned into nature (Bourdieu 1977:78), and I trace these processes through an ethnographic examination of sensing, embodiment, and identity.[9] My starting point lies in efforts to excavate the sensory order of a cultural community, because in the first instance I believe that sensing cannot be understood or defined in any universal way, but involves cultural variation (cf. Classen 1993b; Howes 1991; McLuhan 1962; Ong 1967, 1991; Stoller 1989b; Wober 1966).[10] More important, however, to my theoretical point of view, I believe that in a cultural community's sensorium we find refracted some of the values that they hold so dear that they literally make these themes or these motifs into "body." In other words, a cultural community's sensory order reflects aspects of the world that are so precious to the members of that community that (although they remain largely unconscious and habitual) they are the things that children growing up in this culture developmentally come to carry in their very bodies. So the senses, I believe, are ways of embodying cultural categories, or making into body certain cultural values or aspects of *being* that the particular cultural community has historically deemed precious and dear.

In Anlo-Ewe-speaking contexts, in fact, the notion of *se* or *sese* (which will receive a great deal of focus and elaboration throughout the book) not only is the closest idea we have to the English term for *sensing* but also refers in their world to the idea of *obedience* and *adherence*, which I suggest illustrates the way in which sensing grounds a person in material reality and forms a strong basis for the actual maintenance of sanity. The perceptual framing of that material reality, however, is not without a cultural basis, and hence we return to the problem of how history becomes turned into nature. These embodied forms, then, constitute vital aspects of a people's sense of identity, and within the notion of identity, I believe, are subsumed their ideas and experiences of well-being and their conceptions of the person and the self.

It is here that I feel the significance of this study can be found. We live, these days, with an intense and profound paradox: "difference" is being washed away (in sociological as well as academic and scholarly venues), yet at the same time it is the basis of everything from minor neighborhood and interpersonal tension to full-fledged and full-scale genocide. When an "Anlo person" lives in Toronto, Paris, London, Chicago, or New York, what is it that continues to sustain a feeling, an idea, or a sense of *being* Anlo? If one has lived in the West for twenty years and spoken French or English most of one's life, what is the basis for continuing to identify as Anlo?

I believe this quality of "being Anlo" has something to do with the very sensory orientations one develops in the early years of life, that these ways of sensing and ways of apprehending the material world (or adhering to reality) are formed through "the symbolic mediation of experience" (Shweder et al. 1998:887) and are so deeply inscribed, so "durably installed" (Bourdieu 1977:78), that they are unconscious, habitual, and literally "made body." So I start by trying to understand an Anlo epistemology of sensing—to trace an indigenous theory of sensing, or what seems to be a portion of a more generalized theory of inner states—because in that sensory order I think we will find some of the basic cultural categories used by parents and caregivers in their child-rearing strategies or in the way they shape bodily practices and psychological mentalities. This, I believe, has a great deal to do with ontology or Anlo ways of being-in-the-world. So to understand what it means to be Anlo, I try to trace what is carried in the body (the mind being part of the body) all the way back to how sensory orientations have been conceptualized (historically) and deposited or installed—as if by nature—into Anlo persons.[11]

My study has as one of its precedents a long-standing though minority or even marginalized interest within anthropology in issues of perception. These concerns date back as far as 1883, when Boas's Baffinland study of how Eskimos perceived the color of seawater led him to conclude that the eye was "not a mere physical organ but a means of perception conditioned by the tradition in which its possessor has been reared" (Ruth Benedict quoted in Stocking 1968:145). Subsequent studies have either agreed with Boas or concluded that the most salient aspects of human perception are precultural, and research has not advanced much beyond these two basic claims. For example, at the turn of the century interest in optical illusions led to a series of tests by British psychologist and ethnologist W. H. R. Rivers that led to the "carpentered-world hypothesis" (Bock 1988:10–11). Simply put, this proposal suggests that people who grow up in an environment that is highly carpentered will learn to use angles in perceiving distances whereas those who live in round or oval houses will not develop such perceptual habits. And while additional research has been carried out on the susceptibility to illusion of differing populations (Segall, Campbell, and Herskovits 1966), the conclusions drawn are merely that the basic process of perception is the same for all human groups and that where differences occur it is due to experience rather than a result of inherent "racial" or "biological" distinctions.

Questions about the influence of language on perception were taken up by Edward Sapir and Benjamin Lee Whorf, who concluded that the effects were probably more on conceptual structure than at the actual level of perception (Whorf 1956:158).[12] Hallowell (1951, 1955) was concerned with how the cultural structuring of perception influenced personality organization and the practical experience of the individual, but his ideas were not followed up until quite recently (Csordas 1994b). Other significant contributions to the study of culture and perception include work on proxemics and the ethnography of communication, which clearly demonstrated cultural variation in attention to and use of different sense modalities (E. T. Hall 1959, 1966). At the other end of the spectrum is ethnosemantic research, which suggested that color terminology "evolves" in societies from a simple to complex set in a fairly uniform order—implying a universality to the way human groups apprehend certain "basic" colors (Berlin and Kay 1969). However, controversy over this and subsequent color terminology research continues (see Bock 1988:173–175 and, more significantly, Lucy 1992:177–187 for a thorough review and critique, especially in relation to the question of linguistic relativity), the details of which are somewhat beyond the scope of this study. Two things stand out about this small body of literature. First, most of the work—from Boas to Berlin and Kay—focuses primarily on sight or on audiovisual perception, neglecting other bodily and sensory modes such as touching, tasting, and olfaction (although Hall's work is an exception). Second, while there is good evidence that perception is culturally shaped, it is a research arena that has been neglected by anthropology.[13]

Beyond issues of perception, a second precedent for my study lies in the more general interest within anthropology in the body as an object of study (Blacking 1977) and in the interrelatedness of body and mind (Scheper-Hughes and Lock 1987). An early anthropological awareness of cultural variation in "techniques of the body" (Mauss 1935), plus studies of the links between bodily habit and character (Bateson and Mead 1942) and an understanding of the extent to which metaphor stems from the "natural symbol" of the body (Douglas 1970), all spawned an array of rich ethnographic research in the latter part of the twentieth century. Recent studies range from a focus on the symbolic significance of different aspects of the body (e.g., Obeyesekere 1981; Seeger 1981) to the role of body imagery in health and healing practices and beliefs (e.g., Kleinman 1980; Lock 1980) and even the body as a site where political consciousness is expressed through practices and signs (e.g., Comaroff 1985; Feldman 1991) or as a site where social contradictions play themselves out (e.g., Lindenbaum 1979; Mullings 1984). But while sensing clearly involves something bodily, anthropological studies focusing on the body as an object have paid little explicit or systematic attention to sensory processes or to the way the senses serve as culturally constructed orientational processes.[14]

Sensorial anthropology, because it is concerned with "how the patterning of sense experience varies from one culture to the next in accordance with the meaning and emphasis attached to each of the modalities of perception" (Howes 1991:3), appears, in part, to answer this deficiency. In fact, the senses seem to be experiencing somewhat of a renaissance, with a profusion of works appearing in the past decade from wide-ranging perspectives. Most notable are efforts to define and set an agenda for the anthropology of the senses (Howes 1991) and various sociohistorical analyses of the sensorium (Howes 1992; Classen 1992, 1993a, 1993b, 1997). In addition, sociological analyses of the body and the senses in Western culture have served to excavate the sources of our assumptions about sensing in general (Synnott 1993) and to demonstrate the extensive symbolic power and significance of some of the less studied of the senses, such as smell (Classen, Howes, and Synnott 1994). Since the early 1980s, Paul Stoller has attended to the senses in his ethnographic work among the Songhay of Niger (1980, 1984a, 1984b), and his approach ranges from epistemological challenges to the extreme visualism of the West (1989a, 1997) to sensual ethnography aimed at evoking tastes, smells, sounds, and feelings from worlds that anthropologists attempt to represent (1989b, 1995, with Olkes 1987; also see Seremetakis [1994] for a similar approach). Furthermore, numerous recent ethnographies pay close attention to the role of the senses in illness, healing rituals, and concepts of the body (e.g., Csordas 1994b; Desjarlais 1992; Devisch 1993; Lock 1980; Ohnuki-Tierney 1981a; Roseman 1991), and while not all of these are situated specifically within an anthropology of the senses, they certainly demonstrate the symbolic significance of culturally distinct sensory orientations.[15]

The past two decades have given rise, then, to fruitful studies that explore sensory experience and symbolism, the significance of sensory meanings in cultural descriptions and analyses, and so forth. What seems lacking in this arena, however, is some explicit theorizing about the precise processes by which sensing contributes to cultural difference.[16] So in addition to cultural histories and political economies of sensory experience, we need a better understanding of the role played by culture in developmental and psychological dimensions of sensory perception.[17] My own study revolves around the following questions: What are the basic bodily impressions in a given tradition that constitute something we might gloss roughly as "sensations" or "immediate experiences"?[18] How are the boundaries of the foundational category of immediate bodily experience defined? What components or what experiences do members of particular cultural groups include in this category? What meanings are then associated with the different components? And what are the particular cultural ways in which different senses are thought to synesthetically interplay? In other words, I am interested in the basic cultural meaning system that governs *sensing* within Anlo-Ewe traditions, practices, and philosophical thought. I am suggesting that we cannot address more general problems of how perception and meaning-making take place until we grasp how a cultural group reconciles the set of senses or immediate bodily experiences that warrant attention in the first place.[19] I believe that comparative studies of personhood, identity, and "intentional worlds" (Shweder 1991:74) benefit from an explicit account of sensory orders and sensory engagement. And while this book does not claim to represent a panacea for the problems and questions that I have raised, it is a gesture in our efforts to build an explanatory framework.

Theoretically, the present work draws on several different approaches within psychological anthropology, most notably those referred to as *cultural psychology* and *cultural phenomenology*. It is from cultural psychology in particular that we can hear the strongest critique of general psychology's assumptions about so-called basic psychological principles (Markus, Kitayama, and Heiman 1996). Cultural psychology refers to the interdisciplinary study of how "cultural traditions and social practices regulate, express, and transform the human psyche, resulting less in psychic unity for humankind than in ethnic divergences in mind, self, and emotion" (Shweder 1991:73). It is the study of how "subject and object, self and other, psyche and culture, person and context, figure and ground, practitioner and practice, live together, require each other, and dynamically, dialectically, and jointly make each other up" (Shweder 1991:73,

1999:63). Within this approach, the analytic attention to the "reciprocity and mutual embeddedness of culture and psyche" (Shweder 1999:63) necessitates that certain concepts or principles deemed "basic" by many general psychologists be reexamined for the socially constructed, historically grounded, and culturally variable nature of their makeup (Markus, Kitayama, and Heiman 1996:863–864). These so-called basics include concepts such as "person" and "situation" and also principles and processes such as "representation," "persuasion," "knowledge activation," and "information-seeking" (Markus, Kitayama, and Heiman 1996:864), and to this list I would add sensing and perceiving. So a fundamental assumption in this approach is that "psychological processes are not just 'influenced' but are thoroughly culturally constituted, and as a consequence, psychological processes will vary with sociocultural context" (Markus, Kitayama, and Heiman 1996:859). While not denying that there may be certain psychic universals within the human species, cultural psychologists argue that "psychologists may be prematurely settling on *one* psychology, that is, on one set of assumptions about what are the relevant or most important psychological states and processes, and on one set of generalizations about their nature and function" (Markus, Kitayama, and Heiman 1996:858). This book will examine some of those sociohistorically constructed generalizations about the nature and boundaries of what we refer to as "the senses," while simultaneously describing another cultural way of depicting how sensation functions in relation to perception, meaning-making, and identity.

Cultural phenomenology focuses on how embodied experience, thought, feeling, and psychological orientations all interrelate. Embodiment and orientation are central themes within phenomenological anthropology (Csordas 1994c:340; Desjarlais 1992; Jackson 1996; Stoller 1989b). For now let me just indicate that largely because of its extensive attention to processes of perception (e.g., Csordas 1990:8–12; Hallowell 1951) and its recognition of the body and bodily experience as the "orientational locus of the self" (Csordas 1994c:340; Hallowell 1955), this approach has played a significant role in shaping my methodological strategies and argument. For instance, the assertion that perception begins in the body and ends in objects (rather than the other way around) has been borrowed from Merleau-Ponty and applied to anthropological issues so that we can address the question of cultural mediation in apprehension of one's environment and apprehension of one's own orientational states (Csordas 1990:9), or what Hallowell called (1955) the "behavioral environment of the self." This theoretical premise is not unlike cultural psychology's notion of "intentional worlds" (Shweder 1991:73–76). Here I simply note that while other approaches within psychological anthropology are occasionally brought into the discussion, cultural phenomenology and cultural psychology serve as the greatest influences in this exploration of the social structuring of sensory perceptions and orientations.

Finally, let me say a few words about why I have written this book and what I believe its significance is for anthropology. Identity and ethnic differences in how identity is defined are of enduring concern within anthropology. But presently it is more popular to focus on cultural and transnational flows, on the blurred boundaries between (and the internal diversity within) previously deemed homogenous "cultures" and on the pitfalls of searching for "essences" that definitively *identify* (perhaps stereotype) a specific cultural group. In fact, essentializing a cultural group is probably the greatest faux pas one can commit in anthropology these days. While I agree with many of the efforts to question and challenge certain assumptions about the uniformity of a given people or what (in the past) seemed to produce a static and ahistorical picture of a cultural group, some aspects of the current trend worry me. For instance, anthropology's turn toward greater attention to political economy, history, discourse, and power seems, at times, to be at the expense of attention to culture. What I mean is that it seems all too easy to deconstruct culture or point to things that we cannot claim a group of people share exclusively or share in such a way that they constitute a "cultural group," a "cultural community," or (to use Shweder's term [1999:64]) a "self-monitoring group." But the challenge remains for anthropology to spell out precisely what it is that a given set of people *share* and also how this so-called cultural stuff that they share is acquired or internalized.[20] This book, while not claiming to have a definitive answer to that problem, takes seriously the notion of *sensibility* and the human function of *perception* as distinct aspects of this process that deserve more careful (and more deliberately theoretical) examination.[21]

My interest in the senses and in the notion of sensibility, then, is inextricably tied to anthropological concerns about cultural difference, and I am in agreement with both the assertion that "it continues to be meaningful to talk about different ways of life" and the claim that "the idea of culture invites us to make some kind of distinction between different ways of life" (Shweder 1999:65). So while it may be currently unpopular to allude to notions of core and traditional culture as well as to theorize about what exactly that means, it is that classic and (in my mind) unresolved issue in anthropology that is at the center of this inquiry.

Throughout years of studying and contemplating the nature of cultural difference, certain ideas and concepts continually captured my imagination: orientations, way of life, forms of being-in-the-world, practices and mental states that reinforce each other, habitus, somatic modes of attention, things that are performatively elaborated within a cultural group, intentional worlds, and so forth. These various terms and ideas seem striking in that each is aimed at articulating the complex interrelationships among culture, psyche, soma, and sociality. In this same vein, I want to propose that we think about *sensibility* as a term that unites individual experience with perception, thought, cultural meaning, and social interaction. I am therefore suggesting that a sensibility is a field where habituated bodily sensations link to individual feelings, attitudes, orientations, and perceptions and finally to cultural themes, motifs, and ethos.

THE ARGUMENT

My argument begins with the claim that *sensory orders vary based on cultural tradition, and hence sensoriums may be different from one cultural group to the next.*[22] Chapter 2 provides background on what constitutes Anlo-land and on what I mean when I use the phrases "Anlo-Ewe" and "Anlo-speaking people." Part 1 (consisting of chapter 3) describes the process involved in researching and documenting a *sensory order,* focusing largely on the first step of understanding the local lexicon for the senses and then laying out some of the local Anlo categories for sensory experiences.

My second claim is that *sensoriums also encode moral values in the process of child socialization. Such embodied forms and sensibilities are learned (acquired, internalized, developed) at an early age through child-socialization practices.* Part 2 then focuses on *embodiment* and takes the reader from the language of the senses to some initial ethnographic explorations of the socialization of sensory orientations. Chapter 4 revolves around kinesthesia, or sensations related to movement, and how this domain represents a cultural category for Anlo notions of moral disposition and character. Chapter 5 provides select discussions of birthing and child-raising practices and beliefs that illustrate the sensorial dimensions of socialization routines. This chapter is not meant to be a comprehensive account of childbirth and child-socialization practices in Anlo-land but rather an exploration of my second proposition, which focuses on how cultural categories and sensory orientations are learned at an early age.

Third, *sensoriums help shape notions of identity and of the person*. That is to say, the first two stages of this process help assure that notions of the person both differ culturally and yet appear natural. The third section of the book focuses, therefore, on *identity* and takes up the ontological question of what it means to be a person in particular cultural ways and how the sensorium helps us to understand this issue. Chapter 6 explores how the identity marker *Anlo* (as in their name) derives from an inward turning bodily posture (called ŋlɔ) enacted by an ancestor at a pivotal point in their migration journey three hundred years ago. I subsequently argue that the cultural memory of ŋlɔ kinesthetically and sensually encodes a complex dimension of Anlo ethnic identity: ŋlɔ is thematized and continually rehearsed in the conditioning of sensibilities about what it means to be a person in Anlo ways. Chapter 7 revisits the argument about balance that I mentioned at the opening of this chapter: that Anlo-Ewe people consider balancing (in a physical and psychological sense, as well as in literal and in metaphorical ways) to be an essential component of what it means to be human. Several significant communal rituals are described in chapter 7 and then analyzed for what they reveal about the prominent role that balancing plays (both the practice of balancing and the bodily experience of balancing) in Anlo-Ewe cultural heritage and historical traditions.

Fourth, *sensoriums also help to shape understandings and experiences of health and illness*. For instance, hearing things that those around you do not or cannot hear or seeing things that others deem invisible or nonexistent are symptomatic of insanity and losing one's grounding in reality (or they indicate adherence to an alternate reality). Part 4 therefore focuses on *well-being* and explores what I call intracultural variation in sensory orders.[23] I begin in chapter 8 by addressing cosmological theories as well as religious practices and beliefs, because it is only if we have a grasp of this foundation that we can begin to understand Anlo epistemologies and modes of being-in-the-world. Anlo-Ewe traditional religion is reexamined as a system of the body or as a set of techniques for sensory manipulation. When interpreted through the lens of an indigenous sensorium, *vodu* and other practices appear as external extensions of the interoceptive, proprioceptive modes that are highly valued in other domains of Anlo life. This chapter focuses, then, on how the senses are reflected and incorporated in the cosmological realm and the relationship that holds to perceptions of reality and to how people *know* things. In turn, definitions and experiences of well-being, strength, and health are inextricably tied to spiritual or religious practices and beliefs. In chapter 9 I address initial issues related to being without certain senses in Anlo cultural contexts, such as the meaning and experience of blindness, deafness, a loss of limb mobility and the kinesthetic sense, and so on. I also take up the issue of how speaking is considered a sense by many Anlo people and the ramifications of being mute, as well as how insanity is defined in this context as total loss of one's senses.

The conclusion, consisting of chapter 10, begins with a synopsis of my argument, then moves to a conceptual discussion of the four claims advanced in the book. This explanatory section presents my interpretive framework in abstract (rather than ethnographic) terms so that it might be used by students of culture working in other areas of the world. I then conclude the final chapter with some remarks on the role of ethnography in research on sensory orientations and on how the senses can help us to better understand cultural difference.

CHAPTER 2

Anlo-Land and Anlo-Ewe People

The term *Anlo* is essential to this study of sensoriums and experience, and yet it is not an easy word to translate or define. It identifies a dialect of Ewe, which is a West African language spoken by many of the people who live in southern Togo and the southeastern corner of Ghana. But for many Ewe speakers in Ghana, Anlo denotes a specific group of Ewe people who inhabit the coastal area of the Volta Region, around the Keta Lagoon, and whose traditions and dialect have unfairly been taken (by scholars, missionaries, and other representatives of colonial regimes) to represent Ewe culture as a whole. To complicate matters, this term that variously refers to language, ethnicity, and place has a literal meaning that describes a body posture of rolling up or folding into oneself (akin to what Euro-Americans would call the fetal position). Clearly, the mixture of feelings and interpretations around what it means to be an Anlo-Ewe person is subjective and complex. With that in mind, this chapter provides general ethnographic background for those unfamiliar with the people and lands of West Africa and, more specifically, with late-twentieth-century southeastern Ghana.

HISTORY, POLITICS, AND SOCIAL STRUCTURE

Anlo-Ewe people belong to a large group, or "nation," of more than a million people located in southeastern Ghana and southern Togo.[1] As Anlo-Ewe ethnographer G. K. Nukunya has explained, "Language and common traditions of origin formed the most important bases of Ewe unity" (1969b:1).[2] The Ewe language is a part of the Kwa language group within the much larger classification of Niger-Kordofanian, which spans from the western shores to the southeastern edge of the African continent (Gregersen 1977). Kwa, however, includes a much smaller set of languages spoken in present-day countries ranging from Liberia in the west to the eastern boundary of Nigeria (Greenberg 1973:76). Ewe itself is related more directly to Akan, Guang, and Ga (all spoken in Ghana), plus Fon (spoken in Benin), and Ibo, Ijaw, Yoruba, and Nupe (spoken in Nigeria).[3] Within Ewe proper, then, over a hundred dialects exist, and among them we can count *Anloghe*—the Anlo language.

While the first layer of definitional boundaries for the identification *Anlo-Ewe* is clearly linguistic, the second unifying feature concerns a common tradition of origin for Ewe speakers. It is commonly believed that Ewe-speaking people came from the Oyo Empire and, more specifically, from the political subunit and city called Ketu (Oyo being located in modern-day Nigeria, with Ketu further west in what is currently Benin). Ewe speakers probably left there some time in the fifteenth or sixteenth century due to the advent of war among the Oyo, Borgu, and Nupe states (Locke 1978:8; Asamoa 1986:5).[4] When they fled Ketu, they divided into at least three groups, and some claim they migrated to Wla (in southern Benin), Tado, and Notsie (both located in the southern half of modern-day Togo) (Asamoa 1986:4). Others suggest that in addition to Tado and Notsie, they fled to an area called Dogbo to the northwest of Ketu (Locke 1978:8). Nonetheless, those Ewe speakers who traveled to Notsie are of greatest concern for this study because they are the ancestors of Anlo-Ewe-speaking people. While a fair amount of detail about life in Notsie has been documented (Amenumey 1986; Asamoa 1986; Locke 1978), my interest is in the group that left Notsie, probably in the mid-1600s, and began populating the area in southeastern Ghana now known as the Volta Region.[5] (Chapter 6 recounts in detail the story of their flight and migration as it pertains directly to Anlo symbology, subjectivity, and cultural logic.) Thus, from Oyo and Ketu to Tado and Notsie, some Ewe speakers who are known in the early twenty-first century as *Anlo* began inhabiting and populating their present-day homeland, in southern Togo and southeastern Ghana, a little over three hundred years ago.

At least one hundred twenty different subgroups have been identified within Ewe-speaking populations (Nukunya 1969b:2), which inhabit approximately ten thousand square miles of land (Locke 1978:1). In addition to differences in dialect and locale, these subgroups vary in their social structure too. According to Nukunya (1969b:2), Ewe speakers in Ho have been described as strictly patrilineal, while the nearby Glidzi (Ewe speakers) reportedly passed down some aspects of their personal property from a man to his sister's son, a matrilineal practice. "Because of these differences, generalizations embracing the whole Ewe-speaking group are bound to be misleading unless the sphere or area of their application is clearly delimited" (Nukunya 1969b:2). For these reasons, I limit my discussion to Anlo-speaking subgroups located on the coast of Ghana, about fifteen miles west of the Togo border, and hemmed in on the western edge by the mouth of the Volta River.

Social structure among Ewe speakers in general is well documented (Manoukian 1952), as is that of the Anlo-speaking area alone (Nukunya 1969b). In historical terms Anlo speakers have been patrilineal and have negotiated kinship relations through both clan and lineage organizations.[6] Most Anlo speakers belong to one of fifteen patrilineal clans, or *hlɔwo*—defined as a group believed to be descended from a putative common ancestor and sharing similar totemic and ritual observances (Nukunya 1969b:21). While in a contemporary sense clans are fairly well defined among Anlo speakers, the smaller grouping of lineage proves more problematic. This is due, in part, to the fact that from community to community (or between one village and the next) the Anlo term for "lineage" often varies. Secondly, within one community reside members of numerous lineages (usually deriving from several of the fifteen clans). Nukunya's descriptions seemed to hold true in the area where I conducted research, so I have relied on his explanation of lineage (or *afedo*) as "that branch of a clan found in a settlement which comprises all those persons, male and female, who are able to trace relationship by a series of accepted genealogical steps through the male line to a known or putative male ancestor and theoretically to each other. The genealogical depth of the lineage is about eight to ten generations" (Nukunya 1969b:26).

Political structures within Anlo-land are like those of many other African societies in that they revolve around authority invested in the institution called *chieftaincy*. The head of all Anlo-speaking people is the *Awoamefia*—which Nukunya translates as "King" but whom people in Anlo-land usually referred to as "Paramount Chief." Two royal clans, Adzovia and Bate, alternate in producing the *Awoamefia* (Nukunya 1969b:9). Below the Paramount Chief are three senior chiefs, who traditionally held positions involving military command; the next level involves chiefs of towns and villages; and, finally, there are chiefs who are heads of the local wards and lineages.

When I was in Ghana in the mid 1990s, it had been nearly three decades since Nukunya wrote about Anlo social structure, but the institution of chieftaincy was still fairly intact. On one hand, Anlo-speaking people living in rural areas continued to rely heavily on the expertise and jurisprudence of local chiefs. On the other hand, the authority of the chieftaincy was being eroded or superseded by offices of so-called modern political systems—such as district assemblies, or Ghana's Committee in Defense of the Revolution established under the Rawlings regime. So those people still residing in the Anlo homeland had to choose among several authorities (on a regular basis) in terms of how to orient themselves or where to place their attention and allegiance. In turn, those residing in Accra or in other parts of Ghana, as well as those Anlo people who were living abroad, also had to choose which of the competing authorities they would heed. For example, I received quite conflicting advice about whom I should appeal to for authorization (actual permission or a simple blessing) to work and live in the village where we stayed. Some believed that the district assemblyman was the appropriate individual since he was an elected official; others introduced me to various chiefs since they were seen as representing the different lineages inhabiting the village; and yet another faction took me to meet "the committee man" (an individual placed there as part of the Committee in Defense of the Revolution) since this particular group felt aligned with him (and admitted they had not even voted in the district assembly election). These processes of allegiance and orientation, I would suggest, were integrally bound up with a person's sense of identity, and they help account (in part) for the heterogeneity of perspectives that I encountered in relation to other aspects of life in Anlo-land. In other words, Anlo society was quite multifaceted at the time I was there—in terms of political and social structure as well as in cultural ways. In later chapters I will take up the problem of how processes of identity formation and orientations of the self necessarily involve "effort and reflexivity" (Csordas 1994b) in that choices and alliances are clearly made within the context of a specific cultural community.

So while "language and common traditions of origin" (Nukunya 1969b:1) are a central aspect of what underpins a category of Anlo, it is a grouping that nevertheless contains a great deal of intracultural variation. It would be awkward and even disingenuous, therefore, to refer to this cultural community as the *Anlo*—implying that it is a monolithic and homogenous group. In the text when it seems appropriate to generalize, I use the phrase *Anlo-speaking people* or, more narrowly, *Anlo speakers with whom I worked.* This admittedly awkward phrasing is meant to limit my claims so as not to give the impression that all Anlo speakers think and perceive in a uniform way. In addition, culture is in a constant state of flux although certain themes and signs may be reproduced consistently within a specific cultural community over long periods of time. This point was brought home to me when a supposedly annual ritual was performed in the village in which we lived (it will be described in chapter 7), but in fact this supposedly annual event had not been staged for more than seven years. In addition, it was a rite that was unfamiliar to many people who resided in the neighboring Anlo towns of Keta and Anloga. How should an ethnographer describe a purported "annual Anlo village ritual" that actually seemed to occur haphazardly and only in specific locations but that she happened to witness while doing fieldwork? Certainly it cannot be presented as depicting "the way things are" in Anlo-land. Contemporary ethnographer of Ewe culture Judy Rosenthal has also commented (1998:45–47) on the lack of stability in Ewe social structures and on the variation in practices from one locale to another, even quoting a fellow scholar who frustratedly commented that in describing Ewe culture "you don't know what to write, and you can't make a synthesis of your material, because the culture is not unified."

Working in Anlo-Ewe culture deepened my own belief that cultural anthropology cannot be about the production of scientific documents, but rather what we leave behind are histories. What we write up, after extensive fieldwork, are historically situated texts concerning a set of people in a place during a time when we were present to witness and document the goings on—an admittedly strange blend of subjectivity and empiricism. Along the lines of producing a history, in this text I have opted for a style of presentation that aims for as much specificity in both time and place as I could manage, and I therefore tack back and forth between past tense descriptions and present tense analysis. That is to say, ethnographic descriptions are usually rendered in the past tense, to indicate that I am depicting something that occurred in a specific place, at a specific time, with a specific group of people, rather than suggesting it is a set of behaviors, attitudes, and practices that all Anlo speakers (throughout all time) would recognize and own. Analytical passages, however, are generally presented in present tense for ease in reading.[7]

Such writing strategies do not, of course, solve all problems related to representing a category called *Anlo.* For one, my presentation makes it appear as though language is the definitive characteristic of being an

Anlo person, which is probably misleading or false, and while it is a very significant marker of what it means to "be Anlo," it is not the only sign. Some people, in fact, have grown up in Accra and speak Ga or Twi as their first language but still consider themselves Anlo because their parents were born and raised in the Anlo homeland and their entire lineage and ancestry is Anlo—hence the "bloodline" criteria for identity. Still other individuals speak the Anlo-Ewe dialect and live in the Anlo homeland, but they actually immigrated there from a Hausa-speaking area in northern Ghana. So while I include the former as "Anlo-speaking people" and exclude the latter, clearly language is not the sole criteria identifying those who belong within this group. The point to keep in mind is that Anlo-land is a dynamic place, Anlo-Ewe people are far from homogenous, and this account represents a small slice of a complex cultural world.[8]

LAND AND LIVELIHOOD

Fish, shallots, and salt have traditionally been the major commodities produced within Anlo-land. While other areas of Ghana contain tremendous wealth in gold, timber, cocoa, aluminum, and so forth, natural resources in Anlo-land in the mid 1990s were rather poor. I was often told that for this reason Anlo-speaking people would send their children to school, resulting in a large representation of their people in Ghanaian politics, professions, and civil service (this point will be elaborated in chapter 6).

The terrain of Anlo-land was dominated by a water system of ocean, the River Volta, smaller creeks, and a lagoon. While the size of Eweland as a whole was about 10,000 square miles (Locke 1978:1), Anlo-land alone was merely 883 square miles (Nukunya 1969b:2). The northern portion of Eweland included a hilly (somewhat mountainous) forest zone. The southern (Anlo) area, on the other hand, was lowland with mangrove swamps and bulrush bordering the lagoon and savanna grasslands on the northern fringes of the territory. People talked of the forested areas that used to exist in Anlo-land proper (e.g., see F. K. Fiawoo 1983 about the woods in which criminals were buried), and there was still a small amount of thicket or bush-type vegetation along the rivers and creeks, but one of the most pressing problems Ghana faced in the 1990s was decimation of the forests. This problem was particularly acute in Ghana's central forest zone, but Anlo-land too had been affected by severe loss of trees. A worse problem for Anlo-land, however, was sea ero-

sion, for in the past forty years the ocean had gradually swallowed up
entire sections of Keta, once a booming port town. In fact, the ocean had
cut through the littoral between Keta and the villages to the east, thereby
destroying the road and bringing to a halt the traffic that used to travel
through Anlo-land to Lome and other parts of Togo. Local people continued to travel by canoe across the twenty-by-twelve-mile lagoon
(Nukunya 1969b:5). But Keta's loss of causeway and port status added
to the poverty of the land and further impelled Anlo people to educate
their children in the hope that they would be able to participate in the
national economy and even to migrate to the West.

With such an extensive system of water surrounding Anlo-land,
fishing was historically the major source of livelihood (Nukunya
1969b:6–7). As a significant factor in the history and socioeconomic life
of Anlo people, seine fishing (from techniques to the organizational dimensions of fishing "companies") was significant and has been described
elsewhere (Hill 1986). Although Anlo-speaking people had only been
fishing since they arrived in this area around three hundred years ago
(e.g., see Greene 1988:73 on historical developments of Anlo fishing),
they quickly excelled. In fact, Ewe speakers in general and especially
Anlo-speaking people have been known to migrate to other coastal areas
throughout West and Central Africa specifically for the fishing opportunities (Nukunya 1969b:6; Greene 1985:83).

Shallot cultivation was also a very intensive and widespread occupation in Anlo-land with the products distributed all over Ghana (Hill
1986:40–41). When living in Anlo-land, I was struck by the sheer
amount of shallots produced in this area, and when they were piled in
enormous heaps on the side of a road or in a lorry, the aroma was powerful and pervasive. One scholar noted that "this astonishing industry is
unique in Ghana—yields being remarkable by any standard. By 1962 it
had developed particularly in an area of 1,500 acres near Anloga" (Hill
1986:40). And although dubious about the reliability of this claim, she
states that "yields were said ... to have averaged 4 to 8 tons per acre per
year of dried shallots" (Hill 1986:40). Regardless of the exact quantity
or volume, shallot beds dominated the landscape in certain sections of
Anlo-land.

In addition to shallots, other (mainly subsistence) crops grown in
Anlo-land included maize, cassava, peppers, tomatoes, okra, sugarcane,
and garden eggs. The primary fruits grown in this area included mango,
coconut and banana. Rainfall, however, was scant at an annual rate of
about twenty-five to thirty inches (Locke 1978:4). While most written

accounts of the area claim that heavy rains occur in May and June and
that a second, lighter rainy season transpires around September and October, people who live in the area reported that for many years little to
no rain had fallen during September and October and that the amount
in May and June had dramatically dropped. Some stated that this situation was related to the depletion of the forest. In the absence of rain,
farmers watered their crops with buckets of water drawn from wells dug
throughout the fields.

The lagoon provided salt, which has historically been a major com-
modity supporting Anlo-speaking communities (Greene 1988). The Keta
Lagoon was described as a "brackish water, the coastal fringes of which
evaporate during years of scanty rainfall, leaving large incrustations of
salt which provide a most important article of trade for the locals. In extremely dry years almost the whole area is dried up" (Nukunya 1969b:5).
During those times the salt was collected and stored for later distribution and sale.

People in Anlo-land also engaged in animal husbandry on a small
scale, with the most commonly raised creatures being fowls, goats, and
ducks. Occasionally people reared sheep and pigs, but cattle were extremely rare. Fresh and smoked fish, plus seafood (such as shrimp or
crabs), were far more common as a product for consumption or trade
than were other kinds of meat. Cats were also raised and consumed periodically as a delicacy.

Finally, weaving was another important source of livelihood for many
people in the Anlo area. Baskets, thick mattresses, and thin mats were
all produced from various rushes or reeds that grew on the edges of the
lagoons. Strip woven cloth (the Ewe term was *kete*, but most Ghanaians
called it *kente*) was another aspect of the weaving industry, though no
longer accomplished through the use of locally grown materials. That is,
at one time cotton was grown in the area and was spun and woven into
cloth. More recently, however, cloth in the Anlo area was woven from
imported threads (see Lamb 1975 and Posnansky 1992 on Ewe cloth).

All the various commodities mentioned above were bought and sold
in the context of an extensive marketing system (Dzobo 1995). "These
multiple economic activities, and local specialization in certain products,
result in an exchange system among the various localities, which makes
trading an important occupation, especially for women. Indeed, Westermann was led to observe that 'there is hardly any woman who does
not trade.'" (Nukunya 1969b:7). Each locality's market fell on every
fourth day, so traders made a circuit with their products. However, as

early as the 1960s the implications of the rising water line were noted:
"The Keta market … attracts traders and customers from all over Ghana,
Togo, Dahomey and Nigeria. But its importance is now decreasing, due
to the increasing menace of sea erosion, from which it has been suffering for a long time" (Nukunya 1969b:3). In the mid 1990s the market
at Anloga (the traditional and ritual capital of Anlo-speaking people)
had surpassed that of Keta, but it still did not draw the crowds that used
to converge on Keta.

Many Anlo people also held jobs and occupations that were not directly tied to the land. In the 1960s it was commonly believed that "in
the very near future Anloga will become a major industrial centre because of the rich deposit of oil recently discovered there" (Nukunya
1969b:3–4), but no level of significant development had yet occurred.
Consequently, migration out (to work in Accra and other areas) was
common. Since many Anlo speakers said that their people had always
been good at mixing with other ethnic groups, learning other languages
and other customs, and adapting to new situations, migration was a
strategy used long before their homeland faced erosion due to the sea.
But this tactic had become particularly relevant during the preceding
decades. Keta used to be a booming port town, and the remnants of this
status could still be seen. Ornately decorated cement block buildings—
some constructed during the nineteenth century—lined the streets. But
very few shops were open, creating the feel and look of a ghost town in
certain respects. What little commerce was now conducted in Anlo-land
had shifted to Anloga. Keta still was home to several schools and the district hospital, but Anloga boasted much more activity. So, in addition to
living off the land, people in Anlo-land worked as teachers, shoemakers,
booksellers, pastors, pharmacists, lorry or taxicab drivers, police officers,
tailors, and shopkeepers. The hospital and various clinics employed
nurses, doctors, midwives, medical officers, and additional staff. Other
occupations involved the production and sale of food in restaurants, in
"chop bars," or out of one's home. But there was also a fair amount of
migration to cities (especially Accra) for other jobs and work in the professional sector. In general, Anlo-speaking people pursued education
quite seriously, and considering they comprised only 3 or 4 percent of See
the population in Ghana, a surprisingly large number of Anlo speakers opp.
was in civil service, at the university, in banking, in law, and so forth.
Merely traveling through Anlo-land allowed a person to see the lack of
industry and limited economic opportunities available to Anlo people at
the end of the twentieth century.

RESEARCH SETTING: ACCRA AND THE VILLAGE OF SRƆGBOE

Between 1992 and 1995 I lived for more than twenty months among
Anlo-Ewe-speaking people in southeastern Ghana. Originally I had
planned to conduct a study focused primarily on rural lifeways and based
in a village in the southern Volta Region. I was interested in understanding how traditional medical practitioners *know what they know*—
about the body, illness, diagnosis, and cure—and wanted to study their
use of the five senses. I lived in the former port town of Keta for two
months, traveling across the lagoon and into the hinterlands to interview
people and to search for a somewhat isolated village in which I could
conduct my study. By the end of my three-month pilot study, I had
identified a village that would be suitable. But when I returned to Ghana
at the end of 1993, members of the Anlo-speaking family that had
"adopted" my husband and me opposed our moving to that particular
place. Their stated reasons at the time included not having enough relatives in that area nor a proper house in which my husband and I could
reside, and they preferred that we live in Keta, which they considered
more "Europeanized." But my persistence in wanting a residence in a location they perceived as "typically Anlo" resulted in a compromise. By
the beginning of 1994 my husband and I had settled in a place called
Srɔgboe, which is the site of the family's royal or ancestral home.

Srɔgboe was a coastal village with a population (in 1994) of about
1,200 people. The lagoon bordered the northern edge of the village, a
creek flowed in from the west, and the ocean lay along the southern
boundary. The main road that one traveled to go anywhere from coastal
Anlo-land out (to Accra, to the regional capital Ho, etc.) cut directly
through Srɔgboe and linked Srɔgboe to a line of villages and towns, such
as Anyanui, Anloga, and Keta. At the time I was there, a private clinic
run by a doctor and his wife serviced some members of the community,
though the doctor spent a good deal of his time in Accra, and many vil-
lagers preferred Anlo-style medicine. Srɔgboe had two schools located
in its territory, but children from several neighboring villages also attended these two institutions. The Whuti-Srɔgboe Post Office serviced
both Srɔgboe and the village immediately adjacent to the east. Electricity poles had been raised in the village, but wires were extended to only
a few homes of people who could afford the installation fees and monthly
upkeep. While there was no piped water in the entire Anlo region, the
well system was excellent, so drinking and bathing water (as well as
water-borne diseases) were not a problem.

A small market operated daily in the center of Srɔgboe. Major marketing activities, however, were conducted at Anyanui every Wednesday and at the Anloga and Keta market held every four days. In addition to the traditional forms of work such as fishing, farming, and weaving, Srɔgboe had several small drinking bars, plus tailoring and sewing shops, corn mills, and a "fitter," or auto mechanic shop. The other outstanding features in Srɔgboe were a number of lineage and community-based shrines and several "cult houses" where people who adhered to the religious sects of Yeve or Blekete resided. Finally, a random census revealed that Srɔgboe consisted of approximately 78 single houses, plus 63 compounds (with each compound averaging three houses). I estimated the total population of Srɔgboe to be about 1,200 people in 1994, with a gender ratio of three males for every four females.[9]

Once my husband and I had settled in Srɔgboe, invitations and obligations to attend events and visit "relatives" in Accra began to pour in. At first I considered these demands intrusive and perceived the family that had adopted us as having an undue influence and control over my research process. But gradually I began to realize that this back and forth between the village and Accra, going from one relative's house to another, attending to family obligations and reciprocating the visits of people who had traveled to see us in the village, was an integral part of being a person in Anlo ways.[10] My research gradually took on a rhythm of expansion and contraction: outward toward Accra and the metropolis where I participated in the flow of life of a network of thousands of disbursed Anlo speakers (some visiting Accra from their current homes abroad), and inward to a concentrated setting of village life in the Anlo homeland. Other people who resided primarily in the village were also traveling continually to and from Accra—for reasons of health, business, births, deaths, and basic family obligations.

A network of Anlo speakers in and around Accra, then, became as significant to my research as were the people living in the homeland. My interest in *being a person in Anlo ways* necessitated this shift from my original intention of a purely rural setting (for the project) to one that included the urban sphere—since personhood and Anlo identities encompassed both domains. That is, I could not seem to talk to an "urban Anlo" without mention of the homeland; and I could not seem to talk to a "rural Anlo" without mention of Accra. While I do not want to give the impression that absolutely every individual traveled back and forth (between Accra and Anlo-land) on a regular basis, I would suggest that this process of a contractive and expansive movement definitely affected every Anlo-speaking family. Confirming my own sense of the significance of travel to Anlo worlds, Rosenthal has suggested that "Ewe culture travels and is *a traveling* (similar to the reciprocating motion of a film camera) as surely as anthropology is. Ewe personhood is a travel narrative" (Rosenthal 1998:27, emphasis added). Her development of the metaphor of Ewe culture and Ewe personhood as a traveling narrative (Rosenthal 1998:120) is supported by my own account in which I discuss the significance of movement, walks, the Anlo-Ewe migration story, and references to Anlo-Ewe people who have emigrated to the United States. So, during our longest stretch of fieldwork, from the end of 1993 and into the middle of 1995, my husband and I traveled from Srɔgboe to Accra on a regular basis for both business reasons and to fulfill obligations within the large extended family that had adopted us. In Accra we interacted largely with Anlo and Ewe speakers and kept an apartment in an Anlo-speaking compound in the Kokomlemle section of the city. The longer we stayed the more frequently we were expected to attend funerals, outdoorings, weddings, holiday celebrations, and so on, which required travel back and forth. The more entrenched we became in the society, the more members of the family we met, and the more interactions we had with Anlo-speaking bankers, accountants, lawyers, doctors, civil servants, contractors, architects, auto mechanics, blacksmiths, professors, drummers, traders, economists, engineers, and so forth. I gradually came to understand that it was futile to try and distinguish between research with Anlo-speaking people and this traveling process that is endemic to Ewe culture.

People in Ghana operated largely within ethnic or language-based networks, and our negotiation of practical aspects of life (exchanging currency, purchasing household items, having the tires changed on the car) required a reliance on this network of Anlo-Ewe people. My husband and I became quite close to many of the individuals with whom we lived and worked, and I therefore had a difficult time thinking of them as "informants." Elaine worked with me almost daily—making introductions to people she believed could help me with the study, translating during formal interviews with chiefs, visiting village midwives and herbalists in remote areas, and teasing me about coming half-way across the world to learn about Anlo-Ewe *buffalo affairs* (her code word for my delight in learning their proverbs). At the end of my stay in Ghana in 1995, I explained to Elaine that in the book I would be writing I needed a word that designated the role that she and these others played in the work that we had done. I asked her opinion of terms such as collaborators, teachers, or friends. For two and a half hours, while driving from Srɔgboe to Accra, we analyzed the ramifications of each word. Elaine had read none of the postmodern literature on the reflexive turn in anthropology, but still she managed to articulate most of the objections we might find there for referring to someone like herself as an "informant." Finally, she proposed an Anlo-Ewe word *mɔfialawo*, which refers to people who show or teach you the way. *Mɔfiala* (singular) could be translated into English as "guide," and further underscoring the notion of Ewe culture as a traveling narrative (Rosenthal 1998), we can think of *mɔfialawo* (the plural) in terms of "those who guide you along the path or the road" (*mɔ:* road, path; *fia:* teach, show; *la:* forms the noun agent). Since it was in the context of their culture that I was trying to find my way, throughout the text I use this Anlo-Ewe term— *mɔfialawo*—to refer to people we might otherwise think of as "informants." Finally, I do not use anyone's actual name, and I have concealed individual's identities by changing personal characteristics. In addition, several of the *mɔfialawo* identified in the book are composites of two or more people I interviewed or consulted. In the tradition of certain other Ewe ethnographies, most notably Nukunya's classic *Kinship and Marriage among the Anlo Ewe* (1969b), I have retained actual place names and provided an accurate map. Now let us turn to the language of sensory experiences in Anlo worlds.

PART ONE

Conceptualizing Sensory Orientations in Anlo-Land

CHAPTER 3

Language and Sensory Orientations

ON THE SEARCH FOR AN INDIGENOUS TERM OR CATEGORY FOR "THE SENSES"

Among the many *mɔfialawo* with whom I worked, there seemed to be little consensus about a precise cultural category that we could map into our domain of the five senses. In fact, at one point in the middle of my research, I seemed to have nearly as many configurations of sense-data as the number of people I had interviewed. I was fearful that I would never be able to make sense of the lexical chaos I seemed to have gathered or generated, so I made an appointment to meet with Mr. Adzomada.[1]

Most Anlo people considered Mr. Adzomada to be one of the foremost authorities on their history and cultural traditions, so I was counting on this interview to set things straight. Mr. Adzomada was in his eighties when my friend Elaine arranged for me to talk with him. She informed me that he relished oranges, so I purchased a dozen in the market before traveling to his house on the outskirts of Anloga. At the presentation of the *aŋutiwo* (oranges), he inhaled the fragrance emanating from the bag and I figured we were off to a good start. When I asked him a question about the senses, however, he emphatically replied, "We don't have that in our culture." During this interview and subsequent conversations, no matter how many different ways I tried to broach the subject of sensibilia, no matter which language we spoke, and whether I used a translator or interviewed him by myself, Mr. Adzomada insisted that Anlo-Ewe cultural traditions simply did not involve the cultivation of any kind of reified model of sensory systems that clearly spelled out a theory for *how we know what we know*. He would then move to instructing me in the themes and motifs about which he believed I needed to learn to understand Anlo history and culture.

I was initially discouraged by Mr. Adzomada. Naturally this was somewhat depressing, the more so because the longer I reflected on his position that "we don't have that in our culture" and the more I examined the assortment of pieces and chunks of sense-data that emerged from a wide array of interviews, conversations, and observed events, the more deeply I appreciated the sincerity and truth in what he said. On one hand, Anlo cultural traditions have probably never involved an articulated sensorium—an organized, delineated, almost reified or objectified account of the bodily modes of gathering information—and it seemed almost spurious, then, to write about "an indigenous Anlo sensorium." On the other hand, they were clearly using their bodies to gather knowledge. Mr. Adzomada looked, listened, touched, tasted, and so forth.

This is a classic anthropological problem. Anthropologists use the word *emic* to refer to the use of categories, distinctions, and concepts that are meaningful to people within a particular cultural tradition; by contrast, an *etic* perspective draws on categories, rules, and concepts derived from the outsider's point of view (Geertz 1983:56–57). An outsider, however, is necessarily grounded in his or her own respective emic perspective, so etic perhaps more accurately depicts a point of view based on Western science. Since an etic perspective is implicitly Western and scientific, scholars might therefore argue that it is meaningless to the members of the culture to which the concepts are being applied.[2] However, the real problem is not that dualistic, not really a question of which pole represents authenticity. Anthropology inhabits the interstitial spaces, and I maintain that authentic knowledge can be found both in the claims of my *mɔfialawo*—that "we don't have that in our culture"—and in my own position that there does indeed exist an Anlo cultural category that includes sensory experience.

I decided that to proceed I should use John Lucy's discussion of language variability as a model. In his work on linguistic relativity, Lucy explains, "A domain-centered approach begins with a certain domain of experienced reality and asks how various languages encode or construe it. Usually the analysis attempts to characterize the domain independently of language(s) and then determine how each language selects from and organizes the domain" (Lucy 1997:298). He has argued that studies approached in this way "essentially end up showing the distribution of the world's languages relative to a fixed set of parameters drawn from the Western European scientific tradition.... Language becomes a dependent variable, a device for coding or mapping a pregiven reality, rather than a substantive contributor to its interpretation or constitution" (Lucy 1997:300). In this vein, the grouping or taxonomy of touch, taste, smell, hearing, and sight can be seen as a domain that has been developed largely within a Western European scientific tradition. I decided to collect words used to describe what I considered scientifically as the senses. The lexicon for the senses that I present in this chapter, therefore, could be the result of how these terms are used functionally in referring to the domain of sensory experience, but they may lack "structural coherence on language-internal grounds" (Lucy 1997:299).

Only after having returned from the field and after analyzing much of the information I gathered in that initial trip did I realize that Lucy's proposed "structure-centered approach" is probably more fruitful for research on sensory perception rather than a domain-centered approach (see Lucy 1997 for an overview). A structure-centered approach involves identifying a difference in structure of meaning between two languages (such as Euro-American English and Anlo-Ewe) and then examining the interpretation of reality that is implicit in the structure of meaning that we find in this difference (Lucy 1997:296). We would then look for what the "language forms volunteer" in the area of sensing and perception and through the patterns of meaning try to understand "how the world must appear to someone using such categories" (Lucy 1997:296). From the lexicon, then, I move on to consider the implicit internal coherence of these terms.[3]

Unlike other areas of the world, in Anlo-Ewe contexts there are no ancient (written or recorded) texts that we could peruse for epistemological clues about their sensorium. So the excavating of this indigenous theory of inner states had to be done by combing through dictionaries, by listening to proverbs, and by scrutinizing conversations and notes from my observations of habitual forms of bodily practice.[4] Since a consensus (in the strict use of the term) did not seem to emerge around a specific set of senses, I finally chose polyvocality in my efforts to represent their sensorium. That is to say, after interviews with dozens of people, I still did not have a definitive and finite set of sensory modalities with specific names, and I often found disagreement over terminology and the parameters of individual senses. I found, however, that I could

: a kind of (provisional) inventory of sensory fields, and that is what I present below.

CULTURAL CATEGORIES AND THE
DOMAIN OF *FEELING IN THE BODY*

In the late nineteenth century, Diedrich Westermann compiled an Ewe-German dictionary (published in 1905), which was subsequently translated into English in the 1920s, and the term *sense* was rendered in Ewe as *sidzenu* (Westermann 1973[1928]:214). When I first arrived in Anloland in the early to mid 1990s, I tried to use this term to refer to a domain of experience that includes hearing, touch, taste, smell, and sight, but I soon found myself in the middle of a massive problem of translation. *Sidzenu* meant neither that set of experiences nor did it refer to an indigenous category of immediate bodily experiences that were meaningful to the people with whom I worked. *Sidzenu* instead meant something along the lines of "thing recognized" (*dzesi*: to note, observe, recognize; *nu*: thing) and therefore implied a somewhat mentalistic and cognitive (rather than embodied) process or phenomenon. In addition, within the network of Anlo-speaking people with whom I worked (which included highly educated people who spoke both African and European languages, as well as individuals who had little exposure to either formal schooling or European languages), no *mɔfiala* ever proposed or even passively agreed to the word *sidzenu* as a translation for the English word *sense*. I soon came to realize that one discrete lexical term for "the senses" did not seem to exist in the Anlo-Ewe language.

For example, one *mɔfiala* suggested that senses could be called *nusenuwo* (*nu*: thing; *se*: to hear, feel; *nuwo*: things), which means roughly "things with which you can hear or feel things." Later he expanded the designation to *ŋutila nusenuwo* (*ŋuti*: exterior; *la*: flesh; [*ŋutila*: human or animal body]; *nu*: thing; *se*: to hear; *nuwo*: things), which can be translated as "bodily phenomena with which you can hear (or feel, taste, smell, understand, and obey)." Another person described sensing in general as *nusiwo kpena ɖe mia ŋuti hafi mienyaa nusi le dzodzɔm ɖe mia dzi*, which can be translated as "things that help us to know what is happening (on) to us."[5] Sensing was expressed by yet another Anlo-speaking person with the phrase *aleke nese le lame*, which means "how you feel within yourself" or "how you feel in your body." But the expression that seemed to be used most frequently was the very complicated and polysemous term *seselelame*.

Seselelame (which can be translated loosely as "feeling in the body") is best understood in reference to what Thomas Csordas has called "somatic modes of attention" (1993). By this phrase Csordas is referring to "culturally elaborated ways of attending to and with one's body in surroundings that include the embodied presence of others" or "culturally *elaborated* attention *to* and *with* the body in the immediacy of an *intersubjective* milieu" (1993:138–139). And he elaborates:

> Because we are not isolated subjectivities trapped within our bodies, but share an intersubjective milieu with others, we must also specify that a somatic mode of attention means not only attention to and with one's own body, but includes attention to the bodies of others. Our concern is the *cultural elaboration of sensory engagement,* not preoccupation with one's own body as an isolated phenomenon. (Csordas 1993:139, emphasis added)

Seselelame is an ideal illustration of a culturally elaborated way in which many Anlo-speaking people attend to and read their own bodies while simultaneously orienting themselves to objects, to the environment, and to the bodies of those around them. It is difficult to make a direct translation into English of the term *seselelame,* for it refers to various kinds of sensory embodiment that do not fit neatly into Euro-American categories or words. On one hand, it seems to refer to a specific sense or kind of physical sensation that we might call tingling in the skin (sometimes a symptom of impending illness), but in other instances it is used to describe sexual arousal, heartache, or even passion. In other contexts it refers to a kind of inspiration (to dance or to speak), but it can also be used to describe something akin to intuition (when unsure of exactly how you are coming by some information). Finally, people used it to refer to a generalized (almost synesthetic) *feeling in or through the body,* and it was proposed by some as a possible translation for the English term *sense.*

Many people think of perception as cognitive and sensation as physical, but *seselelame* actually straddles that supposed divide. In learning and employing the Ewe language, I usually translated the verb *se* or *sese* mainly as hearing or feeling (although in certain contexts it could be used to mean tasting, smelling, understanding, or obeying and also could be used in reference to knowing, hearing, or comprehending a language). But an Ewe linguist recently suggested to me that *se* could actually be considered a basic perception verb, and he then translated the term *se-se-le-la-me* as "feel-feel-at-flesh-inside."[6] So if *se* (in very broad terms) is "to perceive," we could also render *se-se-le-la-me* as "perceive-perceive-at-flesh-inside"—suggesting that *seselelame* then houses the cognitive function of perception as well as the somatic phenomenon of sensation (inside the flesh).

In addition, *seselelame* is also used in connection with certain emotional states. As one *mɔfiala* explained (in English): "You can feel happiness in your body, you can feel sorrow in your body, and you can feel other things, like cold. *Seselelame* describes all of these things because it is *hearing or feeling in the body. Mesi le lame* is what we say.[7] So from that we just made a verbal noun: *seselelame.*" And later he explained it through the experience of going to the theater: "You go and watch it, and you feel something inside. You hear music, see the actors act very well, and you feel something inside. You applaud, get up and dance, or shout something. That is a feeling and it comes through *seselelame.*"

Elaine was my main research assistant and translated for me when I conducted formal interviews with chiefs, herbalists, midwives, and so forth. She served as a central guide, or *mɔfiala,* for me in 1992 and then again from 1993 into 1995. In one of our many tape-recorded conversations, Elaine described the range of ways she thinks about experiences of *seselelame:*

> *Seselelame* can be a pain or a pleasure. I can feel pain in the body; I can enjoy another thing in the body. Somebody might be—excuse me—holding my breast and then I feel, you know, I enjoy it. So that's *seselelame. . . . Lame* is the flesh, in the body. *Lame vim:* I'm feeling pains in my body. Oh, *leke nye dokome ɖidzɔ kpɔm:* I am happy. *Nye lame koe ɖidzɔ kpɔm:* I am happy within myself. *Sese* is hearing—not hearing by the ear but a feeling type hearing . . . . Yes, *seselelame* means feeling in the body but *esia kple to* means with the ear. Same spelling, same pronunciation, but different meaning. *Esia?* Do you hear? *Esi le lame?* Do you feel it in your body? . . . Before you know that you are not well, you have to feel something in the *lame. . . .* You wake up and then you feel that, 'Oh, I'm not fine.' That means that you are feeling something inside you. *Seselelame ɖeve. Nye meli nyuie egbe o. Seselelame ema.* [Which means:] 'There is an aching, painful feeling in my body. I'm not well, not feeling fine today. That is that feeling in my body.' . . . Sometimes you feel tiredness or a headache; you feel it through your body—*seselelame.* It's through the body that you know you're not fine.

These discussions reveal that painful and pleasurable sensations along with emotional inspiration and physiological indications of illness are all considered part of the category of *seselelame.* They can often blend together in people's experience or in their ideas about experience. So while different words might be employed at different times (in Anlo-speaking contexts) to distinguish certain phases of experience (such as sensation, cognition, or imagination), attention to the connections seemed to be valued, and *seselelame* was often used as the metaterm for many if not most of these inner states of being.

This point is illustrated in the following quote from an interview with Raphael, whom I often talked with during my visits to Accra. He grew up in Anyako, held two master's degrees from the University of Ghana, and subsequently earned his living as an architect. Here he explains how *seselelame, sidzedze,* and *gomesese* are related (though slightly different) experiences or phenomena.

> If you say *sidzedze*—in this case we are relating it to the various senses that we have mentioned in the Western sense [hearing, touch, taste, smell, and sight]—so if you say *sidzedzenu* we mean in effect that you have actually taken the thing to mind or you have actually observed the situation, analyzed it and realized that no, this is the thing....In every level of the senses you can use it. Because it is like I said: you observe and then you analyze the situation with your brain to find out why that sensation, why that *seselelame*? [For example:] They say that this lady has been knocked down by a car. The man, her husband, is a good friend of mine. Your sense will tell you that you have to visit them and express sympathy. Your brain has quickly worked and actually told you your sympathy is called for at that point in time. So we would say you have realized it yourself. So it [*seselelame*] is like *sidzedzenu*—it [*sidzedzenu*] is an advanced form of *seselelame*.... *Gomesese* is understanding ... and is also not too different because when you have a sensation—some source of *seselelame*—you must analyze and understand what that thing can create within you or within the other inmates of the house. So it is a message, an external message, that you get and you have to—in a way—analyze it properly.

Raphael's explanation demonstrates the close links among sensation, perception, emotion, cognition, and so forth and indicates how *seselelame* is best understood utilizing numerous categories or analytic tools. Defying the divide between physical sensation and mental processes of perception, cognition, and imagination, *seselelame* is an indigenous category that bridges such traditional (perhaps Western-based) oppositions.[8] Secondly, Raphael comments that one must analyze and imagine what the "messages" (messages that might otherwise be called sensations, emotions, and intuitions) create within you and within the other people in the house—revealing the intersubjective characteristic of *seselelame*, or how it is a way of "attending to and with one's body in surroundings that include the embodied presence of others" (Csordas 1993:138–139).

EXPLORATIONS OF AN INDIGENOUS ANLO SENSORIUM

If *seselelame* is a cultural category, then what is contained within this class or domain? The answer to this question is not straightforward. It requires both further research at the ethnographic level and extensive discussion of the assumptions embedded in the "category as container" metaphorical concept deeply entrenched in Western philosophical thought (cf. Lakoff and Johnson 1999:51, 341). Here I will limit my discussion to a cursory account of this issue and then turn to several in-depth examples of specific perceptory domains that will illustrate some of the unique ways in which a category of immediate bodily experiences is delineated and elaborated within Anlo cultural worlds.

One way to think about the kinds of phenomena that fall within the category of *seselelame* is to look at the larger class of words to which sense terms belong. This suggests that as the Ewe language evolved (it is genetically related to the languages Fon and Yoruba), there was an encoding of a perceived relationship among ontological states of sensation, emotion, disposition, and vocation. Sapir suggested (1921:100) that "[l]inguistic categories make up a system of surviving dogma—dogma of the unconscious." In the Ewe language, sense words such as hearing, tasting, and seeing seem to belong to a larger class of words beginning with the prefix *nu-* (which can be translated as "thing").[9] The following sensation terms begin with *nu-*: *nusese* (hearing), *nulele* (touching), *nuɖoɖo* (seeing), *nuɖoɖokpɔ* (tasting) and *nuvevesese* (smelling). In addition, some words denoting emotions or affective states begin with *nu-*, such as *nuxaxa* (grief, sorrow), *nugbenugbe* (pain, rage, being beside oneself with anger or joy), *nublanuikpɔkpɔ* (compassion, mercy, commiseration), and *nuɖodzro* (desirous, covetous). Furthermore, certain dispositional states attributed to persons also begin with *nu-*, for instance *nuvɔwɔla* (a person who sins), *nuvela* (a person who is economical or miserly), *nubiala* (a person who begs and asks for things), *nunyala* or *nunyatɔ* (a person who is wise and knowing), and *nublanuitɔ* (a person who is deplorable, miserable, or unfortunate). Finally, many vocational descriptors also begin with *nu-*: *nufiala* (teacher), *nutula* (blacksmith), *nutɔla* (tailor), and *numela* (potter). While there seems to be a social interpretation implicit in this grouping, such a formal analysis needs confirmation from additional ethnographic evidence of how these ideas are reflected in speakers' behavior (Lucy 1997:296). However, these structural similarities may suggest relationships or associations that are embedded in the language, thereby pointing to an archaic notion (Sapir's "system of surviving dogma") of the links among sensing, affect, dispositions, and vocational qualities.

But reports of immediate bodily experiences associated with *seselelame* that I discussed with various Anlo speakers did not amount to a clear reflection of the structural pattern that I have outlined. Instead, a gestalt of all the bodily experiences and inner states that various *mɔfialawo* offered in relation to *seselelame* includes the following: *nusese:* aural perception or hearing; *agbagbaɖoɖo:* a vestibular sense, balancing, and equilibrium from the inner ear; *azɔlizɔzɔ* or *azɔlinu:* kinesthesia, walking, or a movement sense; also *nulele:* a complex of tactility, contact, touch; *nukpɔkpɔ:* visuality or sight; *nuɖɔɖɔ* and *nuɖɔɖɔkpɔ:* terms used to describe the experience of tasting; *nuvevese:* olfactory action or smell; and finally, *nufofo:* orality, vocality, and talking (the prefix *nu-* in this case means "mouth" rather than "thing"). Furthermore, *seselelame* was provided as a specific sense by many people, in addition to serving as a descriptor for a class of experiences.

Here it is useful to borrow from research on the cultural psychology of emotion in our effort to better understand the cultural grounding of sensation. For example, Shweder suggests (1993:418) that we think about the problem of "What is the generic shape of the meaning system that defines an experience as an emotional experience (eg. anger, sadness, or shame) rather than an experience of some other kind (eg. muscle tension, fatigue, or emptiness)?" The same question can be asked in regard to the senses: What is the generic shape of the meaning system that defines an experience as sensory rather than as an experience of some other kind?[10] For example, a problem I raised in chapter 1 concerns why balance is deemed "sensory" in one cultural meaning system, while it is postural, locomotive, or a motor skill in another. And what does this reveal in relation to an Anlo-Ewe theory of knowing? One point is that their category of *seselelame* may be quite fluid in both temporal and spatial terms, and it may have changed significantly during contact with Europeans—with the influence of European languages, typologies, and categories and with European philosophical thought. How *seselelame* is conceived and employed may also differ significantly from one community of Anlo-Ewe people to the next.

However, most of the Anlo speakers I worked with seemed to think of sensing as "feeling in the body" *(seselelame)* and as "bodily ways of knowing what is happening to you" *(ŋutila nusenuwo).* Their conceptualization of *seselelame* did not specify that the "information," or what was to be known, had to originate in a source outside the body. This is quite different from the Western folk model (but surprisingly similar to some Western sensory scientists). Many Westerners make fairly clear distinctions between external senses (hearing, touch, taste, smell, sight) and internal senses (balance, kinesthesia, proprioception) and then emotion (anger, happiness, sadness, disgust, surprise)—especially in our intellectual models. Anlo speakers did not seem to limit their definition of sensing to a category describing only the physical instruments used for assessing the external environment. Instead, they also included ways of monitoring internal states (interoception) in *seselelame.*

I want to make clear, however, that Anlo speakers can distinguish between exteroceptors and interoceptors, or external and internal types of sensing.[11] Their set of senses could almost be divided into two broad groups: those components that begin with the prefix *nu-,* meaning thing or object, and the ones that do not contain *nu-* (plus an in-between or oddball sense of *nufofo,* or speech). All of the terms prefixed by the *nu-* that means "thing or object" concern apprehending something external (note that the *nu-* in *nufofo* [speech] is pronounced with a different tone and means "mouth"), while the other components (balance, movement or kinesthesia, and *seselelame,* or senses of the skin) concern monitoring internal states.

Finally, while we may be able to say that exteroception is the primary orientation of a sensorium intellectually reified and popularly objectified in Euro-American contexts, it seems to be the case that in relative terms an almost opposite orientation (toward interoception, monitoring and stabilizing the internal environment) is more important within Anlo-speaking contexts. This concern with valuation, or a relative hierarchy of senses, governs, to a certain extent, how the various components of their sensorium are presented in the following section. I do not propose that the list should be seen as a rigid typology or a strict hierarchy, but I am suggesting that some of the initial modalities are more highly valued among Anlo speakers than those discussed toward the end. This issue of ranking and classification, or valuation and privileging, is necessarily complicated and will be taken up again at the end of the chapter when I revisit the sensotype hypothesis of social psychologist Mallory Wober.

Given the various disclaimers just covered, a provisional account of an indigenous Anlo sensorium includes the following components:

nusese: aural perception or hearing

agbagbaɖoɖo: a vestibular sense, balancing, equilibrium from the inner ear *azɔlizɔzɔ* or *azɔlinu:* kinesthesia, walking, or a movement sense

nulele: a complex of tactility, contact, touch

nukpɔkpɔ: visuality or sight

nudɔdɔ and *nudɔdɔkpɔ:* terms used to describe the experience of tasting

nuvevese: olfactory action or smell

nufofo: orality, vocality, and talking

seselelame: feeling in the body; also synesthesia and a specific skin sense

With that overview, I will now turn to in-depth descriptions and discussions of the various sensory fields outlined.

NUSESE: AUDITION AND THE ABILITY TO HEAR

Ewe is a tonal language, and slight inflections of pitch in single syllables or the pronunciation of words can produce dramatic differences in meaning or render an utterance completely incomprehensible. In addition, people evocatively play with the sounds of language for humor as well as for sober events such as funerals (e.g., Agawu 1995; Anyidoho 1983; Avorgbedor 1983, 1994; Awoonor 1975). As a native English speaker, when I express myself in Ewe the utterances are so rich that it feels like singing. Sound, in general, is arguably the most dynamic sensory field in not only Anlo-Ewe contexts but in many West African cultures (see Stoller 1989b:101–122; Peek 1994). Kofi Agawu, in fact, presents a soundscape for his beautiful book describing the rhythmic experience and rhythmic expression of people in northern Eweland (1995). And Daniel Avorgbedor (2000) has written eloquently on the "ontology of sound in Anlo-Ewe culture" and on the "phenomenology of sound and its consequences." Avorgbedor even lays out and describes different classes of sound forms that are appropriate to differing Anlo-Ewe social situations, especially in relation to the use of sound in ritual healing. Given the profound role of sound in the cultural experiences of Anlo-speaking people, it may seem that aurality does not receive enough attention in my study. But this is in part because others have written about music, rhythm, and sound in Ewe contexts, and my book aims to balance the scales by engaging the entire sensorium.[12]

In the areas of Anlo-land in which I worked, the Ewe term *nusese* denoted "hearing" or "audition" in the strict sense of the word, but it also signified a more general "sensibility" or "sentiment," as in a kind of ethos. "To hear" was expressed using the root word *se,* but *se* was not limited to sounds perceived and understood through their entrance into the ear alone. *Se* also was used to express feeling something (perhaps emotionally) or experiencing tastes or smells or to convey a deep understanding: an obedience, compliance, or adherence to some phenomenon. Hearing, or *nusese,* therefore, occurred and was experienced in more parts of the body than simply the ear.

Almost all terms proposed by various Anlo speakers as potential translations for a categorical word for "the senses," in fact, contained this root word *se.* For instance, *seselelame* (*sese:* hearing; *le:* within; *lame:* body, flesh, skin) implied that this sensation occurred more generally within the body (or in the sense organ referred to as skin) rather than merely in the ear.[13] Likewise, the term *ŋutila nusenuwo* (translated as "flesh-embedded or bodily phenomena with which you can hear, feel, taste, smell, or understand and obey") drew on this same *se* as the active aspect, or the dynamic dimension, of the idiom. Therefore, while the term *nusese* in its simplest function connoted "hearing" or "to hear" (things), *nusese* actually permeated (linguistically, conceptually, and phenomenologically) nearly every other zone of the sensorium. In the 1920s Westermann discerned (in compiling an Ewe dictionary) that Anlo-Ewe sensibilities were fundamentally aural or at least fundamentally grounded in a concept they referred to as *nusese* (1973[1930]:262). Etymologically, *nusese* was more akin to older meanings of the English term *aural,* which referred to air, breeze, vibration, radiation, and so forth and which could be discerned as much through the skin, eyes, and nose as through the ear.

Hearing, as we typically conceptualize it in modern Western terms, then, is not a very precise gloss for the more far-reaching *nusese.* For example, many Euro-Americans tend to associate *auras* with a sense of vision, we believe that *aural* phenomena are perceived through the ear, and we consider *aromas* to come through the nose. Our forebears, however, probably conceptualized these sensory experiences as more similar than we do today, which would explain their etymological grounding in the Greek *aer,* which is the term for air. As Classen explains (1993b:56) in her study of the senses and language, a "perceived similarity of sound and scent probably has to do with the fact that both are experienced as carried on the air."

An Anlo-Ewe speaker might comment on how delicious a soup smelled by stating, *"Mese detsi la fe veve."* The customary translation would be "I smell the soup's aroma," but since the sentence contains the lexical term *se,* we could translate the comment into English as "I *hear* the soup's aroma." In fact, I often heard Anlo-Ewe speakers express themselves in English using the term *hear* in circumstances where native speakers would use the word *smell.* It would be easy to dismiss this particular discrepancy as a mere lack of fluency in the English language. But I believe that the larger picture suggested the possibility that different embodied experiences and different cultural logics were at work here. Anlo-speaking people with whom I spoke did not seem to experience or conceptualize perceptual processes as restricted to five discrete channels. Phenomena such as "hearing in the skin" or "hearing odor" were not merely problems of language and translation but suggested a difference in embodied experience or aspects of a different *being-in-the-world* (to use Merleau-Ponty's phrase), which was fundamentally aural (cf. Avorgbedor 2000 for a phenomenology and an ontology of sound in Anlo-Ewe).

AGBAGBAƉOƉO AS A VESTIBULAR SENSE: ON BALANCING AND THE INNER EAR

Many West Africans are often seen (in photographs, films, and in person) balancing an object on top of their heads while walking through a market or down a road: a basket filled with mangos, a bucket of water, a tray of carefully stacked oranges, a bundle of firewood, or even a bag of cement. In Srɔgboe, children often transported their desks atop their heads on the way to and from school.

Agbagbaɖoɖo denoted balancing a load and a sense of balance in the Anlo-Ewe language, and in his dictionary Westermann (1973[1928]) indicated two slightly different applications typically attributed to this term. In the first place the verb *ɖo agbagba* meant "to carry something on the head without touching it with the hands" or "to balance" (Westermann 1973[1928]:82), and the form *agbagbaɖoɖo* then translated into English as "balancing." The second use, however, concerned a stage in early childhood development, explained as "to make the first attempts in walking (of a child)" (Westermann 1973[1928]:82). Anlo-Ewe speakers with whom I discussed this issue corrected Westermann. They explained that it was not the first steps taken in walking but rather a baby's act of raising up on two feet and not falling over, thus another way to describe balancing. This skill, acquired in infancy, was so important that to never learn how to do it indicated the individual was an animal—continuing to crawl or move on all four legs. So for many Anlo-speaking people *agbagbaɖoɖo,* or balancing, was an essential part of their definition of what it meant to be human. In fact, Anlo traditional religious beliefs included an understanding of evolutionary changes that occurred and separated humans from other animal life. That is, some Anlo-speaking people believed that standing upright, balancing and moving on two legs, was one of the major characteristics that distinguished us from other animals.

The vestibular sense, therefore, was an important dimension of the phenomenology of perception among Anlo-speaking peoples. Furthermore, as I will show when discussing "Being without Senses" in chapter 9, some Anlo-speaking people believed loss of hearing was the most grave impairment of sensory perception because with this loss would come a disruption to their sense of balance. Hearing and balance were two of the most valued sense modalities and warrant placement at the beginning of an Anlo sensorium. In fact, Avorgbedor (2000:9) links the two by arguing that Anlo-Ewe people "frequently employ the 'hidden' and manifest properties of a variety of sound forms in their ritual performances that seek to restore balance or health in individual biophysiologies or in an entire village community." For many Anlo people, balance and hearing seem to be closely linked.

AZƆLIZƆZƆ OR AZƆLINU:
WALKING AS KINESTHESIA AND A MOVEMENT SENSE

The English term *kinesthesia* comes from the Greek words *kinein,* which means "to move," and *aisthesis,* which means "perception." Kinesthesia is therefore perception through movement, or more technically understood as "a sense mediated by end organs located in muscles, tendons, and joints and stimulated by bodily movements and tensions, also sensory experience derived from this sense" (Woolf 1977:635). In the West, few people typically recognize or know much about this sense, but it is a phenomenon commonly understood and discussed among dancers. Like dancers, many Anlo-speaking people valued movement and believed that much could be perceived and understood by and about a person through his or her carriage or walk.

Since Westermann (1973[1928]:299) indicated that the Anlo-Ewe word *azɔlizɔzɔ* meant walking, marching, or gait, I initially considered it an inappropriate gloss for a movement sense. However, an Ewe linguist clarified that zɔ does have to do with *movement* first and foremost, so that zɔ is not used exclusively to talk about human walks, but a snake can also be said to zɔ (move).[14] The technical term *kinesthesia* implies perception through movement in the joints, muscles, and tendons of the entire body, not just at the locus of the legs in the course of walking. While additional terms could be used to depict other sorts of movement (such as *vava*), many Anlo speakers associated the phenomena of generalized movement (of living bodies) with the term zɔ— to walk, to travel, to move. In fact, walking *(azɔlizɔzɔ or azɔlinu)* carried such significance that the Anlo-Ewe language contained dozens of ways of symbolically essentializing the style or the manner in which a person walks or moves. For instance, zɔ *lugulugu* referred to walking as if drunk; walking *kadzakadza* implied the majestic movement of a lion. In addition, a person could possess "walking about eyes" *(tsa ŋku)* or "walking about hands" *(tsa asi)*. This issue of a lexicon for essentializing different styles of walk forms the basis of an extended example in the next chapter, but the point here is that movement was considered by many Anlo speakers to fit within a category of *feeling in the body* and to be a significant somatic and sensory experience.

Furthermore, walking was not simply a method of transport or a purely practical thing, for it involved movement and gestural motion that emanated from the whole body. For example, women throughout West Africa strap their infants to their backs within a piece of cloth carefully wrapped around their torsos. One Anlo-speaking *mɔfiala* explained this practice by stating, "You cannot walk if you have a baby occupying your arms." To prove her wrong I promptly picked up her granddaughter, held the child against my shoulder, and walked across the room. She took the child from me and set her on the ground, then molded my arms into a slightly bent position and delivered further instructions in the *proper* manner for an Anlo woman to walk. In this exchange I learned that *azɔlizɔzɔ* was not limited to the propelling action of the legs, but involved choreographic dynamics implicating the whole body. Furthermore, many Anlo-speaking people maintained that a person's character was revealed in his or her walk or mode of comportment: the moral fiber of a person was embodied and expressed in the way that he or she moved. The term *azɔlime* referred literally to the way or style in which a person moved and behaved, while it also denoted manner or course of life, deportment, nature, and disposition (Westermann 1973[1928]:299).[15]

Azɔlizɔzɔ (moving), and bodily gesture in general, were so important to Anlo-speaking peoples, in fact, that they invested this sensory sphere with ideas of morality.

SESELELAME AS SPECIFIC SENSATIONS, AS SYNESTHESIA, AND AS A METASENSE

The term *seselelame* can be glossed as "hearing or feeling within the body, flesh, or skin," a more specific usage than described above. *Se* means "to hear, feel, taste, smell, understand, and obey," and when doubled to *sese* it becomes "hearing or feeling (tasting, understanding, etc.)." *Le + lame* can be interpreted several ways but seems to derive from *le* and *me* (or *le eme*), meaning "within," and *la,* which means "meat, flesh, or skin." *Lame* (in the skin, or in the flesh) can also be a word for the "body" proper, so *seselelame* can be glossed as "hearing [with]in the body" or "hearing or feeling [with]in the flesh or skin." This detailed explanation seems necessary in part because (as I mentioned earlier in the chapter) Westermann did not include *seselelame* in his dictionary. Some of the people I consulted speculated that the word *seselelame* was not used when Westermann did his work in the early twentieth century, but others insisted that *seselelame* was an ancient word that was used by their grandfather's grandfathers ad infinitum. Some people suggested that recognition of this word depended upon which village or locale a person was from, as lexical terms varied significantly in places merely ten miles apart. Nonetheless, every Anlo-speaking person I consulted comprehended the word *seselelame*—though they claimed to employ it in more or less different ways and with differing frequency.

One usage of the term *seselelame* can be illustrated with the following three situations. First, when a person was falling in love or was sexually attracted to another person, Anlo speakers often mentioned physical sensations and charged feelings that occurred simply at the thought of the person or mention of the person's name. They attributed this agitation or these perceptions to *seselelame.* Second, when drummers beat out rhythms such as *agbadza* (a particular Ewe form of music and dance) and a person felt inspired to dance, many Anlo-speaking people suggested that it was *seselelame* that moved the person into the circle. Third, when a person's "bones ached" and he or she felt a tingle in the skin and sensed a sickness coming on, this was *seselelame* indicating that the person was about to come down with an illness or become sick. Each of these three cases contained a clearly physical and tangible dimension and had a certain correspondence to the various ways of conceptualizing proprioception.

In the opening chapter I explained that *proprioception* is an English term that refers to an additional sense modality, and yet different definitions of this term exist. Some people define proprioceptors as nerves that keep a person "informed of what is taking place as he works his muscles" (Hall 1966:55). In more technical terms, proprioception means "the reception of stimuli produced within the organism" (Woolf 1977:924), and psychologists sometimes define proprioception as "the sense of body position and movement" (Aronoff et al. 1970:692). These definitions make it difficult to distinguish kinesthesia from proprioception, as both seem to depict sensations related to motion and movement. In the *Oxford English Dictionary, proprioceptive* is defined as "activated by, pertaining to, or designating stimuli produced within the organism by movement or tension in its own tissues, as in muscle sense," while *kinesthesia* is defined as "the sensation of bodily position or of strain or movement of the muscles, tendons, etc., of one's body." Some people seem to use these two terms interchangeably, but for me they are separable. I think of kinesthesia as (interoception) located primarily in the joints and ligaments, while I think of proprioception as (sensory stimulation) located primarily in the muscles and skin.[16] The sensations would be distinct if a person learned to attend differentially to the stimulated sites. How then does this relate to Anlo-Ewe categories?

To answer the question of whether kinesthesia and proprioception are useful concepts to employ when attempting to understand Anlo perceptual worlds, I must first jump ahead a moment and open the next window, which looks into the sensory domain of tactility, contact, and touch. When many Euro-American people talk about touch they often initially relate it to the fingertips and hands, but upon asking them to consider *skin* as a sensory organ they usually suggest that the skin's function is clearly related to touch. In scientific terms, however, skin actually houses at least three sensory modalities: pain receptors, thermal (temperature) receptors, and receptors for tactility or touch (Pieron 1952; Rivlin and Gravelle 1984:32–33).[17] This implies that humans have the potential to distinguish between the following five discrete sensory fields: kinesthesia, proprioception, pain, temperature, and touch. Anthropological questions would then be whether any or all of these sensibilia have been cultivated within the perceptual orientations of different cultural traditions and how different peoples symbolically conceptualize and delineate these perceptual phenomena. In the case of Anlo-speaking peoples, many in-

dividuals with whom I consulted made the following distinctions: what
Western science calls kinesthesia was a sense by itself, generally referred
to as *azɔlizɔzɔ* or *azɔlinu;* Anlo speakers placed what we consider proprioception, pain receptors, and thermal receptors into a different domain and used the term *seselelame* as a set of more or less specific sensations or what might be better translated as "feelings"; and they
considered most tactile receptors to be *nulele.*

A reference point might be useful here, so before exploring Anlo systems in further detail, I will try to show how many Euro-Americans tend
to conceptualize these five phenomena. We tend to categorize the thermal and the tactile receptors under a word we call *touch;* pain is defined
as something distinct from or completely outside of the five senses; and
proprioception is something very few of us think about or name, but
when we experience proprioceptive stimulation we attribute it to a purely
muscular or mystical source. The meaning of "muscular or mystical"
source for proprioception, will become more clear after I explain various nuances of *seselelame.*

In discussing *seselelame* with Anlo-speaking peoples in a variety of
places, such as Accra, Keta, Srɔgboe, Dzelukɔfe, Anloga, and elsewhere,
I collected a profusion of explanations and examples of what it meant.
One usage of *seselelame* referred rather specifically to a kind of skin- and
muscle-based feeling, like proprioception. A more general usage of *seselelame,* however, was more like intuition or extrasensory perception. This
second type of *seselelame* struck me as rather synesthetic, resulting from
a crossover or combination of senses (so that we might refer to it as a
metasense), and as a repository for somewhat mystical information (even
extrasomatic, so that sensing may be part of a broader indigenous theory of inner states that includes affective and dispositional conditions).
So *seselelame* was sometimes used to refer to experiences that were very
bodily based and that corresponded closely to the English concept of
proprioception. But at other times it seemed to be more akin to "intuition" and even had the flavor of what we in Euro-American contexts
might refer to as "extrasensory perception." Anlo-speaking people often
described sensations for this kind of *seselelame* as uncanny feelings or
messages they received that turned out to be a premonition. Examples
include *seselelame* as a source of motivation to visit a relative right before he died or as confirming the presence of an ancestor at a specific
communal event. A "message" was usually associated with these kinds
of *seselelame* experiences, and for that reason people often linked it to
the English term for "hearing." They spoke of hearing a message or hear-

ing information not through their ears but throughout their entire being; they somehow "knew something" but could not really account for how they knew it. This kind of *seselelame* was considered deeper and more mysterious than specific bodily sensations and was not necessarily attributed to them. This kind of *seselelame* was also more difficult for people to describe than when they experienced, for instance, specific sensations in the skin. Some even expressed a fear of danger surrounding mere attempts to put these experiences into words.

NULELE: A COMPLEX OF TACTILITY, CONTACT, AND TOUCH

While gathering information on sensory experiences in Anlo-land, the phenomenon I think of as "touch" was probably the most problematic. There seemed to be a profusion of expressions for what all seemed to be "tactility." Translation into my own experience and cognitive framework proved to be extremely confusing, and I frequently made mistakes in comprehension, expression, and interpretation. Taking this as a sign of the complexity of this sensory arena, my own model (while representing a distillation of a large array of information about sensations and experiences related to touch) is offered as a provisional scheme.

Five root words appeared over and over again in my observations and discussions about touch, and they are arranged phenomenologically into a kind of continuum of intensity. In its barest simplicity, the continuum consisted of *li* (caress), *ka* (contact), *le* (seize), *tɔ* (push), and *fo* (strike). Initially I was reluctant to accept as *tactility* the last three categories of seize, push, and strike (*le, tɔ,* and *fo*), but people consistently offered them as aspects of *contact* or *touch* and argued for the correspondence with a kind of haptic experience. For instance, as I protested the inclusion of *fo* (which is a verb for "to beat or strike") in an Anlo sensorium, one *mɔfiala* offered the following proverb (which utilizes *fo*): *Alesi tsi fo ame la, womefua dzo nenema o.* A literal translation suggests, "In the manner in which rain beats on a person, he should not warm himself at the fire in this way." Stated more elegantly: "You do not warm yourself according to the severity of your wetness," or "A person does not need to warm himself as much as he was drenched by rain" (Dzobo 1975:191). By citing this proverb, this *mɔfiala* was trying to make the following point: in this context rain was contacting or touching the skin (expressed as *tsi fo ame la*), and the sensation in the skin produced by this experience was best summed up by *fo* (to strike, beat, or pound). The lexical term *fo,* therefore, represented a tactile experience, or it referred to a kind of perception that occurred at the level of skin receptors, and it emerged consistently in conversations with Anlo-speaking people when addressing the phenomenon of touch.

Before explaining additional Anlo-Ewe expressions and experiences concerning touch (identified as *li:* caress, *ka:* contact, *le:* seize, and *tɔ:* push), let me briefly address the question of whether these various terms simply represent differences at the level of language or are experientially and phenomenologically distinct. The problem of precisely how much influence language has on perception is a complex issue and is not directly addressed in this study (for an in-depth examination of the linguistic-relativity question, see Lucy 1992). Here I am looking instead at how the senses that are valued and emphasized in a particular cultural tradition work in symbolic ways to orient the self in a particular direction. Euro-American traditions of the past few centuries have emphasized five senses, and I would suggest that we thereby categorize much of our experience and many perceptual events in our lives in terms of seeing, tasting, touching, smelling, and hearing. The acquisition of language in our early years aids us in differentiating among those five experiences or functions. Anlo-speaking people generally did not have a notion of five specific channels or five specific sensory fields into which experiences were packaged and labeled. In addition, they did not have an overarching term under which all touching, tactility, or contact seemed to be placed. Instead, children learned a variety of terms to describe or reflect on different experiences involving contact or touch. I summarized the array of experiences in the five lexical terms listed earlier, and from this continuum it is clear that there was a great range of intensity in the realm of contact or touch. These various terms represented both language differences and discrete sensations that many Anlo-speaking people considered experientially and phenomenologically distinct.

However, distinctions symbolized by the terms are probably the basis for the phenomenological differences and are therefore intimately linked to cultural logic. For instance, if we Euro-Americans place a hand or fingertips on cotton cloth and then on a brick, we might describe the first sensation as "soft" and the second sensation as "hard," but both experiences are considered "tactile," or both encounters are classified as "touching." For many Anlo-speaking people, however, these constitute two distinct phenomena; a common term like *touch* is not applied to these two distinct sensations. The first is typically described using the term *li* or *nali ekpɔ* (which could also be spelled *naleekpɔ*), and the second situation (describing contact with hard objects such as a rock or book) calls for the term *ka asi enu* or *de asi nu ŋu*. Westermann treated these as verbs with no reference to sensing or sensations. He described *li* as "to rub, touch lightly, stroke, caress, pat" (1973[1928]:153), while *ka* was simply "to touch," and *ka asi nu ŋu* meant "to touch a thing" (1973[1928]:114). Some *mɔfialawo* who also spoke English did not agree with his translations, however, and insisted that these were two different sensations, two different ways of touching and experiencing feedback from interaction with the different classes of objects. Furthermore, they expressed difficulty in finding words in English to express their reflections on the experiences. In light of the fact that Western scientists now recognize or acknowledge that there are different nerve receptors that exist in the skin that allow the human body to distinguish between contact with soft and hard objects, the symbolic and culturally constituted nature of perception is evident here.

Within a continuum of various Anlo-Ewe concepts of tactility, the final two lexical terms are *le* (to grasp or seize) and *tɔ* (to shove or push). Like *fo*, discussed above in terms of "strike," it was difficult to conceptualize "grasping" and "shoving" as sense modalities, yet *le* (in the form of the word *nulele* [*nu:* thing; *lele:* grasping]) was probably the most commonly cited term in the Ewe language that was offered as a way to think about tactility. Westermann (1973[1928]:152) translated *le* as "to seize, catch, hold, or grasp." *Le* was also used to denote "keeping" or "holding," in the sense of maintaining an idea or sustaining a sensory experience in one's mind. In addition, one could catch, grasp, or touch with parts of the body other than the hand, for example, certain sicknesses that affect the whole body are expressed as *dɔlele* (*dɔ:* sickness, disease; *lele:* seizing, catching, holding). In addition, while this will be discussed at length in later chapters, it should be mentioned here that to contain harmful spirits also implicated this sensory realm since the same tactility-oriented *le* was contained in the term *legba* (ritual objects that served as guardians of thresholds). As for *tɔ*, Westermann translated it as "to push, thrust, strike, knock, hit; to touch; to sting, to stab" (1973 [1928]:238), so *tɔ* seemed to represent a kind of focused, active, intentional kind of touching, and this was the term used when making imperative statements. However, the specific part of the body to use in the act of touching had to be stated, so simply commanding someone to *tɔ* an object was meaningless. Instead, it would be expressed as "touch it with your hand" *(tɔ asie)*, "touch it with your foot" *(tɔ afɔe)*, "touch it with your elbow" *(tɔ abɔkugluie)*, "touch it with one finger" *(tɔ asibide)*, and so on. Rather than speaking about a generalized kind of touching or exhibiting a cultural logic that subsumed a myriad of haptic experiences into one basic category, the expressions of many Anlo-speaking people tended to indicate that they experienced a range of intensities and types of tactile contact considered distinctive enough that we are left with the question of whether these are discrete senses or sensations that contemporary science suggests humans certainly have the ability to feel.

NUFOFO AS ORALITY, VOCALITY, AND TALKING

An overlap exists between the sensory component of touch and this sense of *nufofo* (speech) with the common morpheme *fo*. While the basic, root meaning of *fo* is "to strike," this word involves a wide range of derivative uses that include baking bread, cooking soup, shooting a gun, chopping down a tree, and others (see Westermann 1973[1928]:62). In the previous section I discussed how *fo* is used to depict contact or a kind of touching of or being touched by an object or substance, as in one person striking another or in the sense of rain beating or drenching one's skin. This section will explore yet another use of *fo,* which involves a striking action or a striking sensation that Euro-Americans think of as orality, vocality, or talking.

Among Anlo-Ewe speakers, *nufofo* generally referred simply to the act of "talking" or "speaking," and while "talking" is difficult for most Euro-Americans to accept as one of the senses, it was almost always offered as one by my Anlo-speaking *mɔfialawo.* That is, any time I asked a *mɔfiala* to talk to me (in Ewe) about the different ways one can "feel what is happening to oneself" (meaning experience or sense some phenomenon), *nufofo* was nearly always presented among the various sensory fields.

While the English term *oral* certainly means "spoken" and "uttered by the mouth or in words," it also means "of, given through, or affecting the mouth" (Woolf 1977:806). Anlo-speaking people often expressed how their term *nufofo* also had these two levels of meaning. Furthermore, they would elaborate on how substances and phenomena that were "of, given through, or affecting the mouth" created sensations from which one's surroundings (or the world) were perceived and interpreted. In Anlo terms, things that could flow in and out of the mouth included breath, food, saliva, liquid, words, sounds, and so on, and therefore the mouth and *nufofo* were regarded as a site or channel for very powerful phenomena. Furthermore, just as sensing in their language was conceptualized with the more general term *seselelame* (feeling in the body), speaking too fell within a broader category of experience they referred to as *sesetonume:* feeling in the mouth. This category includes sensations involved in eating, drinking, breathing, regulation of saliva, and sexual exchanges and also speech.

Because Euro-Americans tend to think of speech as an "active externalization of data" (Classen 1993b:2) and to think of sensing as a passive receipt of stimulus from something outside the body, and because we think of speaking as learned and sensing as innate, these two bodily experiences or functions are typically considered distinct. But Anlo speakers emphasized similarities and relationships in the experiences of speaking, eating, kissing, and so forth and called these *sesetonume:* feeling in the mouth.

Furthermore, words are not only information or knowledge but also sound, so in addition to their meaning, words have a physical force that operates not only at the site of the ear and mind but throughout the entire body. With the Anlo term for speech and talking *(nufofo)* containing the morpheme *fo* (which means to strike, beat, blow), there is a symbolic acknowledgment of the dynamic power ascribed to the words themselves. While this might simply represent naming the physical thing that happens when people talk, some Anlo people with whom I worked talked about speaking as involving striking or forceful sensations (or *sesetonume:* feelings in the mouth).[18] In an abstract way, words were thought by some to be projected and directed or wielded with force and also with the intention of hitting a mark. Such "launching" or projection could be done with positive, negative, and, occasionally (but rarely), neutral intentions. This idea of the "power of words" has been well documented for numerous African cultures (e.g., Finnegan 1969; Peek 1981, 1994; Ray 1973; Stoller 1984b; Yankah 1995), but here I would like to adhere specifically to the sensorial and embodied dimensions of *nufofo*. Many Anlo-speaking people would agree with the idea that "sound surrounds and penetrates the listener" (Howes 1991:171), since they frequently expressed to me that a listener could simultaneously be the producer of sound when that sound was a result of the listener's own *nufofo*. Therefore, sound produced from within oneself travels through the speaker creating vibrations and force as in *sesetonume*—feeling in the mouth. In *nufofo*, then, there was an implicit collapsing of subject and object in that the producer of the sound was automatically (even if deaf since vibrations can be felt) a listener too.

Speech is therefore classified as a kind of *seselelame* or as involving *feeling* that occurs *within the body*. In many West African contexts speech is believed to have a power or energy independent of its referential quality. This is illustrated by the following quotation from Stoller's essay "Sound in Songhay Cultural Experience," which describes the attitudes of Songhay people of Niger and touches upon the ideas of Wolof-speaking people of Senegal and the Jelgobe Fulani of Burkina Faso.

> Words do not just have meaning—they are breath and vibrations of air, constituted and shaped by the body and motives of the speaker, physically contacting and influencing the addressee. So informants liken the effect of a *griot*'s praise-song on his addressee to the effect of wind upon fire (both metaphorically and literally, since air and fire are supposed to be basic constituents of the body). (Irvine as quoted by Stoller 1984b:567)[19]

Many West Africans believe that when you produce speech you indeed can feel it moving through you (as in *sesetonume*—feeling in the mouth—and as though inspiration comes in an embodied form and can be interoceptively sensed), and as others speak, your body registers or experiences the impact of their speech. So the term for speech *(nufofo)* as "striking thing" symbolizes (or condenses and collapses) at least a strand of cultural logic about the dynamic power that words can contain.

Moreover, in cultures where the written word and other visual modes of representation are not as highly valued as they are relative to other sense modalities (or in comparison to their valuation in cultural contexts such as Euro-America), the aural and the oral are in certain ways inseparable (Howes 1991:8–11). That is, one cannot conceive of hearing without linking it to speech, so they implicitly belong in the same indigenous category of sensing or *feeling within the body* (cf. Yankah 1995 on how the Akan royal orator functions as not only the chief's mouth, but his ears as well). This may seem to contradict the beliefs outlined previously, and in our cultural logic it probably does, but I am suggesting that Anlo speakers simultaneously hold these two views of the existential and functional properties of speech. Among neighboring Fon speakers, "Critical to the activation potential of speech is both its transferential nature and its potent social and psychodynamic grounding" (Blier 1995:77). In Anlo contexts, too, the "transferential nature" of *nufofo* (speaking) included more than imparting meaning, or "mental ideas." Furthermore, words uttered by one person were considered to form a direct link between the speaker and the addressee, so that a circular flow of energy was set in motion.

The essence of this perspective was that a person could not say something (or project something from his or her mouth) without feeling something, too. As an analogy, when one strikes a fist or palm against an object, the contact causes vibrations to reverberate through one's own body as well as having an impact on the object struck; when engaging in *nu-fofo,* the sound waves affect the speaker while simultaneously traveling outward and enveloping the listener. Words in Anlo-land, therefore, were not just thoughts or mental phenomena but came from the body (as well as the mind), and many Anlo speakers believed that there was power not simply in "words as carriers of referential meaning, but in the sounds of the words," too (Stoller 1984b:568). Finally, later chapters will explore some etiologies of disease and how *nufofo* could be the cause of a grave illness many Anlo-speaking people referred to as *enu* (which literally meant "mouth"). *Enu* would often result when bad words and ill will were exchanged in the course of *nufofo,* so that many people believed that the circular flow of energy set in motion (during speech acts) could bring illness upon both speaker and listener but that it most typically preyed upon innocent children who were caught in the cross fire of negatively charged *nufofo* (talking, or speech). Clearly, the mouth and speech were regarded by many Anlo people as a site or channel for very powerful phenomena, and this illness called *enu,* along with other detailed implications, will be taken up at length in later chapters.

NUKPƆKPƆ FOR SEEING, VISUALITY, OR SIGHT

Westermann (1973[1928]:146, 180) translated *kpɔ* as "to see, look, behold; to visit; to notice, observe; to experience, examine; to have, obtain, possess" and *nukpɔkpɔ* as "seeing, sight; possessing, possession, property." However, "the gaze" (to use Foucault's terminology) was not necessarily as highly valued in Anlo-land as many scholars suggest it is in the contemporary West and in relation to the many other sensory fields stressed in Anlo contexts. Anlo-speaking people certainly employed various visual terms or occasionally expressed things through visual idioms, but in the final analysis they had less linguistic elaboration around color terminology, for instance, than they had around textures or about carriage and style of walk. On the other hand, while I placed *nukpɔkpɔ* lower on the list of senses than modalities such as touch, movement, and audition, this does not mean sight was not important to most Anlo people, and in fact, *nukpɔkpɔ* was a complicated phenomenon characterized by nuanced paradoxes.

A well-known proverb among Anlo speakers (and many Ewe-speaking peoples in general) was *Ne ŋku-gbagbatɔ be yele kpe fu ge wo la, nyae be ɖee wo ɖo afɔ kpe dzi:* "If a blindman says he is going to stone you, know

he has set his foot upon a stone." Dzobo (1975:152) suggested this was a
saying that concerned self-confidence and explained it as "a comment on
what somebody wants to do, and in that sense is another way of saying
that the person is sure of his ability to do it. He *knows* what he wants to
do. He is sure of himself." As usual, however, multiple layers of
signification are at work in this saying, and two additional meanings reveal something about ways of sensing among many Anlo-speaking people. The first connotation concerns the sense covered previously, *nufofo,*
and simply warns that *people mean what they say.* The second connotation of the proverb relates to the sense of sight, instructing in the idea that
seeing is not the only modality that allows a person to get something done.
The blind man could employ other senses, such as hearing, movement,
and touch, and despite not being able to see, he could skillfully strike you
with a stone.

While many Anlo-speaking people readily admitted to a fear or ab-
horrence of going blind, they also regularly rehearsed a kind of cultural
logic warning about the limitations of sight. That is, the idea of "seeing
is believing" was not axiomatic among Anlo speakers, who instead
seemed to cultivate a deep respect for *unseen* things. The existence of
"the invisible world" was not suspect for many Anlo speakers, and instead they often held a firm belief in the existence of a whole arena of
things that human beings were simply unable to see. Furthermore, it was
not considered particularly healthy to worry over or question this basic
fact, for when necessity urged a greater knowledge about this realm (a
"sounding out" or "seeing into" invisible domains), one simply consulted a specialist (such as a *bokɔ* or *amegashi*) for divination. But in
general, the existence of a great many invisible things was readily accepted, and other senses (such as hearing, or even *seselelame*) were considered equally reliable when compared with sight and when searching
for confirmation or proof of some phenomenon.

Another illustration of many Anlo-speaking people's belief that there
were deep limitations to relying primarily on sight was the aphorism,
"There is no art to find the mind's construction on the face." Cited by
several *mɔfialawo,* the saying was meant to convey to me that what was
revealed in a person's visage was not a reliable indication of the content
of his mind; no matter how much artistry one possessed, one could not
see what went on inside another person's heart or head. From this basic
idea stem several other beliefs illustrative of sensory orientations and cultural logic. First, other senses (in addition to sight) must be used to read
and understand human beings *(amegɔmesese).*[20] Second, like other

African peoples, Anlo speakers also cultivate what Robert Farris Thompson has referred to as an "aesthetic of the cool." More specifically, and in relation to Yoruba culture, Thompson (1966:86) explains how the "equilibrium and poetic structure of traditional dances ... as well as the *frozen facial expressions* worn by those who perform these dances, expresses a philosophy of the cool, an ancient, indigenous ideal: patience and collectedness of mind." In relation to maintaining cool and to displaying a so-called frozen facial expression, many Anlo-speaking mothers with whom I talked about child-rearing strategies mentioned the importance of teaching their children different ways of hearing and seeing. One such alternate way to hear or see involved taking things in but letting them pass through and remaining "cool." Again, this issue will be taken up in chapter 7 in relation to balance and in chapter 9 in relation to Anlo concepts of well-being.

Finally, while *nukpɔkpɔ* may not have been the most highly valued sense within the whole repertoire, it would be inaccurate to suggest that Anlo-speaking people did not think with vision-based terms, phrases, and idioms. "Insofar as thought depends on language ... the sensory foundations of many of the words we think with demonstrate that we not only think *about* our senses, we think *through* them" (Classen 1993b:8–9). In the Anlo-Ewe language, there were numerous terms and idioms that referred to eyesight or vision. For instance, *kpɔdeŋu* was a term denoting "example" but translated literally into English as "see near it" or "see around and close to it." When warning someone to be careful, one would declare, *"Kpɔ nyuie!"* which meant "Look well!" and was akin to shouting, "Watch out!" And *Mavu ŋku o* (your eyes are not open) was a way of commenting on a person's uncivilized or crude demeanor. So, while the notion of "seeing is believing" did not necessarily hold much weight among many Anlo-speaking people, *nukpɔkpɔ* still held a significant role in Anlo traditions and as a sensory field.

NUÐƆÐƆ AND NUÐƆÐƆKPƆ FOR GUSTATION AND "TASTING TO SEE"

Nuɖɔɖɔ was commonly conceptualized as a taste-bud, tongue-based, bodily type tasting and included a range of flavors such as sweet, salty, bitter, fermented, as well as the sensation of textures that were experienced during the consumption of food. *Nuɖɔɖɔkpɔ* literally meant "taste and see" or "eat a thing and see." This was a metaphorically synesthetic sense differing from straight *nuɖɔɖɔ* in that *nuɖɔɖɔkpɔ* implied more cognitive qualities. Most tasting and eating was not considered to produce mental images, according to many of the Anlo-speaking people with whom I consulted, and was referred to as basic *nuɖɔɖɔ* (tasting) or *nuɖuɖu,* which is the word for "eating." But if food stimulated the mind, then it was experienced as *nuɖɔɖɔkpɔ* (eating and seeing). *Nuɖɔɖɔ* was therefore commonly associated with quotidian consumption of food, whereas *nuɖɔɖɔkpɔ* related sensations of taste to the mind. While not all *mɔfialawo* agreed with this division between *nuɖɔɖɔ* and *nuɖɔɖɔkpɔ,* enough people suggested that there were at least two different ways of tasting (or two distinct and general experiences in relation to sensations of taste) that an Anlo sensorium was best described as encompassing at least these two.

Underscoring the interplay between emic and etic perspectives, which is at the root of my efforts to construct an "indigenous Anlo sensorium," Western science also sometimes divides taste into two categories. According to some psychologists, "Taste, or gustation, may be considered in two ways: as the global sensation or perception that accompanies ingestion or as the specific sensation that accompanies stimulation of specialized organs in the mouth" (Aronoff et al. 1970:284). While not an exact parallel with Anlo cultural logics surrounding gustation, both models suggest thinking about (or through) *taste* in two different ways. Others have suggested that two is even an inaccurate reduction of human gustatory sensibilities: "Taste ... turned out to be among the most complex of the sensory systems" and it is "possible to make a case for considering sweet, salty, bitter, and sour each as a separate sensory system" (Rivlin and Gravelle 1984:17–22). While Anlo-speaking people had separate ways of describing sweet, salty, bitter, and sour, many categorized all four under the sensation of taste. However, many Anlo speakers distinguished between *nuɖɔɖɔ,* which was a type of taste associated with the act of eating, and *nuɖɔɖɔkpɔ,* which related tasting to thought.

Taste is a domain where links between perception and *cultural logic and symbolic life* may be more readily apparent than in relation to other sensory modalities. Bourdieu's (1984) reintegration of elementary tastes for the flavors of food with more elaborated aesthetic and reflective tastes as an avenue to illuminate distinctions and the legitimation of social differences is also relevant to the ethnography of Anlo-speaking peoples. Preferences for certain tastes, as well as the activity of eating itself, were associated by many Anlo-speaking people with distinctions in identity, elements, and terms of well-being and with ritual transformations of ontological states. For example, many Anlo speakers' notions of well-being linked directly to the idea that "you are what you eat." While they had not developed as elaborate a set of beliefs around food as the humoral system of South Asia (e.g., Laderman 1983:21–72), they did hold decided ideas about the strength and weakness of certain foods. *Akple,* the staple grain eaten in most Anlo households, was considered "strong," whereas rice (eaten only on special occasions) was considered "weak." Taste for rice and consumption of large amounts of rice was deemed to both weaken a person and ultimately result in illness.

In terms of links between tastes and identity, in the cosmopolitan setting of Accra, where language was a common marker of ethnicity, many Anlo-speaking people also tended to notice and comment on the food that people consumed in public places. Again, while symbolism encoded in food was not as systematically developed as in South Asia—and therefore did not result in the extreme "gastro-politics" underpinning certain tensions and conflicts in South India (Appadurai 1981)—still, to a certain extent what a person ate in public (in Accra) identified (for many Anlo speakers) where the person was from or the person's ethnic identity. Not just Anlo speakers but Ewe-speaking people in general were a numeric minority in Ghana and consequently exhibited a great deal of sensitivity to issues of ethnicity and identity politics.

A final example of how perceptory tastes link to cultural logic can be explored in religious rituals, which often culminate in the exchange of food, offering of food to the ancestors, or consumption by initiates of certain herbs, liquids, or foods. In a discussion of "medicine cults" adopted into the southern Ewe area in the first half of the twentieth century, Fiawoo (1968) describes a practice referred to as *atikeɖuɖu* (eating the medicine), the final act for initiates of the Blekete religious sect.

> Kneeling before the priest and the *Blekete* altar, the applicant makes the following declaration: "I dedicate myself to you *Nana* and your services. Help my children to live. Save my family from evil influences." The priest shares with the initiate kolanut which has been sanctified at the altar. The chewing of the nut and the shaking of hands makes the reception of the initiate into full membership. (Fiawoo 1968:75)

Missing from this account is any comment on taste, flavor, or the experiential aspect of *atikeɖuɖu* (eating the medicine). While it can be assumed that "chewing the nut" (along with shaking hands) structurally symbolizes or signifies a transformation, is this experienced as *nuɖɔɖɔkpɔ,* or "tasting to see"? In other words, rather than simply *nuɖɔɖɔ* (tasting), or even *nuɖuɖu* (eating), does chewing the kolanut relate sen-

sations of taste (at this pivotal moment of transformation) to images in
the mind? If so, what does this reveal about the powers of the taste
process to assist in the transformation from initiate to member? In my
own research I did not have discussions with members of the Blekete sect
and therefore was not able to inquire about lived and embodied experiences of *atikeququ* (eating the medicine). But these are some of the questions that arise when attention is turned not only to the nuances of an
indigenous sensorium (to understand, for instance, why and how many
Anlo speakers make distinctions between *nuɖɔɖɔkpɔ*, tasting to see, and
basic *nuɖɔɖɔ*, or tasting) but also to the experiential and embodied side
of perception and cultural logic.

NUVEVESE AND NUVEVESESE FOR OLFACTION, SMELL, AND SYNESTHETIC DIMENSIONS OF HEARING AROMA OR SCENT

As with Anlo-speaking people's ordering of taste, there were at least two
conceptually different kinds of *nuvevese*—a term that corresponded to
the English word *olfaction,* or *smell. Nuvevese* was described as actively
trying to know a scent by intentionally and consciously using the olfactory organ (i.e., one's nostrils or nose). The other kind was more passive: an odor or scent flowed around or surrounded a person not unlike
music or sound. Some people suggested that this distinction was reflected
in the two terms *nuvevese* (to smell) and *nuvevesese* (smelling), which on
one hand simply represented different grammatical forms of the same
word but also respectively signified "actively seeking to smell" and "passively smelling." The idea that these were simply two forms of the same
word (and therefore referred basically to the same activity or experience)
was often expressed by Anlo-speaking people who had a fair amount of
formal education. Those with whom I spoke who had less formal education seemed more willing to articulate (or accept) different experiences
being categorized under these two terms: *nuvevese* (to smell actively) and
nuvevesese (passively smelling). Stepping back from the issue of vocab-
ulary, however, most people seemed to believe or agree that there was
not one uniform experience of olfaction, and smelling did indeed involve
active and passive experiences.[21]

The sensation referred to as passive *nuvevesese* was often described
as similar to hearing: when not *trying* to smell an object (for instance,
placing one's nose near or toward a soup or a piece of fruit), one could
still be enveloped by an aroma or fragrance and simply "hear it" in or

with the whole body. A similar conception of olfaction is described in a cultural history of aroma in the Western world:

> Significant advances have been made in the understanding of the biological and chemical nature of olfaction, but many fundamental questions have yet to be answered: is smell one sense or two—one responding to odours proper and the other registering odourless pheromones (air-borne chemicals)? Is the nose the only part of the body affected by odours? (Classen, Howes, and Synnott 1994:3)

Many Anlo-speaking people would probably respond to these questions with the affirmations that smell was definitely two senses and that the nose was by no means the only part of the body affected by odor.[22]

In fact, the second type of olfaction contained a metaphorical (if not literal) synesthetic quality. *Nuvevesese* contains the complex verb *sese,* which could mean hearing, feeling, tasting, smelling, understanding, obeying, and so forth. Some *mɔfialawo* characterized *nuvevesese* as feeling a fragrance or aroma all through and around the body. It was therefore more similar to hearing than sight since one could "hear odors" and "hear sounds" that were behind one's body or even inside an enclosed (hence, invisible) space. And when Anlo speakers expressed themselves in English, some (even fairly educated) people used the word *hear* when they referred to sensing a scent. When confronted with why they used that word when aware of the English word *smell,* they would often explain that they did not mean one was "hearing scent with the ears," but they did indeed mean to say "hearing scent through the nose" (and not smelling it per se in the active sense of "to smell"). They felt an inability to express this nuance in English but thought that using the word *hear* was closer to what they meant than the word *smell.* Therefore, *nuvevesese* signified a more synesthetic type of olfaction that affected or was sensed by more parts of the body than simply the nose and indicated that there were at least two kinds of olfaction within an Anlo sensorium.

This list should not be considered a finished product, but rather it should be seen as a starting point in our efforts toward understanding sensory experiences, consciousness, and development of person and self in Anlo worlds. Toward that end, let me now turn to a discussion of how to break away from typologies, hierarchies, and the impulse to modularize sensory modes and move toward an exploration of the "cultural elaboration of sensory engagement" (Csordas 1993:139) in Anlo-Ewe worlds.

FROM WOBER'S "SENSOTYPE" TO BOURDIEU'S "HABITUS" AND CSORDAS'S "CULTURAL ELABORATION OF SENSORY ENGAGEMENT"

For many people, the list that I generated earlier in the chapter constitutes the end of the story, or represents, in their estimation, what ought to be the culmination of this book. That is, when I converse with people about what I do, or when I present my work in a public forum (including academic audiences) many people want me to outline what we might call "an Anlo sensotype" (even though very few people actually use that phrase in their request). They want to know first and foremost what senses Anlo speakers "have" (and are particularly interested in the notorious "sixth sense," which I discussed in chapter 1). Second, people wonder which senses are most important to them, so they want a hierarchy or a ranking of the sensory modes valued by Anlo people. And finally, some people ask about measuring and testing for the relative abilities to hear, balance, and see (etc.) between Anlo-speaking people and Euro-Americans (or among other ethnically or culturally different groups).

This set of concerns represents one level of work in the arena of culture and the senses. But even if I addressed all of those questions, I am not certain we would have gained much by way of any greater understanding of meaningful differences between cultural worlds. A sensotype is on the surface an intriguing notion and one that fascinated me for a period of time while I was in the field. *Sensotype* was a term employed more than three decades ago by Mallory Wober to refer to a "pattern of relative importance of the different senses, by which a child learns to perceive the world and in which pattern he develops his abilities" (1966:182). According to Wober's claim, individuals tend to develop abilities grounded in senses that are more highly valued or more frequently utilized in the pattern of sensory orientations characteristic of a particular place or within a specific cultural milieu. But let us pretend that at this point I provided you with a conclusive study demonstrating that the average Anlo-Ewe person scored higher than the average Euro-American on a test measuring vestibular skills (the ability to balance while walking across a beam, or the ability to maintain an object balanced on top of one's head, etc.). In the large scheme of things, what would that prove? What significant issue on the world's stage would that piece of information help us to come to grips with? For me, it would answer very little by way of meaningful, palpable differences between two different cultural groups.

To me, the important issue is that in Anlo epistemological traditions and ontological practices, bodily movements specifically in the form of reified kinds of walks are instrumentally tied to forms of thinking and reasoning, especially about moral character. We now move away from any impulse toward sensotyping and instead focus on very local concerns around "somatic modes of attention" and on the "cultural elaboration of sensory engagement" (Csordas 1993). In doing this I will not systematically cover each of the sensory components I laid out previously (which is in part what I mean when I use the phrase "impulse toward sensotyping"), but rather I will focus on those sensory fields that are "performatively elaborated" (Csordas 1993) in the habitus inhabited by those Anlo *mɔfialawo* with whom I worked. It is here that I believe we can come to understand more about how sensory experiences are pivotal in the formation of identity and cultural difference.

PART TWO

Moral Embodiment and Sensory Socialization

CHAPTER 4

Kinesthesia and the Development of Moral Sensibilities

In his work on embodiment, Csordas (1990:40) draws a distinction between his own argument about the body as the existential ground of culture and self and the point of view taken by Johnson (1987), who treats the body as the cognitive ground of culture. While my own use of *embodiment* follows Csordas to a great extent, I am also interested in Johnson's cognitive approach. For Johnson, "the term 'body' is used as a generic term for the embodied origins of imaginative structures of understanding" and "our embodiment is essential to who we are, to what meaning is, and to our ability to draw rational inferences and to be creative" (Johnson 1987:xv, xxxviii). Both approaches inform my own study, which simultaneously explores existential and corporeal reverberations of the sensorium outlined in the previous chapter and attends to Johnson's "rational inferences" or the "imaginative structures of understanding" that correspond to (or even stem from) this culturally constituted sensory order (cf. Lakoff and Johnson 1999). In other words, looking at symbolic life in terms of *cultural logic* as well as *embodiment* involves exploring cognitive inferences that analogically extend from (or are integrally tied to) a culturally constructed sensorium as well as exploring "embodied processes of perception" among Anlo speakers, or what Csordas describes (1990:9) as "the experience of perceiving in all its richness and indeterminacy."

Merleau-Ponty's phenomenology involves a rejection of the empiricist model that suggests external objects stimulate our internal organs

73

such that we register sensory data and instead embraces the idea that perception begins in the body and ends in objects (Csordas 1990:8–9). Merleau-Ponty's concept of the *preobjective,* therefore, suggests that "we do not have any objects prior to perception," or "objects are a secondary product of reflective thinking" (Csordas 1990:9). Furthermore, since a separation of subject from object is the result of analysis, it is independent of (or irrelevant to) the experience of being-in-the-world. The adaptation to anthropology of Merleau-Ponty's approach is conceptualized by Csordas in the following way: "If our perception 'ends in objects,' the goal of a phenomenological anthropology of perception is to capture that moment of transcendence in which perception begins, and, *in the midst of arbitrariness and indeterminacy,* constitutes and is constituted by culture" (Csordas 1990:9, emphasis added). The previous chapter laid out various components of a sensorium as the initial step in mapping how perceptions experienced by Anlo-speaking people "constitute and are constituted by culture." That is, identifying some of the terminology Anlo-speaking people adopt as they learn to isolate and focus (both cognitively and in terms of sensations) provides a window on how (in the midst of arbitrariness and indeterminacy) perception can be seen as culturally patterned among Anlo-speaking people. At the phenomenal level or from the experiential standpoint of being-in-the-world, analytic categories of language, cognition, sensation, perception, culture, and embodiment exist as a complex and sticky web, which the following ethnographic example and extended discussion aims to illustrate.

In chapter 1 I suggested that in a sensorium we find cultural categories or a scheme (an implicit model) for organizing experience; we find that values have become "embodied" and "naturalized" through the course of history and through the practice of traditions; and we find that these embodied forms and sensibilities are learned (acquired, internalized, developed) at an early age through child-socialization practices. Here I explore kinesthesia (a sense located in muscles and tendons and mediated by bodily movement) and the way it is not only highly valued in many Anlo-speaking contexts but is also integrally bound up with Anlo ways of understanding and expressing morality.

Two young boys in our compound, Aaron and Kobla, never seemed to go straight to the well when their mother sent them to fetch water. I often observed them horsing around as they made their way through the compound and out the gate to the community well in the village where we lived. One day, as I watched them running in circles, chasing each other, walking backwards, and swinging their buckets to and fro, I heard their mother shouting in a distressed voice something about how they were walking *lugulugu*. My ears perked up when I heard that adverb, *lugulugu*, as I had recently begun making a list of different kinds of walks or styles of comportment. I already knew that one could *zɔ kadzakadza* (walk like a lion), or *zɔ minyaminya* (walk stealthily, as a person who eavesdrops), or *zɔ megbemegbe* (walk backwards, implying deception). As Kobladada (Kobla's mother) shouted at them from behind her kitchen wall, I watched them darting from one side of the compound to the other, swaying perilously on the outer edge of a foot, feigning to nearly fall down, and evidently mocking their mother for her charge that they were moving *lugulugu* on their way to the well.

Many Anlo people considered *azɔlizɔzɔ*—movement, walking, or kinesthesia—to have sensorial qualities, and they wanted this phenomenon included in my writings about their sensorium. In addition, several *mɔfialawo* had been insisting that I include "morality" among the senses that Anlo-Ewe people held dear. One of the reasons they believed that morality had sensorial qualities was that a close association between kinesthetic sensations (in *azɔlizɔzɔ*, or movement) and dispositional feelings (in *azɔlime* or *zɔzɔme,* one's moral character). Both concepts share the root *zɔ*—to walk, travel, or move one's body generally. Kobla and Aaron's mother's accusation of their *lugulugu* approach to getting water from the well seemed like an opportune incident to probe for the logic behind these associations.

I began by asking Elaine, my research assistant and friend, what *lugulugu* really meant. She explained that while a word such as *zɔ lugulugu* referred in the first instance to bodily motions such as swaying, tarrying, dawdling, or moving as if drunk, it could also be used to refer to a person's character. In response to a daughter's statement that "Kofi is the man I want to marry," Elaine explained that parents might discourage the young woman by exclaiming, *"Oh, ame lugulugu!"* The expression reveals the parents' perception that Kofi was a *lugulugu* man: not simply a person who moved in a tarrying or dawdling fashion, but a person who was not serious—an aimless, irresponsible fellow. An Ewe linguist clarified that *lugulugu* is a "manner-denoting ideophone" that references winding, meandering, zigzagging, and such. He explained that Elaine's characterization is accurate in that a person can move in a *lugulugu* manner, but we can also talk about a road (which does not move) as being *lugulugu* (meandering). In terms of our discussion here about kinesthesia and morality, the point is that in Ewe contexts, words like *lugulugu* are often used to extend ideas about the manner of movement (and for humans, the manner of walking) to manners that sum up a person's behavior.[1]

So were eight-year-old Kobla and ten-year-old Aaron already hopelessly *lugulugu*? I wondered, does a person begin walking *lugulugu* first and then become a *lugulugu* person or vice versa? In response to my inquiries about this, Kobla and Aaron's mother (along with several other caregivers in our compound) made it clear that they had to be vigilant about the possibility of either (on the significance of parental belief systems, see Harkness and Super 1996). That is, a child could develop either a kind of *lugulugu* laziness or *lugulugu* slouch, but either way it would permeate or pervade the person. So in the process of fetching water from the well, when Aaron and Kobla were consistently "going this way and that," fooling around, distracting each other from the task, and stirring up trouble, the concern this evoked in their caregivers was that the phenomenon that was embodied in these displays would begin to dominate their character. The logic expressed was that if you move in a *lugulugu* fashion you experience sensations of *lugulugu*-ness and begin thinking in a *lugulugu* way and become a *lugulugu* person, which is then evident to others from the way your *lugulugu* character is embodied in your *lugulugu* walk. Or, if you consistently think in a *lugulugu* way, you would also move in a *lugulugu* fashion and basically develop into a *lugulugu* person. Clearly, the specific case of a kinesthetic phenomenon called *lugulugu* shows how analytic categories of language, cognition, sensation, perception, culture, and embodiment are not experienced in discrete stages at the phenomenal level or from the existential standpoint of being-in-the-world. Here we see how local understandings of how humans process information (summed up in their categorical term *seselelame*) capitalize on synesthetic modes of knowing.

The point is that in terms of a cultural logic found among many Anlo-speaking people, there is a clear connection, or association, between bodily sensations and who you are or who you become: your character, your moral fortitude is embodied in the way you move, and the way you move embodies an essence of your nature. My Anlo neighbors did not suggest that people saw the child walking *lugulugu* and then thought that he was wayward. Rather, they suggested that the sensations the child would experience in the body (interoceptively, or in terms of *seselelame*) would necessarily involve imaginative structures that would develop in the mind, and that whole would then be perceived by all as a culturally constituted and objectified phenomenon called *lugulugu*. Here bodily habits and psychological outlook are deeply intertwined, rendering categories such as *cognitive, linguistic,* and even *embodied* as analytical and not experientially discrete phenomena.

Perhaps we have a similar cultural logic in our own folk epistemology. For example, in searching for a translation for *lugulugu,* the term "wishy-washy" comes to mind (in addition to "zigzag" and "meander"). Many English-speaking Americans probably believe that if a person feels wishy-washy day in and day out, then the person might actually carry himself with a wavering sort of comportment and in general have an indecisive demeanor. But here I want to argue that in Anlo-Ewe contexts we find a "performative elaboration" (Csordas 1993:146) of movement and moral character that is both quantitatively and qualitatively different from what we find in most Euro-American contexts.

One striking feature of *lugulugu* (as well as other kinds of movement adverbs, such as *minyaminya* or *kadzakadza*) lies in the fact that many of them are ideophones, and many (not always the same ones) are formed through reduplication.[2] In other words, "walks" (which also essentialize one's sense of morality or depict comportment) are often symbolized with "picture words (onomatopes), which attempt to express by their sound the *impression conveyed by the senses*" (Westermann 1930:107, emphasis added). Their language, therefore, reflects the belief that *azɔlinu* (walking, movement, kinesthesia) is eminently sensory. This helps to explain why *azɔlizɔzɔ* (movement) and *azɔlime* (dispositional character and moral feelings) fall into the cultural category of *seselelame* (feeling in the body) for many Anlo-Ewe people.

While the English language certainly contains instances of reduplication (e.g., *wishy-washy,* mentioned earlier), such repetitive constructions are pervasive in Ewe (e.g., Ameka 1999; Ansre 1963; Sapir 1921:76–78; Westermann 1930).[3] Ansre suggests (1963:128) that eight out of every one hundred words spoken in Ewe are reduplicated terms. In a more recent study, Ameka indicates (1999:78) that Ansre's estimate about reduplication in Ewe is probably too low. Furthermore, Samarin (1967:35) makes the fascinating observation that in the written version of a particular Ewe-language play, there are few ideophones, but when he attended a performance, "the actors ad libbed by adding ideophones to the prepared script" (Samarin 1967:35). This undoubtedly enhanced the sensory quality of the experience (which the performers of the play seemed moved to do).[4] Ideophones have been described as "vivid vocal images or representations of visual, auditory and other sensory or mental experiences" (Cole 1955:370). They have also been defined as "nouns of sensory quality" (see Newman 1968:109 n. 11) and as words that describe sound, color, smell, manner, appearance, state, action, or intensity (Cole 1955:370). Evans-Pritchard called ideophones "poetry in ordinary language" (1962:143). In a technical sense, reduplicated forms are distinct from the ideophone proper, and here I want to make clear that I am not trying to take up the linguistic debate about what precisely the *ideophone* is or does (e.g., Ameka 2001b; Newman 1968; Noss 1986). What I do want to stress is that both the reduplication strategy and deployment of ideophones function at a certain level to sensorially evoke that which they represent. Indeed, when I witnessed Kobla and Aaron swaying and tarrying and swinging and when I heard their mother shouting *lugulugu,* I experienced a very visceral (rather than merely intellectual) realization of what was going on—which takes us back to the issue of reduplication specifically in the arena of movement or walks.

Earlier I mentioned that while I was in the field I compiled a list of Ewe terms that indicated styles or types of comportment. This list is not meant to be read as a classification system per se nor as an exhaustive or complete program of movement terms from the Anlo-Ewe language. But this sample illustrates the richness of an Anlo-Ewe lexicon for movement and walks:

azɔlizɔzɔ: walking or moving in general

azɔlime: style of walking, shaping character and way of life

azɔlinu: walking, "walking thing"

zɔzɔme: implies the same as *azɔlime,* but literally means "in walking" or "in movement" (comportment) and represents a kind of short hand for talking about your character, your manner of life

zɔkɔɖui: walking with your shoulders bent, hunched over, hobbling along like an old person

zɔkloloe: walking a long distance alone; walking straight on without stopping

zɔgbozɔe: moving back and forth, coming and going, to the right and to the left; a loitering, lingering, up and down sort of approach

atsyɔzɔli (zɔ tsyɔzɔli): walking affectedly, putting on pretense or airs, moving majestically, proudly, with style, like a king or queen

lugulugu (zɔ lugulugu): walking or moving in a swaying, tarrying, or dawdling manner; moving as if you are drunk *megbemegbe (zɔ megbemegbe)*: walking backwards; backing up (leaving deceptive footprints); not wanting to attract attention, a person simply steps backwards a bit

minyaminya (zɔ minyaminya): moving gently and stealthily like a cat, gliding without making noise; used in eavesdropping

kadzakadza (zɔ kadzakadza): moving or walking like a lion, decidedly and with power; moving in a vigorous and furious manner

hanyahanya (zɔ hanyahanya): walking as if one "has a load"; the kind of movements people make when needing to relieve themselves

bafobafo (zɔ bafobafo): the walk of a small man, his body moving briskly

bɔhobɔho (zɔ bɔhobɔho): a fat man's heavy, laborious walk

ɖocɔcɔ (zɔ cɔcɔcɔ): walking slowly or leisurely; sauntering

mi eme: passing by intentionally, keeping in motion without stopping or saying hello

atizɔti: literally a walking stick, but can also be a person who serves as your walking stick: an assistant, a crutch

tsadzadzɛ: restless or inquisitive; a busybody

tsa asi: "walking about hands"; feeling, groping with one's hands

tsa ŋku: "walking about eyes"; letting the eyes wander, search; undercover investigating

zɔ amɛ gɔme: to spy on a person, to find out his secrets (literally, "walk inside a person")

mezɔ ɖe ŋuwo: respectful greeting when arriving at a person's house: "I walked well getting to your house"

In addition to these kinesthetically related terms that I recorded in my fieldnotes, Westermann compiled (1930:107–109) a set of adverbs that can modify *zɔ* (to walk) "according to the manner of going." The following are excerpted from his sample:

zɔ behebehe: describes the slouch of a weak man

zɔ biabia: the walk of a long-legged man, who strides out

zɔ bulabula: to walk without looking where one is going

zɔ ɖeɖe: a free, breezy style of walking

zɔ ɖaboɖabo: to walk shakily like a duck

zɔ gblulugblulu: to walk looking to the front like a buffalo

zɔ hloyihloyi: to walk with many objects, clothes, etc., dangling round one's body

zɔ kaka: to walk straight, without moving one's body, proudly

zɔ kodzokodzo: to walk with the body bent forwards, stooping

zɔ kpaɖikpaɖi: to walk with limbs joined closely together

zɔ kpuɖukpuɖu: the hurried walk of a small man

zɔ takataka: to walk without care

zɔ tyenɖetyenɖe: to walk, moving one's belly, and with slightly bent hips

zɔ tyaɖityaɖi: to walk dragging one's body, with a slight limp

zɔ tyɔtyɔ: the stately, energetic walk of a tall man

zɔ wudɔwudɔ: the weary walk of a stately person, especially women (respectful)

zɔ vɔlavɔla: to step lightly, hurried, unhindered

zɔ vɔuivɔui: to walk quickly

These lists—a kind of cultural catalog of comportments—indicate that there are more than fifty terms in Ewe representing different kinesthetic styles: from zɔ bafobafo and zɔ bulabula to zɔ kodzokodzo and zɔ lumɔlumɔ.[5] The sheer number of ways one can talk about essentialized kinetic modes (different styles of azɔlinu or zɔzɔme) alerts us, on one level, to the significance of this domain in Ewe cultural worlds. And the fact that most of these terms are onomatopes or ideophones (see Westermann 1930:107) indicates a kind of "performative elaboration" (Csordas 1993:146) of the sensory dimension of azɔlizɔzɔ (movement) and azɔlime (moral essence). Or, as Sapir commented in relation to reduplication: "the process is generally employed, *with self-evident symbolism*, to indicate ... plurality, repetition, customary activity, ... added intensity," and so forth (1921:76, emphasis added). *With self-evident symbolism*, then, Ewe speakers refer to kinetic modes, styles of comportment, or simply "the way you walk" with language that is saturated with sensory valuation. In fact, when I was in Ghana for only a few months in 1992, I did not have time to adjust to the pace of the culture and was always rushing around trying to get things done. Several *mɔfialawo* commented on my zɔ dziadzia style—walking with purpose, moving intently, as if on a serious mission.

In their essay "Sounding Sensory Profiles," David Howes and Constance Classen suggest that in the realm of language (only one of many avenues to studying the senses), "the number of terms for each of the senses is an indicator of the relative importance of that sense, or else of the different ways in which it is understood to operate" (1991:263). Here I am suggesting that in the Ewe language, the number of sensory words (onomatopes, ideophones, picture words, icons, etc.) used in the kinesthetic realm or to depict the feel and image of the ways in which people move is an indicator of the extent to which movement and walking (or kinesthetic activity) is deemed a sensory experience in Ewe worlds.

A brief consideration of *color* in an Euro-American context may deepen our appreciation for how complex *kinesthesia* was to Anlo speakers. Through forays into a paint store in the process of redecorating a house, or in playing with a child and her Crayola crayons, many Euro-Americans develop the idea that, given the opportunity or motivation, one could learn (to perceive, identify, and name) distinctions among tones labeled pink, red, blue, purple, magenta, fuchsia, lavender, scarlet, and so forth. Within the Anlo-Ewe language, color terminology was limited to several basic words for primary colors, with more exotic hues described by employing "like" or "similar to" and pointing out or referring to an object with a comparable shade. But in Anlo-Ewe contexts there was a large repertoire of terms for the way a person walks or moves. Clearly, humans are capable of experiencing and manifesting a multitude of kinesthetic motions and postures, but the predilection for essentializing and labeling these patterns is limited to those cultural traditions that have placed a high premium on kinesthesia and proprioception.

Fafa Ocloo presents a case in point. One afternoon while I was working with my research assistant, Elaine, in the front room of our house, we heard a commotion as Fafa Ocloo appeared in the compound to pay respects to her aunt, Adzoa Kokui, and to pour libations to their ancestors. The driver had parked her Mercedes outside the gate, and Fafa strode in, gracefully negotiating the sand with her high heels. A slit up the back of her fitted skirt allowed Fafa to walk. Her skirt was matched by a purple and bright green Dutch wax-print blouse embellished by the signature balloon-shaped sleeves of West African women. As a headwrap, Fafa donned the same wax-print, her face adorned by starched wings jutting up toward the sky. I wondered aloud who this visitor might be, and Elaine commented (largely in jest) *"Ele zɔzɔm atsyɔzɔli ŋutɔ!"* (She is "walking *atsyɔzɔli*" very well).

Atsyɔzɔli, it turned out, was an affected comportment generally involving *atsyɔɖoɖo,* a highly revered form of adornment and dress. Elaine explained, "It is walking majestically. When you put on fine clothes and are going to church or to a ceremony—*atsyɔzɔli*—you walk like a queen. I cannot make *atsyɔzɔli* in these clothes." She gestured toward her everyday garb. "I must wear *kente* or fine clothing. You must wear fine clothes—or be a person who is very proud—to *atsyɔzɔli* on a daily basis." I asked Elaine, can *anyone* be or do *atsyɔzɔli?* "Yes, but you must put on the clothes and the airs. Some people do it all the time. Most people only do it on special occasions. Some people are born to walk like that. They say, Eh, as for that woman, *Esia ko zɔ tsyɔzɔli loo!* That's just how you walk [she demonstrated]: swing your arms, walk slowly, turn your head to the side, smile a little, look at those as you pass, a faintly snobbish air. That's *atsyɔzɔli.* Oooooo. Um hmmm. That's how Fafa Ocloo walks! She doesn't say bye-bye when you are going. She doesn't walk with you to the roadside."

So was *atsyɔzɔli* a positive or negative thing? Elaine explained, "If you are endowed with the natural and the material things to *atsyɔzɔli,* no one will abuse you. People kind of enjoy it, or admire it. But if you are snobby along with it, then people don't like it. That's *atsyɔdada*—people say you are vain." (In Westermann's dictionary, *atsyɔdada* is translated as "a dandy" [1973[1928]:262].) Elaine said, "It depends on the other qualities of the person. If the qualities are snobby, then people don't like it. But if your other qualities are fine, then people enjoy and admire *atsyɔzɔli.*" Fafa Ocloo, according to Elaine, was teetering on the brink between *atsyɔɖoɖo* (adornment, embellishment, display) and *atsyɔdada* (putting on pretenses, vanity, being a snob). At this point in our tape-recorded conversation, Elaine laughed heartily and mused: "You can't balance when you're focused on *atsyɔzɔli.* No, *agbagbaɖoɖo* and *atsyɔzɔli* don't mix!" It is not clear to me, in retrospect, if Elaine was speaking in literal or metaphorical terms. I was too caught up in the joke, laughing uproariously with Elaine, to seriously question her intent. But the fact that she made an association between the two (balancing and walking affectedly) is remarkable, and her laughter and tone of voice betray a playfulness and a level of philosophical significance to this comment that the bare words on this page fail to convey. She concluded, "It is difficult to *atsyɔzɔli* if you have a load on your head. Some people can, but it will hurt your neck." Here she snickered mischievously. "Your head and hands and eyes must be free to move. It is better to move quickly, set down your load, and then *atsyɔzɔli.*"

The other extreme was expressed as *zɔgbozɔe* (*zɔ:* walk; *gbo:* come; *zɔe:* walk). In Accra, a *zɔgbozɔe* man lived in our compound for several months. His aunt would send him to the market to buy cassava, pepper, and fish; he would return carrying a can of condensed milk. His uncle asked him to repair some wiring in my room one afternoon. He appeared with a screwdriver, spent an hour removing the plate, then left for town to go and purchase the wire. When he returned, several hours later, he had neglected to bring the cutter. By evening the plug in my room still did not work. *"Tsyɔ! Ame zɔgbozɔe,"* his aunt complained. (Going and coming, cannot get the job done, a sorry and pathetic sort of guy.)

I have described the character or disposition of some individuals as summed up by terms simultaneously used to depict how they carry themselves or walk. Many of the adjectives and adverbs discussed here can be used not only to describe movement but also a person's eating behavior, the way the person laughs, general mannerisms, and so forth, and people seemed to comment liberally (using terms from the lists presented earlier) on such demeanor.[6] Comportment, then, was of concern to many Anlo-speaking people with whom I worked. Many believed that bodily movement both shaped character and revealed demeanor. It is striking how two prominent Anlo-Ewe poets, Kofi Anyidoho and Kofi Awoonor, also attend to walks or kinesthesia in their work. Anyidoho dedicated his book *AncestralLogic and CaribbeanBlues* to several women "for *walking in balance* back home" (1993, emphasis added). In the opening of Awoonor's novel *This Earth, My Brother ...* (1971), he introduces each of the characters largely through highlighting their walks: "He was marching up and down with a long bamboo cane. He stamped his feet in military precision just to impress and frighten us" (p. 3). Another character "hurried onwards in his jerky walk in which his heels did not touch the ground" (p. 10). And, "the second day my father said, You look like a sleepwalker" (p. 4). As for the woman, she could "read my steps from afar.... In her sleep she knew it when I walked towards her room" (pp. 1–2). Awoonor acknowledges that traditional Ewe cultural-aesthetic forms serve as deep inspiration for his writing (1975:202–217). To that last description he could have added that with *seselelame* "she read my steps ... she smelled me from far away." It was that feeling in the body *(seselelame)* that allowed her to "read my steps at all hours," to *know*—even in sleep—"when I walked towards her room."[7]

In 1995, shortly before I left Ghana, a man shot and killed an Ewe man for collecting sand from the footprints he had made earlier in the day. That is, the Ewe man was caught picking *afɔke* (foot-sand) from the other man's prints. In fear for his life, believing the Ewe man in his front yard would work powerful *juju* with the sand that held a residue of his body and his walk, the man shot the other and pleaded self-defense. Here Bourdieu's habitus encodes aspects of the world that are precious and dear or deemed so valuable by members of a cultural group that they literally make these themes or motifs into "body." In Anlo contexts, the cultural elaboration of the way one moves represents a way of being-in-the-world that is socially reproduced and imbued with moral meaning. Eventually I came to realize that this entwinement explained why many of my *mɔfialawo* (including Mr. Adzomada) were reluctant to focus completely on sensing in their discussions with me and instead wanted to teach me about their history, folklore, and traditions. I asked about tasting and touching; they wanted to talk about *zɔzɔme* and *azɔlime* (comportment and moral disposition). As I listened more closely to what Anlo speakers wanted me to know, I began to see the bridge between the two agendas—between my concern with excavating an indigenous Anlo sensorium and their focus on Anlo-Ewe traditions or core cultural values. In many ways that bridge is built around the concept of *seselelame,* which I translate loosely as a kind of interoceptively oriented feeling in the body, because *seselelame* has a direct bearing upon how self-awareness is produced in this cultural context. Moreover, balance, movement, and a more generalized feeling in the body *(seselelame)* are critical components of an indigenous theory of inner states. Now we turn to the way these understandings are embedded in the child's earliest experience.[8]

Young entrepreneur in Anloga with his roulette wheel

Mother back tying her daughter while stirring soup

Political rally in Anloga for President J. J. Rawlings, whose heritage includes Anlo-Ewe ancestry

View of the Keta Lagoon on the northern edge of Srɔgboe and Whuti, with young Anlo boys taking their boat out fishing

Farmers weeding and watering family shallot fields near Anloga. Shallots have been a commercial crop since the late nineteenth century, partially replacing the copra industry when disease wiped out coconut palms.

Girls harvesting cassava, one of the staple foods of West Africa

Woman cooking Anlo-Ewe staple food known as *akple*

Merchant's storefront closed for the day

Market women in Anloga waiting for customers to purchase their chickens

Seamstress working in the Anloga market. She is pointing at a locally woven basket known as a *kevi*.

Young Srɔgboe seamstresses in their shop

Two girls head-loading in Srɔgboe-Whuti

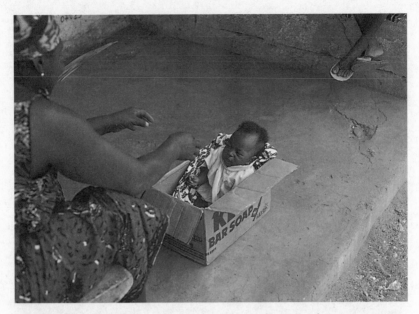

Grandmother reaching for baby in a box to prop her up and encourage greater bodily balance

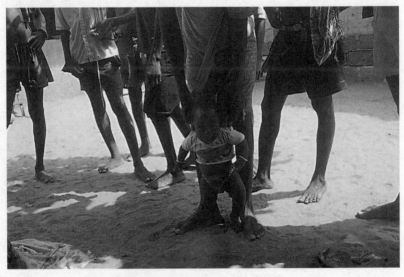

Father supporting his baby with a cloth thread through the child's armpits, encouraging the not-yet-toddler to stand and walk

Srɔgboe children sitting on a bench. The girl on the left is exhibiting proper posture.

Two women both engaged in *atsyozɔli:* walking with style

Vodu ceremony in a sacred grove in Srɔgboe during the Tɔgbui Apim festival

Legba empowerment object (guardian of thresholds) in a Keta alley

Older ladies at the Hogbetsotso festival enacting their ancestor's escape from Notsie in the mid-seventeenth century. Each woman on the left displays an old-style *atsibla* (pillow strapped to the buttocks); perfumed skin applications on their arms and backs are referred to as *atikeveve*.

Author-ethnographer conferring with an Anlo-Ewe scholar

Elderly couple in their home

Sensory Symbolism in Birth and Infant Care Practices

In many human societies, ideas about health, personhood, and social relations extend into the period before a child is even born, and in this arena Anlo-land was no exception. Conception, pregnancy, birth, and the first weeks and months of a baby's life were surrounded by ideas about sensory symbolism and meanings ascribed to various interactions and practices that involved different sensory modes. Human beings are ushered into (Bourdieu's phrase is "durably installed" with) their culture's sensorium, which, as I have suggested, reflects some of the most fundamental values. The ushering in begins symbolically in the (ritually packed) birth event itself and continues during early childhood experiences. In this way, phenomena em-bodied, or made body, are "placed beyond the grasp of consciousness, and hence cannot be touched by voluntary, deliberate transformation, cannot even be made explicit" (Bourdieu 1977:94). They are some of the most "ineffable, incommunicable, and inimitable" aspects of being, and as Bourdieu suggests (1977:94), there is nothing "more precious, than the values given body, *made* body by the transubstantiation achieved by the hidden persuasion of an implicit pedagogy" embedded in cultural and socialization processes.

This chapter does not purport to be a comprehensive account of childbirth and child-socialization practices in Anlo-land, but rather a sampling of those elements that the *mɔfialawo* with whom I worked stressed as significant dimensions of their culture and those elements that illustrate the connections between sensory socialization and embodiment. A more systematic examination of child-socialization practices should provide much richer ethnographic information to further support the following claims, and additional research needs to be carried out to more deeply understand how children internalize cultural meanings (Strauss and Quinn 1997) about sensory categories. But this chapter provides initial information on how sensory valuation is reflected in pregnancy and birth rituals and enacted in child-socialization routines.

POSTURE AND BALANCE:
TREATING THE PLACENTA AS A STOOL

Birth attendants and village *vixelawo* in Srɔgboe, Whuti, Atokɔ, and Kplowotokɔ sometimes called the placenta *zikpui,* which is a term referring to a traditional African stool on which chiefs sit. While they were clear that in the Ewe language the word *amenɔ* was the technical or literal term used to describe the afterbirth, I often heard them talk about the placenta as a stool *(zikpui).* Before elaborating on the significance of calling the placenta a stool, let me note here that I distinguish between three different categories of people who deliver babies. When I use the term "midwife," I mean a person who has received biomedically based training as a nurse-midwife. The term "traditional birth attendant" is reserved for those who have participated in a brief government-sponsored training program to upgrade their delivery skills. I use "village *vixela*" to refer to other people in the rural area who deliver babies on a regular basis but who have not received formal or state-sanctioned training.[1]

Many traditional birth attendants and *vixelawo* reported imagining the baby sitting on a little stool inside the womb, and after delivery they would talk about waiting for the "baby's seat" to emerge. This belief was not literal; they were amused by my questions about whether they really thought the baby was sitting upright (on top of the placenta) inside the womb, and they clearly understood that a preferable presentation during delivery was head (rather than feet) first. The symbolic expression is striking, however, in the association it conjures to stools (which hold profound spiritual significance in Anlo-land and throughout West Africa) and to posture and balance. There is an imagined baby composing or arranging her body into a still and balanced form, poised on an African stool, even in the womb.

Those experienced in the meditative arts of yoga might readily understand the underlying concept here, but to truly appreciate the sensory experience symbolized by *zikpui,* perhaps one needs to have sat on a carved wooden stool and felt how resting in such a (balanced) position stills the body's proprioceptive and kinesthetic sensations. Nonetheless, the image of the baby atop a *zikpui* or "placental stool" drew on cultural categories of balancing *(agbagbaɖoɖo)*, kinesthesia and movement *(azɔlizɔzɔ)*, and the more general sense of *seselelame* (feeling in the body, flesh, and skin).

I hasten to add that this is not all that is involved. The symbolism suggests that the baby is linked to the mother via the placenta as the individual is tied to the lineage through the ancestral stool.[2] An ancestral stool is considered a symbol of heritage and authority, being a "seat of power," and it plays a significant role in religious rituals of the lineage, or clan. Amoaku (1975:119–120) explains "the symbolic significance of the ancestral stool as the source of all traditional political and spiritual power among the Ewe." In ritual contexts, stools are even "fed" and "given drinks" (Glover 1992), which is suggestive of a nourishing capacity paralleled by the placenta being the life-support system for a baby. Stool festivals (called *zikpuinu* or *afedonu*) involve offerings of food and drink to the ancestors (Nukunya 1969b:27), often literally in the presence of or while standing before the ancestral stool. While I do not know how conscious these connections may have been on the part of the various traditional birth attendants and village *vixelawo* who referred to the placenta as a stool, the symbolism suggests that just as it is from the placenta that the baby derives nutrients, oxygen, and blood, it is in relation to the ancestral stool that members of the lineage sustain themselves (by knowing who they are and to what group they belong). Just as the ancestral stool is treated reverentially, the placenta is typically buried somewhere in the compound that serves as the baby's lineage ground. It is a place to which most Anlo-speaking people return regularly to pay homage to their ancestors and is therefore instrumental in the formation of identity.

CRAVING AND CONSUMING *EYE*

A second pregnancy practice with relevant sensory symbolism revolved around beliefs about and consumption of a clay or earthen substance known in the Ewe language as *eye*. Throughout markets in Keta, Anloga, Anyanui, Anyako, and so forth, a small number of women ran stalls from which they sold an assortment of usually oblong or egg-shaped pieces of baked clay. Conversations with village *vixelawo*, traditional birth attendants, and midwives indicated that pregnant women often ingested these substances as a way of coping with nausea, heartburn, excess saliva, and vomiting. The physiological causes and consequences of this worldwide practice (variously described in the literature as *geophagia, pica,* and *cravings*) have been debated among anthropologists, cultural geographers, and medical practitioners (Reid 1992). Typically viewed as pathological in the context of Western medical traditions, Reid (1992) found little evidence for the efficacy of geophagia in cases of anemia but concluded that the adaptive value of consuming clay seemed to lie in its antidiarrheal, detoxification, and mineral supplementation possibilities. Specifically in West Africa, although Vermeer (1966) suggested that consumption by pregnant women among the Tiv might be explained as a source of mineral supplementation (of calcium and magnesium), a similar study among Ewe speakers (Vermeer 1971) did not reveal a clear-cut physiological need. Given Reid's (1992) more recent and more extensive study of geophagia, the case among Ewe speakers most certainly deserves revisiting, but the biomedical implications of this phenomenon did not interest me as much as simply what people in Anlo-land thought about this practice. Who was inclined to consume *eye?* Under what circumstances or for what purposes? Was this seen as a positive, negative, or neutral phenomenon? What were the perceived benefits, consequences, or outcomes of eating *eye?*

In Anlo-land I never observed or heard of male consumption nor did I encounter much about nonpregnant women eating *eye.* Vermeer, however, reported (1971:66) on a small number of Ewe-speaking men consuming the clay for medicinal purposes, simply for pleasure, or in the context of ritual practices. Consumption was almost always described as a response to either pregnancy cravings or as a palliative for the nausea and acid indigestion that occur during pregnancy, and in two different instances I was even suspected of being pregnant when I was observed purchasing and later unwrapping my parcel full of differently shaped pieces of *eye.* Opinions as to its neutrality, detriment, or benefit varied widely. Midwives tended to perceive it as a harmful practice. As one midwife, who I am calling Janice, explained, "It just makes the women constipated. They have a craving for it. And if they can't get *eye,* they just eat dirt. It's very bad for them." Traditional birth attendants often reported that previously they thought it was all right to eat small quantities of *eye* for morning sickness and other discomforts of pregnancy, but then they learned in their government training courses that ingesting *eye* was counterproductive. A few village *vixelawo* with whom I discussed the practice seemed to feel quite neutral about the subject, which I attributed largely to their not having been instructed that it was detrimental to a woman's health.

Women in the rural area in general had a good deal of sympathy for the practice. It was believed to help calm an upset stomach and the vomiting that occurred with such frequency during pregnancy. One woman reported that sometimes they did not even eat the *eye*, but "just want to smell it, crave the scent. We just bake it, put it in the oven and bake the *eye*. Or we also bake sand to smell that too." Vermeer (1971:69–70) commented similarly: "Informants repeatedly related that the scent of the clays is a strong factor motivating purchase and consumption, especially on wet, rainy days. Presumably the aromatic quality of the clay is akin to the smell of the 'good earth' on wet days among rural inhabitants in Western societies, and this may have a possible bearing on the initiation and perpetuation of the practice." In addition to the appeal of the aroma, Vermeer made further observations (1971:70) about the symbolic value of certain visual (and even haptic) attributes: "The shape of *eye* seems further related to the ... condition of pregnancy. Traditionally *eye* has the shape of an egg, a food which in Ewe culture is ascribed the attributes of promoting long life, health, well-being, and fertility. Ingestion of *eye*, therefore, imparts these qualities to the pregnant female who considers herself in a subnormal condition and prone to illness."

What village *vixelawo* and traditional birth attendants consistently told me, however, was that excessive ingestion resulted in a buildup of the substance covering the baby's skin. This idea is illustrated in the following translated excerpt from an interview I conducted with a traditional birth attendant in Tegbi Ashiata.

TBA: The women just feel they must eat it. I don't care whether or not they eat it. It's up to them.

KLG: Do you notice any effect it has?

TBA: Yes, it sticks to the baby's skin.

KLG: So when the baby is born you can actually see it?

TBA: Yes, the baby comes with *eye* on it. Then we have to use soap and *akutsa* [a sponge made from a locally grown creeper] to push it off during the first bath. When they eat a little, it doesn't show. But when they eat plenty, it shows. It covers the whole body of the baby. It doesn't affect the baby, as such, but it sticks on the baby for a long time. You wash the baby and it still does not come off. It takes several days, weeks, even months before it finally comes off. And if it doesn't come off, then it leaves an everlasting scent on the baby.

KLG: You mean it is in the skin? And you can smell it on the baby?

TBA: Yes.

KLG: When you say "everlasting," what do you mean?

TBA: For years—if you don't give a good bath. You have to scrape it all
during infancy. When it [the baby] is growing and does not get a
good bath, it [the *eye,* the scent] stays. So, it's not good for them.

This "everlasting scent," traceable to the state of the neonate, was referred to as *ʤigbeʤi* (*ʤigbe:* birthday; *ʤi:* dirt, filth), or "birth dirt."
While some people reported that *ʤigbeʤi* was essentially a strong body
odor that certain individuals possessed as a result of a weak first bath,
more extensive discussions revealed that for many people *ʤigbeʤi* symbolized a more generalized improper upbringing.

Nearly all the birth attendants and village *vixelawo* with whom I
worked believed that the greasy or cheesy coating on a newborn was due
to the mother's ingestion of *eye,* while Anlo-speaking midwives invariably understood it to be *vernix caseosa* (a medical term for the substance
that covers the fetus in utero). This was evident in a dialogue that ensued when Janice took me to the village of Lume-Avete to talk with several birth attendants during the summer of 1992. While traditional birth
attendants had a great deal of experience delivering babies and had been
through a two-week government-sponsored intensive training course,
Janice (in her capacity as a dedicated midwife and a very active member
of the Ghana Registered Midwives Association) continued to visit and
instruct a number of traditional birth attendants in the vicinity of her
Maternity Home. In accompanying her on one of these visits, I asked the
birth attendant what she thought of the substance on the baby's skin
when it was first born. She replied that she used to think it was caused
by pregnant women eating too much *eye,* but on a number of occasions
she asked her clients and they denied having engaged in the practice, so
she began wondering if it came from something else.

At that point Janice interjected (with a bit of frustration) that all the
traditional birth attendants seemed to think the *vernix caseosa* was from
eating clay or dirt, and in turn they would scrub the baby vigorously (out
of fear it would leave *ʤigbeʤi,* the everlasting scent). Janice stated that
she had been trying for years to get them to "drop this belief," and she
expressed frustration that she continued to find this idea to be widespread. She then took time to instruct this particular traditional birth attendant about the natural coating that a baby acquires while in the womb
and to explain that the whitish gray film on the skin had no relationship
to a pregnant woman's consuming clay or dirt.

Two years later, when I had returned to Anlo-land and attended approximately fifteen different births, I saw that there were still conflicts over the coating found on many newborns. Since many traditional birth attendants were instructed that consumption of *eye* was a detrimental practice for pregnant women and they associated the amount of mucus on a neonate's skin with the level of ingestion of clay on the part of the woman, I witnessed several instances of intense scolding by the traditional birth attendant as she wiped and washed the *vernix caseosa* off the baby's skin. None of the delivering mothers protested that they had not consumed *eye*, so that seemed to further support the idea that they were perceived to be related.

The association here links a gustatory practice or craving, the visible and textural covering on some newborn babies, the everlasting scent that would be embedded in the skin and plague a person for the rest of his or her life, and badness. It is indisputable that the clay known as *eye* resembles in both color and texture the *vernix caseosa* coating a newborn's skin. Even I had to give pause in a couple instances when I observed the heavy substance covering a neonate and listened to the discussion between the birth attendant and the mother. Yet it seems likely that the local sensorium enhanced the connection.

In ontological terms, an association existed for many people between eating something *(eye)*, seeing and feeling it affect one's offspring (a coating on the baby's skin), and the potential for a condition of great social stigma *(dzigbedi,* or the everlasting scent). Similar to the case of *lugulugu,* the concerns expressed about *dzigbedi* were largely rooted in the cultural category of *seselelame*—a complex notion weaving together physical sensations with moral sensibilities, emotional states, and intersubjective relations. *Dzigbedi* is particularly striking because of how it necessitates a conditioning quite literally of the skin. The foundational logic of *seselelame* (feeling in the body, flesh, and skin) combined with the ideas about the potential harm of birth dirt helps explain a social practice (the ritual first bath) that if not properly performed could affect the entire family by signifying that they had not given the individual a proper upbringing. The epistemological and ontological properties of these beliefs and practices illustrate the quotidian affect of a culturally constructed sensorium.

BATHING THE NEWBORN AND REMOVAL OF *DZIGBEDI*

Turning to the customary first bath, let me first address the importance of bathing and cleanliness in general. Nearly thirty years ago, in a study focusing on how Ewe-speaking children learn practices, traditions, and morals emphasized within their own cultural heritage, Egblewogbe (1975:24) explained:

> Ewe people lay great emphasis on cleanliness. Children are washed at least twice a day. Older ones are taught how to wash themselves. Splinters or twigs of soft-wooded trees are used as chewing sticks. Clothes are washed at least once a week on days when no farming is done. It is the duty of children to sweep the rooms and the compound early every morning and to fetch water from the wells....Any woman who does not keep her house clean...is referred to insultingly as one covered up with dirt, and this detracts very much from a woman's integrity.

While many older Anlo-speaking people complained to me that standards of cleanliness and hygiene (both personal and environmental) had deteriorated significantly in the last few decades, I found Egblewogbe's statement to still ring true.

Shortly after I arrived in Srɔgboe, I jotted down the following observation in my notes: "This evening Fortune [a four-year-old girl] was standing in a pan in front of her house covered from head to toe in white foam. She was squealing and splashing the water. Her grandmother was giving her a bath. This is a child who almost always looks grimy, filthy, as if she just rolled in the mud. But I see that she is bathed (SCRUBBED!) thoroughly at least once a day." A few months later I wrote the following generalization based upon observations of more than five different families and twelve to fifteen children with whom we shared a compound: "Children are bathed frequently and often 'in public'—that is, in front of their house, in full view of the entire compound. They are covered with soap and scrubbed, and they are scolded for going too long without a good bath."

The bathing of children in this context was more of a social than an individualized phenomenon. Not only were children often publicly bathed in front of other families but the implications of poor hygiene extended far beyond the individual self. That is, whether uncleanliness was seen, smelled, felt, tasted, or heard about, the stigma of bad hygiene tended to adhere to a person's relatives as much if not more than it pertained to the individual self. Families were blamed for not having trained the child well or for having failed to begin as early as the baby's initial bath.

While living in Srɔgboe I attended more than a dozen births and witnessed the bathing routine given to neonates. The following is an excerpt from my fieldnotes that specifically describes this practice. The baby's bath was preceded, of course, by several hours of labor, rupture of the membranes, actual birth and issuance of the placenta, cutting and tying of the umbilical cord, and bathing of Adzoa (the delivering mother) by her own mother and the traditional birth attendant (referred to simply as "B"). The baby was initially called Kwaku, which was the day name for a boy born on Wednesday.

B wiped up some of the floor, but the flies were beginning to amass in the room—attracted by the fluids and blood. About that time two elderly ladies came in, and then K [another traditional birth attendant] came in. By then there were also children coming in and out of the room—some to look, some to help B carry water, stools, etc. B asked K "Where have you been?" She then explained to me that they were going to bathe the baby. K picked up the wash basin full of bloody water from Adzoa's bath and carried it outside on her head. More buckets of water were brought into the room, along with a clean basin, and a bench for the elderly ladies. They sat to my left. B was across from me and K sat near her. B placed the basin directly in front of herself, then placed her legs out straight across the basin and with her ankles and calves resting on the opposite edge. She placed the baby across her legs. She then told me I should bring my husband in to watch the bath. I went out to get him. A young boy brought a chair for my husband to sit on and placed it right next to my stool. K took the bar of soap and lathered up a sponge that was shaped and textured like a net. She handed it to B who began scrubbing the baby's head. B held him with her left palm across his chest and her thumb and fingers under each of his arms. With her right hand she scrubbed his head with the sponge and plenty of lathery soap. She lathered, scrubbed, and rinsed his head, all the time talking with the elderly ladies and K. Meanwhile at least 6 to 10 children had come inside and lined up behind the elderly ladies to watch, but everyone remained quiet. After Kwaku's head was rinsed, B placed him on his stomach across her thighs and lathered and scrubbed his back, buttocks, and legs. This section was rinsed thoroughly and then he was placed on his back across her legs and his stomach, neck, underarms, genitals, legs, feet, and so forth were thoroughly cleaned. After rinsing the front, B repeated the entire routine—head, back, then front—one more time. Kwaku was relatively calm and cried very little during this "work-out." B then dipped the sponge into warm to hot water and pressed it against Kwaku with more force than she previously used. She pushed against his legs, especially at the knee joints. She pulled on the legs with her left hand and pressed the sponge against him with her right hand. He started putting up a bit of a fuss at this point. His skin began turning more pink. He was on his stomach across her thighs; she pulled on his legs, then placed his arms behind his back, crossed the hands and pressed against the elbow joints. All the while she kept placing the sponge in and out of the warm or hot water. She then pressed and rubbed the sponge from the front to the back of his head. She also thoroughly cleaned the umbilical cord with the antiseptic liquid in the jar containing the strings used to tie the cords. This last section of the bath was rougher than the beginning and Kwaku cried a bit, but it only lasted a few minutes. Soon B was drying him off, and rubbing shea butter into his skin. She also powdered him with talc or baby powder of some sort. And she cleared the passageway of his throat by pressing her finger down beyond his tongue. When she finished and pulled her finger out, he was quite calm and just made a small and brief crying sound. Finally, Adzoa and her sister were rummaging through a bag of baby clothes to find a suitable garment. They gave B a blue and white feminine looking dress which she rejected since he was a boy. B pointed to a pink colored simpler garment. Adzoa handed it to her. Kwaku was lying on his back across B's legs at this point, and his arms were sticking straight up into the air. B laughed and said, "He's ready!" since she was able to slip the sleeves right over him. She buttoned it down the back, then picked up a cloth that was the same pattern as the one Adzoa was currently wearing, and she wrapped Kwaku in the cloth. She held him up and everyone smiled and nodded affirmations. B handed Kwaku to K who handed him to me. The two elderly ladies left. Three little girls sat next to me smiling and watching Kwaku. Meanwhile B and K helped Adzoa get up and wipe off a bit more. They helped her change the cloth that was absorbing the blood still flowing from her. She then wrapped herself back up in the cloth that matched Kwaku's and she lay down on the straw mat and cushion. I handed Kwaku to B and she set him down next to Adzoa, right near her head. We closed the window since the sun was streaming in and falling directly on Adzoa's mat.

This bath was fairly typical of the many I observed, though variations could include pouring of libations, the use of a local sponge (akutsa) instead of the plastic net–like cloth, and more pressing and shaping of the head. Also, when the birth was difficult or dangerous, additional rituals were often performed to ensure the health and safety of the mother and new child.

While the potential for ɖzigbeɖi (the everlasting scent) was believed to be the most extreme outcome of not administering a proper bath and the presence of eʋe made scrubbing all the more urgent, in general people believed that if the family and the traditional birth attendant (or vixela) did not cleanse the baby well, as the child grew to an adult he or she would retain and exude some degree of scent. Furthermore, failure to flex the joints would result in poor posture and coordination, and failure to massage the skull would result in an oddly shaped head. In regard to the skull, the fear was that without proper attention the two parietal bones would migrate apart, leaving a gap between them. To complicate matters, however, certain Anlo-speaking individuals did not believe or accept this point of view. Janice (the midwife) was quite vehement in her opposition to this practice, stating that people often used water that was much too hot, they caused pain to the baby with harsh brushes and vigorous scrubbing, and it was dangerous to apply hot water and pressure to the skull (in their efforts to shape the baby's head). She believed the entire ritual was completely unnecessary and had nothing to do with the health and well-being of the child, but was simply a "traditional practice" that was almost impossible to convince people to forego.

Finally, two things become clear to me in these discussions about hygiene and bathing. Many people believed they could know things about each other and about the moral status of various families from the sensory dimensions of hygiene in that when uncleanliness was seen, smelled, felt, tasted, or heard about, the stigma was attributed to the failings of the family at large.[3] Second, bathing was an explicitly social phenomenon. While Kwaku's entire birth event involved numerous members of the family, the baby's bath attracted the largest number of observers. The ritual could even be described as a "performance," with those watching (such as the elderly ladies, the children, my husband, and myself) as an "audience." One's hygiene and, by extension, one's health was a matter of social concern, and this began with life in the womb and during the birth event itself.

The importance of cleanliness and its relation to health extended not only beyond individuals to their families but to the larger sphere or the body politic we might refer to as Anlo. At the Hogbetsotso festival (which will be discussed at length in chapter 7), Togbui Adeladze (the Paramount Chief of Anlo-speaking peoples) declared in his speech, "Cleanliness is next to godliness and helps to eradicate diseases, so let's keep our environment clean." In J. J. Rawling's speech, which followed shortly after the Paramount Chief's, the president also made note of the significance of hygiene and sanitation in Anlo traditions. He declared that the area of Anlo-land used to be the shining example in Ghana of people taking care of their environment. He bemoaned the deterioration of those previous standards, citing garbage strewn along the sides of the roads and in the town as well as the riddling of many beaches with human waste as examples of eroding moral values and a significant compromise to the health and well-being of not only Anlo people but the nation at large. Clearly, a baby's first bath was perceived as not only preventing *dzigbedzi,* or an everlasting scent, but also served to symbolically usher the child into a way of being-in-the-world with ramifications extending far beyond the individualized self.

A final point about the ritual first bath revolves around the issue of making flexible bodies and the development of adaptability as a character trait. In the sketch of Kwaku's first bath in the excerpt of fieldnotes presented earlier, I described how the traditional birth attendant "pushed against his legs, especially at the knee joints. She pulled on the legs with her left hand and pressed the sponge against him with her right hand.... He was on his stomach across her thighs; she pulled on his legs, then placed his arms behind his back, crossed the hands and pressed against the elbow joints." This specific routine (focused on the knee and elbow joints) was not limited to the first bath alone, but was repeated by many Anlo-speaking families throughout the first few months of a baby's life. The ritual massage was intended to enhance flexibility, which was thought to be best initiated and rehearsed at a very early age.

Many people believed that flexing the joints, stretching and manipulating them as part of daily bathing of an infant, would produce in the individual an agile and elegant bodily shape, posture, and movements. While this practice was aimed at an embodied aspect of being, it seems to me also related to the high value placed on adaptability. Under the rubric of Anlo forms of being-in-the-world, in chapter 6 I will introduce the proverb *Ne neyi akpɔkplɔwo fe dume eye wotsyɔ akɔ la, wo ha natsyɔ akɔ* (If you visit the village of the toads and you find them squatting, you must squat too) and explore how altering one's body posture symbolizes adaptability and how the saying relates to the value placed on flexibility. As I argue there, adaptability in dealing with other cultural or ethnic groups throughout Ghana and West Africa was a character trait many Anlo-speaking people prided themselves on exhibiting. Experiencing and knowing *flexibility in an embodied dimension* and at an early age (through manipulation of the joints during an infant's bath) helped to produce *flexibility in one's character* and psychological outlook. While living in Anlo-land I spent a great deal of time in the company of Mrs. Sena Ocloo, who was a retired school teacher, and her husband, Mr. Kobla Ocloo, a retired medical officer. In the following tape-recorded conversation, the discussion moves from bodily massage aimed at physical flexibility to Mr. Ocloo's comment about flexibility in character and in social interaction.

> KLG: At some of the baths I've seen, they manipulate or massage the elbows and knees.
>
> Mrs. Ocloo: Aha. That's how we do it—take the elbows and knees and flex them. That's how the baby becomes supple. First you start with the head ...
>
> KLG: [I describe Mrs. Ocloo's hand gestures.] Round, form, or mold the head?

> *Mrs. Ocloo:* Yes. Then after that, the arms. You put the baby on its stomach, across your legs. Then you get the two arms: place the hands together behind the baby's back. You try to straighten the elbows. Do the same for the legs, also.
>
> *KLG:* And what is that for?
>
> *Mrs. Ocloo:* They say babies…well, they don't want the elbows sticking out. So they want it supple…so that when you are moving… well, you watch a typical Anlo…a typical Anlo woman walking, just swinging the hands like this [she stands and demonstrates]…With the elbows placed like this [she bends her arms slightly, elbows pointed forward, arms are no longer passively hanging against her sides].
>
> *KLG:* So right from the beginning you flex the baby's arms so that…
>
> *Mrs. Ocloo:* They don't get stiff. It's our tradition. Right from the start the child gets the routine.
>
> *Mr. Ocloo:* We want our people to be supple. They need to be able to move freely…Not rigid in their body or their thinking. Our people have to go live with the Fanti, the Ga, the Ashanti, and they have to be able to get along with them. So you start early, make them flexible from the beginning.

This is very similar to how the sense of *azɔlizɔzɔ* (walking or movement) was directly linked to *azɔlime* (one's character and way of life), or how in many Anlo contexts the way a person walked and moved symbolized the moral stance of an individual's life. Again, in the context of this cultural logic, no rigid distinction exists between the development of bodily habits and psychological outlook. One flexes the baby's joints to impart both somatic agility and adaptability of character.

OUTDOORING AND THE NAMING CEREMONY

Approximately seven days after a baby's birth, many families performed an "outdooring," or "naming ceremony," for the child. Usually, the baby was first carried out of the house, then back inside, and over the threshold in this manner seven times. Placed on the ground, one of the relatives (preferably someone who shared the baby's day name) would approach the baby and query, "Who is this I have found in the wilderness? Does this baby belong to someone?" The mother of the child then declared, "Yes, it is my baby, it belongs to us." The mother then paid the finder a token few *cedis* (like pennies) to get the baby back, to bring the baby into the family and out of the wild, or to join the child to a human group. If the family still had a thatched or corrugated iron roof, they might splash water on the roof and let it sprinkle down onto the baby's face. With the sun and the wind, the dripping water introduced the child to "the elements"; this was to assert that he was still a creature of the natural world. Finally, since *nufofo*, or speaking, was considered by many to involve important sensory qualities, many outdooring ceremonies included dropping a bit of gin, schnapps, or something pungent like salt water onto the baby's tongue to ensure that the child developed a sharp edge in his pattern of speech.[4]

Not all families in Anlo-land performed this ritual for the newborn or orchestrated the ceremony in precisely this way, and there was disagreement as to which components were borrowed from neighboring groups and which were traditionally practiced in Anlo areas. Nevertheless, this particular version of the ritual exhibits a tension between two different ways of being: feeling water, sun, and wind on the skin symbolizes that you are a child of nature, while at the same time hearing it declared that you belong to a family lets everyone know you are not a creature of the "bush."[5] This symbolism will be revisited later in relation to *agbagbaɖoɖo*, or the human capacity "to balance." While a number of *mɔfialawo* stated that the final segment of the birth ritual was an Akan custom that Anlo-speaking people had recently adopted, it symbolically displays an association between tasting a pungent flavor and speaking sharply and clearly, or being articulate and quick with one's tongue, which are values shared by many West African peoples.

CARRYING THE BABY ON THE BACK (VIKPAKPA)

Not limited to the Ewe-speaking area, throughout West Africa there is a widespread practice in which women attach their small children to their backs by wrapping the children in a cloth bound around their abdomens and breasts. This is referred to in the Ewe language as *vikpakpa*. In support of a functionalist interpretation, one *mɔfiala* explained that in Anlo contexts women placed their baby on the back to free up their hands to grind corn, to work at the farm, to cook, and to perform other everyday tasks. In addition, however, many Anlo speakers argued that the close contact and position on the back created a strong bond or attachment between mother and child; the child felt safe and secure strapped to the mother's back and accompanying her for prolonged periods throughout the day. Another *mɔfiala* said, "Since we carry babies on our front during their first year, by the time they are born we have to place them on our backs in order to straighten ourselves out." While it was not clear how widespread these beliefs were among Anlo-speaking people, it was clear that the practice of *vikpakpa* (carrying the baby on the back) was associated with the highly valued senses of balance and posture *(agbag-baɖoɖo)*, kinesthesia and movement *(azɔlizɔzɔ* or *azɔlinu)*, and flexibility in general.

Mr. and Mrs. Ocloo spent many hours, during 1994 and 1995, helping me contemplate and write about different aspects of Anlo culture. When I asked them tell me about *vikpakpa*, one of the first items they offered was the phrase *Vinɔko menya kpaɖo*. The saying literally meant something along the lines of "a baby cradled in the front *(vi:* baby; *nɔ:* mother; *ko:* stomach) would not know *(menya)* the cloth used to carry a child on the mother's back *(kpa vi:* to tie a child on one's back; *ɖo:* country cloth, possibly a Dahomean or Fon word)." While I never heard this phrase used in conversation or in a natural context, the Ocloos explained it as a very serious insult used by parents or grandparents to remind a youngster not to be impertinent because he probably did not really *know* what he was talking about. For instance, Mrs. Ocloo suggested that if a child from a wealthy family made fun of one of her peers who was less well-off, the parent might scold *Vinɔko menya kpaɖo* and elaborate by telling the child that, while her family may possess money at that point, when she was a baby they did not have even a cloth to tie her to her mother's back (and, hence, she was cradled on the front). Or perhaps, Mrs. Ocloo embellished, the parent would tell the child that she was wrapped and carried in a rag *(ɖo vuvu)* rather than a fine woven cloth *(kete)*!

The implications of the *Vinɔko menya kpaɖo* interaction described by the Ocloos begin with the deep insult of claiming a child was carried at the mother's front, since it is believed that *vikpakpa* (back tying) is in part what establishes strong bonds between child and mother, strong connections between a child and his or her lineage, and a general sense of security and attachment. So, if carried in the front, the very nature of your being has been compromised in that you did not develop the strong bonds with your mother and the relations with your family that are perceived to be the result (in part) of prolonged attachment at the back. This point was further grounded for me during a conversation I had with Adzoa Kokui, my elderly neighbor, after she had spent the previous week in Accra. She asked me if all Americans carry their babies on their stomachs, even after they are born. I was not sure what she meant and asked for clarification, so Adzoa explained that while she was in Accra she had seen an American woman carrying her baby in a kind of pouch at the front, and she felt sorry for them.

I later followed up on this exchange during an interview with her. In that more in-depth conversation Adzoa Kokui described how a woman's body was not meant to carry the baby in the womb for almost a year and then continue carrying the baby (once born) in front, but rather *vikpakpa* (back tying) ensured that a woman's body would be balanced out after the process of childbearing. Second, she stated that the baby would simply not develop properly if strapped to a woman's front. The baby that she had seen in Accra was facing out, with his back against his mother's stomach, and Adzoa expressed mortification at what a baby must experience in the process of being exposed to the world in this way—moving along in front of his own mother when only two months old! I told her that many times the baby would be carried facing in or even cradled in a kind of swing wrapped over the woman's shoulders. Despite my explanations, Adzoa insisted on the superiority of *vikpakpa* (back tying). She emphasized that in terms of *seselelame* (the sensory and emotional feelings the infant would have), clinging to the back was the best place. It provided the baby with a way to move through the market, travel along the road, or ride in a canoe across the lagoon with the *feeling in the body* (feeling in the flesh or the skin) of his mother there in front securing the way. Adzoa Kokui's rationale for the merits of *vikpakpa* (back tying) provided an interesting comment on somatic modes of attention to movement, balance, and the blend of sensory and emotional feelings in the body *(seselelame)*.[6]

To return to the *Vinɔko menya kpaɖo* interaction (the insult that if you were cradled on your mother's front, you would not know the cloth used to carry you on the back), it also implies that you do not know your own family's past. That is, the insult essentially accuses the child of not *knowing* some fundamental things (with the symbolic implication that one develops this knowing through the connection and the attachment that develops by being carried at your mother's back). More broadly, the insult is aimed at reinforcing the importance of knowing where you come from, or understanding the details and sources of your identity. This kind of knowing involves a sensibility grounded in bodily forms and bodily experiences such as being carried on your mother's back in a particular kind of cloth. Here we encounter a specific notion of *how we know things* that suggests it is built up (in part) from the tactile sensations prominent in the mother-infant bond. In addition, it implies there would be certain "durably installed" understandings about the distinction between being wrapped and carried in a rag *(ɖo vuvu)* compared with a fine woven cloth *(kete)*. Those early sensations need to be sustained, it is believed, to truly know where you came from and to cultivate a healthy sense of identity. The moral metaphors associated with *vikpakpa,* therefore, illustrate yet another area where somatic modes of attention and sensory experiences are directly linked to cultural logic and issues of the nature and relations of being and the grounds of knowledge.

In direct relation to *vikpakpa,* over the years Anlo-speaking people have utilized an object variously referred to as *atsibla, atibla,* or *atufu.* Appearing like a perch or a shelf on which the baby (strapped to the back) might rest, this was indeed one of the original functions of *atsibla,* though it is seldom (if ever) used that way today. Not in daily use in the early part of the twenty-first century, these days an *atsibla* is typically employed during festivals as a "display of traditional flavor."[7] In the early 1900s, however, when Westermann compiled his dictionary, he described *atibla* as "a cushion which women tie on their back when carrying a child" (1973[1928]:231) or "a cushion worn by women in their dress at the back, on which children are carried" (1973[1928]:248). By the 1960s the function of *atsibla* seemed to have changed in that Nukunya explained in his ethnography: "*Atsibla* is a kind of undergarment for women worn immediately above the buttocks, and is made by tying several pieces of cloth around the back end of the waist-line beads. It has the effect of hiding the actual shape of the buttocks by making the protuberance of the rumps more pronounced" (1969b:89). The evaluation and meaning of *atsibla* changed through the years from being functional (the early 1900s description of a cushion for carrying the baby) to being merely a piece of clothing (the under-garment version described in the 1960s) to being purely ornamental in the 1990s (a decorative object worn only on special occasions).

Indeed, some older women reported to me that carrying a child on one's back *(vikpakpa)* was easier when they used *atsibla* and that their posture remained straighter, more "in line," or balanced. They commented that it was a strain to carry the baby without *atsibla,* and it was harmful to the constitution of the young women who persisted in doing so. This deeper dimension of *atsibla* links it to an evaluation of the body that puts the kinesthetic and vestibular senses at the forefront of experience and appreciated form. Westerners might perceive an *atsibla* as a merely decorative (and visually appreciable) object, and indeed some Anlo speakers may even embrace that point of view, but the older and more traditional aspects of *atsibla* were far from purely visual and decorative. Instead, *atsibla* was meant to be *used* (not simply viewed), and it enhanced bodily movements and experience in sensory terms (kinesthetic and vestibular as well as *seselelame,* or a more general *feeling in the body*) already shown to hold great value for many Anlo-speaking people.

A proverb that drew on the symbolism of *atsibla* claimed that *Vi vɔ nyo wu atufu ga* (A wicked child is better than a big cushion, or a big *atsibla*). In the first instance, this saying was clearly meant to illustrate the high value placed on children that is characteristic of most African societies. However, in discussions about this proverb with a number of Anlo-speaking people, many restated or interpreted the meaning as a preference for *feeling the weight of the baby* (even if it was a wicked child) over walking around with an empty pillow (though the *atsibla* by itself would certainly be lighter on one's back). Their evaluation downplayed the visual sense and drew largely on kinesthetic and haptic sensibilities as well as on the more generalized state of *feeling in the body,* or *seselelame.* That is, an outsider might read or interpret this proverb as meaning that it would *look* or *appear* foolish to merely wear an *atsibla,* and people would thereby *see* that you were childless or barren. In discussions with Anlo speakers, however, issues of *appearance* or what it would look like to others if they had no baby on the back were never offered. The concern signified by the proverb was interpreted in terms of a bodily sensation, a feeling within and through the body, or in relation to *seselelame:* the emotional and sensory import of being childless.

EMPHASIS ON LEARNING TO BALANCE

In addition to being carried on a mother's back, children were often placed on mats in the center of our compound and encouraged to sit up, to crawl, and to begin trying *ɖo agba* (an imperative term used to encourage the infant to balance—which was done at this stage with the assistance of an older sibling or parent). These stages were precursors to walking and eventually balancing a load on one's head.[8] Balancing *(agbagbaɖoɖo)* was considered a vital component in each stage, such that sitting up properly involved balance, as did teetering on the feet while a sibling held hands or fingertips raised high above the baby's head. In fact, the conflation of these different bodily actions with balance seems to have led Westermann to a slight misunderstanding in his translations. For the term *agbagba,* or the verb *ɖo agbagba,* Westermann recorded (1973[1928]:82) two different meanings in his dictionary: (1) to carry something on the head without touching it with the hands; to balance; and (2) to make the first attempts in walking (of a child). When I tried to use the term according to his second rendering, however, I was consistently corrected. Ðo agba, I learned, was not the first attempts at walking but rather the stage prior to even the first step—the critical point when a baby mastered standing and *balancing* on his own two feet while the sibling let go of his hands. Walking usually followed shortly thereafter, but the skill of balancing on one's own was deemed a critical moment in a baby's development.

Moving forward required further refinement in a baby's ability to balance, but very quickly after the child was able to get around, they placed an object (often a small pan) on top of her head. So the sense of balancing *(agbagbaḍoḍo)* was integrally bound up with the practice of headloading, or carrying packages and cargo on top of one's head. As I watched children in my compound develop this understanding and learn the skill, I wrote in my fieldnotes:

> Yesterday I asked the children to help me fill the huge barrel in our bathroom (for toilet flushing) with buckets of water carried from the well. Afi and Aaron were the main assistants. Mawusi and Kodzo helped. But most remarkable was the fact that Peter made all 6 or 7 trips with us, carrying a small pan on his tiny 2 year old head. I was impressed. Children seem to observe and begin practicing head-loading from a very early age. They begin to do it themselves without any real prompting. Or actually, Peter got lots of positive strokes and encouragement for what he was doing. Afi and Aaron cheered him on. We all stood in the doorway (after we had all poured our water into the barrel) waiting for Peter who was struggling along, his small body carrying a load of water on top of his head. We smiled, encouraged him, and waited until he finished before we all set out for another load.

I chose to include this particular excerpt from my fieldnotes in part because I corrected myself in the middle of documenting and reflecting on my own observations. That is, I first wrote down that the children engage in this practice spontaneously or "without any real prompting." I then retracted and wrote that in actuality, in this cultural setting children were actively persuaded and inspired to balance during various stages in the development of motor skills. What appears to be a kind of "natural" development of abilities is culturally elaborated or augmented through habitual practices and everyday discourse. All over the world children learn, of course, to walk in a balanced manner and to carry objects. But in this setting, balancing seemed to be emphasized to a degree not found in all cultural groups, and after a certain point in a child's de-velopment in Anlo-land, head-loading, balancing, and walking became nearly inseparable.

The following is a discussion I had with Mr. and Mrs. Ocloo con-cerning how the baby learns to walk, which culminates in a comment about more philosophical dimensions of the human capacity to balance.

KLG: In Srɔgboe, some of the mothers and the older sisters say ɖo agbagba to their babies.

Mr. Ocloo: Yes, agbagbaɖoɖo [he corrects my pronunciation]—it means balancing.

Mrs. Ocloo: Toddlers…when the child is being taught how to stand…

Mr. Ocloo: To step: to stand and step.

Mrs. Ocloo: They say agbagbaɖoɖo.

KLG: Usually the baby was sitting down on the mat, on its rump, when the girls and ladies in Srɔgboe said it.

Mrs. Ocloo: So you raise it up, "Aɖo agbagba…agbagba kede…agbagba kede!!!" So he also gets up. You say that when you are raising the baby up on its feet. Yes. "Agbagbaɖo agbagba…. Agbag-baɖo agbagba"…so the child tries and then gets up, gets up on his feet.

Mr. Ocloo: Balances himself. Stands.

Mrs. Ocloo: After that you say "Ta, ta, ta!" And he tries to walk.

KLG: "Ta" means what?

Mrs. Ocloo: Just "ta, ta, ta" [she said this as she put one foot in front of the next]. It describes the movement. Or tabulatabula. That's how a toddler moves: zɔ tabulatabula…zɔ tabulatabula. [She crept ahead gingerly, wobbling like a small child trying to learn to walk.]

KLG: So ta is just the sound of the footsteps, of the feet, and tabulatabula the movement of the body.

Mrs. Ocloo: [She continued to demonstrate.] "Ta, ta…ɖo agbagba kede… ta, ta, ta…ɖo agbagba kede…ta, ta…" until he does it.

Mr. Ocloo: But before then, you say "Ta, devia ta tum, ta tum" which means he is crawling on his knees. That one is done before the agbagbaɖoɖo because they have to crawl before they can stand up.

KLG: So when they first start to move…

Mr. Ocloo: …on the knees…that's "devia ta tam."

KLG: And then it starts—ɖo agbagba.

Mr. Ocloo: Tata is "to crawl." Tatam: crawling.

KLG: Tata…tatam…devia tatam: the baby is crawling…And isn't another meaning of agbagbaɖoɖo to carry things?

Mrs. Ocloo: Aahhhh. You have *to balance* the thing on your head. *Gbagba:* it's the same thing.

Mr. Ocloo: It's a balance: Just as a child stands and tries to balance itself on its legs, so you have to balance the article you are carrying on your head and leave it. Balancing like that, getting up on two legs, that's human.

KLG: If you cannot balance like that, do people say anything? Is it awkward if you live here and you don't have the ability to carry things on your head?

Mrs. Ocloo: [Laughs.] You see, formerly when we were carrying loads, you would learn easily to do this thing...learn to...

Mr. Ocloo: Ɖo agbagba!

Mrs. Ocloo: But these days lorries are carrying the things, and you have porters carrying the things, so these days it is not. But formerly, as you go along, with your friends, going to the market, or going to the water, and all that...you will be conversing and then you will ɖo the *agbagba*...you will put the thing on your head. You will learn it naturally. So there weren't people, really, who couldn't do it.

Mr. Ocloo: But you know, it is cumbersome to hold the thing with your hands on top of your head.

KLG: Holding it with your hands is cumbersome?

Mr. Ocloo: Yes, holding it with your hands! So when you ɖo agbagba you feel free and you can go. That's all. You have to let go.

KLG: So it is basically that you begin, as a child, putting things on your head, and then you find as you grow and go along that you get tired if you leave your hands up there to hold it?

Mrs. Ocloo: Yes. That's it.

KLG: So you learn to drop them, your hands, and go free.

Mr. Ocloo: You learn to drop them and go without using them, with the load on your head. It's about balance...and it's good training for life.

Our conversation then turned toward the meaning of that comment: that physically balancing things on your head was "good training for life." Mr. Ocloo admitted that his own *ahanoŋko* (drinking name) included the word *agbagbaɖoɖo* and that it was considered a virtue to remain balanced and even-tempered (on the meaning and significance of drinking names, see Avorgbedor 1983). Mr. Ocloo believed there was a fairly explicit connection between the physical practice of balancing and a temperamental quality of being level-headed and calm.

Not only for Mr. and Mrs. Ocloo but for a number of *mɔfialawo,* balancing was described as one of the ultimate symbols for being human.

They considered upright posture, the ability to balance and move on two legs, as part of what separated humans from other animals. Consequently, despite Mrs. Ocloo's comment that there were no Anlo people who could not balance, some people reported worrying over children who had initial difficulty mastering this physical skill. Adzoa Kokui explained that if a child was not able to balance, he was considered a wild animal or a creature from the bush *(gbemela)*. Wildness was in general associated with the bush and not the village—the village being the place that some Ewe people deemed the "place of quintessential humanness" (Rosenthal 1998:109). While not focusing specifically on the somatic mode of balance, this distinction between becoming a human or remaining a wild animal, or living in the bush, was also addressed in direct relation to Ewe child-socialization practices:

> The ideals for which the Ewe people strive in the education of their children are reflected in the way the society assesses individual character: A well-behaved person is spoken of as *ewɔ amε* or *enye amε,* meaning roughly "he or she is a person." In the first of these expressions, which literally means "he makes a person," the stress is on "becoming" (he makes or has made himself a person). In the second, emphasis is on being (essence as opposed to existence). Education for the Ewes is, therefore, the *making* of a child to *become* what the society accepts as a person or human being *(amε)*. Indeed anyone who behaves contrary to the rules of the society is referred to simply as an animal: *edzo la* or *enye la* (he is an animal, i.e. a fool); or *dzimakplε* (born-but-not-bred, i.e. ill-bred). (Egblewogbe 1975:21)

Becoming a person, making a child into a human being, involved development of other sensory fields in addition to balance. For instance, learning to hear, listen, and obey *(nusese)* was of primary importance in parent-child interactions around discipline and development. Children were instructed and corrected in a variety of sense modalities, but to understand and comply was synonymous with hearing. Parents asked, *"Esia? Esia?"* which meant not only "Do you hear?" but usually implied "Do what I told you to do" (hence, "Obey!"). Many older Anlo speakers used a proverb, *Vi masenu aŋɔkae kua to ne,* which meant, "The ear of the disobedient child is always pulled by a vine thorn." To be disobedient or obstinate was referred to as having "hard or strong ears" *(tosεsε),* and the term for *punishment* was equivalent to "ear pulling" *(tohehe).* Thus, aurality was emphasized early in a child's life, which would be consonant with the fact that the Ewe language is tonal and therefore requires development of finely tuned auditory abilities.

In summary, many pregnancy and child-raising practices illustrate the cultural elaboration of sensory and somatic modes of attention. I have shown how everyday routines such as removal of ʤigbeɖi (birth dirt), flexing the baby's joints, or carrying infants on the back *(vikpakpa)* illustrate ways in which (symbolic) values are "given body, *made* body by the transubstantiation achieved by the hidden persuasion of an implicit pedagogy" (Bourdieu 1977:94). In other words, embedded in these socialization processes are some of the values that are so dear, so precious that they literally make this ideology into body with each generation. In this process the sensory order is reproduced through sensory engagements in routine practices and the enactment of traditions. Persons are thereby "durably installed" with the sensory orientations and the "thematized aspects of the world" (Csordas 1994c) that serve as a vital aspect of Anlo identity and sensibilities.

But these processes are neither automatic nor mechanically implanted into passive individuals. They are what constitutes the stuff of experience, the feelings that make up the micro-level of social interactions (or sensory engagements). They are, as Csordas says, "self-processes" or "orientational processes in which aspects of the world are thematized" (1994c:340). The self, he says, is "neither a substance nor entity, but an indeterminate capacity to engage or become oriented in the world, and it is characterized by effort and reflexivity" (1994c:340). We become persons in the midst of complex social relationships and interpersonal power dynamics as well as in the midst of continuous historical and cultural change. We all have individual stories and narratives that reflect congruence with and disparity from others in our cultural group. These self-processes, including those of sensory attention and orientation, require effort or agency and intentionality, some kind of engagement with the process of life. We move to this dynamic next.

PART THREE

Person and Identity

CHAPTER 6

Toward an Understanding of Anlo Forms of Being-in-the-World

In this chapter I concentrate even more intensely on aspects of the world that are thematized in Anlo contexts, beginning with perceptions of their homeland, their migration story, and the ŋlɔ of their appellation but then turning to issues of morality and personhood.[1] I explore the themes and motifs consistently presented to me as dimensions of Anlo core culture (categorized in anthropological terms as *emic*) in terms of the *etic* issue of the dovetailing of the senses, culture, and identity. Thematized aspects of Anlo personhood are probed for what they reveal about sensory, emotional, somatic modes of attention and processes of the self. Just as part 2 did not purport to contain a comprehensive account of child-socialization practices in Anlo worlds, part 3 is not meant to be an exhaustive account of the topic of personhood and the self. Rather, it is an analysis involving my third working proposition: that the local sensory order affects the concept and experience of being a person in the world.

We have seen how a local theory of immediate bodily experience, summed up by the term *seselelame*, highlights or culturally elaborates interoceptive as well as exteroceptive sensory fields. To really grasp the meaning of personhood and self processes in Anlo contexts one must appreciate the emphasis placed on interoception or internal sensory modes. Anlo sensibilities and Anlo forms of being-in-the-world involve a cultivation, I would argue, of interoceptive modes.

PAST AND PRESENT, BODY AND LAND

Some time in the late 1980s, several years before I first traveled to Ghana, an Anlo-Ewe friend of mine named Kwame related two pieces of what he considered vital information about his people. The first item concerned his ancestors' escape from slavery, three hundred years ago, and how they came to inhabit what is now the southeastern corner of the Volta Region in Ghana. Late colonial and postcolonial times constituted the setting for the second item. By this time, Kwame's account detailed, his people were no longer slaves, but rather they made up a prominent and vocal political force in contemporary Ghanaian society.[2] Linkages between the two parts of his account are at once rooted in the land (the terrain and soil often referred to as an Anlo homeland) and in the body (the ways in which their name, Anlo, has its origins in a body posture we refer to in Euro-American contexts as "the fetal position").

"As place is sensed, senses are placed; as places make sense, senses make place." Steven Feld calls this assertion of his a "doubly reciprocal motion" (1996:91), and Edward S. Casey invokes Feld's phrase to make the point that we are simultaneously "never without perception" and "never without emplaced experiences" (1996:19). Kwame described the place that he grew up as poor. By *poor* he did not mean culturally deprived, because he often spontaneously danced *Agbadza* and maintained that American jazz and other Western art forms derived from the music and inspirations of his very people.[3] But by *poor* he meant that the sandy soil on the coast of southeastern Ghana consistently failed to produce more than "small-small garden eggs" (eggplants), bitter oranges, dry tomatoes, "hard-time corn," and so forth. His perceptions of Anlo-land as *poor* seemed to be shaped by two other significant factors. First, he contrasted his Anlo homeland with the land held by the more famous ethnic group of Ghana, the Asante, which readily yielded the lucrative products of cocoa, timber, and gold. Second, Kwame lamented the point in the 1960s when his hometown of Keta was overlooked in favor of Tema as the site of postcolonial Ghana's national port. In his youth Keta thrived as a port town: the docking of European ships provided Keta with a continual flow (in and out) of cloth, beads, vegetables, spices, and so forth. His mother was a bead trader and his father served as a manager in the United Africa Company. The bustling atmosphere of business and trade in Keta that Kwame remembered from childhood came to an end when Tema, a town closer to the capital city Accra, was designated the national port. From then on Keta was neglected, and as sea erosion increased and the nation failed to erect a barrier wall, miles and miles of Keta and other parts of the Anlo homeland were lost to the water.[4]

As I entered the Anlo homeland for the first time in 1992, how much of Kwame's sense of the place of his childhood did I carry with me? Kwame's perceptions, built through emplaced experiences, were of a poor, almost disintegrating place, and the *feelingfulness* (to use Feld's phrase) in Kwame's portrayal of the destitute situation of Anlo-land would be hard to shake. His brother drove the Mercedes that I rode in, and I remember being awed (shortly after passing through Dabala Junction) by specific silk-cotton trees majestically standing alone in an expanse of grass and then again (once we had reached the coast) by luxuriant green carpets of flourishing shallots. But I put aside the pleasant and sensuous associations I gleaned from those isolated items and instead concentrated on perceptions of "poorness" that I felt obligated to feel and see. I did this because by the time I made my first trip to Anlo-land, in addition to Kwame's account, several Anlo people (in the United States and then in Accra) had conveyed to me with deep sadness the adversity they felt their relatives lived with in a *poor* place that was dissolving into the sea. In fact, on the morning of my first day in Keta, Kwame's cousin took me to meet one of their elderly relatives, who we found sitting on a chair on the porch of his house as water washed up the steps and spilled onto his feet. His house would be gone in a matter of months or a year, but he refused to abandon his home. His relatives checked on him daily to make sure he had not washed out to sea along with the portal.

"As place is sensed, senses are placed," according to Feld (1996:91). What were the implications for Kwame and other Anlo people of the disintegration of their natal place? In 1994 when I had returned to Ghana I met an American linguist who had been working with Ewe speakers on and off for twenty-some years. We had a brief conversation, but I will never forget his asking me, "Don't you find Ewe people rather *morose?* I feel exhausted and depressed as I work through translations of their poems and songs and as I listen to narratives about their ancestors and traditions—because they seem so invested in the woe that they associate with their history and lives." I was startled not by the content of his observation but by his frankness and his use of the term *morose.* I felt reluctant to generalize or characterize an Anlo or an Anlo-Ewe ethos in such a way, not simply because generalizations tend to be unacceptable in anthropology these days (for example, see Abu-Lughod 1991 on anthropologies of the particular) but also because of the very hearty sense of humor possessed by many Anlo and Ewe people that I knew. *Morose* was the initial term he used, but what resonated for me was a kind of melancholy—a sorrowful and mournful affect—that he attributed to many of the Ewe individuals with whom he had worked over the years. I later heard non-Ewe Ghanaians characterize Ewe people (especially Anlo-Ewes) as inward, philosophical, and introspective.

THE FLIGHT FROM ŊƆTSIE AND
THE TELLING OF A MIGRATION MYTH

Shortly after this encounter with the linguist, I began to notice that a shift had occurred in my response to their migration story. As I noted earlier, I had originally heard this story some time in the late 1980s (in the United States) from my friend Kwame.[5] And in the course of research on Ewe culture and history, I had also read brief accounts of the flight from Ŋɔtsie in numerous sources.[6] But once I arrived in Accra and began spending time out in the rural areas around Keta and Anloga (at first in 1992, and later for a longer stretch through 1994 and 1995), more than twenty additional people related their migration story to me. Perhaps it was simply that I was a newcomer to Anlo-land, but I was not prepared for how often I would be told this story. I even felt annoyance, sometimes, at having to sit through it yet another time. I knew all the twists and turns of the narrative by heart—trying to make rope from clay that contained thorns, throwing water against the wall, walking backwards out of the city, and so forth—and in retrospect I was clearly failing to appreciate, during those initial months, the significance of this story to their sense of identity as well as to the questions at the heart of my own research.

After the conversation with the linguist, however, I realized that I had begun responding to their story by curving my own body inward (often in sync with the rolling-up gesture of the storyteller) at the point in the narrative when the person described how their ancestor, Tɔgbui Whenya, folded into himself out of fatigue. Here is one oral account of their migration story told by a middle-aged gentleman I will call Mr. Tamakloe, who allowed me to tape-record as we spoke in English at his home in the town of Anloga.

> We Anlo were not always here; we once lived in Ŋɔtsie, or Hogbe, which is located in what's now Ghana's neighboring nation of Togo. But back in the seventeenth century our ancestors lived in the walled city of Ŋɔtsie. We weren't called the Anlo then, but Dogboawo. Most of the kings of Ŋɔtsie were benevolent, but then Agokoli took power some time around 1650.

Agokoli was a tyrant who took delight in tormenting his people by ordering them to make rope out of "swish" (or clay) filled with thorns. Well, as
for that, no one can make a rope from a pile of mud, especially when your
hands bleed, so our ancestors suffered under Agokoli's rule.

They began plotting their escape. It was a walled city, you know. And
Agokoli had plenty, plenty soldiers keeping watch over his workforce.
Many people say our ancestors in Nɔtsie were slaves. But it wasn't the
same kind of slavery that happened when they were forced onto ships for
Ablotsi—your place—so I'm going to call them his workforce.

The day for escape began with vigorous drumming. The men drummed
to entertain and distract the soldiers while the women packed minimal necessary items into their *keviwo* [head-loadable baskets]. For days the women
had been throwing their wash water against one small section of the wall.
Some even say they urinated on the wall to make it soft. By midnight the
drumming was at its peak and the soldiers had wandered away to sleep off
their *akpeteshie* [an alcoholic drink]. An old man named Tegli offered up a
prayer that the wall break open easily, and then he stabbed a machete into
the softened mud. The wall fell and all the women and children went
through first with the leaders. The elderly men followed, and finally the
young men and the drummers escaped, and they walked backwards—*zɔ
megbemegbe*—to make footprints that would deceive the soldiers. The
tracks would make it appear as though the walled city was under siege and
cause the soldiers to search inside for the intruders, giving our ancestors
time to travel far from Nɔtsie long before Agokoli realized they had
escaped.

Some traveled directly westward from Nɔtsie to the central part of the
Volta River. Their descendants are the northern Ewe living around Kpando
and in and around Ho. Most of the Dogboawo went southwest from Nɔtsie. Tɔgbui Whenya and his nephew Sri were among those who led their
relatives south. It was a long, long journey; many hundreds of miles on
foot, carrying their babies on their backs, balancing loads on top of their
heads. Tɔgbui Whenya and his followers established Wheta-Atiteti and
then moved on to settle Keta, Tegbi, and Woe. Finally, when Whenya
arrived at the place we now call Anloga, he collapsed and said, *"Nyeamea
meŋlɔ afiaɖekeyiyi megale nunye o"*—which means "I am rolled or coiled
up from exhaustion and I cannot travel further." So Whenya's followers
stopped right there, and somehow the place has been called Anloga—Big
Anlo—since that time.

As Mr. Tamakloe conveyed those final few sentences, he wrapped his
hands around the outside of his arms, folded his head over toward his
knees, and curled up into a ball—simulating Tɔgbui Whenya's weariness
or fatigue upon reaching the piece of land that was subsequently referred
to as Anloga.[7] As I had become conditioned to anticipate this climax, I
also rolled up. But after the conversation with the linguist, this seemingly
small event of folding into oneself became magnified in my mind. As the

place they call their homeland was beginning to make sense to me, I was beginning to wonder about how the sensations experienced in curling up into what I knew as "the fetal position" could influence or *shape* one's consciousness of *place* (*place* being culturally as well as materially constituted). In other words, in applying Casey's (1996) notion of "emplacement" to Anlo contexts, was there a relationship between the nearly barren landscape of the Anlo homeland and the inward-turning bodily motion of ŋlɔ that we find encoded in their name?

ON THE POETICS, AESTHETICS AND ICONICITY OF ŊLɔ

"Ŋɔtsie is to the Ewe what Ife is to the Yoruba," wrote Ewe scholar William Komla Amoaku (1975)—with Ife representing a kind of Mecca or Jerusalem. "Ŋɔtsie represents the 'symbolism of the center,' where their spiritual and political power originated. The history of their dispersion from this center is, therefore, often told under oath, for it is regarded as sacred history" (Amoaku 1975:88). No oaths were ever sworn when the story was narrated to me, which may be accounted for by the differences in location and time. That is, Amoaku's work was conducted in the early 1970s primarily in northern Ewe-land, around Ho, where he grew up, whereas I conducted research more than twenty years later and worked primarily with southern Ewes and people who referred to themselves as Anlo. The story seemed to be presented to me more as a legend with a secular quality, so if any Anlo people regarded it as "sacred history," I had teetered on complete impudence in the irreverent attitude I had taken toward hearing about Tɔgbui Whenya rolling up into a ball. But herein lies part of the paradox that will be elaborated later when I flesh out the second piece of information Kwame had related to me in the late 1980s. While doing fieldwork in Anlo-land, when I would point out that they were named in honor of "rolling up" with fatigue, I was inevitably met with a response of hearty laughter. This occurred even in the context of recounting the migration story. So while I cannot say that the migration story from Ŋɔtsie was a "sacred history" with the people who hosted me, the sheer number of times I heard the story was testimony to its significance.[8] In addition, the story was probably told differently in the north, since the climax would not be Tɔgbui Whenya arriving at the coast and rolling up. But Tɔgbui Whenya's *"meŋlɔ"* was certainly a focal point in the telling of the story in the south (as well as among Anlo speakers in Accra and in the United States), so the force and the meaning of *"Nyeamea meŋlɔ ... "* and their name Aŋlɔ will be examined now, and I will return later to Amoaku's observation of Ŋɔtsie's association with *the center*.

In the Ewe language, the utterance of ŋlɔ (also *meŋlɔ* or Aŋlɔ) results in a very interesting effect on the body—an effect that is best understood in terms of synesthesia, onomatopoeia, and iconicity. To speak of *meŋlɔ* or Aŋlɔ requires a formation in the mouth and a sonic production that trigger a rolled-up or curled-up sensation and resonance throughout the body.[9] The iconicity resides, in the first instance, in the curling of the tongue to duplicate the rolling up of the body that is being signaled by the term ŋlɔ. But beyond this basic iconicity, there is an aural dimension to ŋlɔ (stemming largely from the nasal ɔ rather than from the curling up of the tongue to produce the ŋ phoneme) that synesthetically prompts feelings of a kind of texture and timbre of roundness. In his work on lift-up-over sounding, Feld (1988:82) defined *timbre* as "the building blocks of sound quality" and *texture* as the "composite, realized experiential feel of the sound mass in motion," and I am suggesting here that there is an "experiential feel" of a poetic round, rolling, or curling-up "sound mass in motion" when Ewe speakers say Aŋlɔ or make the statement "*Nyeamea meŋlɔ....*" So while the action or gesture of folding into oneself does not in any literal sense produce an accompanying sound—such that the word ŋlɔ could be considered onomatapoeic in a technical sense—it synesthetically creates an "experiential feel" of roundness or an inward-spiraling kinesthetic return to the center.[10]

When Mr. Tamakloe curled up as he depicted and discussed Tɔgbui Whenya's fatigue, it was quite clearly an "iconic gesture" in that his action bore a close formal relationship to the semantic content of the narrative about their flight from Ŋɔtsie and their ancestor's exhaustion (see McNeill 1992:12–15 on iconic and metaphoric gestures). So on one level, we are dealing with an instance of kinesic behavior: a movement of the body that served to illustrate what was being verbally conveyed (Knapp 1978). In addition, we could also simply say that Mr. Tamakloe's rolling up was a display of affect, for while it is usually in a facial configuration that one looks for an affective display, "the body can also be read for global judgments of affect—for example, a drooping, sad body" (Knapp 1978:16). Clearly iconic and affective, here I want to explore how ŋlɔ is far more than that, and it may be said that Aŋlɔ itself is metaphoric for a sensibility and a way of being-in-the-world.

More than six years after I taped that interview with Mr. Tamakloe, I phoned a friend in Houston who considers herself an Anlo-Ewe person—even though she grew up largely in Accra and has lived in the

United States for more than twenty years. Her parents had been raised in Anlo-land, she grew up speaking the Anlo dialect of the Ewe language, and she periodically visited relatives in the rural Anlo homeland; hence, she had always and continued to identify as an Anlo-Ewe. I phoned her and very directly posed the following question: "You know how the term *Anlo* literally means to roll up or curl up in the fetal position?" She laughed and said, "Yesss?" I then asked, "What does it mean to you to be part of a people whose name means 'rolled up'?" In her lengthy response was the phrase "resentment and respect." She said that curling up in the fetal position is something you do when you feel sad, when you are crying, when you are lonely or depressed. She said that being Anlo meant you felt that way a lot, but you always had to unroll, or come out of it, eventually, and that gave you a feeling of strength. I told her that I had used the phrase "persecution and power" in one discussion I had delivered about the name Aŋlɔ (Geurts 1998:129–136), and I asked if that fit with what she meant. She confirmed that it did.

Resentment and respect. Probing such a sensibility, or an orientation in the world, led me to tracing the linkages between the two items Kwame had told me about: his account of their ancestors' escape from slavery and the migration to the coast, and then their ascendance to a position of influence (and resentment) in contemporary Ghana. The connections seemed to coalesce poignantly around feelings associated with ŋlɔ—and here I have glossed ŋlɔ as "the fetal position," but this translation does not map perfectly from one language and cultural context to the next. While ŋlɔ refers to a bodily position in which one folds or rolls up (curving inward as is customary for a baby in the womb), ŋlɔ does not directly correspond to the posture of a fetus, nor is it reified or objectified in the same way that "the fetal position" is in the discourse commonly associated with Euro-America. Here we can borrow from the phenomenological anthropology of Michael Jackson (1996:1) in refusing to "invoke cultural privilege as a foundation for evaluating worldviews or examining the complex and enigmatic character of the human condition." While I suspect that "the fetal position" is recognized by most if not all human groups, what it means, in what circumstances it is invoked, how it is encoded in local languages, and the ways it is elaborated or repressed are just some of the issues we can wonder about as we resist the assumption of equivalence from one cultural world to the next. With Tɔgbui Whenya's "*Nyeamea meŋlɔ* ... " as a critical moment in their migration story and with Aŋlɔ as both a toponym and a label they readily assign to their own "ethnoscape" (Appadurai 1991), I am led to ask about the consciousness of *ŋlɔ* in its "lived immediacy" among people who grew up attending to and orienting themselves toward *ŋlɔ*.

EMBODIED CONSCIOUSNESS

Toward that end, I want to now shift our notion of *ŋlɔ* away from that of "the fetal position" and ask what does it mean to grow up with *ŋlɔ* as an underlying theme (albeit on an unconscious level) of one's cultural history, identity, and ethnicity? How does a person make sense of *ŋlɔ* as a fundamental aspect of Aŋlɔtɔwo (one's people), Aŋlɔga (one's ancestral homeland), and Aŋlɔgbe (the language one speaks)? I would suggest that as a historically constituted object, *ŋlɔ* paradoxically symbolizes *freedom* from enslavement and *exhaustion* from the flight, *joy* for the arrival at a new homeland and *sorrow* for those who died along the way. It is emblematic of *comedy* in the sense that people often laugh when discussing the fact that their name means "rolled up," and *tragedy* in the sense that *ŋlɔ* signifies aging, returning to the fetal position, folding into oneself and then into the ground. Merleau-Ponty (1962:148) surmised, "To be a body, is to be tied to a certain world, ... our body is not primarily *in* space, it is of it." Anlo-Ewe people are of that time-space of Ŋɔtsie on to Keta-Anloga-Anyako (etc.), of the Anlo homeland to Ghana and West Africa in general to living in Europe and the United States, and they are still telling that story of the flight from Ŋɔtsie and Tɔgbui Whenya rolling up. What interests me is how *ŋlɔ* constitutes and is constituted by the existential condition of being Anlo (of people who grow up as or identify as Aŋlɔ).

The migration story was told to me on numerous occasions and by a variety of individuals.[11] Furthermore, when it was recounted, certain individuals imitated Tɔgbui Whenya's rolling into himself, thereby literally rehearsing this somatic mode of attention reflected in their name. What happens to a person's *being-in-the-world* when she "rehearses" (re-lives, re-enacts) Tɔgbui Whenya's *ŋlɔ*? The experience could be reduced to a cognitive process of intellectual reflection in which Tɔgbui Whenya and his behaviors are objectified, or treated as an historical and cultural object distinct from the storyteller. But the question that arose in my mind was why in more than a dozen instances people did not simply explain to me in words how Tɔgbui Whenya coiled up; instead they spontaneously reenacted (and relived) this almost primordial somatic mode referred to in their language as *ŋlɔ*. I also became intrigued by how, as the months proceeded and I became *sensitized* to Anlo *sensibilities*,

my own bodily response to the climax of the story was to join in with
the rolling up when Tɔgbui Whenya expressed his exhaustion. The point
here is that among many individuals who participate in an Anlo
ethnoscape, there exists an attention to ŋlɔ—a probably unconscious and
clearly somatic mode of attention—that defies delineation in our traditional analytic categories.

I turn to the argument that one way to treat this culturally constituted
phenomenon is to return to the phenomenon itself and to fully embrace
the *indeterminacy* of ŋlɔ. Csordas explains (1993:149) that the " 'turning toward' that constitutes the object of attention cannot be *determi-
nate* in terms of either subject or object, but only *real* in terms of intersubjectivity." Consequently, ŋlɔ becomes "real" in a time and space
between body, mind, self, other, subject, and object (rather than exclusively in one of those domains). Such indeterminacy as is illustrated here
is an essential aspect of one's existence in the "lived world of perceptual
phenomena" that constitutes Anlo ethnoscapes and Anlo selves. A
methodological approach of "embodiment" (Csordas 1990) suggests we
ask, when "turning toward" or attending to ŋlɔ, not only what is gleaned
cognitively (which may turn out to be the least fruitful analytic category
in relation to ŋlɔ) but what is experienced in terms of intuition, emotion,
imagination, perception, and sensation (cf. Csordas 1993:146–149). The
next section will begin to address this concern and will lay some of the
groundwork for my contention that a "turning toward" ŋlɔ is a fundamental though mostly unconscious dimension of self processes in Anlo
contexts and in the development of Anlo sensibilities, for to many Anlo
people, ŋlɔ holds something chthonic or "primordial" (if you will) about
human existence.

RESENTMENT AND RESPECT

I have described several dualistic phenomena that inhabit or constitute
the idea and experience of ŋlɔ: *freedom* and *exhaustion, joy* and *sorrow,*
humor and *grief.* While this portrayal connotes a holistic and balanced
essence for ŋlɔ, I believe that in general ŋlɔ tends more toward the exhaustion, sorrow, and grief side of the equation. Earlier I suggested that
this is in part due to the iconicity of ŋlɔ and the way that the utterance
itself can synesthetically create an "experiential feel" of roundness or an
inward-spiraling kinesthetic motion toward the center. This is not to suggest that most Anlo-speaking people are completely inward or morose
(as was the feeling of the linguist immersed in translating funeral dirges

and laments), but I do think that "being Anlo" (or *Anlo-ness*) involves a certain sense of persecution and a feeling of being misunderstood, maligned, and feared and that this dimension of their identity (or of an Anlo sensibility) is embodied in the melancholy and inward-turning somatic expression *ŋlɔ*. This raises the question of why some Anlo speakers feel persecuted and misunderstood and how this relates back to the two pieces of information I first heard from my friend Kwame.

The migration story recounted earlier indicates that Anlo-speaking people have lived in their present homeland for about three hundred years and came there due to persecution by King Agokoli, who ruled Nɔtsie. Histories of Ewe-speaking peoples prior to their life in Nɔtsie also focus on movement westward out of Oyo and then Ketu presumably as a result of persecution. Hence, the telling of histories among Anlo-speaking people rehearses (almost mythologically) stories and collective self-images revolving around experiencing persecution and fleeing from oppressive situations, triumphing in escape and freedom, and facing persecution in yet another place.

One can judge the pervasiveness of this view from a small pamphlet (Barawusu n.d.) I purchased at a bookstore in Anloga. The pamphlet was written and produced by a secondary school student named Solomon M.K. Barawusu and is entitled *The Hogbetsotso Festival: A Comparison between the Liberation of the Ewes from Slavery in Notsie—Togo—under the Wicked King Agorkorli and the Liberation of the Israelites from Slavery in Egypt under the Wicked King Pharaoh*. The opening lines of Barawusu's poem in free verse are as follows:

> If there have ever existed
> Any twin nations of the world
> With astounding records of similarity
> In their struggle from slavery to freedom
> Such twin undisputable nations
> Are the Israelites and the Ewes
> The Bible and Ewe history
> Prove them sisters in terms of slavery
> Brothers in terms of leadership
> Comrades in terms of liberation
> And friends in terms of escape
> Both had common obstacles
> That stood in their way to freedom
> The Israelites had a wicked Pharaoh
> After serving under kind ones
> The Ewes also had a wicked King—Agorkorli
> After serving under kind ones ...

I quote this pamphlet simply to make the point that the self-image of persecution was sufficiently prevalent among Anlo-speaking people that in the 1990s a secondary school student could write and sell locally (through distribution in bookstores) a document such as this. The historical accuracy or the validity of the comparison between Ewes and Israelites is not what matters here, but rather what is of interest is the ethnic imaginings that correspond easily to ŋlɔ as a rolling, coiling-up kind of somatic mode that attends to and expresses the melancholy and sorrow that pervades Anlo-Ewe stories and myths about the past.

Historians attest to the reality of this experience of persecution, which is the heart of the second item that was first told to me by my friend Kwame and which had been reinforced by additional Anlo people that I had since met. Numerous Anlo people have commented to me on how the Anlo-Ewe homeland is devoid of any rich natural resources (particularly in comparison with the gold, cocoa, and timber prevalent in the areas occupied by Asante peoples who live in the forest zone of Ghana). Sandra Greene (1985:83) points out that "after the advent of colonial rule the Anlo sought to overcome the limited opportunities available to them in their own area by emigrating to non-Anlo/non-Ewe districts in Ghana." She then explains that "while few studies exist on Anlo relations with other ethnic groups, it appears that it was not uncommon for the Anlo and other Ewes in diaspora to be the subject of rumor and suspicion" (Greene 1985:83).

Then Greene discusses several specific historical incidents that could certainly be interpreted as "persecution" of Anlo-Ewe speaking people (such as the burning of villages), and she explains how other ethnic groups in Ghana consistently perceive Anlo-Ewe speakers to be "thieves, kidnappers, sorcerers, and ritual murderers" or as people who dabble in "sorcery and evil medicine" (Greene 1985:83–84). Her review of several studies led to the conclusion that "[i]n systematic surveys among and interviews with Ghanaian university and secondary school students, as well as 'the general adult population' about the images of members of other ethnic groups, all respondents consistently described the Ewe in some of the most negative stereotypical terms" (Greene 1985:84). The historical and cultural factors underpinning this situation of animosity certainly deserve careful and lengthy consideration, but a full exploration of relations among various ethnic groups in Ghana is clearly beyond the scope of this study.[12] The point I believe this material makes is that while negative stereotypes of Ewe speakers seem to be generally cultivated by other ethnic groups, they also serve to feed Anlo speakers' self-perceptions of persecution. Relevant to our discussion here, therefore, is how various Anlo-speaking individuals explained Greene's conclusions and what these explanations then reveal about the ways in which "culture and psyche make each other up" (Shweder 1991:73).

Anloga is the ritual capital of Anlo-land, and the place or the site where three hundred years ago their ancestor Tɔgbui Whenya is said to have experienced the emotional and sensory feelings of ŋlɔ when he bent over and curved his body inward with arms and legs drawn toward his chest, resting and determining that his people would rest there too. In ŋlɔ itself we find an indexical sign of a central feature of what we might call an Anlo sensibility: the perduring mood of sorrow and woe that is counterbalanced by the sense of strength and vigor when springing back out of this position. As one *mɔfiala* explained, "There is an Anlo proverb which states that *Amea ɖeke metsɔa anyiɖefe wɔa mlɔfe o*—Nobody makes the place he fell his sleeping bed. Tɔgbui Whenya may roll or curl up but he will surely spring back with strength, power, and energy to resist every form of enemy persecution and domination. *Nyeamea meŋlɔ* has defined our worldview as far as fear of subordination by other ethnic groups is concerned" (Adikah 2000).

Many Anlo-speaking people with whom I worked began their explanations of persecution with reference to the dearth of natural resources in their own homeland. They explained that since the land provided limited opportunities for livelihood or for inheritance of wealth, the place of Anlo-land itself was a source of depression. While it remained a place that they held close to their heart because it was the ground of their heritage and childhood (in the case of many individuals), Anlo-land did not provide a ready source of sustenance, with its sandy soil and lack of industry, in the late twentieth century. Due to these conditions, many Anlo speakers have stressed education for their children and the development of skills that would allow them to work in other areas and to mingle with other ethnic groups. For instance, many Anlo speakers pointed out how they typically learned various other languages spoken in Ghana (such as Twi, Ga, Akan, or Fante) but they very seldom encountered an (ethnically) non-Ewe Ghanaian who could speak Ewe. One *mɔfiala* told me that an Ewe professor once said to him, "Kofi, *agbalea srɔm haa?* You know that we have nothing. It [studying] is the only mineral resource we have." This emphasis on education has led to perceptions of Ewe-speaking people in general and Anlo speakers in particular playing the role of what some call the "intelligentsia" in contemporary Ghana.[13] What they meant was that although Ewe-speaking people (and especially

Anlo-Ewes) were a minority in Ghana, they were also conspicuously active and present in the professional and educated sector of the nation. A number of people explained that while other ethnic groups claimed this was due to nepotism or "tribalism," among Anlo speakers it was perceived as resulting from the higher percentage of Ewe speakers (compared with other ethnic groups) who achieved advanced levels of education and who were therefore qualified for civil sector and professional occupations. Anlo speakers often expressed that they pursued work in the civil sector due to limited economic opportunities in their homeland, and the self-perception of being Ghana's intelligentsia was considered as burdensome as it was beneficial—hence the connection back to a *mythos* summed up in the trope of *ŋlɔ* (coiling up or rolling into oneself) as a somatic and kinesthetic mode that attends to and expresses a sensibility featuring melancholy and sorrow. As my friend in Houston explained, "Being Anlo, for me, is about respect and resentment: on one hand they respect us for being so industrious and hard working, but then they turn around and resent us when we succeed. It just makes me sad."

Another explanation about why Ewe-speaking people in general were feared, disliked, or negatively stereotyped revolved around their classic ritual practices and moral code rooted in a complex religious system commonly referred to by outsiders as *voodoo* or *vodun* (for background see Blier 1995; Gilbert 1982; Meyer 1999; Rosenthal 1998). All over the world the English term *voodoo* elicits pejorative images and thoughts that illustrate why practitioners were frequently labeled as "thieves, kidnappers, sorcerers, and ritual murderers" (Greene 1985:84). *Vodu* is an ancient metaphysical philosophy and set of sacred practices involving the use of herbs, incantations, sculpture, and so forth to reinforce Anlo-Ewe moral codes (see Blier 1995; Geurts 1997; Rosenthal 1998), and it will be discussed in more detail in chapter 8. The fact that Anlo speakers themselves realized others in Ghana perceived aspects of their classic religion in a very negative light is evidenced by the deeper issue being addressed by Greene in the work referred to previously about ethnic relations in Ghana.[14] Greene suggests an explanation for why the office of the Paramount Chief (known as *Awoamefia*) was once clearly associated with religious and ritual practices, but more recently these associations have been omitted or dropped in most oral accounts of traditions and history surrounding the Paramount Chief.

> Most place emphasis in their discussions of the nature of the Anlo political system on the non-religious aspects of the *awoamefia* office; they also omit or downplay any reference to the role of religion in any of the other politi-

cal offices as well. Instead they focus on those features in the political system that they themselves note are quite different in kind, but nevertheless
share some common characteristics with the perceived predominately secular Akan political culture which has come increasingly to dominate the
popular image of southern Ghanaian culture in general. This, I believe, is
not an unconscious act of omission, but reflects the concerns of these scholars not to focus on information that can be misinterpreted and misused to
besmirch the image of the Anlo. (Greene 1985:84)

Since Anlo-Ewe religious practices were feared and viewed in a negative
light by many Ghanaians, West Africans, and "outsiders" in general, associations between such actions and the Paramount Chief (as well as
other politically oriented items) were gradually downplayed.

In other circumstances, however, fear of the ritual powers of many Anlo
speakers was exploited, since stories abounded among Ghanaians about
the potency of Ewe *juju*. A vignette from my fieldwork in 1994 may illustrate this point more clearly. Marion, a young American researcher I knew
in Accra, purchased a twelve-foot piece of *adinkra* (cloth) in the marketplace of the Center for National Culture, but when she delivered the cloth
to her seamstress (who was an Anlo-speaking woman with whom I was
also acquainted), Marion learned that the cloth was very old and would
soon begin shredding or tearing apart. Indeed, the seamstress showed me
the very cloth, and as she pulled gently on the threads, she demonstrated
how the weave of the *adinkra* was very loose. Marion's Ewe-speaking
friend, neighbor, and occasional research assistant, Rejoice, suggested that
Marion had been cheated and that they should return to the market and
confront the merchant from whom she had purchased the cloth.

Several weeks later they recounted to me how they went to the market
together and Rejoice appealed to the merchant while speaking a combination of English and Twi (the national lingua franca), but the merchant and
her partners refused to exchange the *adinkra* for a newer, more durable
fabric. The dialogue escalated into a heated argument, but the merchant
refused to budge. Rejoice then began escorting Marion toward the exit,
stopped, turned around to face the merchant, and declared loudly and *in
Ewe*: "*Miekpɔge loo!*" This translates simply as "You will see!" but is closer
in meaning to the English phrase "Just you wait!" and connotes a curse or
impending recourse to sorcery. They then turned and exited the market.
Approximately five minutes later a young man from the stall (probably the
son of the market woman) came running up to them with a splendid piece
of *adinkra,* beseeching them to exchange it for the old and tattered cloth.
The transaction was completed and they left.

The point of this story is that once reason failed to produce a positive result, Rejoice made it known to the merchant (and others in the market) that she was an Ewe (-speaking) person, which in and of itself signified access to the powers of a potent curse based in *vodu*. This display thereby exploited, to a certain extent, general perceptions of Ewe-speaking people: that they could and would resort to using a curse (or *dzosasa*, as it is called in the Ewe language) to get their way. These ritual practices thus have a quality of indeterminacy; they were simultaneously a source of persecution and power. Here *resentment and respect* hold an indexical relationship to ŋlɔ as a rolling, coiling-up kind of somatic mode that attends to and expresses a melancholic Anlo sensibility.[15]

GRASPING THROUGH TO THE MYTHOPOEIC

To further probe this association I want to return to the issue of what Bourdieu calls the "socially informed body" and to begin to raise some questions about cultural memory. The *body* that we encounter in Bourdieu is not divorced, of course, from either the mind or the social environment, but rather he insists that "every successfully socialized agent ...possesses, in their *incorporated state,* the instruments of an ordering of the world, a system of classifying schemes which organize...practices...." (1977:123–124, emphasis added). The incorporated state at question here is one of Anlo ontology. That very Anlo ontology begins, in a word, with the migration story or mythic account of how Tɔgbui Whenya led his people out of slavery and then folded into himself (and declared "*Nyeamea meŋlɔ... "*)—a story that may have been circulating for three hundred years.[16] Bourdieu has suggested (1977:124) that "to grasp through the constituted reality of myth the constituting moment of the mythopoeic act is not, as idealism supposes, to seek in the conscious mind the universal structures of a 'mythopoeic subjectivity' and the unity of a spiritual principle governing all empirically realized configurations regardless of social conditions." Bourdieu's argument is that grasping through to the constituting moment of the mythopoeic act involves instead a reconstruction of the principle of the *socially informed body,* which is a principle that unifies and generates practices and which is inextricably cognitive and evaluative. His notion of evaluative, of course, opens the floodgates of the sensory, for evaluation involves taste and distaste, compulsion and repulsion, and the attentiveness and tuning out that is done through all sensory fields. Here I am suggesting that ŋlɔ is a part of the socially informed body of those who share in the heritage and sensibility of being Anlo, or those who participate in and are oriented to an Anlo ethnoscape.

But we cannot seek the mythopoeic subjectivity of ŋlɔ merely in the conscious mind. We have to break away from our own ethnocentric attachment to a dualistic split between conscious and unconscious and be willing to play with the indeterminate space between those categories that are often not meaningful in other cultural contexts. So without backing down from the interpretation of ŋlɔ that I am putting forth here, I can acknowledge that ŋlɔ is forced into what Bourdieu calls "rational systematization and logical criticism" by virtue of the very methodology he critiques. That is to say, Bourdieu argues (1977:123) that when a person lacks the symbolic mastery of schemes and their products, the only way such a person (an observer) can participate is by creating a model. As an anthropologist and a person who inhabits at most only the fringes of an Anlo ethnoscape, I construct a model of ŋlɔ because it is "the substitute required when one does not have...immediate mastery of the apparatus" (1977:123). My model of ŋlɔ, then, is aimed at approximating a phenomenon at work in Anlo worlds, which I am suggesting cannot be reduced to a word *(ŋlɔ)*, an event in a story (Tɔgbui Whenya's declaration and performance of *"Nyeamea meŋlɔ... "*), a body posture (curling or folding into oneself), an emotional-sensory state (exhaustion, sorrow, depression), or a cognitive concept (ŋlɔ as a mere metaphor of persecution). *Ŋlɔ* is part of the "system of classifying schemes," part of the "instruments of the ordering of the world," in an Anlo habitus—an Anlo habitus that has been recapitulating a history of Tɔgbui Whenya's ŋlɔ such that we are forced to confront what this means about how *history is turned into nature*.

Merleau-Ponty suggested that in the philosophy and phenomenology of consciousness, the concept of "institution" could serve as a kind of hinge. By *institution* he meant "those events in experience which endow it with durable dimensions, in relation to which a whole series of other experiences will acquire meaning, will form an intelligible series or history—or again those events which sediment in me a meaning, not just of survivals or residues, but as the invitation to a sequel, the necessity of a future" (1963:108–109). *Ŋlɔ* might be that kind of hinge, that kind of institution. As an eminently polysemous symbol, it "sediments a meaning" not just of an event three hundred years ago when Tɔgbui Whenya rolled up, but rather it sediments a meaning that is an "invitation to a sequel." It invites the recapitulation of the sensations Tɔgbui Whenya felt when he landed at the ground that has been perceived as Aŋlɔ-land ever since. And as an institution, in Merleau-Ponty's sense, ŋlɔ allows for a whole series of other experiences to acquire meaning. As one *mɔfiala* explained in a letter to me:

> The Ŋɔtsie story and *Nyeamea meŋlɔ* invokes a participatory emotion in us. *Meŋlɔ* conveys an image of a curling-up hedgehog. It conveys a nostalgic feeling of tiredness, fatigue, weakness and sadness borne out of never-ending journeys across mountains, rivers, and more significantly of breaking-free from subjugation. "At last I can relax my tired bones!" Tɔgbui Whenya decided to ŋlɔ not only because he was tired but also he might have gained a nostalgic moment and the satisfaction that his people, hedged in by the sea and the lagoon, were well protected from enemies. Ŋɔtsie represents the genesis of our subjugation, our heritage, our ancestry and *Nyeamea meŋlɔ* represents the climax, the conclusion after long years of suffering. Ŋɔtsie is the beginning; Anloga the finishing point. When my grandmother danced backwards and later curled up with excitement written all over her face, it was a dramatization of ... being Anlo." (Adikah 2000)

ŊɔTSIE AND THE CENTER: EMPLACEMENT AND AN AESTHETICS-POETICS OF ŊLɔ

Amoaku (an Ewe scholar) suggested that for many Ewe people Ŋɔtsie is metaphorically the sacred mountain, the *axis mundi,* or the place where heaven and earth meet. He tells a story of visiting the site where Ŋɔtsie used to exist[17]—of standing amidst the debris of the wall—and he explains that before he left the site he engaged in washing his face with water and herbs as a "symbol of communion with our ancestral gods" and as a means of atoning for "deserting them" or abandoning and separating from his ancestors.

When certain Anlo people present the story of their own flight from Ŋɔtsie (Amoaku is from Ho, not Anlo-land), the event is accompanied by what for me is one of the most profound physical gestures the human body can perform: the folding inward or coiling up of ŋlɔ. When I first tried to write about witnessing Anlo-Ewe people coil forward as they told me about Tɔgbui Whenya, I was reminded of Jackson's (1989) essay "Knowledge of the Body." He opens with an account (1989:119) of beginning to practice yoga in his mid-thirties. Initial work with *asanas* (postures) was like "unpicking the locks of a cage" because prior to this his body "passed into and out of my awareness like a stranger; whole areas of my physical being and potentiality were dead to me, like locked rooms" (cf. Stoller 1997 on the "scholar's body"). I had been practicing yoga for more than fifteen years before I first sojourned to Anlo-land,

and I mention this because it is possible I was struck by ŋlɔ in large part because of this dimension of my own biography. It is commonly understood in yoga that "forward bends" (such as what one does when folding into oneself or gesturing ŋlɔ) are known to produce sorrow, nostalgia, and grief. During one particular class I began to spontaneously weep, for reasons totally unknown to me, in the middle of a session on forward bends. My teacher quickly removed me from the group engaged in forward bends and instructed me to initiate back-bending postures. Along the lines of a principle of the obverse, forward bends in yoga must be countered or complemented with backward motion.[18] This anecdote is offered as a way of making two points. First, it is to acknowledge my own predisposition to having attended to or focused on this specific aspect of Anlo worlds, whereas other researchers may have glossed over it. Second, the yogic philosophy of forward bending asserts that rolling up or gesturing in the manner of "the fetal position," or ŋlɔ, will necessarily generate sorrow, introspection, even grief, providing a precedent for an association of ŋlɔ with sadness, sorrow, and their stories about the past.

So, from ŋlɔ as an iconic gesture and the onomatapoeic and synesthetic qualities I suggested accompany the utterance "Nyeamea meŋlɔ ..." to the yogic implications of this forward bend, I want to extend this exegesis out one final ring. I want to suggest that when certain Anlo people present their migration myth and we reach the moment of Tɔgbui Whenya declaring "Nyeamea meŋlɔ...," we are dealing with a "direct presentation of the feelingful dimension of experience" (Armstrong quoted in Feld 1988:103) that characterizes what Robert Plant Armstrong means by his term "affecting presence." To explore this idea, let me direct our attention to Feld's (1988:103–104) synthetic distillation of Armstrong's three works on aesthetics, consciousness, and myth. Feld explains that Armstrong "wishes to examine works of affecting presence as direct forces and sensibilities, through which one might grasp '... the very consciousness of a people, the particular conditions under which their human existence is possible'" (Armstrong 1975:82, quoted in Feld 1988:103). Anlo and Ewe people lived in oral societies for centuries before the Ewe language was transliterated, and storytelling as well as other verbal arts have a robust history and continue as vital forms of cultural production across West Africa.[19] The myth or legend of Nɔtsie, or the prose narrative concerning their migration out, first struck me as just some story that certain people wanted me to know, but after years of reflecting on how and how often it was presented to me, I have come to regard the tale itself as a "work of affecting presence" (in Armstrong's terms) and the moment of gesturing Tɔgbui Whenya's curling up as an "enacted metaphor." Feld highlights (1988:103) Armstrong's argument about how "affecting presences, as works or events witnessed, are 'constituted, in a primordial and intransigent fashion, of basic cultural psychic conditions—not symbols of those conditions but specific enactments—presentations—of those very conditions—the affecting presence is not a 'semblance' but an actuality … in cultural terms it presents rather than represents.'" When Mr. Tamakloe folded into himself, it was an enactment, a presentation of the condition of "being Anlo" for more than three hundred years. Ŋlɔ emerges, then, as a trope, an enacted metaphor for a melancholy sensibility, an embodied consciousness with its obverse: ŋlɔ as persecution and power; ŋlɔ as resentment and respect.

One final insight from Armstrong and Feld sheds light on these interpretations of ŋlɔ especially in relation to seselelame. Feld suggests that through his interpretive matrix, Armstrong is able to transcend a false dichotomization of cognition and emotion or body and mind: "For him, it is never that the viewer's affect is caused by the artist's sensibilities packed into work; it is that the viewer's feelings are drenched in comprehension of enacted sensibilities that live in the work" (Feld 1988:104). In the course of a myriad of presentations about the flight from Ŋɔtsie by Anlo interlocutors, when I began to roll or curl up myself, I believe that my feelings had finally become "drenched in comprehension of enacted sensibilities" rooted in seselelame. Here I have tried to describe how beginning with "emplaced experiences" in a land washing out to sea, there arose an attentiveness to Ŋɔtsie as the center and to Tɔgbui Whenya's never-ending and somatically expressed "Nyeamea meŋlɔ…," which poetically and aesthetically captures a vital dimension of the condition of being-Anlo-in-the-world.

STRAIGHTNESS AND TRUTH: ASPECTS OF MORAL KNOWING

Decades ago Victor Turner employed (1967:43) the phrase "biopsychical individuals" to suggest the inextricability of physical sensations (the phenomenal dimension of experience and knowing) and psychological orientations (the noumenal dimension of experience and knowing). The goals here are not unlike Turner's penetrating insight into the multiplex (and largely unconscious) ways in which symbolic phenomena are experienced by individuals. While Turner's specific focus at that point was on ritual contexts, this study includes quotidian life as well as ceremonial settings.

Moral knowing among Anlo-speaking people is a complex topic. Here I introduce three of the more extreme deterrents that people readily mentioned as reminders of the consequences of unethical actions: a tradition in Anlo-land of burying criminals alive (Tɔkɔ Atɔlia), prohibitions on wealth acquired through immoral or illegal means *(ga foɖi mawo)*, and a form of restitution in which the lineage must provide (in perpetuity) a young girl to serve in a shrine *(trɔxɔviwo)*. They are dimensions of an Anlo moral code that individuals internalize through discourse about these themes and through actions, deeds, and daily conduct (practices). Growing up in Anlo contexts means attending to these themes of Tɔkɔ Atɔlia, *ga foɖi mawo,* and *trɔxɔviwo.* The attending and orienting in turn contribute to the development of an Anlo sensibility, or what we might think of as a perduring mood, a disposition, or an orientation that is "patterned within the workings of a body" (Desjarlais 1992:150). And as one *mɔfiala* stated, this sensibility determines or guides "how you walk through life, how you carry and conduct yourself." Here again we see the association of movement, one's comportment and walk, with one's moral character.

These deterrents are understood to work in the end because of the importance of balancing, or *agbagbaɖoɖo,* which we saw figure into childsocialization routines. Many Anlo speakers told me that they refrained from indulging in destructive deeds (alluded to previously) even though they had access to malevolent powers because of their concern with maintaining balance.

Tɔkɔ Atɔlia (The Fifth Landing Stage)

"The fear of Tɔkɔ Atɔlia is very real," explained one *mɔfiala.* "To know that stealing or sleeping with another man's wife could land you in the ground, buried alive, made me listen well to my parents. It wasn't just that I thought stealing was wrong, I felt scared of the crows picking out my eyes—like Agbebada, you know—and of the thirst. My mouth goes dry thinking of being buried alive; of feeling each moment of my death." In my conversation with this young man he made direct reference to a character, Agbebada, in a five-act play called *Tɔkɔ Atɔlia* (or *The Fifth Landing Stage*), written by F. K. Fiawoo (1981, 1983).

The title of the play refers to a piece of land in the settlement of Anloga where the forefathers of those in Anlo-land buried criminals alive according to the *nyiko* custom (Fiawoo 1959a:104–111). Previously forested, by the 1990s the area was a grassy field located behind the Anloga police station and used as the central site of the annual Hogbetsotso festival (a festival that will be discussed in chapter 7). In the play's introduction we learn:

> Our forefathers detested crime and showed relentless severity in exacting the penalty from the guilty. In those days there were no police in our land nor public prisons. Each member of the community was concerned to guard against social disorder, aiding the unwritten laws of the country to operate severely on those who habitually infringed them. Some of these offenders were made by the State to pay fines, others were banished, some were reduced to serfdom, while others were buried alive according to the gravity of the offence.... Concerning stealing, adultery, and the evil practices of sorcery, they said that these acts were responsible for the destruction of nations. They based their view upon their experiences from the days of their migration from Hogbe to Anlo land. (Fiawoo 1983:7)

Numerous elderly people I interviewed expressed the belief that Tɔkɔ Atɔlia was "something of the past" and had no effect of deterrence on the "immoral behaviors of today's young people." However, young people themselves did not necessarily hold that perspective, as indicated by the words of the young man quoted previously. Perhaps due to the influence or currency of Fiawoo's play, young people themselves often referred to *The Fifth Landing Stage* as they discussed what it meant to grow up in Ghana as "an Anlo person." That is, they perceived this site and tales of criminals buried alive in that soil as symbols of the strict code of ethics adhered to by their people. So the young man quoted previously explained that as he grew up he eventually came to understand that the custom was no longer in practice, and he was therefore not really in jeopardy of being buried alive. But he noted that as a child he remembered feeling terrified not simply of the idea but of the actual sensation of being buried alive.

People literally shuddered, therefore, as they talked with me about Tɔkɔ Atɔlia, and they usually spoke in hushed tones. People seemed pressed to make me understand that Tɔkɔ Atɔlia did not represent cruelty or perversity on the part of their forefathers, but rather it was the last resort in their criminal justice system and was a protective and preventive element in maintaining community stability and health. While this practice of burying criminals alive was no longer in effect in the 1990s, I would suggest that stories and memories of Tɔkɔ Atɔlia continued to have a *biopsychical* hold on many Anlo-speaking people with whom I worked. This hold was not merely on the elderly, and numerous young people held an almost somatic understanding (hence, the shuddering of the body and the memories of fear from childhood) of the consequences of committing a crime.

Ga fodi Mawo: *Prohibitions on "Dirty Money"*

The phrase *ga fodi mawo* literally meant "dirty monies" and was commonly used to express an ethics about the pursuit of wealth. Earlier discussions covered the issue of the dearth of resources and opportunities for lucrative work in the Anlo traditional homeland. Because of this situation, people commonly ventured out of the area to Accra, other parts of Ghana, throughout West Africa, and beyond, planning and hoping to create an enterprising and successful business. Such initiative was encouraged among many Anlo-speaking families, and several people summed up the prevailing attitude in the following piece of advice they delivered to young people: Go forth, work hard, be industrious, and don't come home empty-handed [i.e., bring back wealth!], but make sure you are not carrying "dirty money." The belief was that "dirty money" was acquired through nefarious means, and people in the family would begin to die if a member brought such money home.

This concept was not so different from *dzigbedi,* or retention of "birth dirt," and here I would suggest that a similar quality marks the phenomenon of "dirty money." There was a kind of dirt or soiled state that could not be washed out of either human beings or money, and the presence of this filth ultimately represented a morally compromised condition. *Dzigbedi* (birth dirt) was often identified by an odor emanating from an individual, and the conclusion drawn often revolved around the idea that the person had not received a proper first bath (as an infant) or a proper upbringing in general, and this resulted in a compromised condition not simply in relation to physical hygiene but to the moral and social status of the individual as well. "Birth dirt" left on an infant could never be washed out. *Ga fodi mawo* (dirty monies) also could not be "cleaned" no matter how much "laundering" the monies were subject to. While "dirty monies" were not identified through olfactory perception like *dzigbedi,* they were perceived in divination and by the "recurring decimal" of death in a given family. That is, if one engaged in bribery and corruption or in accumulation of wealth by immoral means (including employment of *dzoka* or "juju"),[20] people began to die throughout the family. There were very few ways a family or lineage could put a stop to this "recurring decimal," but one form of propitiation was *troxoviwo.*

Trɔxɔviwo: *"The Trɔ (Spirit or Deity) that Takes Your Child"*

A *trɔ* was conceptualized as a tutelary god, spirit, or deity, and throughout the Ewe-speaking area shrines and devotional communities existed
to serve a variety of *trɔwo*.[21] *Trɔxɔviwo* was one such category of temple or sanctuary, and its name derived from how the spirit demanded a
(usually female) child from the lineage as a way of atoning for a sin or
as cosmic restitution for a specific criminal act.[22] Unlike Tɔkɔ Atɔlia (the
burying of criminals alive at the "fifth landing stage"), which was no
longer practiced in the latter half of the twentieth century, *trɔxɔviwo*
temples were still in existence at the time I lived in Anlo-land. In the
1990s, although the practice was rare, young children (usually virgin
girls) were still turned over to become devotees of a *trɔ* and to live at the
shrine.[23] It was an extremely controversial subject throughout Ghana,
as evidenced by the appearance of frequent articles in the national news-
papers (where it was referred to as the Trokosi Cult), and the debate usually focused on whether the practice should be banned. What follows,
however, is an exploration of the functions of *trɔxɔviwo* (specifically in
Anlo-Ewe contexts) and how this phenomenon related to moral knowing, somatic and sensory modes of attention, and ideas of personhood
and well-being.

One *mɔfiala* explained *trɔxɔviwo* as "a deterrent sort of thing. It de-
terred people. They didn't want you to go there, so people lived a *straight*
life. If you went there, it meant other people would be following you.
Even when you were dead, they had to replace you." This *mɔfiala* was
referring to the following system described in its "ideal" (but not necessarily actualized) format, which was believed to enforce moral codes.
When a person committed a crime such as murder or theft of a significant
amount of money (*ga foɖi mawo*: dirty monies), the victims of the crime
would travel to a specific sanctuary or holy place and appeal to the appropriate *trɔ* for recompense. The perpetrator would be identified
(through divination) and then summoned to the shrine. It was commonly
understood that the penalty for crimes of that severity involved a female
member of the perpetrator's family (or lineage) "serving the *trɔ*," which
meant working and living at the shrine. The girl (who had to be a virgin) would "ritually marry" the priest of the shrine, so the family was
required to provide a sizeable dowry and the funds for an elaborate ceremony. However, if during the subsequent years a man saw the young
woman at the shrine and wanted to marry her, he could "buy her out of
the shrine" (in a sense) by supplying a bride-payment to the priest and

the shrine. Under those conditions, a departure ceremony would be staged for the young woman, who would then leave the shrine as a wife of the man who dispensed the bride-payment.

Marriage to a man outside of the shrine was the only sanctioned mechanism by which the girl could retire or withdraw from the shrine. In the event that no man ever asked to marry her, or if a man did but he failed to provide the bride-payment, the young woman would spend the remainder of her life in the shrine. Under those circumstances, once she came of age, or began to menstruate, she would bear the children of the priest at the shrine. Regardless of whether she remained in the shrine or left, the family was obligated to bring another virgin girl at the time of her death. The debt to the *trɔ* never ceased; the sacrifice had to be made continuously. The procedure often broke down if a young woman left the shrine to marry an outsider since it was not at that point that the family was supposed to "replace her," but rather they were to bring another young woman to the shrine years later when the original "servant" died. That is, by the time she reached old age and died, families often had forgotten her role in the shrine years earlier and thereby failed to send her "replacement." With the breach would come a rash of deaths in the family, and a diviner (*bokɔ* or *amegashi*) was usually consulted. In cases of a "recurring decimal of death," divination would usually reveal that the family had failed to sustain the sacrifice for a major criminal offense. This could be a recent breach, or it could reach several generations back. The family would therefore be instructed to resume sending a virgin girl to serve in the shrine. As previously explained, the policy was that there was no way to expunge the culpability for a capital crime like murder or theft, and the family would "pay" for the violation for eternity. If they stopped "making payments," family members would begin to die. It is for this reason that the *trɔxɔviwo* system was perceived as a very strong deterrent to criminal behavior and why one *mɔfiala* explained, "They didn't want you to go there, so people lived a *straight* life. If you went there, it meant other people would be following you. Even when you were dead, they had to replace you." The sensory content here is more attenuated, but it is none the less important.

As indicated, "people lived a straight life" for fear of getting (themselves and their family) caught up in *trɔxɔviwo*. The use of the word *straight* by this *mɔfiala* was not insignificant, for it alluded to the bodily dimension of moral knowing that was integrally tied to the highly valued sensory experiences of balance and movement and to the topic of comportment and morality. It will be recalled that *agbagbaɖoɖo* (balancing) and *azɔlizɔzɔ* (walking, movement) involved posture and gesture, which in turn were read and experienced along a continuum ranging from "crooked" (immoral) to "straight" (ethically sound). The cultural logic underpinning *trɔxɔviwo,* I would suggest, contributed to somatic modes of attention centering on straightness, morality, and truth. In terms of symbolic value, the institution of *trɔxɔviwo* had a deep grip on its "adherents" as well as a strong hold on people who grew up knowing that *trɔxɔviwo* was right down the road (so to speak) if they diverged from the straight (moral) path.

Ewe scholar N.K. Dzobo's work on the phenomenology of knowledge and truth among Akan and Ewe peoples of Ghana directly addresses the issue of straightness and truth. He explains that the most commonly used word for truth in the Ewe language is *nyatefe.*

> Etymologically the word is made up of *nya* and *tefe. Tefe* which means "place" or "spot" is a common suffix in the Ewe language.... And so *nyatefe* literally means *the statement/word that is at its place, i.e. a correct statement.* A statement is said to be correct when it describes accurately the state of affairs as it is. Another way of saying that a statement is true in Ewe is to say *Nya la le etefe:* "The statement/word is at its place," and this is usually said about the report of an eyewitness.... the report of an eyewitness can be trusted to be true because such reports normally give accurate accounts of the state of things. For this reason when the elders at a court want to question the validity of a report of a person they ask him ... *"Eno nya la tefea?"* Literally it means: "Did you sit down (witness) at the place where the event occurred?" (Dzobo 1980:95)

While Dzobo's linguistic and ethnographic data was generally derived from the northern Ewe-speaking area of Ghana (in and around the town of Ho), this particular item also pertained to customs and dialect of many southern (Anlo) Ewe-speaking peoples. In fact, in the same way that English-speaking people might utter (in response to another's commentary), "That's the truth," Anlo-Ewe speakers might respond with the word *"Nyatefe,"* which literally meant "The word is at its place." Truth, in metaphorical terms, had a kind of kinesthetic-proprioceptive quality in that it concerned placement and position. The inquiry *"Nyatefea?"* meant "Is that the truth?" but in essence the question asked whether the word was at its place (meaning proprioceptively positioned).

Furthermore, Dzobo pointed out that the phrase *Enɔ tefea,* or *Enɔ nya tefea,* was the common and colloquial expression among Ewe (and I would include Anlo) speakers when eliciting an eyewitness account. He translated this phrase as "Did you sit down (witness) at the place where the event occurred?" While *nɔ* did not exactly mean "sit down," it certainly referred to a *somatic presence,* and such bodily attendance was perceived and experienced as an integral part of one's ability to "witness," or to know something and recount it.

However, in the phrase *Enɔ nya tefea* and in the cultural logic surrounding truth and moral knowing there was not exhibited much concern with *eye*-witnessing. Dzobo used the term "eye-witness," of course, to translate an Ewe concept into a Western idiom, for visually based knowing might represent what many Westerners would understand best. And certainly Anlo speakers might also ask, "Did you see it?" which would be expressed as *Ekpɔ etefea* and would mean "Did you see the place (where the event happened)?" Such phrasing was not as common, however, as putting it in terms of words, speech, or in relation to one's knowledge of a talking-oriented matter (hence, *nya* and *nyatefe*). In the Ewe language, the whole phrase rested in an idiom of *bodily presence* and *sound* (hearing of words), which was a kind of somatic and aural "witnessing" (or knowing) rather than an *eye*-witnessing. The more somatic and aural rendition, of course, exhibited a direct correspondence to a sensorium in which auditory and kinesthetic perception was culturally elaborated. To elicit the truth, then, the elders might ask, *Enɔ nya tefea* or *Enɔ nya la tefea:* Were you *present* (*somatically*) when the *word* (which was an aurally based signifier for *event*) was at its place?

Another common way of expressing truth was *nyadzɔdzɔe,* which derived from *nya* (word, matter, speech) plus *dzɔdzɔe* (straight, upright, fair).

> Truth as *nyadzɔdzɔe* therefore means literally "straight statement/word," and so falsehood is referred to as *nyagoglo* or *nyamadzɔmadzɔ,* meaning "crooked statement/word." ... The knowledge of normative truth-statements is acquired through long years of experience and is also passed down from generation to generation. In non-literate societies the memory is the repository of truth as *nyadzɔdzɔe.* (Dzobo 1980:97–98)

Truth as straightness reverberates back to the explanation given by one *mɔfiala* that "people live a straight life" in part because of their fear of *trɔxɔviwo.* Righteousness, fairness, and moral knowing were culturally construed as straight words, straight statements, straight behavior, and even (referring to the discussion of *azɔlime* in chapter 4) a "straight walk."[24] *Trɔxɔviwo,* therefore, symbolized the ultimate penalty for the morally compromised condition of "lack of straightness," or divergence from a moral and truthful life.

Additionally, *trɔxɔviwo* represented an intricate convergence of self, society, and cosmos, which will be taken up in greater detail later and which was alluded to over thirty years ago.

> Closely related to the ordeal but probably more exacting is the custom of *fiasiɖixexe*, a sort of penal servitude by which a criminal is bonded to serve for life in a cult house in atonement for his crime. In lieu of deciding guilt or innocence by simple ordeal, where the gravity of the offense warrants it, one of the "convent cults" (*trɔxɔviwo*, lit. cults which take in children) may be sworn. Where perjury is established by the god concerned, the person involved engages in what is known as *fiasiɖixexe* or ritual expiation. He enters the cult house and dedicates himself to the service of the cult as a cult servant. If he dies in service, it is the responsibility of his family to make replacement. If the original crime is murder, his life may be claimed immediately by the cult, but the family responsibility to the cult remains unchanged. The understanding is that the family has entered into a perpetual covenant with the cult to the effect that a member of the lineage shall always be in attendance. Negligence in this ritual obligation is visited continuously with death in the family until the contract is honored again. *Fiasiɖi* thus poses a grave threat to the survival of members of a family; it may even cause the extinction of a whole family. The severity of this form of atonement is enough to restrict, if not deter recourse to *fiasiɖi*. It is an effective means of the ritual proscription of crime. (Fiawoo 1959:116–117)

While D. K. Fiawoo's details varied slightly from how the practice was explained to me, relations among the individual, the family, and the spirits *(trɔ)* were basically the same. That is, "personal, social, and cosmic fields of Being" were considered to be inextricably woven together (Jackson and Karp 1990:23), so that the actions of one individual "may even cause the extinction of a whole family" (Fiawoo 1959a:117). The cultural logic and embodied experiences surrounding *trɔxɔviwo*, then, contained deep principles about being a person in Anlo ways, beginning with the fact that the *well-being* of "selves" (or biopsychic individuals) was integrally tied to the health and balanced nature of social and cosmic bodies.

While the example of *trɔxɔviwo* might be an extreme manifestation of this principle, it demonstrates how a person existed only in the sense of how they were related to other persons. If a person committed murder or theft (on the scale of *ga foɖi mawo*), penance did not end with any imagined boundaries around the individual, but plagued the lineage for eternity. In this way personhood was defined in part by intersubjectivity, by the connections among the body-self and sociofamilial conditions and spiritual concerns.

Moral knowing in Anlo contexts, therefore, was situated in the truth-fulness of these principles, and this *knowing* was not simply a cognitive experience but was carried around at the level of sensation and emotion. As we saw in the young man's reflections about Tɔkɔ Atɔlia, people did not experience the fear and effects of something like *trɔxɔviwo* only at an intellectual level, but somatically and affectively retained this under-standing and knowledge. This example of somatic modes of attending to straightness and truth (as an aspect of moral knowing among Anlo-speaking people) begins to demonstrate how bodies, selves, and others are ontologically and epistemologically interwoven.

TRƆNA ZUNA: SHAPE-SHIFTING AND MYTHIC LEGENDS OF TƆGBUI TSALI

Fiagbedzi the teacher referred to Tɔgbui Tsali as "Jesus Christ of the Anlo people." Startled by this characterization, I asked Fiagbedzi to clarify what he meant. He explained that Tsali was a powerful person capable of miraculous and magical deeds and then recounted a famous story I had heard from other *mɔfialawo*. When Tsali was young and still under the tutelage of his father, Akplomada, a day came when Tsali's sense of his own power got the better of him. Akplomada regularly removed his intestines to cleanse and dry his internal organs as a method of keeping them healthy. During one of these routines, Akplomada handed the in-testines to Tsali and asked his son to help dry them out. Thinking he could outwit his own father, Tsali changed himself into a hawk and flew up into the sky with the entrails.

Dismayed by the incorrigibility of his own son, Akplomada decided to teach the young boy a lesson. He knew the bird would have to land on a tree before eating the entrails, and he calculated that Tsali would choose the tallest perch around. Akplomada promptly shifted his own shape to that of a *vuti* (silk-cotton tree), and Tsali (in the form of a hawk) descended onto the highest branch of the disguised figure of Akplomada. Tsali placed the intestines across the bough, not knowing it was actually his father's arm. Akplomada immediately transformed back into his own shape, they both landed in a heap together on the ground, and Akplo-mada declared, "*Ðevie nenye, nyemefia nuwo kata wo vɔ o: nyemefia vuzuzu wo o*" (If you're a child, I have not yet finished teaching you all things; I have not taught you how to change [or shape-shift] into a silk-cotton tree) (Mamattah 1976:328). Tsali's father wanted him to understand that while Tsali had already acquired great prowess with the *am-lima* (magical powers) he had gained, Akplomada would always be superior to his son.

Tsali grew up to be what some call the greatest mystic in Anlo history. His use of herbs, magic, and spiritual healing were the basis of dozens of stories concerning his exploits. It is his shape-shifting abilities that interest me for what this indicates about somatic changeability and an associated philosophy or cultural logic concerning the tension between adaptability and essential form. Another famous story about Tsali focused on his role in the flight out of Ŋɔtsie—the Anlo migration story recounted earlier. After all the people had fled the walled city and footprints had been planted in the soil facing the gates (to suggest the city was under siege), Tsali supposedly turned himself into a small striped mouse so that he could crawl in and out of the footprints, leaving tiny traces of mouse tracks. This second level of deception created *etsɔ afɔ wo* (yesterday's old looking footprints) and was aimed at causing chaos for the Ŋɔtsie soldiers and guards.

Such legends abound of Tɔgbui Tsali's continual use of shape-shifting to accomplish magical feats. Referred to as *etsi amlima* (magic) or, more specifically, as *trɔ zu* (to turn, to change into, to become), he had the capability of altering his body or transforming his somatic construct as a means of accomplishing an end. In the process, however, he never lost his essence and always returned to the original form or shape of Tɔgbui Tsali. Shape-shifting, of course, can be found in the myths of many peoples. Nonetheless, I would like to suggest that tension between flexibility—even at the corporeal level—and maintaining some kind of ontological essence symbolizes an important dimension of Anlo sensibilities, especially in relation to personhood and identity. Two contrasting and complementary proverbs may further support this point.

One day early in our fieldwork when my husband was complaining about the taste and texture of the Anlo staple food called *akple* (a dough made from ground cassava and corn), Adzoa Kokui (who delighted in abusing and joking with my husband) instructed him with a proverb: *Ne neyi akpɔkplɔwo fe dume eye wotsyɔ akɔ la, wo ha natsyɔ akɔ.* My husband (whose facility with the Ewe language was negligible) asked me to translate what it was that she was haranguing him about that day. Even when Adzoa repeated the phrase I wasn't able to fully comprehend what she said, but I recognized the word for "toads" and heard something about "if you go to their town," but the rest of her sentence was lost on me. Sounding suspiciously like a proverb, I looked in Dzobo's (1975:21) book for something about toads and found the saying, "If you visit the village of the toads and you find them squatting, you must squat too." Confirming with Adzoa Kokui that this was indeed the advice she had delivered to my husband, I then found myself reflecting on the fact that while his complaint had to do with food (hence, the sensation of taste), the saying drew on the image of altering one's body posture as a symbol of adaptability.

If we take proverbs to be illustrative of certain facets of cultural logic and habitus, this one certainly not only indicates that you should be able and willing to squat or alter your form when required but also displays a strong value concerning flexibility. Adaptability when dealing with other cultural or ethnic groups was a character trait I heard many Anlo-speaking people discuss as something they prided themselves on exhibiting. Since this was not a comparative study, I do not have any information to suggest whether Anlo speakers as a group were actually more or less flexible than other Ghanaians, but they definitely perceived themselves to be an adaptable people (both as individuals and as a group). In another non-Anlo, but Ewe-speaking context, Ewe personhood has been described as involving "practices of camouflage" that take part in "a larger aesthetic of masking and changing identities, and in Ewe selfhood it is 'masks all the way down.' Such masks, costumes, camouflage, and make-up are not indications of artificiality but rather of diverse dimensions of agency" (Rosenthal 1998:81). Changeability, or a "chameleon capacity," was a characteristic perhaps more widespread than just among Anlo people, possibly marking Ewe personhood more generally.

But specifically in terms of what I am referring to as Anlo forms of being-in-the-world, adaptability was a theme I encountered in many contexts, and it relates back to the description in chapter 5 of the practice of flexing a baby's joints so as to make her into a flexible, supple person. However, while the proverb emphasized adjusting to the ways of others, doing things as others did them even at the level of attending to alternate somatic modes (squatting with those whose habit was to squat), the proverb did not suggest that one's essence, then, somehow became that of a toad.

In perusing Dzobo's extensive record of Ewe proverbs, I noted a second saying that seemed to indicate a notion of limitations on completely shifting one's shape: *Siande titi ŋui ɖe kɔ ŋu, mezua zi o* (If a black antelope rubs herself against an anthill, she does not become a deer as a result) (Dzobo 1975:149). After discussing this with several Anlo speakers, I learned that it was not a phrase commonly used in the southern area since antelope and deer were creatures of the woods and not typically found living in the terrain of the Anlo homeland. Several *mɔfialawo* suggested that it was probably recorded among Ewe speakers near Ho but that the logic was still definitely applicable in Anlo contexts. The proverb demonstrated that if you were a black antelope, no matter how much brown color you rubbed upon yourself (from the anthill), you would not become a deer as a result. You could change your color to be like the deer, or alter your shape when among toads, but that did not erase the essence of who you really were. As often as Tɔgbui Tsali transformed himself into another shape, he always returned to his original form of Tsali. The two proverbs illustrated a cultural logic that embraced tensions between essentials and changeability, between self-acceptance and willingness to adjust to others. And both proverbs drew on imagery of somatic or sensate aspects of being to symbolize the lessons on identity they aimed to teach.

"Not stable, being is highly changeable, always in transformation." These are words written to describe an Ewe philosophy of personhood (Rosenthal 1998:174) but could equally be applied to Tɔgbui Tsali and all that he represents specifically in Anlo-land. This theme of essence and changeability, then, is present in other Ewe contexts as well. In a wider sense there seems to be a tension between an "essence of Eweness" and the "constant absorption of things-supposedly-not-Ewe by Ewe people, their implicit refusal of essence and of identity" (Rosenthal 1998:29). Regarding Ewe personhood in general others have commented on a "radical indeterminacy of the person" (Rosenthal 1998:174), which further underscores the account I have given of specifically Anlo people in a large Ewe cultural complex.

Many Anlo-speaking people believe deeply that there is something essential about being a person in Anlo ways. Many Anlo speakers migrate to other regions of Ghana, West Africa, and throughout the world, and they pride themselves on adaptability such that if they *visit the village of the toads,* they attend to *squatting.* But even when living in another cultural setting, Anlo persons usually carry (in their being) the essence of Anlo: they carry the complex sensations of *seselelame,* they carry the embodied paradoxes of *ŋlɔ,* they carry the memory of criminals buried alive at Tɔkɔ Atɔlia, they carry embodiment of the story of escape from Nɔtsie, and they carry the knowledge of the shape-shifting abilities of their mythical ancestor Tɔgbui Tsali. While this is but a brief and cursory look at Anlo forms of being-in-the-world, it begins to illustrate linkages between cultural models and the social experience of the individual, for many Anlo speakers believe that maintenance of these forms (these memories, morals, logics, and ways of being-in-the-world) are essential to their personal and collective identity and well-being.

The next chapter will turn to an examination of Anlo rituals that reinforce the somatic mode and philosophical notion of balance. But it will begin with an exploration of the meaning and significance of the phrase *Meɖu dze o* (You've not eaten salt), which bemoans the tragic state of an Anlo person who does not know or cannot make use of such *thematized aspects of the world* as ŋlɔ, Tɔkɔ Atɔlia, *ga foɖi mawo,* Tɔgbui Tsali, and so forth. *Meɖu dze o* (You don't eat salt) represents another emic theme that many older *mɔfialawo* insisted I record as an Anlo way of referring to those who do not know their own language, history, and culture.

CHAPTER 7

Personhood and Ritual Reinforcement of Balance

REFLECTIONS ON PERSONHOOD IN ANLO-LAND

To understand Anlo notions of personhood, I find it useful to meditate on water and salt. Water surrounds their homeland. And as the twentieth century came to a close, the Atlantic ocean was engulfing Anlo-land. If the ground itself disappears, what becomes of Anlo-land? Or if a person does not actually reside on Anlo soil, what is Anlo-land to him or her? Is it a place or a state of mind? Is it a psychological orientation or a state of being? Pace Bourdieu, is Anlo-land so much a part of *being,* so "durably installed," that it actually *has body?*

Salt, too, has been central to experience in Anlo worlds. With a lagoon at the center of the Anlo homeland, harvested salt has played a significant role in their economic history for several hundred years (cf. Greene 1988 and Amenumey 1986). When the lagoon periodically dried up, people spent months gathering and bagging salt. And older Anlo speakers used a phrase concerning salt to capture something about tradition, well-being, and the self. They would say *Meɖu dze o!* which translates as "You don't eat salt!" Not being "salted" meant that a person did not know his own language, culture, and history, and older people frequently expressed concern over this problem among the young.[1] Salt and water index certain things about Anlo soil and about an Anlo ancestral homeland, and they play a role in the constitution of Anlo sensibilities and development of self.

In the last chapter we learned that the term *Anlo* itself has been shown to have a complex set of references, including "folded into oneself," with associated feelings of resentment and respect or persecution and influence. Straightness and truth, prohibitions on "dirty money," and the knowledge of their (criminal) ancestors buried alive at Tɔkɔ Atɔlia are some themes stemming from an Anlo code of morality. And this is where *Meɖu dze o* comes into play: not eating salt is a phrase signifying a failure to consume or take in the meaning of these various themes.

Self processes among Anlo speakers involve orientations toward a set of topics or themes. Even if a person represses, rejects, or denies any of these aspects of the world, they remain cultural motifs that require an individual's attention at some level. This is one of the reasons many *mɔfialawo* insisted that I learn about and record these various themes: they believed that without that set of core cultural motifs I could not begin to comprehend what was involved in being a person in Anlo ways. Regardless of how an Anlo speaker engages with these various themes, it requires some amount of effort and reflexivity. And in this process we can observe a kind of objectified thing (though not really a substance or entity, but a kind of capacity) we might refer to as Anlo personhood. So within Anlo worlds, many *mɔfialawo* articulated a notion of personhood that (to a great extent) parallels that of Csordas: the thematized aspects of the world that they insisted I learn help to constitute the objectified dimensions of the self that make up Anlo persons who have "a cultural identity or set of identities" (Csordas 1994c:340). But *Meɖu dze o* (you don't eat salt) warns of the failure to attend (through effort and reflexivity) to thematized aspects of Anlo worlds; when *you don't eat salt* (symbolically speaking), you fail to develop a sense of identity or a sensibility grounded in these themes.

In addition, the last chapter explored how the actions of an individual have powerful consequences for those around him to the extent that unethical behaviors can result in a spirit taking one's child *(trɔxɔviwo)*. This "sociocentrism" will be explored later through a discussion of how everyday life for most Anlo speakers involves dealing with definite "ties that bind" *(sasa)* or the inextricable relationships individuals hold with ancestors and kin. Almost in contrast to such binding relationships, however, a flexibility or adaptability (toward other ways of life) is also cultivated. Chapter 5 described the practice of flexing the baby's joints as one of the endeavors involved in creating an adaptable person, and the last chapter elaborated on this cultural theme by examining proverbs and philosophical notions of essence and changeability. So while Anlo children are raised to be able to adapt to other cultural worlds and to affiliate with members of different ethnic groups, a balance is desired between such affiliations and a grounding in a kind of Anlo sensibility or knowledge of one's own history, language, and culture. This theme of balance as a central dimension of sensibility will therefore be taken up more directly in this chapter, and the reinforcement of balance through ritual practices will be explored.

Balancing in general is a theme with many associations for Anlo speakers, including the notion that to be human means developing the ability to balance. In fact, one religious sect (Yeve) supposedly requires initiates to engage in a ritual of balancing *(agbagbaɖoɖo)* a tray containing thirty-six articles of life *(agbegbaɖoɖo)* as a way of reinforcing the symbolic importance of equilibrium.[2] In this context the ability to balance the tray represents a culmination of skills acquired through initiation. In addition, Avorgbedor has suggested (2000) that Anlo-Ewe people practice a selective integration of a wide range of sounds as they work to sustain (or restore) the balance of personal and social health. Here I will address some implications of these kinds of performative and cultural elaborations of balance. By highlighting this dimension of Anlo worlds, I do not mean to imply that balancing is absent in the daily or ritual practices of other cultural groups. As a fundamental bodily mode and bodily experience, balance undoubtedly serves as a basic-level category in many (if not all) societies and provides a platform on which is built a great deal of metaphorical reasoning (cf. Lakoff and Johnson 1999, especially 290–306). But what I am interested in here is the way that balance is ideologically reinforced through embodied practices and sensory engagement in this particular (Anlo) cultural context. We begin with an account of two community rituals aimed at reconciliation and health.

HOGBETSOTSO FESTIVAL'S NUGBIDODO

Some time within the past forty years Anlo-speaking people began staging an annual national ritual named Hogbetsotso.[3] The purpose of the rite was largely to celebrate and rehearse their migration from Notsie— a place also referred to as Hogbe, hence the festival's name, which meant "coming from Hogbe." Staged annually during the first part of November, Hogbetsotso consisted of more than a week of festivities, performances, and ceremonies, which included plays, dancing and drumming performed by school children, a reenactment of the flight from the walled city of Notsie (performed at midnight), workdays aimed at cleansing and purifying villages and towns, and a tour of historical places in and near Anloga. The festival culminated in a grand durbar attended by Anlo-speaking citizens from near and far, other Ghanaians, and an assortment of foreigners. In 1994, Ghana's president J. J. Rawlings and his entourage of government officials also attended the durbar. Truly the most magnificent ritual (if only in terms of size, scale, and the magnitude of preparations) that occurred in Anlo-land during my sojourn there, Hog-betsotso deserves a book unto itself.[4] However, since my concern here is mainly with sensory embodiment and its relation to socialization, personhood, and health, I will focus on one particularly relevant phase of Hogbetsotso, which is Nugbidodo, or the Peace-Making and Reconciliation Ceremony.

Nugbidodo was performed on the Thursday prior to Hogbetsotso's grand durbar, and it took place in the ceremonial center of Anloga. Its stated purpose was "to bring peace and harmony among all the people of Anlo before the festival" (Kodzo-Vordoagu 1994:15). The Paramount Chief *(Awoamefia)* of Anlo-Ewe people dressed as the Nyigbla Priest of State (Nyigbla will be described in greater detail in chapter 8), entered the ground in a ritualized procession and rested out of the sun beneath the thatched roof of a round gazebo. Libations were poured and the ancestors and gods were beseeched to bestow blessings, health, and peace on all the people of Anlo both at home and abroad. A ritualized airing of grievances was then performed and complaints were "packed into" or "placed under" herbs. The herbs were subsequently mixed and cleansed with water and then distributed into fifteen ceramic pots, which were taken back to each of the fifteen clan houses to be sprinkled and splashed as a part of the operation of settling grievances and restoring national well-being and peace. Finally, three rams were sacrificed and slaughtered (one for each division, or wing, of the Anlo state) and prepared along with other foods as a reconciling communal feast.

As in any ritual, the sensorial aspects of Nugbidodo were abundant. For instance, the healing and reconciling of grievances involved speaking *(nufofo)* aloud and listening *(nusese)* to various complaints along with the sounds of ritualized "crying out" performed by a special group of women. Gustation *(nuɖɔɖɔ)* could be explored in relation to the communal feast. And we could also inquire about the sensations of splashed water used to "wash away the sin that is now a part of his [a person's] body" (Fiawoo 1959a:223). However, one aspect of Nugbidodo that exhibited an array of sensorial issues with implications for personhood as well as for states of well-being and health was actually *the form of dress* required for participation in this event. To gain entry to the ceremonial grounds, everyone was required to remove his or her shoes; the regulated women's attire consisted of one cloth around the waist and a second cloth wrapped across the breasts and through the armpits, exposing bare shoulders; men were required to wear cloth in a togalike wrap, with a section of the twelve-foot piece draped across the left shoulder. Western styles of dress in the form of trousers, shirts, shoes, and so forth, were not allowed.[5] Treating clothing as attached to or something of *an extension of the body*, here I will briefly explore what was symbolized by and experienced in the rituals around dress in relation to Nugbidodo.

Western-style clothing was symbolic of a complicated set of historical influences and changes that Anlo-speaking people continually negotiated from precolonial to present-day times (cf. Perani and Wolff 1995). As a brief example of this, other than the Paramount Chief, "no one else (before the turn of the century) was privileged at Anloga ... to wear European clothes" (Fiawoo 1959a:223). The simple explanation for this regulation was that the Paramount Chief (in his capacity as Nyigbla's priest) regularly donned a "long loose gown" resembling European attire. Citizens dressing like Europeans were then considered "impostors impersonating Nyigbla or his chief priest" (Fiawoo 1959a:223). But the implications of this regulation are hinted at in a footnote where Fiawoo explains, "This taboo which practically sealed off Anloga and villages to the west from the German missionaries might have been responsible for the late evangelization of Anloga and neighboring villages. When Keta celebrated a Church centenary in 1953, Anloga had not yet attained her Golden Jubilee anniversary" (Fiawoo 1959a:223). This is to say that Anloga and Anlo-speaking communities to the west (which included Srɔgboe) resisted a variety of European influences, including body ornamentation and style of dress. While Nyigbla's role and the "religious" reasons for this custom were undoubtedly important, political considerations also should not be overlooked since a ban on European clothing was integrally related to other forms of resistance utilized at that time against the missionizing and colonizing efforts of Europeans. By the late twentieth century, the ban had long since been lifted, and Western-style clothing as well as "hybrid styles" were common throughout Anlo villages as well as towns. In Hogbetsotso's Reconciliation Ceremony, however, the prohibition was revived.

But what did this symbolize about sensory and somatic modes, about self processes and Anlo personhood? Jean and John Comaroff demonstrate (1997:218–273) the significance of clothing for the colonial project in southern Africa by arguing that the process of re-dressing Africans in European fashions was tantamount to "insinuating in them a newly embodied sense of self-worth, taste, and personhood." In those same terms of self-worth and self processes as well as in relation to tastes and desires, I am suggesting that quite distinct sensorial and embodied experiences come from wearing Anlo traditional cloth compared to Western-style dress, especially if we think of the body as "the existential ground of culture and the self" (Csordas 1994a). This is particularly true in the practice of resistance as integrally bound up with the psychosocial well-being of both individuals and the body politic. That is, when one style of dress reaffirms a sense of tradition, history, and identity, it can empower people in a very embodied way, while another form can serve to oppress and defeat. More specifically, thinking in this way allows us to explore the effects of the tactile, kinesthetic, vestibular, proprioceptive, and visual experiences of clothing or dress in terms of identity and of health.[6]

When discussing differences between Anlo styles of dress and those imported from the West, in the haptic realm (and especially for men) people focused less on texture than on "draping" as distinct from "fitting." The fitted and snug nature of sleeves, cuffs, collars, trousers, and waistbands (referred to by Jean Comaroff as "the straightjacket of Protestant personhood" [1996:26]) were contrasted with the flowing sense of a togalike garment characterizing the traditional or precolonial mode of dress. Continually hoisting up the cloth and tossing the end over one's left shoulder was reported to feel almost "majestic," and the practice was even likened to a male lion shaking his mane. Posture, comportment, and gait were also reportedly different depending on one's style of dress, which harkens back to the discussion in chapter 4 that highlighted the profound significance (or "performative elaboration") of movement and walk. I observed that one particular neighbor seemed taller and even proud when he donned African cloth. My husband and I would often joke with him about this perception, but during a more serious moment our neighbor confessed that he felt dignified, more balanced, and upright when dressed in cloth that represented his own cultural heritage. He referred to *zɔ kadzakadza* (which meant "walking or moving like a lion") to describe the sort of *seselelame,* or feeling in the body, that came with dressing in African cloth.

This specific example requires teasing out the difference between influences of the context verses the cloth since this particular man usually wore pants, shirt, and shoes when he fished and farmed, but he wore an African robe or wrap when attending a ceremonial event. Perhaps laboring in the heat and sun was as much the cause of an "oppressive" or "defeated" feeling as were sleeves and collar, while celebration and ceremony contributed to the sense of "uplift" he described. This very point, however, underscores the symbolic nature of this phenomenon. I am not suggesting literal links between a shirt or blouse and a gross state of oppression (although an argument could be made about the "straightjacket of Protestant personhood"), but rather I am pointing toward a subtle and complex web of symbolism and sensation that illustrates my focus on embodiment and somatic modes of attention. In Terence Turner's discussion of "the social skin" (1980), he suggests that clothing imprints cultural categories and a "social project" onto the body while simultaneously serving as an expression of what is inside, or a statement from within. It is that two-pronged force that makes clothing such an effective medium for remaking the self. In the context of colonial evangelism in southern Africa, the Comaroffs have argued (1997:220) that clothing "made the 'native' body a terrain on which the battle for selfhood was to be fought, on which personal identity was to be re-formed, re-placed, re-inhabited." The verity of this statement would not be lost on the people of Anlo-land, who are known for their history of resistance to the political authority of the Danes and British at a time when colonization was in full force in other areas of the Gold Coast (cf. Amenumey 1968). So while it would be very interesting to examine the role of clothing in Anlo relations with missionaries and the changes in fashion that can be linked to colonial evangelism, in order to return to the subject of Nugbidodo as a ceremony of reconciliation and restoration of peace, I will leave this historical issue aside here.

As I said earlier, during the rite of Nugbidodo, all participants experienced this event while wrapped in cloth in the traditional or local style. (Some of the fabric itself was undoubtedly manufactured in Europe or abroad, but the dress code at least was reminiscent of a precolonial heritage.) I have raised the question of what was at stake in terms of the sensorium, embodiment, and personhood, and I have suggested a continuity with certain elements of resistance to Westernization, colonization, and missionization that existed in parts of Anlo-land during the nineteenth century. Nugbidodo as an act of reconciliation was ultimately about healing the body politic; insisting upon a return to wearing Anlo garb contributed to a reconciliation at the level of the body, a balancing out of the effect of outside influences in everyday life. This took the reconciliation beyond the cognitive domain to a redress that could activate one's senses and thereby create an embodied experience. What was at stake, it might be argued, was the potential for improved states of psychological well-being (through a stronger sense of identity and history) in part via the sensorial experience of the very clothing that people wore.

The following is from a conversation I held with an English-speaking weaver whom I call Mr. Dunyo, this section focusing on a particular pattern of strip-woven cloth called *Takpekpe Anloga*. We do not specifically relate our discussion to Nugbidodo, but in this excerpt he comments on what it feels like to wear African cloth.

> *KLG:* So the name of this pattern means "Meeting of the Anlos"?
>
> *Mr. Dunyo:* Yes, *Takpekpe Anloga:* Meeting at Anloga or Meeting of the Anlo people. It is an old pattern and I try to get the good threads, silk and cotton, when I make this one.
>
> *KLG:* Does the thread make a difference?
>
> *Mr. Dunyo:* The cloth must flow well to wear it, it cannot be stiff. This depends on the thread, and people will say it depends on my skill. They will complain to me and abuse me if the cloth is hard or stiff, but many don't want to spend the money for the good thread.
>
> *KLG:* What happens if the cloth is stiff?
>
> *Mr. Dunyo:* Oh, no one wants it to rub and scratch their skin. They want it to feel smooth and soft. That's fine. Besides, good cloth moves with the person, it catches the sunlight, and these golden threads will shine [he points to specific areas of the pattern].
>
> *KLG:* I noticed that with this particular cloth—*Takpekpe Anloga*. I could see how at first you see the blue, and then when the person turns you can see what's almost an undercurrent—the black or darker color. Then the yellow almost sparkles. All these currents. I wondered if that's where the name came from—you know, the "behind the scenes" stuff that goes on at meetings.
>
> *Mr. Dunyo:* [Laughs while saying] I don't know. You may be right. It's just named that. I thought it was because this is the one the big men like to wear to the meeting. But maybe you're right.
>
> *KLG:* Do they only wear it to—what? Council meetings? Or to other events as well?
>
> *Mr. Dunyo:* Oh, mostly for funerals, the durbar, Hogbetsotso. It's for *atsyɔɖoɖo*—for bedecking oneself, dressing beautifully. They put it on and feel proud, they feel Anlo.
>
> *KLG:* They feel Anlo?

Mr. Dunyo: Yes, they wear the traditional cloth and it makes people feel proud of our past. They remember their forefathers, their ancestors, where they came from. It's not really easy to wear this cloth. [He stands up and begins wrapping the cloth we are looking at—*Takpekpe Anloga*—around himself.] You see, here ... [he is throwing or maneuvering it over his shoulder] ... you have to stand upright, you have to assume a dignity to keep it from falling off [he chuckles]. It kind of brings everything home, maybe because we wear it to funerals so much, and to solemn occasions, but this cloth makes you feel that you belong to Anlo. It's very different than wearing a suit and tie.

KLG: In what way is it different?

Mr. Dunyo: It's softer and stronger at the same time. A suit is tight and makes you feel stiff. But this cloth, well, it flows around me, it moves along with me as I walk. But then at the same time I have to keep checking on it, pay attention to it, adjust it on my shoulder, and that keeps reminding me of, well, it makes me know I'm not a Frenchman, at all, or a Englishman. It's African. This cloth is definitely African. When I wear *Takpekpe Anloga* I feel that.

Here Mr. Dunyo makes clear associations between what one wears and a certain sense of identity. While not clearly spelling out what it feels like to "be African" or to "be Anlo," and while not making any direct reference to principles of balance, still it is clear that he has a sensibility about his identity being connected to the way the cloth—or this particular kind of clothing—feels on his body.

In his argument about clothing and bodily adornment as a symbolic medium ("the social skin"), Turner argues that in the case of the Amazonian Kayapo, the bodies of individuals serve as a microcosm of the body politic (1980:121). I am suggesting something similar for this situation among Anlo speakers, that one of the effects of Nugbidodo involves a balancing out of the inward- and outward-looking paradox that is constitutive of what I have called an Anlo sensibility. That is, I have suggested that one of the things that characterizes an Anlo sensibility is an attention to being flexible enough to live with other people, to adopt their ways, while at the same time maintaining an orientation to one's core being or those "thematized aspects of the world" that constitute Anlo identity. Turner suggests (1980:139) that the surface of the body serves as a very complex boundary "which simultaneously separates domains lying on either side of it and conflates different levels of social, individual and intra-psychic meaning." Clothing is then quite intentionally deployed in Nugbidodo to engender a particular setting and an embodied commemorative mode. While everyday life involves the incorporation of modes of dress from outside, the ceremony aimed an reconciliation and restoration of peace, harmony, and health, attempts (in part) to rebalance this account. In an interesting parallel to Anlo attentiveness to balance, Turner suggests that for the Kayapo, balance is "the most fundamental structural principle of Kayapo society" and that "balance between opposing yet complementary forces ... is systematically articulated and, as it were, played out on the bodies of every member of Kayapo society through the medium of bodily adornment" (Turner 1980:139). While the performative elaboration of balance in the context of Nugbidodo is admittedly subtle, in the next section we will examine a much more explicit demonstration of balance. The description of ritual that follows will also provide an additional platform from which to explore issues of sensory engagement and commemoration.

TƆGBUI APIM CEREMONY IN SRƆGBOE

While Hogbetsotso's Nugbidodo was a socioreligious event performed for the entire Anlo "nation," the following description of a more localized or community-based ritual took place in the village where I lived. The event was referred to as Srɔgboe's Tɔgbui Apim festival, in honor of "Grandfather Apim," who safeguarded the ancestors of Srɔgboe citizens in a battle or war hundreds of years in the past. The ritual involved propitiating the "local *Du-Legba* whose chief sphere of activity [was] to protect the village or town from misfortune, evil, sickness, and such-like and to act as a messenger between man and some of the gods" (Cudjoe 1971:188). Not unlike Hogbetsotso's Nugbidodo rite, but on a much smaller scale, the ultimate purpose of the Tɔgbui Apim festival was to ensure the health and well-being of the body politic. In this analysis we will examine how commemoration evoked in the Tɔgbui Apim rite is connected to personhood and self processes in Anlo contexts.

During a formal interview with one of the chiefs of Srɔgboe, he explained that it was not really known whether Tɔgbui Apim was an actual person or a spirit, but they currently referred to him as a *trɔ* (the word *trɔ* means deity or god and will be covered in chapter 8). The name of the village, Srɔgboe, meant "place of the *srɔ* trees," and Tɔgbui Apim's shrine was located near the lagoon side of Srɔgboe's borders, underneath the only *srɔ* tree still in existence in that area. Closely related to Srɔgboe's *trɔ* (named Tɔgbui Apim) was the *Du-Legba,* or "empowerment object-cum-threshold guard," who protected the entire village. *Legbawo* in general will be discussed at length in chapter 8, but this ritual specifically concerned the *du* (town) *legba* at the threshold of Srɔgboe. In her work on *Du-Legba* cults, Cudjoe (1971:199) explains, "A *Du-Legba* has neither a special festival nor dances. A *legba* which is associated with a god takes part in the festival or dance held for that particular god." In this week-long festival staged to honor and appease Tɔgbui Apim, Srɔgboe citizens also paid homage to the *Du-Legba* situated at the entrance to their town. The clay *Du-Legba* figure for the Srɔgboe community sat protected within three stone walls and under a corrugated iron roof along a pathway leading between Srɔgboe and the neighboring village called Whuti. Cudjoe continues (1971:188, 191): "a *Du-Legba* must be at the entrance of the town to prevent sickness from entering," and it is believed that the *Du-Legba* is "able to repel illness." Unlike other Anlo assemblies (such as the Paramount Chieftaincy and divisional wings of government or even the Yeve religious sect), the *Du-Legba* association was not highly organized (Cudjoe 1971:196–197). However, the purpose was clear in that it was "a cult devoted to the welfare of the whole community. By the very fact that one is a member of the village one has a vested interest in the local *Du-Legba* whose chief sphere of activity is to protect the village or town from misfortune, evil, sickness, and such-like and to act as a messenger between man and some of the gods. It serves as the 'root' of the town" (Cudjoe 1971:188). The Tɔgbui Apim festival contained these various characteristics of what Cudjoe called *Du-Legba* cults, so while it was not officially labeled a *Du-Legba* festival or rite, it seems fair to assume that it could be classified as such.

Public activities of the 1994 Tɔgbui Apim festival lasted approximately one week and featured four major ceremonies. The first event on Monday focused on feeding or offering sacrifices to Srɔgboe's *Du-Legba*. The second event lasted from morning to evening on Friday and involved a procession from the beach to Tɔgbui Apim's shrine. The subsequent day was dominated by very heated dancing and drumming characterized by frequent spirit possessions of many of the human participants. And the finale on Sunday was distinguished by subdued, cool dancing performed mainly by members of voluntary associations. Fund raising for community development projects occurred at a table placed as a kind of backdrop to the drumming and dancing, which was manned by several elders and village chiefs.

One of the striking things about this ritual was "the sequencing of the sensations" (Howes and Classen 1991:279), or the progression of sensory emphases (and repressions) in the various stages of the Tɔgbui Apim event. While a variety of senses were implicated and experienced in every situation, each of the four events contained a kind of dominant modality. The first ceremony focused on senses of the mouth (taste and speech) in that goat meat and *ɖekplε* (a corn meal mixed with palm oil) were given to the *Du-Legba* and fed to a few dozen participants while incantatory prayers were pronounced and libations were poured (see Cudjoe 1971:198 concerning the appetites of a *Du-Legba*). Acoustical stimulation was absent in this first event, and since drumming was prevalent at ritual gatherings in Anlo-land, the lack of music was conspicuous in this section of the ceremony.

The second day began with hundreds of people gathered in the morning on the beach. We surrounded a temporary circular dwelling constructed from green palm fronds and covered in white plasticized rice sacks sewn together. Amid drumming, singing, and dancing, from the dwelling emerged a man clothed in a towel from the waist down, balancing a large wooden bowl on top of his head. The bowl contained various calabashes and ceramic pots covered in white muslin cloth, and the entire "package" was fastened together with meshed fabric resembling a net. The carrier's face was covered with a white or ash-colored powder. Muskets were fired sporadically and filled the air with explosions of smoke and sulphurlike odors; people drummed, chanted, and danced as the carrier staggered in the sand across the beach. For the next five or six hours crowds followed the carrier (who was guarded by approximately ten people holding sticks), as he wove in and around the alleyways and roads of Srɔgboe and neighboring villages. All this time he balanced the wooden bowl filled with containers on top of his head. The carrier appeared to be possessed by a spirit and reportedly Tɔgbui Apim directed his movements.[7]

The procession eventually led to the Tɔgbui Apim shrine, which was surrounded by benches on which sat several drummers and other musicians performing with sekere rattles and bells, and they were accompanied by a small number of people engaged in singing and dancing. The majority of the crowd, however, were merely spectators. The carrier entered from an alleyway into the shrine's clearing, and continued holding the bowl on his head, staggering and swaying about while still surrounded by a group holding sticks. After circulating about the clearing and passing by the lagoon, the carrier eventually returned and entered the shrine. I was not witness to the proceedings within the shrine, and the chief who I later interviewed suggested I not ask about it since he was not at liberty to divulge precisely what occurred (see note 7 for this chapter). Respecting the limits of my access to various aspects of this ritual, what was readily apparent about this phase of the ceremony was the intense focus on the vestibular and kinesthetic senses while other senses were somewhat downplayed. That is, while a certain amount of visual stimulation (from costumes, colors, and general processioneering) along with sounds (from music, muskets, and occasional shouting) were certainly present, a great amount of attention was focused on the balancing of offerings for Tɔgbui Apim. In contrast, balancing was not the focus of the final two days. However, before engaging in a deeper analysis of the "sequencing of sensations" and the ordering of senses as an expression of cultural values (Classen 1993b:5), I will briefly describe the events of the final two days.

During the following day—dominated by a kind of heated and vigorous dancing—people gathered in the village center or marketplace, where around two trees were positioned two circles of benches within which drummers, other musicians, and acrobatic dancers began to perform. If the costumes from the previous day were visually stimulating, those worn by the dancers inside the circle were even more impressive. The performers donned a variety of flowing skirts made from purple and green straw, from multicolored scarves, or from bright cloth often in red, blue, and white stripes. Most faces were covered in a mask of blue or white powder or clay. Even more spectacular than the costumes, however, were the actions: dancers wielded machetes and knives, alternately slicing at leaves or the bark on the tree, and then turned the blade to their own skin. That is, performers demonstrated the razor-sharp status of blades by searing through leaves or wood, but when applied to their own bodies, the knife failed to cut their skin. The absence of any punctures in the skin (and the absence of blood) signified that the individual had adhered to the taboos of his religious sect (members who were reportedly mainly from Kɔkuʋu, but some individuals evidently belonged to other groups such as Blekete and Yeve). Those who bled, therefore, were exposed as unfaithful.

In addition to these knife and machete displays, other "heated" activities included periods of exceedingly rapid rhythms produced by the drummers, resulting in very hectic, almost frenetic styles of dancing; individuals produced bottles of *akpeteshi* (locally brewed gin) or other alcoholic beverages from their pockets and poured liquid down the throats of other dancers; cigarettes were lit and puffed sometimes four at a time or placed in peoples' ears, and some dancers blew smoke along other dancers' skin; canisters of powder were also used to produce clouds of smoke, and performers applied variously colored powders to their own and others' bodies, faces, and hair; finally, performers' bodies were frequently taken over in states of possession trance. (For another ethnographic account of hot *vodus* who dance with knives, see Rosenthal 1998:65).

This third day of dancing was rigorous, or "heated," when compared to the performance of the fourth day, which was nearly opposite and characterized by a subdued, or low-key style. That is, the final day of the festival (Sunday) involved cool and calm dancing in which members of the circle tossed a towel at a spectator on the outside, who was then obliged to join the group and perform a duet with the individual who threw the towel. The "guest" returned to the outside of the circle after the duet was complete, and the larger group (which constituted a voluntary association)[8] proceeded with a methodically slow and organized rotational dance around the tree. During both days a panel of chiefs, elders, and district assemblymen oversaw the collection of donations for development programs to improve the health and welfare of the Srɔgboe community.

When contemplating the four outstanding parts of this Tɔgbui Apim rite, the sequence in which the senses were engaged began with taste and speech, then emphasized balance, and finally highlighted dancing, movement, or kinesthesia along with aurality as the dominant senses (though with different degrees of intensity) in the final two parts. Sight and the gaze were clearly implicated in each phase too, especially in relation to this textualized version (based largely on my own observations) of the event. But I would like to try here to move beyond an analysis of only the visible and attend to the other senses as well. Toward that end, what did this sequencing indicate? Was the heightening of some senses as important as the suppression of others? How does the sequencing of sensations evoked by the ritual help us to understand how commemoration comes into play in Anlo worlds? The ritual specialist at the center of the entire event (the carrier of the offering for Tɔgbui Apim, or the one who embodied Tɔgbui Apim) was distinguished by his reliance on *balancing* as one of the most dominant modes of his engagement and display. It was apparent that balancing was a much stronger, deeper, more pervasive theme than is superficially apparent, for three reasons: (1) the "heated" and the "cool" dancing of the last two days constitutes a *balancing* of temperature and intensity, (2) an incident occurred during the ritual that illustrates issues of "homogeneity" and "diversity" and a "*balance* of persons" in the local community, and (3) the dominant senses at the beginning of the ritual oppose and *balance* out the dominant senses displayed at the end of the event.[9]

Balancing was clearly an essential component in the central activity of the ritual since an offering to Tɔgbui Apim was *balanced* on top of the carrier's head for the greater part of a day, and crowds of people focused their attention precisely on this *balancing* act. However, the final two days of the ritual also exhibited a kind of balance. The dominant senses displayed during those two days were drumming and dancing. However, with the first day's "heated" dancing and the second day of "cooling off," there was a balanced experience and display of kinesthetic sensations (in the dancing) and aural perceptions (from the music and sound), so that between the two days both poles of intensity were represented.[10] This is in keeping with Robert Faris Thompson's claim (1966:97) that balance is "one of the most important canons of West African dance," and he links this to a concept that he refers to as "the aesthetic of the cool." While we see this expressed in dancing, music, and other art forms of West Africa, this is a principle applicable not simply to processes of art. By this phrase Thompson means "a philosophy of the cool, an ancient, indigenous ideal: patience and collectedness of mind" (1966:86). He argues for the interrelatedness of epistemology and dance in West African contexts and suggests that distilled in their choreographies are complex ways of thinking "comparable to Cartesian philosophy in point of influence and importance" (Thompson 1966:86). So the stoic faces of performers in a heated dance and the equilibrium maintained by a twirling dancer reinforce this emphasis on a cool, even-tempered stance. Thompson cites (1966:86) Yoruba myths that draw on the "mediating principle in cool water" and the "mediating principle in a cool, healing leaf" to suggest that they all "posit water, certain leaves, and other items as symbols of the coolness that transcends disorder and without which community is impossible." In this orientation we find the symbology of water and coolness as a route to personal and social equilibrium, which is important not only to Yoruba peoples but is also a central aspect of the definition of health and well-being in many parts of Anlo-land.

The two different types of dancing that occurred in the Tɔgbui Apim ritual reflect the heterogeneous nature of Srɔgboe or a kind of "balance of persons" within Anlo-speaking communities (which is not unlike the hot and cool personalities of the spirits of a pantheon discussed by Rosenthal 1998:115). Prior to this event I was under the impression that Srɔgboe was rather homogeneous. While certain customs practiced within Srɔgboe often varied slightly from those of neighboring villages (like Atɔkɔ) or towns (such as Keta), Srɔgboe was a village of merely one thousand to fifteen hundred people and seemed (to me) to be comprised of a fairly unified group. During the festival, however, a greater assortment of persons within the Srɔgboe community participated than I had previously realized were there. On Saturday afternoon I was observing the very "heated" dancing of the various religious sects. An elderly woman who had gone out of her way on several occasions (over the course of the previous months) to do favors for my husband and me took me by the arm and pulled me into the circle where the Kɔkuʋu dancers were stabbing their bodies with knives. Fearful of the slashing action of the blades, I nevertheless felt indebted to this woman and therefore followed her lead in dancing with several older women and putting on a short display for the leaders of this group. My participation continued for about twenty minutes, until a woman from my compound (who had been enlisted to look after my husband and me—by the family that had adopted us, so to speak) came and yanked me out of the circle and escorted me away. She scolded incessantly and declared how bad it was for me to be dancing with these people who cut themselves with knives. The following day she dressed in a fairly formal outfit (consisting of a blouse sewn from a bright green wax-print fabric with a matching wrap of cloth around her waist) and actively performed in the "cooler and calmer" dancing of the voluntary associations. On several occasions she tossed a towel at me (or my husband), which signaled us to join the group and engage in one short round of the dance.

These two contrasting styles of dance, and what they reveal about sensory symbolism and the "cultural elaboration of sensory engagement" (Csordas 1993:139), can be approached phenomenologically, and I will begin this analysis by reviewing some of the issues raised by Csordas in developing his analytic framework of embodiment. While the following comments might prove difficult to follow outside their original context, it is important to note Csordas's distinction between a focus on the body as an object and an examination of the *appropriation of bodiliness* as significant in the process of becoming a person and internalizing aspects of the social group to which one belongs. He suggests that the "argument that the appropriation of bodiliness is the fundamental matrix or material infrastructure of the *production of personhood and social identity* elaborates the notion of the body as existential ground of culture and self" (Csordas 1994a:13, emphasis added). He goes on to make a "distinction between the body as a set of individual psychological or sensuous responses and as a *material process of social interaction*" (Csordas 1994a:13, emphasis added). It is the latter approach—treating the body as a material process of social interaction—that characterizes an analysis that makes use of the methodological tool of embodiment. In the social interactions described previously, there is an "appropriation of bodiliness" by various factions within the small community of people living in Srɔgboe, and these practices serve (in part) as the "material infrastructure of the production of personhood and social identity." Bodily practices such as applying a knife to the skin or dancing in a "heated" fashion resulting in possession or movement into a trance state are a material infrastructure of some kinds of Anlo persons. On the other hand, "cool" dancing, which makes use of "passing a towel" and a European-influenced style of dress, is a "bodiliness" that is the fundamental matrix of yet another kind of Anlo identity.

While it was made clear to me which kind of person I was expected "to become" (in the process of my enculturation into a way of life), that aspect of the account is not of central concern for this discussion. It certainly illustrates the importance of alliance with a particular set of bodily practices in the "production of personhood and social identity," but what is of importance in this event is the larger purpose of the ritual: to ensure the health, welfare, and protection of the Srɔgboe community. In the bodily practices displayed in the various dances of the Tɔgbui Apim festival there was an emphasis on balancing various opposing forces. Rather than relying solely on discourse about this festival, approaching it through the standpoint of embodiment allows us to see how *agbagbaɖoɖo* (balancing) played a central role in this event. The ritual seems to suggest that the health and well-being of the community involves an integration and equilibrium among various kinds of Anlo persons and identities.

While it is supposed to be performed biennially, the 1994 Tɔgbui Apim rite was reportedly the first time in approximately six years that it had occurred. The expense involved in staging it was cited as a major reason for delays, and more than five or six years had passed since the last festival. One of the chiefs explained that he was hospitalized with a serious illness when someone came to visit him. The person told the chief, "You will get well, but you must go back and organize the people to stage the Tɔgbui Apim festival." The chief reported to me that the spirit from the calabash (which was one of the central objects utilized during the ritual) had entered that person and sent him to the hospital to advise the chief. When this chief did indeed recover from an illness he thought might kill him, he hastily began mobilizing the community to propitiate Tɔgbui Apim. In many ways this illustrates Csordas's (1993:146) suggestion that bodies are often "not a function of the individual 'self' as in Euro-America, but of the community," for it was the breakdown of one individual's body that served as a catalyst for the renewal of community sensibilities around practices they had to perform to ensure the well-being and health of the local body politic.

Phenomenological philosopher Edward Casey (1987:223) lays out four formal features that he attributes to the ways in which ritual informs commemoration: reflection, allusion to an event or person, bodily action, and collective participation. The Tɔgbui Apim rite is an interesting case study in that it provides an occasion for that act of reflection, the contemplation or meditation being about a commemorated person (their ancestor named Apim) and event (his mythic protection and defense of their land and community). Bodily action and subjectivity are central to this process: the body does not simply represent the commemoration, but it may "become a *commemorabilium*" and it always serves as "an *expressive sign* of that which is commemorated" (Casey 1987:245). This is not simply in the case of the ritual specialist balancing the calabash but also for all participants in the rite, for this occurs through identification. In chapter 6 we saw how some Anlo people roll up or fold into themselves when commemorating Tɔgbui Whenya's exhaustion from escaping slavery; in this chapter we discussed how Anlo people of Srɔgboe assembled at the Srɔ Tree in honor of Tɔgbui Apim. Focusing momentarily on Tɔgbui Whenya and Tɔgbui Apim, we can consider that "to identify with someone . . . is to merge not only with that person's mental or psychic being. It is also to assimilate his or her corporeality in its full emotional resonance" (Casey 1987:246). This mythic encounter with their ancestor—this occasion for an act of reflection on the role of Tɔgbui Apim in their lives—does more than simply conjure an image: it allows for an incorporation of the past into the identity and sensibilities of contemporary Srɔgboe people. In the context of a commemorative event such as the Tɔgbui Apim ritual, there is an "incorporative action of identification" and through this process, Casey suggests (1987:240), "I interiorize the other, set him or her up *within me* as an abiding presence." Cautioning against reducing this to a case of narcissistic assimilation of self and other, he indicates that "[a]s I take the other in, I am essentially altered, aggrandized. I gain increased psychic structure by means of greater internal differentiation" (Casey 1987:240). So the commemorative taking in of Tɔgbui Whenya or Tɔgbui Apim involves an identification that is critical in the self processes associated with Anlo personhood. One of the striking things about ritual commemoration of both Whenya and Apim is an attentiveness to balance in the commemorative actions. When Whenya is invoked and some people roll up into the fetal position, ŋlɔ is counterbalanced by unrolling or coming out of the inwardness (an interoceptively focused bodily position) and associative meanings are spun about the power or invigoration created through the back and forth of this bodily move. Commemorative attention to Apim explicitly forces the issue of balance in that his appearance and his embodiment come in an iconic form: the calabash carried, balanced, and spotlighted so that Srɔgboe people could "interiorize" him in this form, "set him up *within* as an abiding presence."

In summarizing, let me return to the communal dimension of the Tɔgbui Apim event as well as Nugbidodo so as not to falsely reify a kind of individualist psychology that I would argue has little explanatory power in Anlo worlds. In Casey's discussion of the ways that ritual contributes to commemoration, he also describes (1987:237) the putting aside of private wishes and private desires, the "joining together" that ritual engenders and the creation of *"communitas."* Casey cites Victor Turner's account of the Ndembu chief-to-be who was told, "We have granted you chieftainship. You must eat with your fellow men, you must live well with them.... Do not be selfish, do not keep the chieftainship to yourself: You must laugh with the people.... You must not be ungenerous to people!" (Turner quoted in Casey 1987:238). This mandate is close to that received by the Srɔgboe chief who was ill and instructed by Tɔgbui Apim to bring the community together in 1994; it is also similar to the cultural edict fulfilled by the Paramount Chief of Anlo-land when he entered the gazebo-like structure for Nugbidodo. People of various parts of Anlo-land were allowed to hurl abuses at him for a brief period of time, to air grievances and engage with him before the rancor was contained in ceramic pots and covered with herbs. In regard to the Ndembu example, Casey notes (1987:238) that "it is striking that the most concrete activity here recommended is to 'eat with your fellow men.'" In terms of our analysis of the sensory dimension of these rituals, "the opening onto this past is provided by a sensation of taste" because this particular sense modality is "surely the most thoroughly participatory form of body memory and contrasting, in this very respect, with visual memory" (Casey 1987:252).

Both Anlo rituals made use of *sesetonume* (feeling in the mouth) in feeding the *Du-Legba* at the beginning of the Tɔgbui Apim rite, in generating animus-packed saliva to deposit under the herbs, and in the communal feast that brought Nugbidodo to a close. This kind of "eating together" can be said to represent

> just what happens in the ingestion of eucharistic sacraments. In such shared activity of incorporation, the injunction to "live well with [others]" is most concretely realized. Moreover, the common partaking of food and drink acts to suspend rigid distinctions of rank and status that obtain in society at large. In a *communitas,* where unity is less important than fellowship, all who come are welcome whatever differences of class or education obtain otherwise. As much as the Ndembu ceremony so tellingly described by Turner, the rite of the Eucharist offers a blend of "lowliness and sacredness, of homogeneity and comradeship." (Casey 1987:238)

While the partaking of food is highlighted here, I would hasten to add that in some of the other forms of sensory engagement—such as the dancing and kinesthetic exchanges that occurred during the Tɔgbui Apim event and the exchange of saliva and negative words of Nugbidodo—we also encounter a "suspension of rigid distinctions" of rank, status, lineage, and religious affiliation. The ritual commemorating Tɔgbui Apim worked at blending and balancing people within the community who belonged to secret societies or religious sects (such as Yeve, Blekete, Kɔkuʋu) in addition to people who belonged to secular voluntary associations; Nugbidodo brought together people from all corners of Anlo-land as well as from abroad. This chapter has attempted to examine how the sensorium is reinforced, in part, through these processes. The blending occurs both communally and psychically; it is simultaneously a sociological and a psychological process, which illustrates cultural psychology's claim that "culture and psyche make each other up." In an effort to sum up both this and the last chapter, let me make some observations about cultural memory, identity, and the body.

An Anlo man who has lived in North America for more than twenty years reflected with me on the erosion of the coastal section of Anlo-land. He considered the impact of global warming and the impending rise in sea level across the world, then noted that sooner rather than later Anlo-land as an actual place will cease to exist. "All Anlo will live in diaspora," he noted. "We will still be Anlo, but we will no longer have a place." So what is it that he continues to "have" or to remember that makes him an Anlo person when he has been away so long? And if Anlo-land itself ceases to exist as an actual piece of ground, why does he believe that "being Anlo" would still be meaningful? In ceremony and in commemoration we often find an element of celebration that "connotes not only an affirmation of there being, or one's having, such a past as is being commemorated, but above all an honoring of this past, a paying homage to it" (Casey 1987:226). An Anlo past, this *mɔfiala* believes, will continue to be commemorated and honored. Without doing that, without sustaining some kind of cultural memory, a sense of identity and a grounded sensibility become impossible. "At every level, the human psyche is constituted by identifications ... the mind is radically non-solipsistic: it is something shared and non-solitary from the start" (Casey 1987:244). The *shared* dimension of constituting psyche through identifications occurs in practices, and these practices involve sensory engagement.

The regular practice of these various *somatic modes of attention*—bathing the baby, flexing the joints, folding into oneself like Tɔgbui Whenya, head-loading and balancing, dancing, and so forth—results in an internalization of generative principles such that these are clearly features of the habitus of certain Anlo worlds. In these various ethnographic examples we can see that the way people learn to attend (somatically) to their surroundings, both in everyday life and in the context of ritual events, forms the material infrastructure of the person. Cultural memory, identity, and the body coincide in interactions with others (sensory engagement with relatives, neighbors, ancestors, and gods, as we have seen in parts 2 and 3), which in turn create *identifications* that are essential to being human. That is what I believe many *mɔfialawo* were trying to convey to me by insisting that I learn certain "core" dimensions of their cultural heritage. If "mind is fashioned from without" and the "interpsychic" is essential to the constitution of any kind of "intrapsychic" (Casey 1987:244–245), then the meaning of *Anlo* in historical and sociological terms becomes vital to the ways in which identifications are played out (constructed) in contemporary settings. *Seselelame* as a form of "feeling in the body" that links sensations to emotion and disposition is crucial to this process. Identifications are mediated through the senses, through sensory engagements, which (in the words of one Ewe scholar) are aimed at "the *making* of a child to *become* ... a person or human being *(ame)*" (Egblewogbe 1975:21). Much of this "becoming," I would argue, involves *the appropriation of bodiliness,* and such *bodiliness* has a distinct cultural grounding.

Sensory engagements at play in Anlo contexts, or a sensorium that makes up part of the "instruments of an ordering of the world" or the "system of classifying schemes which organize practices" (Bourdieu 1977:123–124) in an Anlo habitus, are striking for several reasons. There is an interesting attention to inner sensations such as those generated in balancing and kinesthesia, which seems to parallel the internal, inward-looking aspects of their cultural heritage (their emphasis on retaining a core identity). This is not to the exclusion, of course, of recognition of the external perceptory fields, which links to their principle of counterbalance exemplified by focusing outward, on living in diaspora. Ŋlɔ signifies well this dimension of Anlo being-in-the-world. Ŋlɔ commemorates an elaboration of interoceptive states while forcing the counterbalance of attention outward, hence reinforcing the balance we saw elaborated in the two rituals described here, which is central to what many Anlo people believe makes a decent person. Personhood is tied in local and specific ways to sensoriums, to the immediate ways one learns to hold and orient one's body, to the tastes and distastes one acquires in the formative years, and to the way these embodied practices link up to the development of self-awareness and a sense of identity. Part 4 will explore how the sensory order not only shapes the meaning of personhood but also how the nature of reality and the experience of well-being and health are linked to a cultural phenomenology of the senses.

PART FOUR

Health, Strength, and Sensory Dimensions of Well-Being

CHAPTER 8

Anlo Cosmology, the Senses, and Practices of Protection

Here I argue that the local sensorium affects the experience of health and illness and that when we approach their traditional religion as a system of the body, as a set of techniques for sensory manipulation, we better understand the ways in which they *know* things *in* and *about* the cosmos. I hope to demonstrate that definitions of personhood and engagement with other intentional persons are central to health and well-being and so directly tied to or based in a cultural group's sensorium. In addition, certain illness states may involve grounding in a sensory order that is different than the orthodox sensory order of any given cultural group. To understand the implications of this in Anlo contexts, we must examine the way the nature of reality has been represented in Anlo cultural traditions. We turn now toward a more intense examination of how Anlo-speaking individuals situate themselves in relation to their family, community, society, the gods, and the cosmos.

Among Anlo-Ewe people, well-being is not achieved within the confines of the individual, but is dependent upon the flow of energy, matter, substances, and information throughout many aspects of the individual's world. And it is precisely in these interchanges that "the senses" come into play, for such transactions are experienced and occur largely through sensory channels and sensory engagements.

Like other peoples throughout the world, Anlo speakers hold very complex cultural models that guide their experiences of self and other (animal and human as well as divine) beings. These models present well-being (in the form of coolness, stability, and balance) as transactions that occur between self and other. Selves, in fact, in West African contexts are very "porous"—to borrow an idea expressed by Achille Mbembe.[1] He suggests that a West African porosity of the self can be understood in terms of an openness to influences; a person exists only in the sense that she is related to other (animal, human, and divine) beings. More specifically, in Ewe personhood, according to ethnographer Judy Rosenthal, we find a nonboundedness and a lack of the kind of unitary wholeness of being that is characteristic of certain Western psychologies of the self (Rosenthal 1998:174). She explains (1998:157–188) how this plural personhood or indeterminate selfhood exists in Ewe in part because numerous psychic components (such as life sign and ancestral soul) as well as social relationships are understood to be central to the arrangement of self. Her characterization of personhood also rings true for the Anlo contexts in which I worked, and here I go on to argue that to be a healthy person involves sharing common interpretations and understandings of what is real, perceivable, imagined, fantasized, and so forth. Not unlike the Gorovodu adepts in Rosenthal's account of another set of Ewe people, the "intentional worlds" (Shweder 1991:73) of many Anlo mɔfialawo with whom I worked included complex notions of that which was beyond the visible realm, about influences and forces sensed and "known" to those who had grown up in the area but that were beyond the reach of—and even "non-sensible" to—outsiders. This dimension of Anlo life constitutes a complex theological system that deserves far more attention than what I can accomplish here, as my focus is specifically on sensory experience and well-being.[2] This discussion is limited, therefore, to three basic elements of their cosmology: an explanation of the structure or hierarchy of the cosmos, the role Nyigbla plays in the system, and a brief account of the phenomena of *legba, vodu,* and *dzoka.*

Beginning with Evans-Pritchard's (1976[1937]) highly sympathetic account of Azande witchcraft and magic, traditional religion has been approached in a number of African settings as an intellectual system that makes sense on its own terms (e.g., Griaule 1965). In addition, cognitive approaches have drawn analogies between African theories of knowledge and Western scientific thinking (Horton 1967) as well as demonstrating the culturally relative semantic fields of notions such as *knowledge* and *belief* (Kopytoff 1981). Victor Turner's work (e.g., 1967, 1968, 1974) emphasizing the social drama at play in Ndembu ritual took account of the psychological state of patients and healers in addition to highlighting the tension (antistructure) and resolution *(communitas)* in African religious practices. Recent studies have also emphasized the role of power and discourse in the genealogy of African "gnosis" and the ways in which knowledge is (culturally) ordered, while arguing that identity issues cannot be understood without archaeologies of specific (African) modes of philosophy and thought (e.g., Gyekye 1987; Mudimbe 1988).

Building on but diverging slightly from these earlier approaches to the study of African philosophy and African thought, here I want to treat Anlo-Ewe traditional religion as a system of the body involving sensory engagements (cf. Stoller 1989a, Stoller and Olkes 1987, and E. Turner et al. 1992). When we reexamine Anlo religious systems through the lens of an indigenous sensorium, or critically analyze this specific *mode of knowing,* we find that it is a kind of outward extension of the interoceptive, proprioceptive modes that are highly valued in this cultural setting. *Vodu* and other ancient Anlo-Ewe concepts and practices (such as *dzosasa*) reflect a philosophy about how the external world can be manipulated in order to affect the internal environment—and vice versa. *Vodu,* through this lens, appears to be a kind of sensorium beyond the body yet continuous with it; it is an extension of the inner sensorium and one that is manipulable; and the senses play a vital role in sustaining ties between the human world and that of the ancestors, gods, and supreme being.[3]

SUPREME BEING, LINEAL ANCESTORS, AND SPIRITS OF NATURE

For many Anlo-speaking people the cosmos was perceived as inhabited by nature spirits or a pantheon of deities (referred to in the Ewe language as *trɔwo*); ancestors or spirits of humans who had led exemplary, godlike lives (generally called *tɔgbuiwo* and *mamawo*); and a supreme being or an omniscient, omnipotent, omnipresent force that was variously termed Mawu, Mawu-Lisa, Segbo-Lisa, or Mawu-Segbo-Lisa. Mawu (or "God") was considered remote and inaccessible to human beings, while the *trɔwo* (nature spirits) hovered close to earth and interacted with humans on a consistent basis. The ancestors were somewhere between: they were closer to Mawu and more remote than the *trɔwo,* but they were not as distant or as unapproachable as the supreme god.

This three-tiered hierarchy represents the basic idea that most Anlo-speaking people seemed to hold, although devout Christians generally proclaimed the nonexistence of either *trɔwo* or the ancestors and replaced these ideas with notions of Jesus Christ, the Holy Spirit, the devil, angels, and so on. Fiawoo (1959a) deals with some of the issues that arise for Anlo speakers in the collision of these different perspectives, but it is a topic that needs further research and exploration. Fiawoo's work sets the stage for our interest in the *experiences* of those who continue to acknowledge the existence of *trɔwo* and ancestors—whether in combination with Christian beliefs or without adherence to Christianity.

As stated previously, the god concept held by many Anlo-speaking people was variously referred to as Mawu, Mawu-Lisa, Segbo-Lisa, and Mawu-Segbo-Lisa. The various components of the name itself and the nuances of meaning each obtains provide initial insight as to the nature and complexity of this force. While Christians tended to refer to God as simply Mawu,[4] this translation deprives the term or utterance of its rich and multifaceted original meaning.

> The Ewe ... have a dual name for the High God ... either as *Mawu-Lisa,*
> *Segbo-Lisa* or *Se-Lisa* ... two names in the androgynous ... are never to be
> separated. *Mawu* is the female principle and *Lisa* is the male principle ...
> and the two form a unity in duality. In translating the Bible into Ewe, how-
> ever, *Mawu* was severed from *Lisa* and used to translate the various
> Hebrew and Greek names for God, which in many cases are male
> principles and thus stand for half-truths, i.e. from the African ontological
> point of view. (Dzobo 1980:85)

The first problem in reducing the god concept to merely Mawu is the divestiture of its original balance of masculine and feminine qualities. While Dzobo states that "*Mawu* is the female principle and *Lisa* is the male principle," my own research and the accounts of various *mɔfialawo* suggest rather different and much more elaborate associations.[5] One *mɔfiala* explained that "*Mawu* is a combination of *Mawu-Segbo,* masculine, and *Mawu-Lisa,* feminine. *Segbo:* that is heat, the sun, strength, vigor, and all these things. *Lisa:* that is the coolness of night, gentility, and things of that nature.... So when they say *Mawu-Segbo-Lisa,* then they are calling *Mawu* the sexless god or *Mawu* the combination of masculine and feminine." Underscoring this account, Mawu and Lisa are a *couple* in certain *vodu* orders (Rosenthal 1998:61).

The etymology of *segbo* and *lisa* enriches matters even further and embellishes the characteristics associated with each gender. Westermann translates *se* as essentially "a deity" (1973[1928]:209) but it can also be glossed as "destiny" or even "trajectory," while *gbo* denotes "strong, vigorous, powerful, violent ... stubborn" (Westermann 1973[1928]:91). The meaning of *li* is "to exist" (and relates to existence and existentialism in general) (Westermann 1973[1928]:153), and *sa* can be glossed as tie, join, unite, bind, entangled, impenetrable, and inextricable (cf. Westermann 1973[1928]:206). Segbo can therefore be conceptualized as a vigorously powerful force, the masculine dimensions of the universal energy, heat and sun, and supreme strength and vigor, while Lisa refers to inextricable ties that bind, labyrinthine and intertwined aspects of existence, and the feminine associated phenomena of coolness, nighttime, and the moon. As for the etymology of *Mawu* itself, *ma* alone denotes "that or that one" (Westermann 1973[1928]:160), while *wu* means "to surpass, excel, exceed, outdo, overcome," the superlative, or "to be more than" (Westermann 1973[1928]:285–286). Consequently, in an absolute, literal sense, the etymology of *Mawu-Segbo-Lisa* is: that one *(ma)* + surpasses, exceeds *(wu)* + destiny, trajectory *(se)* + power, force, vigor *(gbo)* + existence, consciousness, being *(li)* + intertwined, inextricably entangled *(sa)*. Therefore, God's name (Mawu-Segbo-Lisa) is the proclamation: That one that exceeds or surpasses destiny and total power and that exists inextricably entangled and intertwined. From this it becomes clear that conceptions of god held by many Anlo speakers indicate that even the comprehensive grasp of these contradictory phenomena is surpassed in the notion of *supreme being*. In turn, this supreme-state-of-being-which-is-god is the ultimate exemplar of wholeness, well-being, and health. Supreme (well-) being achieves the melding of night and day, the blending of coolness and heat, and the marriage of a still pool of water and the fire of a shooting star. Whereas *se* (of the masculine Segbo) is trajectory, path, course, destiny, experienced like a straight line, *sa* (of the feminine Lisa) feels like binding, tying, intricate connections, and knots.[6] There is a balancing principle implicit in this concept of ultimate well-being.

The concept and experience of *sa,* in fact, was of central concern in the role the ancestors played in the cosmic system. Westermann's translation of *sa,* it will be recalled, was in part "to be tied, joined, entangled, impenetrable, confused, inextricable" (1973[1928]:206). In Anlo-speaking contexts, people were tied to ancestors in a variety of ways: individuals held an inextricable bond with the ancestor they had reincarnated, the ancestors joined the human to the cosmic realm since Mawu-Segbo-Lisa (or "Supreme Being") was too remote, and the ancestors were the ultimate source of entangled familial lines. The ancestors were generally referred to as *tɔgbuiwo* and *mamawo* (also the kin terms for "grandfather" and "grandmother"). Other terms were also used, however, such as *tɔgbeŋɔliwo,* which more accurately translated as "souls of the ancestors" or simply "ancestral spirits" (Fiawoo 1959a:61–67).

Nonetheless, the *sa*-oriented experience of inextricability was one many Anlo speakers held with ancestral beings. That is, while the ancestors were thought of as residing close to god, they did not remain aloof and detached but were instead entangled, confused, intertwined *(sasa)* into earthly experiences and into persons themselves (which could be likened to Western science's conception of genes).

In her work on *African Vodun,* art historian Suzanne Preston Blier uses the ideas of "enactment, reenactment, and substitution" to describe the ties that bind parent and child among the Fon, Ewe, and related groups (1995:178). Like actors, people are conceived of as capable of embodying another person while at the same time maintaining their selves. She explains (1995:178) that "each baby is at once a unique individual and a representative or substitute (replacement, mask) for an engendering parent(s)." This idea goes hand in hand with Ewe and Fon notions of reincarnation, in which babies are believed to be assisted or guided by an ancestor as they return to earth. That "ancestral sponsor," as Blier designates it, plays a vital role in the child's identity and personality formation. The Anlo-Ewe term for this ancestral sponsor is *amedzɔtɔ,* which means "agent of the person's birth" (*tɔ:* agent; *dzo:* birth; *ame:* person). Blier describes (1995:178) how a child's birth engenders an appeal to Fa to find out whom the baby resembles since the belief holds that "all new children resemble a person who is deceased."

The resemblance factor is, to a certain extent, the reason I liken this phenomenon to a model of genetics. The idea that traits are reproduced and reappear in individuals throughout the lineage, somehow linking past to present and connecting invisible realms to physical and visible matter, is prevalent in both models. Furthermore, in the same way that the notion of genes is a cultural model "linked to the social experience of the individual" (Jackson and Karp 1990:12) in Euro-American contexts, the concept of ancestral spirits fashioning and influencing the makeup of individuals is operationalized in a daily and personal way. In a sense many Euro-Americans pay homage to genetic factors in a similar way to how many Anlo speakers pay homage to ancestral spirits. The amount of discussion and attention paid to inherited genetic predispositions (to a variety of diseases and conditions) in contemporary Euro-American contexts is somewhat akin to the concern and regard paid to the force that ancestral spirits bring to bear on life's regular events among Anlo-speaking people.

However, in regard to reincarnation and the role of *amedzɔtɔ* or the agent of the person's birth, it is not only physical attributes but also character traits and emotional dispositions that one inherits through this process (Blier 1995:181). In addition, it is important to clarify that a person who may have his "grandparent's dzoto [ancestor soul] most probably does not have the same kpoli [life sign] as the grandparent. Thus certain aspects of the person must be radically different from those of the forebear" (Rosenthal 1998:178). I often asked Anlo-speaking people what they perceived to be "inside a person" or what "made up a person" beyond flesh and blood. This discussion was different from what I presented earlier. What Anlo speakers wanted me to understand were vital aspects of what goes into the *"making* of a child to *become* what the society accepts as a person or human being *(amɛ)"* (Egblewogbe 1975:21). That process focused on development of character traits and sensibilities that honored or incorporated Anlo themes and notions of morality. Here we enter into discussions that open the window more directly onto a local psychology. All of the items listed, with their tentative translations into English, were given at one time or another by Anlo speakers as what they considered to be "inside a person."

amɛme: an inner person; a person inside of a person; the deeper, inner part of a human being; this was distinguished from *amɛŋume,* which is the outer person (perhaps the persona) as well as those very close to you, relatives, or people who orbit very close to your being

dzodzome: the character of a person, natural qualities, or those traits that come along with the person "in birth"

ŋutila alo gbɔgbɔ fe nɔnɔme: one's constitution, or literally the "body and breath's form" of a person

luvo: shadow or soul, which is thought of as not confined to one part of the body or being but pervading the whole entity

aklama: a personal guardian spirit, conceived of by some as "inside a person" and by others as "outside the self"

amedzotɔ: reincarnated ancestor inhabiting or possessing one's being

dzitsinya: conscience, or literally "heart *(dzi)* + tell *(tsi)* + word *(nya)*" or matters spoken/voiced in one's heart

A few *mɔfialawo* stated that inside a person were also things like *tamebubu, tamesusu, nunya, lamenusese, seselelame, gɔmesese, sidzenu, lamesese,* and so forth (the relevant translations will be provided momentar-

ily). One person explained that while every person has all of these, some
traits are more developed or prominent than others in a single individual. The most salient inner states among the people I consulted were *tamebubu,* which I have glossed as "thinking," *lamenusese* (feeling), *seseile-
lame* (sensing), and *gomesese* (intuiting). In addition, Rosenthal's
ethnography of Ewe *vodu* presents (1998:175–187) an interesting parallel discussion of all the components of the person, but there is a striking
contrast between her account and my own that could benefit from further investigation. The Ewe people with whom Rosenthal worked were
by and large adepts of a *vodu* order (Gorovodu) and her "different experts' inventories"(p. 175) reflect a decidedly spiritual base to the components inside a person. In turn, even though these qualities may be the
dominion of an ancestral sponsor in the reports of my own *mofialawo,*
in abstract terms the items offered to me have a more secular tone. Are
there differing psychological theories at play among *vodu* adepts in comparison with other Ewe people? One way or another, the two differing
accounts make abundantly clear that all these components or all these
"things" that Ewe people report exist inside of a person indicate a complex concept of personality, self, and psychological structure.

In the midst of a discussion about the ancestors, why address the psychological complexity of persons? Blier explains (1995:181–182) how
the ancestral sponsor fashions not only the physical aspects of the person but also the psychological dimensions and even the moral character.
The word in Fon for character or behavior *(jijo)* has as its root the word
for birth *(jo),* which then underscores "the role that ancestral sponsors
(joto, 'master of birth') play in the formation and conceptualization of
the child's personality." In everyday life, the attention paid to the ancestral sponsor and to the relationship between the child and his sponsor, helps to shape and influence the child's demeanor. (Also see Rosenthal 1998:157–194 for details on this influence.) People consistently talk
to the child about his sponsor so that "a sort of diffuse education ensues
that gives to the latter the moral, psychological, spiritual, and sometimes
even physical attributes of the ancestor.... Through this means one traces
a program of life for the child" (Blier 1995:181–182). My point, therefore, is that all the components of persons, or the "parts inside of persons," are to a certain extent the province of ancestral spirits.

During one of my visits with Mr. Adzomada, he told the following
story about his *amedzoto* (the "agent of his birth," or reincarnated ancestor). At the time of Mr. Adzomada's birth, his father consulted with
a *boko* (diviner) about the baby's *se* (destiny), and the diviner explained

that the ancestor who had been reincarnated was wearing shoes. Mr. Adzomada's father was startled and said to the *bɔkɔ,* "What you have seen simply cannot be. There is no educated person in our family." The *bɔkɔ* insisted, however, that the ancestral spirit he perceived was wearing shoes, and the presence of shoes signified a person of learning. His parents subsequently investigated their family history and finally discovered that on his father's side, several generations back, had lived an educated man. Mr. Adzomada's parents were instructed to give him special treatment since this educated ancestor had evidently returned as the baby's *amɛdzɔtɔ.* When indeed Mr. Adzomada grew up and eventually told his father that he wanted to go to school, this was confirmation that the *bɔkɔ* had been right. In fact, if he had not been treated as a thinking-oriented person—a person in whom *tamebubu* was the dominant function—he would eventually have fallen ill. If the ancestor's will were not honored, if a person's destiny *(se)* were ignored or opposed, then disruptions, imbalances, and sickness would commandeer or confiscate (possess) the person's being.[7]

In discussing Mr. Adzomada's story with other Anlo speakers, the links among sensation, emotion, disposition, and vocation became more clear. People explained that if Mr. Adzomada had not been allowed to go to school as a child (which was the direction or course in life signified by his *amɛdzɔtɔ*'s shoes), his feeling in the body *(seselelame)* would not have been right. He would have had "pains and bad thoughts," which (a number of *mɔfialawo* suggested) was what caused people to use "bad *juju*." Painful sensations and illness, along with negative emotions, were associated with failure (on the family's part) to attend to the directions of an ancestral sponsor and mismanagement of the personal destiny (vocation) of the child. When such a disruption to *seselelame* was set in motion, and one's *se* (destiny, vocation) was derailed, a rotten disposition was considered inevitable. *Seselelame* was the idiom of illness for many Anlo people.

The last level in the cosmic realm was occupied by the *trɔwo,* or spirits of nature. Imagining the cosmos as a pyramid, Mawu-Segbo-Lisa would be situated at the pinnacle, the ancestors directly beneath god, and *trɔwo* or "nature spirits" at the bottom in the space immediately above the human and earthly realm. In a sense *trɔwo* constituted a pantheon of deities or tutelary gods, and some Anlo speakers referred to them as *Mawuviwo,* or "the small gods."

> The word *trɔ* suggests a troubler or a confuser; it implies a god or spirit being who confounds its client or worshipper with an ever-growing number of demands, some of which may be conflicting ... *trɔwo* are the intermedi-

aries between *Mawu* and men. They are the children of *Mawu* and are
sometimes referred to as *Mawuviwo*. Unlike *Mawu* to whom nothing but
goodness is ascribed, the *trɔwo* are capable of good and evil. They minister,
but they also kill. They are imagined to have animal or human forms. They
have hands and feet and are *endowed with the five senses*. Each spirit is
symbolised by a collection of odds and ends—beads, stones, bones, parts of
dead animals, etc.—each of which has its own special value, and
collectively they express the essence of the particular *trɔ*. (Fiawoo
1959a:51, emphasis added)

While Mawu-Segbo-Lisa governed supreme (well-) being of the universe
and everything it contained, and the ancestors were intimately involved
in a person's destiny and constitutional (physiogenetic) makeup, *trɔwo*
played a significant role in day-to-day troubles and fortunes, illnesses
and rehabilitations. *Trɔwo* intervened and participated in minor events
of mundane existence and influenced the well-being and health of persons and whole communities. Fiawoo described (1959a:55–56) public
trɔwo as guarding the welfare of both kin and political-territorial groups,
while personal health and wealth were matters for the *trɔwo* of families
and individuals. They conferred benefits such as "rain, human and soil
fertility, warding off dangers, sickness and epidemics" (Fiawoo 1959a:
55–56). Interactions with *trɔwo*, therefore, focused largely on health
maintenance, protection, and general matters concerning well-being.
Conceptualized often as "spirits," *trɔwo* manifested physically in a variety of ways, including the possession of a person, with its consequent
displacement of personality, as well as "the material god-objects that are
constructed with sacred recipes, secret and protected from the hands of
the uninstructed. Sometimes these god-objects are called the vodus or
tros; sometimes they are said to be the skin, the body, or the house of
the vodus" (Rosenthal 1998:47).

Perceptions of what both *trɔwo* and the ancestors needed and desired
reveal certain things about sensory valuation. *Trɔwo* were "imagined to
have animal or human forms. They have hands and feet and are *endowed
with the five senses*" (Fiawoo 1959a:51). Whether possessing five senses
or more, *trɔwo* were considered sensate beings, and this perception or
belief conditioned how people appealed to and engaged with them.

Each Thursday morning during the time we stayed in Srɔgboe, lineage elders gathered in the center of the compound in which we lived. Our
residence was in the *afedome* (ancestral home) of a particularly prominent family, and approximately ten or twelve elders assembled each week
and performed a set of lineal rites. In the first instance they paid hom-

age to the ancestors by pouring libations and expressing praise, but inherent in this performance was also an appeal to one or more *trɔwo*. As Fiawoo explained (1959a:92–93), "A lineage *trɔ*, like the lineal ancestor, provides for the well-being of the group, individually and collectively. The *trɔ* cult group thus coincides with the ancestral cult group and helps reinforce lineage solidarity by common worship or regardful attitude to a common deity." The weekly performance of ancestral rites invariably involved verbal expression of praise accompanied by ceremonial drinking and offering of liquid (through the pouring of libations from a calabash). That is, the ancestors and *trɔwo* wanted *to hear* (on a regular basis) the vocalization of human praise and gratitude. More than anything else, the verbal expression of honor and appreciation was performed by the lineage elders that corresponds to the idea that *nusese* (hearing) was one of the more highly valued components of the sensorium. Occasionally food was prepared and dancing performed (implicating gustatory and kinesthetic sensations), but in this specific context the sensory field consistently used for interaction between the human and cosmic realm involved sound.

NYIGBLA: HEAD *TRƆ*

Nyigbla was considered the "head of all the Anlo Ewe nature gods *(trɔ)*" (Gilbert 1982:64).[8] He held connections to both thunder and war and was imported into Anlo-land in the mid-eighteenth-century as the Dzevi clan gained acceptance as members of the Anlo polity (Greene 1996:59).[9] For many Anlo-speaking people (those who lived in rural areas as well as those who resided in Accra), Nyigbla was one of the main arbiters of life and death. While Mawu (God) held the ultimate power to kill or create, Nyigbla was the *trɔ* (or spirit) whose dominion was the protection or execution of human beings. Nyigbla was probably summoned into Anlo-land to help in wars with neighboring groups and as a common deity around which Anlo speakers could rally (Fiawoo 1959a:221–222). During the second half of the nineteenth century this *trɔ* (symbolized as a piece of iron in the shape of an anvil) was flourishing at Gbugbla (near Accra). The Anlo council of chiefs sent messengers there to persuade Nyigbla "to leave Gbugbla altogether and come to settle permanently in Anlo," and they then "introduced Nyigbla as a national cult" (Fiawoo 1959a:221–222). Nyigbla could be symbolized by a piece of carved wood (as at Afife), and was perceived by many Anlo speakers as the "lord of water," who sent rain, and as the "lord of life," who provided children to Anlo-speaking people. Nyigbla's special province, however, was warfare, where he was seen mounted on a horse, leading the warriors, and brandishing a bow and arrow (Fiawoo 1959a:221–222).

One *mɔfiala* stated that Nyigbla was the lightning and his wife Sofia was the rumbling thunder that followed, beseeching Nyigbla to be merciful. Nyigbla would ruthlessly strike people with a bolt of lightning, but Sofia would try to temper his approach. Discussing Nyigbla one evening in our compound in Accra,[10] this *mɔfiala* (a professional who held a master's degree in business) explained, "The four of us could be sitting here at the table, and if Nyigbla was after one of us, the lightning would strike him dead and leave not even a trace of harm on the rest of us." He also suggested that this was one of the major differences between the Christian system and that of the classic Anlo religious scheme: in Christianity there was on-going mercy and forgiveness (even for a person who had committed murder), whereas in the ancient Anlo system one was not given a second chance in relation to a capital offense, for Nyigbla would simply strike the person dead.[11] A religion such as Christianity allowed people excuses, this *mɔfiala* suggested, whereas the moral system of ancient Anlo was (and continued to be) more effective in motivating ethical behavior in human beings.

The fear of being struck by lightning and the symbolic magnitude of such an event was great. As another *mɔfiala* explained: "People are afraid that when they go to steal, *thunder will come into the family* and people will be disgraced." An individual's death by lightning (referred to by some as *tohonɔfui*) was a reflection on all his kin since it signified a transgression of such import that Nyigbla involved himself. This phenomenon illustrates the intricate connections among self, society, and cosmos; when a person heard the crash of thunder or witnessed the night sky light up like day, the shudder that reverberated through his body was not simply a "personal" experience of fear, but rather that shudder embodied the sticky web of relations linking individual, social, and cosmic fields of being (cf. Jackson and Karp 1990). Lack of attention paid to *agbagbaɖoɖo* (balancing) created disruptions in these links (largely through violations of moral laws) and resulted in serious illnesses and general *xexeme gbegblɛ* (ruin or destruction of the world).[12]

In addition, one *mɔfiala* explained to me that as he sat in his family house at Anloga, he experienced Nyigbla flying above the lagoon from Anyako to Alakple. This young man described the experience as beginning with a tremendous rumbling, like the galloping sound of horses running in the distance. Next appeared a white light in the sky, which gradually took the shape of a horse mounted by a human being. I asked him to explain the difference between thunder and lightning in relation to this manifestation of Nyigbla. His response focused on the feeling he had *(seselelame)* and how his family knew it was Nyigbla because of the semi-paralysis that set into his body immediately after this experience. The paralysis and stupefaction disappeared only after various purification rites were performed. This situation did not simply present an impending storm with dramatic thunder and lightning. Nyigbla's presence was known through the feeling in the young man's body or his compromised state of health.

An Anlo-speaking person's perception of the distinction between Nyigbla and common lightning could be compared to the difference in our culture between turning on the television to a fictionalized movie as opposed to turning on the television to a newscast announcing a tornado touching down a half mile from our house. How do we know the difference? Is it only through what we can see? What is the nature of the aesthetic difference in our perception and ability to distinguish? These are questions that can be more fully addressed through attention to the sensorium. Metaphysical forces within Anlo worlds were perceived and known largely through the sensory fields, with particular attention to a synesthetic ability they valued in *seselelame*.

Nyigbla therefore represented a very complex phenomenon (from a historical, psychological, and sociological point of view), and the image and definition of Nyigbla varied to a certain extent in the imagination and perceptions of individual Anlo-speaking people. In fact, it would be difficult to simplistically categorize Nyigbla as "the god of thunder" or "the god of war," because his image, duties, and powers were transformed accordingly. While I stated above that one *mɔfiala* perceived Nyigbla as thunder (his wife being Sofia, and lightning) and I referred to Fiawoo's comment that Nyigbla was represented with a piece of iron, an older *mɔfiala* disagreed and stated that Nyigbla was a national *trɔ* (deity or spirit) for all Anlo-speaking people and that he governed the domain of war. He believed that Nyigbla had nothing to do with thunder per se, and his "wife" was not Sofia since that term *(sofia)* simply referred to the feminine aspect of god (and was complemented by the masculine side, called *sodza*). He explained that *sofia* also referred to stone hand axes found in the ground and was associated with Yeve devotees.[13] Furthermore, Nyigbla was not represented by iron, according to this *mɔfiala*, for that would be Whanyevi, the "deity of iron," who oversaw blacksmiths and was attended to by one division of the Dzovia clan.[14]

These discrepancies are not meant to cause confusion or to suggest that Anlo speakers themselves are confused, but rather to highlight the very dynamic nature of these phenomena and the multiplicity of ways in which *trɔwo* (a pantheon of deities) can be interpreted. Nyigbla's multifaceted nature, therefore, is not unlike the "many faces of Ogun" (Barnes 1989:1–26), although I am not suggesting that Nyigbla parallels Ogun in either stature or renown. As I struggled to understand Nyigbla's exact domain, however, I came to realize he combined attributes of Ogun, Sango, and even Esu-Elegba. While "Ogun is popularly known as the god of hunting, iron, and warfare," fusions occur periodically, which then add additional layers of complexity and can result in an overlap of characteristics between two figures (Barnes 1989:2, 7–8). For example, in a poem that employs the image of electricity, Nigeria's Nobel laureate Wole Soyinka combines Sango (deity of thunder and lightning) with Ogun (Barnes 1989:7–8). And while in general Sango and Ogun are quite distinct among the Yoruba, they have converged into one deity, or *loa,* in Haiti (Brown 1989:78). Similarly, Nyigbla was known in Anloland primarily as the god of warfare: he sometimes stood with that identity alone, but sometimes the attributes of other deities were fused onto Nyigbla. First, he was sometimes merged with the god of thunder and lightning, or that god would sometimes be distinguished and called Sogbla or Xebieso. Second, Nyigbla was occasionally fused with the god of ironsmithing, or that god was sometimes separated and referred to as Whanyevi. And finally, Nyigbla was also sometimes associated with the trickster figure or the god of crossroads, but threshold spirits were sometimes distinguished and referred to as *Legba.* Decidedly, for my *mɔfialawo,* Nyigbla held many faces like Ogun, and he consistently played a dynamic role in their lives.

As complex as he is, Nyigbla deserves an entire volume devoted solely to him, however, my final observation about this important figure concerns his function as what Barnes (1989:2) refers to in Ogun as the destroyer or creator archetype. Anlo-speaking elders decided to appropriate Nyigbla (in the latter half of the eighteenth century) to protect and empower the Anlo state and its people during war. In that context it is difficult to imagine Nyigbla striking down an individual unless he was a traitor to the Anlo state. How then do we make sense of my *mɔfiala's* explanation that four people could be sitting at a table and Nyigbla could summarily execute a single person? That is, why would Nyigbla do such a thing? To understand this, it is necessary to look more closely at the concept of "protection" or "empowerment," which then relates to local notions of well-being and health.

Nyigbla was believed to wage war. When the Anlo state was at war with neighboring and foreign powers, throughout the end of the nineteenth century and into the twentieth century, Nyigbla led or inspired military maneuvers of an offensive as well as a defensive nature. Then, in the 1950s an Asian influenza epidemic assaulted or infiltrated "Anlo territory," and people claimed it was Nyigbla who protected them and "waged war" on this deadly disease (Fiawoo 1959a:221–226). In the 1990s, some people said, there was general and severe *xexeme gbegblε* (worldly demise or something rotten and amiss in the universe). But *xexeme gbegblε* was even associated with Nyigbla back in the 1950s:

> Among my informants, opinion varied as to the present status of *Nyigbla*. There were those who accepted my present analysis in terms of declining status and role, but pointed to corresponding maladjustments or what was styled *xexemegbegblε*: personal and family privations, economic difficulties, disease and the relatively short life-span, the jealousies and intrigues of the modern world; these have been the writings on the wall, announcing the vengeance of *Nyigbla* for negligence in ritual observance. (Fiawoo 1959a:225)

Forty years after Fiawoo's observations, I would suggest that reference to *xexeme gbegblε* was perhaps more prevalent, as I frequently heard this phrase uttered with worry about environmental degradation, poverty, infant mortality, AIDS, and so forth. Several older *mɔfialawo* expressed that the younger generations simply *did not listen* to the wisdom of their elders (as well as the wisdom of *trɔwo* and ancestors), and they lacked structure, knowledge of self, discipline, strength, and health.[15] Furthermore, they jeopardized the entire family as they involved themselves in dubious activities (such as those discussed in chapter 6 in relation to *ga foɖi mawo,* or prohibitions on dirty money). In this context, Nyigbla would serve Anlo-land as a whole by sometimes (in a warlike fashion) "surgically striking" one person, or removing an individual who was compromising the well-being (and balance) of the entire group. Listening or hearing *(nusese)* and balancing *(agbagbaɖoɖo),* two highly significant sensory fields for many Anlo speakers, could be seen as the operative values in this discussion. That is, *nusese* concerned listening, hearing, understanding, and obeying, and people would talk about *xexeme gbegblε* (something rotten and amiss in the universe) as related to human failures in hearing and balance: individuals not listening to their elders, people in general not listening to (and obeying) the *trɔwo*, the ancestors, and god (Mawu-Segbo-Lisa). Nyigbla, therefore, as the ultimate arbiter of life and death (the "destroyer/creator archetype" mentioned previously) was perceived as upholding his duties of protecting and empowering Anlo-speaking people by "warring on the disease within" or balancing out the forces of good and evil that permeated the Anlo body politic itself.[16]

LEGBA, VODU, AND DZOKA

In terms of Anlo theosophical beliefs, this chapter has thus far covered Mawu-Segbo-Lisa (a god concept), *tɔgbuiwo* and *mamawo* (ancestors), Nyigbla, and a pantheon of *trɔwo* (deities, small gods, or spirits). Additional dimensions of the cosmological system that are important in obtaining an understanding of how the cosmos relates to sensory aspects of well-being include the phenomena of *legba, vodu,* and *dzoka,* because they are utilized in everyday practices and routines. I suggest conceptualizing these three phenomena in the following way: *legba* as a guardian of entryways and thresholds, *vodu* as an introspective philosophy and interoceptive system of the body based on *power* gleaned from "resting to draw the water" (cf. Blier 1995:40), and *dzoka* as transformative arts. However, experiences of *legba, vodu,* and *dzoka,* along with experiences of *trɔwo* and Nyigbla himself, are rarely as neat and clear as the distinctions I have made. A little background is in order.

Just as it would be difficult for many Euro-Americans to explain precise differences in experiences they have had with ghosts, spirits, angels, the Holy Ghost, souls, demons, apparitions, and so on for Anlo speakers the lines blurred between perceptions of *trɔwo* and *voduwo* and among *legbawo, voduwo, dzokawo, ŋɔliwo, gbɔgbɔwo,* and so forth. Furthermore, different individuals held different relationships to these various entities or phenomena. But a cultural pattern of introspectiveness that we examined in chapter 6 has a continuity here with what struck me as widespread interest in and attention to invisible but interoceptively sensible phenomena.

In her article "Mystical Protection among the Anlo Ewe," Gilbert (1982:66) admits to her confusion about terms such as *alegba, vodu,* and medicinal *atike* cult personages, explaining that in her interactions with Anlo-Ewe speakers these terms were sometimes used interchangeably and at other times very emphatic lines were drawn between the different entities. She indicates that scholarship on the matter did not help since it was replete with contradictions. Gilbert states (1982:66) that a "certain *trɔ* (nature deity) that was 'technically a *vodu*' according to Fiawoo (1959a:91) would probably have been called an *alegba* by my informants. Conversely, Cudjoe refers to a *du-legba* called Sakpata who punishes wrong-doers with smallpox (1971:195)." But Gilbert herself found that Sakpata would be considered a *vodu* among her informants. In the Gorovodu (medicinal *vodu* order) of which Rosenthal writes (1998:60–61), "Tro, vodu, and fetish refer to the spirit and host during possession ceremonies as well as to god-objects."

For the Ewe language in general, Westermann (1973[1928]:152) translates or defines *legba* as "idol, figure representing a deity, a demon." Cudjoe-Calvocoressi (1974:62–63) suggests that for Anlo-speaking people a *legba* is like a *vodu* and is a messenger to the gods, which distinguishes them both from *trɔwo,* which can never be messengers, for they are small gods themselves and do not act as intermediaries between the human and cosmic domain. She believes that *vodu* are from the Fonspeaking area of West Africa and in the context of Anlo culture they can be bought (Cudjoe-Calvocoressi 1974:62–63). As a means of distinction, *trɔ* (plural *trɔwo*) either possess a person or are inherited, but (unlike a *vodu*) a *trɔ* cannot be purchased (Cudjoe-Calvocoressi 1974:62–63).

In regard to *trɔ* and *vodu* (but also including the term *fetish*), Rosenthal suggests (1998:60), "These three terms are usually interchangeable, although tro appears to be used more often among western Ewe [this would include Anlo], and vodu is heard more often among eastern Ewe, Adja, Oatchi, and Guin." In support of such lexical interchangeability, Westermann's translation or definition of *vodu* is simply "*trɔ,*" and for the term *trɔ* he then gives the words "deity, tutelary deity, or demon" (1973[1928]:269, 245). I have only encountered the term "demon" in Westermann's work. Finally, *dzo* has been translated as "charm, magic" and the word *dzoka* as "a charm-string" (Westermann 1973[1928]:26–27). Cudjoe-Calvocoressi further suggests (1974:62–63) that *dzo* comes from the Fon-speaking area and "functions automatically" in response to methodically ritualistic attention (or observation of sacrifices and taboos).

These various efforts to clarify each term or, more important, each phenomenon still leave us a bit confused and lacking any real feeling for what *legba, vodu,* and *dzoka* really are or how they have been experienced. I am interested in sensorial and experiential aspects of these phenomena and not just ideal types, but in the first instance it is important to understand how difficult it is to distinguish among *legbawo, trɔwo,* and *voduwo* and how these distinctions are in part related to specific lo-

cales in the Ewe cultural complex. In addition, while a discourse of visuality was rarely used by my own *mɔfialawo* (their idiom centered more
on *seselelame*), it has frequently been employed by scholars. So while
legba, vodu, and *dzoka* all seem to be a kind of supernatural or cosmic
force (power, deity, spirit), at some level each is a discrete entity to the
people who experience and identify them. Here I would suggest that a
cultural elaboration of introspectiveness and a performative valuation
of interoceptive modes allows us to map these phenomena in a slightly
new way, with *legba* as a guardian of thresholds, *vodu* as power gleaned
from "resting to draw the water" (in Blier 1995:40), and *dzoka* as transformative arts. This slightly new spin I am taking stems from treating
Anlo theosophical beliefs and practices as a system of the body—with
that system directly reflecting their sensory order.

LEGBA "EMPOWERMENT OBJECTS":
GUARDIAN OF THRESHOLDS

Wherever thresholds existed in Anlo-land, one was likely to find *legbawo*. At the entrance of towns, villages, compounds, houses, and to a
certain extent in relation to "thresholds of the human body," one found
what Blier (1995:4) deemed "empowerment objects." In the Fon language these "empowerment objects" were referred to as *bociɔ*, which literally translated as "empowered *(bo)* cadaver *(ciɔ)*" (Blier 1995:2).[17] Indeed, beneath or behind the surface of *legbawo* sculptures, figures, or
shapes were buried "powerful medicinal and sacred herbs *(ama),* and in
some cases, humans" (Gilbert 1982:60).

The following recounts one version of the etymology of the word
legba, highlighting not only the visual rendering of a clay figure but also
the possible kinesthetic and movement based roots of the tradition.

> There was once in the village of Kedzi ... a very ferocious man by the name
> of Akɔli of whom everyone was terrified. Finally the villagers in a joint ef-
> fort were able to tie him up with an exceptionally strong rope and to bury
> him beneath the mud. Over the hole the villagers erected a clay figure in the
> form of a human being. People said in relief *ele egbea* (he has gone today)
> referring to Akɔli. From this time onwards clay figures in human form be-
> came known as Legba. People swore oaths on this clay figure and when it
> was realized that it had power, legbawo became more widespread. (Cudjoe
> 1971:192)

The visible clay figure is only the surface; an invisible dimension, se-
mantically captured by reference to his movement (*ele egbea*: he has gone

today) is the more potent force. As one of my own *mɔfialawo* explained: "*Legba* is a tutelary god that offers protection. When they make it, they put a hole in it from the head down to the bottom and there are herbs and things buried underneath it. *Legba* is just a symbol; underneath it are so many things." While these "many things" were invisible, many *mɔfialawo* (even Christians) reported being able to feel (in terms of *seselelame*) the charged and powerful energy held within *legbawo*.

Cudjoe states up front that the story she cites represents a very localized (and perhaps peculiar) version of the etymology of the word *legba*, and in fact the derivation that has more currency is "seize and collect at one place" (*le:* to seize, catch, hold, grasp; *gba:* to collect or keep at a place).[18] This refers to Legba's capacity to patrol entry- and exit-ways, and to monitor the forces passing in and out, again highlighting movement and kinesthetic sensory modes. Cudjoe describes (1969:51) some of Legba's versatility: "*Legba* has many spheres of activity. He acts, however, mainly as the guardian of the town and the house. He can, for example, either attract or repel all that is evil and unpleasant. He can prevent illness entering the village and protect it in times of war. *Legba* is also fond of causing quarrels between good friends." So, as well as monitoring the entry- and exit-ways through which "all that is evil and unpleasant" can be either "attracted or repelled," Legba also functions as a trickster in "causing quarrels between good friends." In this capacity he is clearly functioning in the role associated with the archetypal trickster figure known in Africa and its diaspora variously as Legba, Eshu, Esu-Elegba(ra), Ananse, Ogo-Yurugu, Papa La-Bas, and so forth (Pelton 1980; Gates 1988).

The deceptions of the trickster are indeed consonant with Legba's other characteristics, which I sum up here as "empowerment object," guardian of thresholds, gatekeeper of welfare and health. Community *legbawo* (called *du-legba*) protect entire villages, settlements, or towns, and can trick contagious diseases hovering at the threshold and "dissuade them from executing their plans" (Cudjoe-Calvocoressi 1974:59). When an evil spirit wishes to enter the community, *legbawo* reportedly invite them to be guests and then subvert the spirit's plans by manipulating their movements. In the 1970s Cudjoe-Calvocoressi (1974:59) remarked, "It is still very firmly believed that the *Du-Legba* is able to prevent sickness from entering the town. Diseases are envisaged as entering a settlement in the form of spirits."

These remarks open the door to issues about perception, experience, and cultural logic. My own inquiries about perceptions and experiences with *legbawo* yielded a complex range of responses and beliefs, the subjective nature of which was clearly beyond the scope of what Cudjoe addressed in her brief articles. And yet, to a certain extent Cudjoe's statements still seemed to endure. While a number of *mɔfialawo* emphatically stated that *legbawo* were "fetishes which Christianity has shown us must be abolished" (and these individuals often claimed to feel no effects whatsoever from the presence of *legbawo* everywhere they turned or walked), most people held nearly the opposite opinion and were reluctant to even discuss the role *legbawo* played in their experiences and lives. Such "empowerment objects" were a delicate subject, and many people were understandably reluctant to discuss it with foreigners, who had historically misportrayed their beliefs and practices as "primitive." But from the deference people paid to the *legbawo* that populated Srɔgboe and neighboring communities, it was clear to me that they still sustained a lively role in the (health-oriented) affairs of most Anlo-speaking people and that their movements were attended to and palpably felt. The following account may illustrate more clearly what I mean.

Legbawo "empowerment objects" held various forms, ranging from visibly dramatic and well-defined statues (see Cudjoe 1969 and Gilbert 1982) to amorphous and almost indiscernible objects, items, or "blobs." Compounds were typically enclosed spaces, surrounded by either a palmfrond fence or a cement-block wall, and outside the entrance to most would sit a *legba*. Indeed, underneath a corrugated iron roof immediately outside the compound in Srɔgboe where I resided sat a *legba*. I expected to see occasional alterations to this *legba*'s environment, such as the appearance of liquids, chicken feathers, or herbs in his enclosure. While such objects were frequently there, I was never present when they were placed on or near the *legba*. Inside the compound, however, near my neighbor's doorway, was a more puzzling object not particularly comprehensible to me since it did not look the way I thought a *legba* should appear.[19] It resembled a stone embedded in the earth, with a round (approximately eight-inch diameter) section protruding through the dirt. One day I drove into the compound, and as I approached my house the tire of the car passed over this "rock." I was startled—feeling a strong jolt in my body—and then felt rather uneasy for the next few days. My husband told me that he was quite certain that rock was a *legba,* but as time passed I let the experience slip from my mind.

Months later we were in Accra visiting with two members of the family—a journalist and a customs officer employed by the government. Abruptly the journalist asked, "All the time you drive the car in and out

of the compound, have you ever run over that stonelike object in front
of Kuya's house?" Startled by the question, I answered in the affirmative
and then asked why he wanted to know. But my question went unan-
swered and a rather heated discussion ensued between the journalist and
the customs officer as to whether or not this "violation" was serious and
warranted further attention. They eventually determined that since I was
an outsider and had virtually no knowledge or understanding of this object, the normal rules did not really pertain. They instructed me to re-
frain from running the car over the stone and then changed the subject
of our discussion (cf. Geurts in press for a lengthier account of this event).

Soon after that I recounted this series of events to my friend Raphael.
He explained that in the first instance what I had experienced while driving over the stone would fit in the realm of *seselelame*: hearing, feeling
some phenomenon through the body, flesh, or skin. Raphael explained
that while I could not necessarily *see* the trappings of any kind of sacred
or "empowerment object" around that specific stone (which I later
learned is technically called an *afeli* [Adikah 2001] but which functions
like a *legba*), I had felt or heard its power in some other way. I related
the story to Raphael during a discussion about invisible forces, thresholds, *seselelame, legba,* and *ʤoka.* When one crossed a threshold and
there was something amiss, he explained, one experienced *seselelame*:
hearing or feeling through the body. One did not necessarily know what
it was and usually neglected to "think" about or recognize the experience, but then the person might become sick shortly after the event.
Thresholds were places of vulnerability where invisible forces could lurk
or hide and attack unsuspecting people as they arrived home. For this
reason the protection of Legba was important. "So, if you become sick,"
I asked, "could you go to Korle-Bu (the largest public hospital in Ghana)
and explain to the doctor that you had this *seselelame* one day as you
came in, and then a couple days later you began to fall ill?" Raphael
laughed at my question and replied, "No, you would not talk like that
to a doctor at Korle-Bu. You would simply report to him that you had
fever and had been feeling certain aches and pains."[20]

As our conversation progressed, however, Raphael began to appreciate why I asked this question. "Yes, I may get sick and go to Korle-Bu,"
he commented, "but then remember the *seselelame* from a few days before as I came through the door. I would not discuss it with the doctor,
but just take what the doctor prescribed and then additionally go to consult with *ŋkuetɔtɔwo* or *etogatɔwo.*" *Ŋkuetɔtɔwo* (*ŋku*: eye; *etɔ*: three;
tɔ: agent; *wo*: plural) were people who could see beyond what ordinary

human beings could see, or people with a third eye; and *etogatɔwo* (*(e)to:*
ear; *ga:* large, great; *tɔ:* agent; *wo:* plural) were people with magnified
hearing or a large ear, people who could hear things that ordinary people could not hear. After consulting with ŋkuetɔtɔwo or *etogatɔwo*, the
person might return to the threshold and detect (through observation,
touch, smell, or taste) traces of a black powder or some other substance
that they had not seen or perceived when originally coming through the
door.

Thresholds, then, were for many people an eminently dangerous site,
an area where highly charged and typically invisible forces could lurk
and attack.[21] This perception held true for the threshold of a community, compound, household, or an individual person, so Legba was called
upon to monitor (and even to "seize and collect at one place") what
passed over the thresholds of these various domains, manipulating senses
of movement. Furthermore, that which passed over thresholds had the
potential to harm or seriously impair the household or community's
health and well-being, and so "empowerment objects" were often employed to protect people from such threats. Finally, sight was not the
sense to rely on as one crossed a threshold; other senses or other aspects
of *seselelame,* such as hearing a faint sound or noting an unusual smell,
might indicate that something was amiss. Only a fool, many people expressed, would pay attention to merely those things perceived by the
eyes. How was one to cope with the demands of all these potential invisible powers lurking around thresholds and hovering about in other
spaces and corners? For many Anlo-speaking people, the answer lay in
practices of *vodu* and in related philosophical notions that emphasized
interoceptive and internal modes of knowing beyond the five fields of
sight, touch, taste, hearing, and smell.

VODU METAPHYSICS: POWER GLEANED
FROM "RESTING TO DRAW THE WATER"

Ewe and Fon are closely related languages, and the term *vodu,* or *vodun,*
refers to ancient concepts and philosophical views that were pervasive
among Anlo speakers with whom I worked and that seem to be widespread among many Ewe and Fon speakers in coastal areas spanning
Ghana, Togo, and Benin. One of Blier's Fon-speaking informants explained to her (1995:40), "Life is a pool that humans come into this
world and find. We must be patient. When you are born in a family you

must learn patience. If an adult is speaking, you must open your ears and listen. If you are patient and hear what one says, the pool that is the source of life, you will take from it. It is for this reason that one says *vodun, vodun,* 'rest to draw the water; rest to draw the water.'"

Little agreement existed among my Anlo-speaking *mɔfialawo* about the precise meaning or designation of the Ewe term *vodu*. As mentioned earlier, it was interchangeable in many people's minds with other words such as *trɔ* or *legba*. One can appreciate this divergence by considering how many Euro-Americans might argue over exactly what constitutes a *spirit* as compared to a saint, ghost, phantom, demon, apparition, god, deity, angel, and so forth. Etymologically, however, we can better understand the term *vodu* by analyzing its component parts. In Ewe, *vo* is said by some to mean "to be at leisure, be disengaged and free," or "to rest and be at ease" (Westermann 1973[1928]:268), while *du* is often translated as "snatch away, tear, pull," and *du tsi* refers to "fetching or pulling water" (as from a well) (Westermann 1973[1928]:17). (But for an alternate etymology of *vodu,* see Rosenthal 1998:174). Embedded in these morphemes are glimpses of what Blier's informant meant by his statement "*vodun, vodun:* rest to draw the water," which harken back to our analysis of *ŋlɔ* as a sign of a cultural preponderance for inward focus. Why then has *vodu* often been translated or conceptualized (particularly among scholars) as a cult, a religion, a god, or even reduced to a material object such as a charm or statuelike idol (a fetish)?

My own research reveals that many Anlo-speaking people perceived and talked about *vodu* more as a philosophy than as a religion or even a spirit. An epistemological comparison of *vodu* with two other cosmological phenomena—*trɔ* and *legba*—may begin to establish the distinctiveness of what I call "*vodu* metaphysics." At first glance the following discussion by Gilbert seems to suggest that *vodu* has a tangible and visible dimension (or that *vodu* can be conceptualized as representationally embodied small gods), but a deeper reading actually supports an alternative view, that *vodu* is much more amorphous and indeterminate than other cosmic phenomena such as *legba* or *trɔ*.

> *Vodu* ... are protective gods brought from Benin and Nigeria; they can be bought and owned by certain individuals. *Vodu* may be represented in the form of a big calabash or merely by a bunch of herbs in a small container, but they can also take the same form as *alegba* or *du-legba.*...Like *alegba* and *du-legba, vodu* images are found along the roadside or outside the entrance to houses. They are sometimes grouped with *alegba,* but one visual

> distinction is often made between them. While *vodu* are sometimes left un-
> covered, as are *alegba,* usually they are completely enclosed inside a conical
> thatched hut. *Alegba* and *du-legba* are never so enclosed. (Gilbert 1982:62)

My own experiences in Anlo-land require making this distinction more
emphatic: *vodu* were rarely (if ever) left uncovered and probably always
"completely enclosed inside a conical thatched hut." Therefore, while
Gilbert provides a hint of the perceptory distinctions we find among
vodu, trɔ, and *legba,* I would take it further and suggest that a *trɔ* was
generally perceived as having a kind of "personality" as well as bodily
features and actual sensory abilities or sensibilities (Fiawoo 1959a:51).
Fiawoo even goes so far as to state (1959a:76) that "anthropomorphic
character and personality are without question ascribed to the *trowo*"
(trɔwo is the plural form of *trɔ).* In contrast, *vodu* fell more in the realm
of metaphysics, being more like a power, a philosophy, or even a *state-
of-being* harnessed through "resting to draw the water" and interoceptively known. In informal discussions some Anlo-speaking people characterized *vodu* as "some kind of power," whereas others refused to make
clear distinctions in their daily experiences. Thus I agree with Gilbert
(1982:62), who writes that "*Du-legba, alegba,* and *vodu* relate to many
facets of Ewe experience, details of which may not always be readily ver-
balized by the people themselves."

These issues of perception, distinction, or ability to verbalize their experiences of *vodu* are illustrated in an interview I recorded with a man
I call Mr. Tamakloe, who lived in Anloga. Our discussion, edited extensively for inclusion here, suggests that *vodu* represents something like
"practices and rituals," which is consonant with Blier's (1995) portrayal
of *vodun* and with a deeper and more complex perspective on *vodu* as
a metaphysical power and manipulation of the senses through practices
rooted in "resting to draw the water."

> *Mr. Tamakloe:* With the Anlo, we have all these things: the *trɔ,* the *vodu.*
> All of them are intertwined. There is an element of *vodu* in
> *trɔ:* things like that.
>
> *KLG:* So how would you translate *vodu* into English?
>
> *Mr. Tamakloe:* Vodu, hmmm. It's very difficult to translate. Practices. Ritu-
> als. And with the *trɔwo,* rituals are there. It is very difficult
> to draw a line between the *vodu* and the *trɔwo.* Very
> difficult. Because some things that are used with the *trɔ* can
> be used over here too [he explained this while motioning
> from one hand to the other].
>
> *KLG:* So the *trɔ* are mostly deities?

Mr. Tamakloe: Yes, deities.

      KLG: And then the *vodu?*

Mr. Tamakloe: Practices and rituals. *Vodu* is more or less the combination of these cult practices.

      KLG: *Vodu* would encompass the *trɔ,* the shrine that concerns a specific *trɔ?* [I tried to understand].

Mr. Tamakloe: Well, another aspect of the *trɔ.* Like *voduda* [a snake]: *voduda* is part of Yeve. And some other ones, like Kɔkuʋu.

      KLG: Kɔkuʋu? The people who use knives?

Mr. Tamakloe: Yes, Kɔkuʋu. That is a *vodu.*

      KLG: That's a *vodu?* I'm not sure I understand. You are saying that *vodu* means certain rites, certain practices that people in the Kɔkuʋu sect engage in?

Mr. Tamakloe: Yes, practices. *Kɔku* is the knife. They begin to cut, but it doesn't bleed [if the devotees have been faithful].

      KLG: So some of what they do is *vodu?* [I tried to clarify].

Mr. Tamakloe: Right.... In most cases *vodu* is related to herbal knowledge. Some herbs you can use for this thing, others for another thing. They can put it at the place where a shrine is. When you get deep into *vodu,* it is herbal knowledge.

      KLG: So when you build a *legba,* you use *vodu?* You put something under it?

Mr. Tamakloe: Yes, you put something into it. But they won't tell you how they made it. It's secret knowledge.

In this exchange it became apparent that *vodu* was conceptualized as practices, rituals, customs, and conventions of the various sects—or "orders" in Rosenthal's (1998) parlance—and it was integrally tied to herbal or *secret* knowledge. Thus, in this way *vodu* was drawn on in constructing *legba* figures; *vodu* was drawn on in communicating or interacting with a *trɔ;* and *vodu* was drawn on for empowerment within the context of various religious sects such as Kɔkuʋu, Blekete, or Yeve.[22] When examined through the lens of the sensorium, *vodu* strikes us as a culturally patterned way of manipulating sensory engagements—with other persons, with animals and plants, with nature spirits, with lineal ancestors, and so forth—in order to affect well-being and health.[23]

While experiences with *vodu* seemed to range from very positive to extremely negative, the health of most Anlo-speaking people depended (to a certain extent) on what I call a "metaphysics of *vodu.*" Positively employed, *vodu* was like prayer and meditation, working as a leveling effect on the body and the mind (or in terms of the nondualistic *sesele-*

lame), empowering one's sense of both balance and well-being. Negatively experienced, however, *vodu* was a source of disturbance, terror, and fear. Either way, few Anlo-speaking people could truly escape an awareness and knowing of *vodu,* for as a metaphysical orientation it maintained a deep conceptual and embodied hold if largely in the unconscious. The following vignette, related to me in 1992 by a midwife I call Janice, makes this point.

Janice grew up in the Volta Region of Ghana, in and around what was deemed the Anlo homeland, but as an adult she spent about twelve years in Britain training as a nurse-midwife. She then returned to her hometown in the Volta Region and built a "maternity home," or what we might call a "women's health clinic." When I worked with her she was an active and high-level member of the professional organization known as the Ghana Registered Midwives Association, and she continued to travel abroad to conferences and for pleasure. While Janice professed mostly scorn and disbelief in *vodu* and related phenomena, she took me to meet a priest of a *vodu* center near her clinic and home. She felt that as a student of Anlo-Ewe culture I needed to be exposed to all facets of life, but she did not conceal her belief that this man was ignorant, superstitious, and backward. She also knew that he was opposed to her efforts to bring "development" and health-care services to this area. In serving together on a local district council, she felt that he blocked her efforts to educate and improve the quality of life of young women and was against her efforts to disburse information about family planning, contraception, and AIDS. She felt his attitudes were directly related to his "traditional religious beliefs," which included the relegation of women to childbearing and domestic service. Accordingly, I was received by this *vodu* priest in a less than warm and cordial way, and the meeting was quite brief and uneventful. However, as we left the center, Janice recounted the following story.

When she returned from Britain in the early 1970s, Janice had cause to interact (on a number of occasions) with various members of this *vodu* center. At the end of one particular meeting they suggested she bring a goat to sacrifice at the shrine. Holding strongly negative beliefs about such "sacrificial rituals," Janice went home and forgot the request. A week later she became ill, visited the (hospital) doctor, took several courses of medicine, but failed to improve. Janice explained that she felt not only fatigued but also "hounded by something" as if it were "hovering" about her or "following" her around.

One day shortly thereafter Janice ran into an acquaintance who had studied the art of "spiritual healing." Without her reporting anything to him about her illness, the man suggested to Janice that something was following her. He expressed intense concern, explaining that it was invisible so he did not expect she could see it but wondered whether she had been experiencing some kind of "shadow effect." He asked if she had made a promise and failed to fulfill it. Despite her surprise at his acute perception of her sensations, Janice remembered no promise and the sickness endured. Weeks later she suddenly recalled the demand for a goat made by members of the *vodu* shrine, and she realized this "coerced promise" fit her healer friend's notion of the etiology of her illness. She promptly delivered a goat to the *vodu* priest, and after months of having felt desperately ill, Janice reported that she recovered within two or three days.

This story illustrates a continuity between the experiential and the ontological. For Janice, *vodu* had an unconscious though clear link to her sense of well-being, even though she had strived (in a more or less cognitive or intellectual way) to disavow it, in part because of her adherence to Christianity. The metaphysics summed up in this experience involving *vodu* indicates in yet another way that *vodu* is not a superficial idea that can be easily discarded, nor is it a religious cult that can be joined. Rather, *vodu* is a deeply embodied phenomenon residing largely in the domain of *seselelame* while being pervasive in Anlo cultural logic: an idea reminiscent of Bourdieu's habitus (1977:78–95) as "history turned into nature."

In its purest meaning of "gleaning power from resting to draw water from a well," *vodu* calls upon Anlo-Ewe (and Fon) philosophical ideas about strength and resolve, or physical balance and health, deriving from an ancient reservoir symbolized by water deep in the earth. The symbology of water in Anlo contexts is quite powerful. One of the first cultural practices I learned during my sojourn in Anlo-land was to offer a cup of water to a guest immediately when she arrived at my home. Initially thinking of this as simply a practical gesture in such intense heat, only later did I begin to reflect on the symbolism of water, rituals of offering water to ancestors and guests, and the point I raised at the beginning of chapter 7: the fact that Anlo-land itself was surrounded by water. The Atlantic Ocean, the Volta River, and the Keta Lagoon: all bodies of water that provided essential sustenance and nourishment in Anlo worlds. Furthermore, in many outdooring ceremonies (which introduced a child to the family, community, and universe) water was sprinkled on the baby's body, thereby exposing the child to essential elements. When I asked the seemingly straightforward question of why water was important, people were incredulous. "We must have water, we are made of water, our bodies would perish without water," one person impatiently declared. After the birth of a baby in Kplɔtɔkɔ, family members, the midwife, and I poured libations, and I asked once again why water was used as an offering to the ancestors. "Water is precious. We come from water before we are born. And when we die they put us in the ground where we are back with the water. We all need water, and we must share water with all those we encounter—including the ancestors." The task of "fetching water" was one of the ways many children learned to master a sense of balance, through repeated efforts at placing a bucket on top of the head and carrying a load of water. In these and other ways, the recognition of water as tantamount to life itself could be observed in rituals and daily habits.

Experiences with *vodu,* then, ranged from very positive (among people who actively cultivated its powers) to extremely negative (among people who felt they had fallen victim to its force). Yet whether *vodu* was experienced as negative or positive, for Anlo-speaking people health was almost invariably related to metaphysical notions of *vodu.* Janice believed that *vodu* was not a legitimate or real thing. But when we analyze her perceptions and her experience and look at her story in ontological and epistemological terms, despite conscious efforts to disavow herself from *vodu,* Janice was involuntarily entangled in this metaphysics. To sustain one's health, Janice and many Anlo-speaking people maintained a consciousness about the potential of *vodu* and protected themselves from the negative side of *vodu* forces and power—as Janice did through her sacrifice of a goat. Protection was in part accomplished through employment of *dzokawo* or *dzosasa,* so the discussion will now turn to an examination of transformative arts.

DZOSASA: TRANSFORMATIVE ARTS

While living in Srɔgboe I had a dream that took place in a chemistry lab. In the dream a person handed me a stone (which fit perfectly into my hand) and then explained, "You can turn this into anything you like." Several days later I recounted the dream to my friend Raphael, and he stated simply, "That's *dzosasa.* You were dreaming about *dzosasa* or *dzoka.*"

The Anlo-Ewe word *dzo* has commonly been translated into English as "magic" or "charm" (see Westermann 1973[1928]:26), or it has been glossed using the more generalized West African term *juju*.[24] Variously conceptualized as fetish, amulet, sorcery, or medicine, at the root of *dzo* is the artistry, science, or sensibility of transformations of material and psychological states. Blier (1995:205–238) suggests similar interpretations for certain *vodun* art forms (especially *bociɔ*) in Fon and Ewe culture, demonstrating that many of the practices associated with these objects are intended not only to transmogrify matter but also (and perhaps more important) to alter mental and emotional states. Here I argue, therefore, that *dzosasa* can be conceptualized as transformative arts, and is a cultural practice aimed largely at manipulations of *seselelame*. Then in chapter 9 we turn to how *dzosasa* can be linked to sensory perception and (in fact) how *dzosasa* (as transformative practices) is emblematic of experiential connections among cosmic, social, and personal fields of well-being.

The section on *vodu* metaphysics raised the issue of the need for protection from malevolent forces and how this can involve employment of *dzoka* and manipulation of sensory fields. Fiawoo explains (1959a:76), "The term *dzosasa* encompasses the whole field of magical charms for both destructive and protective ends. A charm is normally a mixture of varied ingredients, including animal, mineral or vegetable matter." He lists (1959:77–81) eighteen classic "charms" aimed at transforming conditions such as the inability to conceive, the vulnerability of a newborn baby, weakness in battle, lack of success in love, and so forth. Blier's explanation of the relation between *bociɔ* (sculptural) forms and well-being among the Fon also illustrates the role of *dzosasa* in many Anlo-Ewe contexts, especially in regard to healing. Many people who practice arts such as *dzosasa* are focusing on what seems to be a contradictory valuation of both "constancy and transmutability" and this (Blier suggests) "corresponds with the principle aims of *bociɔ* sculptures in maintaining life and encouraging well-being, particularly by transforming and dissipating situations of difficulty or potential trauma" (Blier 1995:209). These "situations of difficulty or potential trauma" that need "transforming and dissipating" could include those listed previously or could involve something less formulaic than the "classic charms" cataloged by Fiawoo. For instance, my interest was in how people *perceived* situations of difficulty or potential trauma that needed dissipating or transforming. What kinds of phenomena were experienced and perceived as either the workings of *dzo* or in need of the influence of *dzo*? The following accounts are merely two from dozens described to me by various *mɔfialawo*.

Account One: A family moved into a house for which they had paid five years rent in advance. At night they *heard* the voices of people conversing on the first floor, they *smelled* the aroma of various soups and freshly cooked *akple* (a staple food for Ewe people, made from cassava and corn dough), and they *heard* the sounds of pots and pans being moved about in the kitchen. When they descended the stairs and entered the kitchen, however, they could *see* nothing out of place. Despite numerous consultations with diviners and specialists, nothing they did (no *dzokawo* that they employed) could combat this force, and they eventually moved out of the house.

Account Two: A student moved in with a middle-aged woman—a remote relative—when he first attended college. He began suffering from severe headaches and an inability to concentrate upon sitting down to study. Aspirins and other medically prescribed pharmaceuticals failed to relieve his symptoms. He consulted a diviner who was able to *see* the woman placing various *dzokawo* in his quarters. The diviner explained that the woman wanted her own son to succeed in school and had previously employed *dzosasa* to sabotage other young men staying in her house. The college student returned home, looked to *see* that a *dzoka* or two were indeed hidden in his room, and promptly moved out. He also employed his own *dzoka* to then prevent this situation from arising again.

The anecdotal nature of these accounts is readily apparent, and I did not even attempt to verify the "reality" of pots and pans moving in the night or to measure any markers of the headaches' etiology since authentication was not my goal. Rather, I was interested in the issue of *perception* and how cultural models connect to the social experiences of individuals (Jackson and Karp 1990:12).[25] *Dzosasa* was an old and important idea for many Anlo speakers, and when people experienced or perceived something they classified as *dzosasa* they were standing at the confluence of personal, social, and cosmic fields (of [well-] being). That is, a person might see, hear, feel, smell, or intuit something that in one circumstance might be perceived as a routine social phenomenon (cooking occurring in the kitchen) and in another situation as an extraordinary event (cooking occurring in the kitchen with no human beings present). With the addition of that last component (no human beings present), this phenomenon automatically became a "situation of difficulty or potential trauma" that needed "transforming and dissipating," so sensory manipulation was accomplished through *dzosasa*.[26]

In conclusion, this chapter outlines three dimensions of the cosmological system of many Anlo-speaking people: the basic structure or hierarchy of the cosmos, the role Nyigbla plays in the system, and a brief account of the phenomena of *legba, vodu,* and *dzoka.* It provides an exploration of how the senses manifest in the cosmic realm and how this influences or relates to the general province of health. At the beginning of the chapter I suggest that well-being is based in a consensus about or a common notion of sensed phenomena, sensed and perceived "realities," and interpretations of what is real, perceivable, imagined, fantasized, and so forth. I then explore some basic aspects of Anlo cosmological perceptions, such as Mawu-Segbo-Lisa as the experience of supreme (well-) being or as god, Nyigbla's ability to strike people dead, the role of one's *amedzoto* (ancestral sponsor) in shaping an individual's sensibility, and so forth. I suggest that a reinterpretation of their religious system, including a new analysis of specific components such as *vodu* and *dzosasa,* allows for an understanding of these as *practices and techniques for sensory manipulation aimed at influencing the balance of health.* In addition, approaching their traditional religion as a system of the body—as a metaphysics that emphasizes the interoceptive and introspective valuation highlighted in chapter 6—allows us to better understand the psychological influence *vodu* obtains throughout Anlo cultural worlds and not simply for individuals who state an explicit belief in *vodu.* This discussion focusing on the senses highlights some of the forces (many invisible) that are "known" to those who have grown up in the area and brings to the foreground specific sensibilities at play in Anlo-Ewe "intentional worlds."

I argue that many Anlo-speaking people hold complex notions of that which is beyond the visible realm, and they utilize multiple sensory fields (coalescing in *seselelame*) to discern what is happening around and inside of themselves. Their preponderance for the proprioceptive and interoceptive sensory modes that we saw exhibited in the discussion of the etymology of their name (from *ŋlɔ*) is repeated here in the focus on *vodu* as a system of metaphysical maintenance (keeping the inner world balanced). And *vodu* functions, in many ways, as a set of manipulable arts, ways of working with sensory fields to maximize knowing and maximize balance in regard to *seselelame.* For example, the account of a diviner perceiving Mr. Adzomada's *amedzoto* (ancestral sponsor) to be wearing shoes is enriched through understanding the local epistemological links between the sensory-emotional and the dispositional and vocational aspects of an individual's life. *Vodu* and other spiritual practices are thus shown to operate as a kind of sensorium beyond the body (some would call this a *virtual reality*), while holding a clear relationship to the sensorium instantiated in the body during child socialization. The ex-

ternal world is manipulated (through ritual and spiritual practices in
vodu and *dzosasa*) to affect the internal world (the *milieu intérior*); and
the inner world (psycho-emotional-sensory states, or what Anlo people
refer to as *seselelame*) is manipulated to change circumstances in their
external environment.

Clearly this discussion could be taken much further, and I therefore
suggest that this chapter simply opens the door to further research that
could delve into much deeper portrayals of the sensory dimensions of
Anlo and Ewe religious experience. But what has been accomplished here
is to demonstrate that well-being is inextricably tied to the cosmological, in many different ways, and the ontological ramifications of this
point are better understood with a grounding in local notions of sensory
fields and an Anlo-Ewe category (for feeling in the body) called *seselelame*. And finally, when we approach their traditional religious system
through the lens of the local sensorium, we find that the senses are deployed in culturally patterned ways to provide avenues for knowing and
engaging with lineal ancestors, nature spirits, and god.

CHAPTER 9

Well-Being, Strength, and Health in Anlo Worlds

I suggested in chapter 7 that well-being in many Anlo-speaking contexts is dependent on something that Thompson (1966) refers to as "an aesthetic of the cool." He argues that this principle of a cool, even-tempered stance is not only an important facet of Yoruba art, music, and dance, but it is "comparable to Cartesian philosophy in point of influence and importance" throughout West Africa (Thompson 1966:86). In the last chapter I took this focus on the "mediating principle in cool water" further with a reinterpretation of the local meaning of *vodu*. I showed how an ancient philosophy of *vodu* emphasizes the process of obtaining personal strength through "resting to draw the water," or meditating on the critical and sensual role that water plays in everyday life and health. What I have described for a *vodu* metaphysics in Anlo contexts parallels Thompson's point that the Yoruba "posit water, certain leaves, and other items as symbols of the coolness that transcends disorder and without which community is impossible" (1966:86). Toward that end, in chapter 7 we explored the balancing of heated and cool dancing at a local ritual in Srɔgboe, which was aimed at restoring the community's health and equilibrium.

An "aesthetic of the cool" can also be seen in certain child-rearing practices. Chapter 5 touched on the importance of aurality in a child's enculturation and described how "listening well" involved minding one's parents. Disobedience and obstinate behavior was sometimes dealt with (especially by older people) through "ear pulling" *(tohehe)*, which symbolized the importance of the ear and the emphasis on listening well in the process of becoming a moral person. In this vein, parents talked to me about teaching their children to hear certain things and let them pass right through the body, to remain cool and keep a collectedness of mind. To maintain stability and not become ill, it was important for children to learn a kind of maintenance or regulation of *seselelame* (hearing, feeling in the body) such that imbalances and overstimulation did not lead to impulsive and excessive behavior.

This chapter examines how well-being is integrally bound up with sensory experience and sensory engagements. I develop the ideas introduced in the last chapter by directly addressing various kinds of illnesses and afflictions, including the loss of certain sense modalities, in an effort to examine links between a sensorium and theories of disease. Here I am suggesting that recognition of the social basis of health and healing compels us to take account of variations in sensoriums because certain illness states may involve grounding in a sensory order different from the orthodox sensory order of a cultural group.[1] For instance, hearing things that those around you do not or cannot hear or seeing things that others deem invisible or nonexistent are symptomatic of insanity and losing one's grounding in reality, or at least indicate adherence to an alternate reality. In Anlo-Ewe speaking contexts, the notion of *se* or *sese* (as in *seselelame*) not only is the closest idea we have to the English term for *sensing* but also refers in their world to the ideas of *obedience* and *adherence,* which I suggest illustrates the way in which sensing grounds a person in the "intentional world(s)" shared with others. Conditions of insanity were expressed by many Anlo speakers as equivalent to the loss of all one's senses, and, conversely, sensing (as those around you sense and perceive things) forms a strong basis for the actual maintenance of sanity and adherence to what people think of as material reality. So I begin this chapter by laying out some general information about illness concepts but then move to an example of a specific affliction that involves the "sense of speech" *(nufofo)* and feelings in the mouth *(sesetonume).* This leads to further discussion of the somatic and sensory mode of attention that involves an "aesthetic of the cool," or keeping balanced and calm in an effort to prevent sickness.

ON *DƆTSOAFE* AND *GBƆGBƆMEDƆ:* "NATURAL" AND "SUPERNATURAL" TYPES OF DISEASE

When an individual became ill, it was usually referred to in Anlo-Ewe as "catching" or "seizing" sickness *(dɔlele).* Broadly speaking, there were two different categories of disease, described as "*dɔtsoafe* or sickness of natural causation and *gbɔgbɔmedɔ* or sickness of [a] supernatural" cause (Fiawoo 1959a:285). While Fiawoo used the English terms *natural* and *supernatural* to characterize the division, I was concerned that this distinction represented less how Anlo speakers thought about different sicknesses and was more of "a dichotomy that often appears in Western comments on non-Western medical theories" (Laderman 1991:15). Etymologically, *dɔtsoafe* (*dɔ:* sickness, illness; *tso:* from; *afe:* home) signified a common, everyday, household-type sickness, while *gbɔgbɔmedɔ* (*gbɔgbɔ:* spirit, ghost; *me:* in; *dɔ:* sickness) literally meant "a spirit in the sickness." Furthermore, *gbɔgbɔmedɔ* was not exactly considered "un-natural" since the spirit world was an organic and normal part of everyday experience. But illnesses labeled *gbɔgbɔmedɔ* were definitely not as common as those labeled "illnesses from home" *(dɔtsoafe);* and the former were somewhat unusual in that they posed a challenge for human beings in search of a cure. When I asked Anlo speakers to translate *gbɔgbɔmedɔ* into English, they usually said "a spiritual sickness" (rather than a "supernatural" or "unusual" illness). The salient feature of *gbɔgbɔmedɔ* seemed to be that embodied in the illness was almost literally a spirit; or, a spiritual component was a major aspect of this type of disease. This in turn implied that its cure was beyond the jurisdiction of humans, including many of the healers.

The determination for whether a disease or illness was classified as *dɔtsoafe* or *gbɔgbɔmedɔ* was rather complicated and circumstantial. However, in hoping for a neat and clear delineation, I asked whether *dɔtsoafe* would not include such illnesses as minor stomach aches *(dɔmeɖui),* headaches *(taɖuame),* and coughs *(kpe)* that dissipate or do not linger as well as malaria *(asra),* dysentery *(kpeta),* measles (*gbaɣi*), chicken pox (*aɖibaku*), and so forth. I suspected that *gbɔgbɔmedɔ* must cover inflictions such as infertility and *ɖikuiɖikui* (*ɖi:* to bear; *ku:* to die), in which the children of one woman consistently died, as well as *tohonɔfui,* contracted when a person was struck by lightening, or *gudɔ,* which constituted a puffiness or bloated condition associated with *enu* (a condition called "mouth," which will be described momentarily). The distinction was not what I anticipated, however, since any stomach ache, cough, or bout of malaria (for instance) could mutate into a spiritual sickness under various (and idiosyncratic) circumstances.[2] One specific kind of illness, called *enu,* illustrates how sensory models are integrally tied to health and loss of health, whether from spirits or sickness from the home.

ENU SEIZING THE MOUTH IN CASES
OF ANIMOSITY AND BAD WILL

Numerous times when I observed deliveries managed by a traditional birth attendant in and around Srɔgboe, I witnessed the effects of something Anlo-speaking people referred to as *enu,* or literally, "mouth." In cases where labor pains were severe or when there was a delay in labor, the traditional birth attendant usually brushed the woman's abdomen with a twelve-inch whisk in an effort to discard the causes of *enu. Enu,* they explained, was a very bad sickness that usually seized children but could also attack pregnant women. The cause of this illness, I was told, was bad will or enmity among household members or between people within the same family. Despite being closely associated with "the home," whether *enu* was classified as *dɔtsoafe* or *gbɔgbɔmedɔ* always depended on the specific case.

While the most common meaning of the word *enu* was simply "mouth," it could also be glossed as "opening, entrance, edge, brink, point; end, contents, amount, quantity; effect" (Westermann 1973[1928]:177). Why was this word used to describe this specific affliction? A child (or pregnant woman) would be seized with *enu* because of disrespectful, wicked, or evil things that passed through the mouths of people in the household. The state of *enu* (the sickness called "mouth") symbolized, to a certain extent, enmity and bad will flowing through openings and entrances and having an effect on the vulnerable—pregnant women and children in the house. (This is reminiscent of the significance of thresholds and our discussion of *legba* in chapter 8.) *Nufofo* (the sense of speaking) was thus believed to be one of the primary forces and channels involved in the etiology of *enu.*

Chapter 3 explored how *speaking* is not considered a sense in most contemporary Western cultures but that many societies do indeed count speech as part of their sensorium. Whereas our five-senses model reinforces the idea of the senses as natural faculties and as "passive recipients of data" and we think of speaking as involving "an active externalization of data" (and to be an acquired or learned skill), for many cultural groups the senses in general are conceived of as "media of communication" (Classen 1993b:2). We use our sensory apparatus not only to receive data (as in perceiving and "reading" other people and phenomena in our environment) but, as sensate creatures, we also employ our senses in acts of communication. In the same way that we touch not only to apprehend something but to make statements, many Anlo speakers conceptualize or imagine *nufofo* (speaking) in both active and passive modes. If *enu* results largely from *nufofo* (or from some aspect of or quality in the sense of speech), it illustrates how certain cultural models of sensing and embodiment are "linked to the social experience of the individual" (Jackson and Karp 1990:12).

That chapter also presented a cultural model in which *nufofo* (speaking) involved sound waves affecting the speaker while simultaneously traveling outward and enveloping the listener. Words in Anlo-land, therefore, were described as not simply thoughts or mental phenomena, but coming from the body as well as the mind (see Houston and Taube 2000 for similar claims about ancient Mesoamerica). As in other West African contexts, many Anlo speakers believed there was power not simply in "words as carriers of referential meaning, but in the sounds of the words" too (Stoller 1984b:568). Among the neighboring Fon speakers, "Critical to the activation potential of speech is both its transferential nature and its potent social and psychodynamic grounding" (Blier 1995:77). The "transferential nature" of *nufofo* (speaking) included more than imparting meaning or "mental ideas," for in *enu,* speaking was one of the culprits in the transference of emotional, psychological, and physiochemical disturbance. That is, when bad will or enmity was expressed in verbal exchange, it was not simply the meaning of the dialogue that caused children and pregnant women to fall sick, but rather children *sensed* the animosity and rancor and it was transferred to their very bodies in part through the striking action of the speech.[3] In regard to this "notion of speech as wielding an unknown potential: 'Speech is irreversible; that is its fatality. What has been said cannot be unsaid, *except by adding to it*'" (Blier 1995:76–77).[4] Once speech containing animus was externalized, children (and pregnant women) began absorbing the negative energy. In fact, through *sesetonume* (feeling in the mouth) one could absorb one's own bad speech, so speaking was believed to be one of the primary forces involved in the etiology of *enu.* Children, on the other hand, were not believed to contract *enu* from their own *sesetonume,* or feelings in the mouth, but rather through bodily absorption of the physical power of the words.[5]

These acrimonious exchanges, characterized locally as *enu,* generally resulted in a serious illness such as one that some Anlo-speaking people called *gudɔ.* While I never observed a case of *gudɔ,* it was described for me as a condition in which the person exhibited "puffiness," was swollen, inflamed, or "blown up." Westermann (1973[1928]:79) defined it as "a sickness acquired by committing a wrong," but some *mɔfialawo* I consulted deemed that description incorrect. That is, if *enu* seized a child and it resulted in *gudɔ,* it was the wrong-doing of *other members of the family* that caused the disorder and not a transgression on the part of the child himself. The way in which Westermann's explanation was acceptable to certain *mɔfialawo,* however, was twofold. First of all, he translated it as "dropsy," or edema (Westermann 1973[1928]:78), which people considered an accurate gloss for the "puffiness" they perceived when children absorbed the animosity. Second, and more to the heart of philosophical issues, people did not become ill all on their own, but rather sickness was due in part to the influences of those around the individual. With these elements of the cultural model firmly in hand, several *mɔfialawo* agreed with Westermann's observation (1973[1928]:78) that *gudɔ* was a result of trespassing "against acknowledged laws of decency, respect or reverence," and they added that when the family as a unit committed such a wrong, someone was bound to suffer from *gudɔ* or to acquire *enu* of another form. The transgressions of the family were appropriated into the body of the child (or occasionally a pregnant woman); these individuals thereby contracted *gudɔ* or exhibited symptoms from another manifestation of the larger category of afflictions referred to by many Anlo speakers as *enu* (see Riesman 1992:109 for a similar condition among the Fulani).

How was *enu* diagnosed and cured? *Enu* could be detected by any of the main types of Anlo healers: *bokɔ,* or Afa priests; *amɛgashi,* or diviners; *gbedala* and *atikewɔla,* or herbalists and "root doctors"; and also by *vixela* (midwives and traditional birth attendants). Whether the average person without special training or experience could recognize *enu* was not very clear, though most people seemed to believe it was necessary to consult a specialist. Often a child was initially taken to a clinic, but after injections and pharmaceuticals failed to produce results, the family would confer with a diviner, herbalist, or another popular medical practitioner. Ultimately, I was informed, the proper authority was a member of the Amɛ clan. Indeed, Nukunya explained in his ethnography that members of the Amɛ clan "have the prerogative of settling any dispute between kinsfolk that has resulted in sickness for one or both parties *(nugbidodo)*" (Nukunya 1969b:196). Included among the various taboos prescribed for this clan, members were not allowed to "be *held by the ear.* If held by one ear by mistake the other ear must also be held" (Nukunya 1969b:195, emphasis added). Those who performed reconciliation could not let their auditory organs be pulled, tampered with, or harmed. With the root of *enu* (or a major dimension of its cause) being "mouth" and *nufofo,* or speaking, it was striking that those people charged with the responsibility of curing this affliction (or laying the groundwork of reconciliation that would allow healing to take place) had to guard their own aural channels.

Several different rituals seemed to be applicable in cases where *enu* had occurred. One *mɔfiala* explained that "you perform arbitration and rites. You put herbs into a bowl. You 'say your say' [speak the things that you have grievances about] and drop them into the bowl [actually an earthenware pot]. The other party does the same. You both wash your hands in the water. This heals the enmity." Another *mɔfiala,* Fiagbedzi the teacher, described two different rituals (one involving fire, the other based in the potency of saliva), which I observed performed on numerous occasions. In the following quote from an audiotaped interview, Fiagbedzi used the term "incinerator" to mean the designated area in the compound or ward where garbage was routinely burned, and by "pot" he meant the covered barrel or clay pot in which drinking water was stored within the home.

> [E]*nu* kills very quickly. It is a spiritual disease, but you see it physically in that a child can be vomiting, or have swelling. You use certain herbs, or you take the child to the incinerator. You put the child near the incinerator, then you use the broom. You can put something on the ground early in the morning, or late in the evening, and place the child on it. Then you start to say some words, all the things that you have been doing: if they are the things which have been worrying the child, they must go into the incinerator, to discard the bad will, discard or destroy the "garbage." Mostly children get *nu*, not many adults. You don't see it clearly (or much) among adults. It is in the children, almost all the reflection goes into the children: it is there that we get to know the parents [or other members of the household, compound, family] are not on good terms. They do things that they shouldn't do to each other.
>
> During birth there must be certain rituals. The pregnant woman may not be on good terms with others in the house. That [bad will] can prevent the childbirth. They must take the pregnant woman near to the pot. She must take the water and spit it onto the pot three times—thinking that everyone goes there to drink the water, and therefore you are now trying to reconcile with other people. You take the water into you, and you spit it out three times, onto the pot, so we assume you have settled any dispute with others....
>
> During festivals, at Hogbetsotso on reconciliation day, they are doing the same thing—reconciliation—because it is also *nu*. The paramount chief may be doing bad things which the subchiefs cannot see. He knows that certain things may have gone on all over but they cannot come to him and say it, so it is because of that he goes there to say it: "You people have been doing this, this, this, and it has been making me angry but I couldn't say it,

so it is today that I want to let you know it is bad, the things you have been doing are bad." Then a subchief will stand up and say all the things that the paramount chief has been doing which have annoyed the subchiefs, and they couldn't say it. "All these things we have been doing against each other! We must have peace." So they bring those things together, and spit onto themselves. Then peace has come. All these things are called *enu* or just plain *nu* from the word for "mouth."

In efforts to deal with *enu* in both childbirth and in reconciliation ceremonies of the body politic, I frequently observed ritual spitting or spraying water from the mouth. Among the neighboring Fon, "in the saliva *(atan)* that one spits, accumulate the mysterious magical forces that emanate from humans" and "[t]o put saliva on someone or an object constitutes ... the accompaniment of a wish" (Blier 1995:78). Furthermore, in conversations with numerous Anlo-speaking people about important practices that their children were required to learn, rinsing the mouth immediately upon waking in the morning (before greeting or speaking to anyone) was consistently offered. Again, a similar practice has been documented among the Fon: " '[T]he mouth as an organ of speech charged with power, should, to expulse the harmful magical forces that accumulate in the saliva at night, be vigorously rinsed in the morning before addressing the greetings to no matter whom. The filth of the mouth *(nugbe)* designates the words of quarrel between adversaries' " (Blier 1995:380). What *enu* illustrates is a cultural model for what Blier calls the "activation potential" of the sense of speech. An individual's experience of speech occurs in the context of the recognition that enmity or bad will can become embodied in the affliction called *enu* and can literally kill.

Not in Anlo culture per se, but among Ewe people devoted to Gorovodu, there exists an ethics of speech that reflects the notion that "speech is not just one's words or a repetition of other's words; it also involves accents, scowls and tears, rage and seduction, all sorts of (everybody's) gestures. Speech is also the mass of words inside, thoughts and plans that must finally come out" (Rosenthal 1998:191). There is a sanction against acting without thinking in Gorovodu and support for consulting with the gods. Anlo-Ewe people with whom I worked also stressed the strong links between speech and *seselelame* (feeling in the body) and the importance of letting rancor or negativity pass right through.

The sense of speaking among both Anlo-Ewe and Fon speakers clearly holds a "transferential nature and ... potent social and psychodynamic grounding" (Blier 1995:77). Therefore, a proverb used occasionally in Euro-American contexts, "Sticks and stones may break my bones, but words will never hurt me," would probably not ring true for many Anlo people. So the "transferential nature" of *nufofo* (speaking) includes more than imparting meaning or "mental ideas," for in *enu*, speaking is one of the culprits in the transference of emotional and physiological disturbance, especially to children. In the presence of an acrimonious verbal exchange, it is not simply the meaning of the dialogue that causes children and pregnant women to fall sick, but rather it is perceived as a phenomenon of *seselelame* (feeling in the body), and the animosity and rancor are transferred to their bodies in part through the striking action of the sound of speech itself. It is not simply the hearing of an argument and the consequent psychological effect that are at stake here, but rather the notion that once speech containing animus is externalized, adults can absorb their own anger through *sesetonume* (feeling in the mouth) and children absorb the rancor through *seselelame* (feeling in the body, flesh, or skin). To prevent such absorption, one older *mɔfiala*, Adzoa Kokui, explained that it was important for children to learn to hear things and let them pass right through the body. This perspective illustrates how a central notion of well-being involves maintaining an "aesthetic of the cool" discussed earlier, or a regulation of sensory stimulation. Speech in this context moves out of the cognitive or purely psychological domain, and the sensory and bodily dimensions of verbal exchange come to the foreground.[6]

BEING WITHOUT SENSES: EXPERIENCES AND SYMBOLISM OF "ALTERNATIVE SENSORY MODES"

Are blindness, deafness, or the inability to walk illnesses? Here I examine how Anlo-speaking people conceptualized and treated sensory and somatic modes that were different from those of the norm in their "indigenous sensorium."

Chapter 5 introduced the idea that flexibility was highly valued among Anlo-speaking people through a discussion of how babies are massaged and their joints flexed early in life in order to create supple, lithe bodies and flexible people. Chapter 6 took this topic further by noting connections between this somatic mode of attention to flexibility and a cultural logic emphasizing adaptability and accommodation to differing ways of life. While I am not suggesting there is a simplistic causal relationship between mothers flexing the joints of newborn babies and Anlo-speaking adults then holding a flexible psychological orientation, I am suggesting that an interest in and attention to flexibility is a cultural value that exists among many Anlo-speaking people on a physical level and as a theme elaborated in various areas of their cultural logic.[7] In terms of alternative sensory modes, this attitude and approach based on a kind of pliability is also revealed in the stance many people took toward blindness, deafness, and so on. As one *mɔfiala* explained, "There are no throw-away people in Anlo society; everyone counts." Therefore, despite a person's inability to hear, see, or move about on both legs, many people expressed that the individual could still function in some vital role within the community.

The Grave Implications of Tokuno, or Deafness

Responses to the inquiry of which sense modality was the worst to lose were very idiosyncratic. Some *mɔfialawo* said that sight was the worst physical loss, others perceived it to be easier to operate without being able to see than to function without the ability to hear, and a few talked of their misery when (due to an illness) they temporarily lost sensations of taste and smell. It would therefore be misleading to suggest that all Anlo-speaking people held a unified, homogenous attitude toward the problem of which sense was the worst one to lose. The graveness with which people spoke of the condition of being deaf, however, was quite striking.

Interviewing Elaine one day, I asked her to explain a saying from a book of Ewe proverbs (Dzobo 1975:204), which seemed to suggest something about the value of hearing: *foleatikɔe be sese kple ame ɖokuisinɔnɔ* (The kite says that hearing and readiness go together). She answered, "Oh, that is another dialect. We Anlos say *Avako be sese kple ɖokuisinɔnɔ. Avako* is a hawk (and also the word for kite). Anlos don't like this bird. When it cries over your head, this means that bad news is coming. Or when it lands two or three times on your rooftop, there is bad news coming. So, yes, 'hearing and readiness go together.' When you hear the *avako* cry, you must brace yourself and be ready. Or when you hear the gunfire blast, you must run away. If you don't hear the noise of the gun, they will capture you. So if you are deaf, it is a handicap: you cannot be ready, you cannot respond. If you can't hear, you will stay there, and then the buffaloes will chop you!" (meaning that you would be eaten by wild animals).

Indeed, a prominent Anlo-speaking scholar suggested that being without hearing was the worst state since it caused complete disorientation.

He would probably be in agreement with the idea that in regard to "the sensorium of the blind and deaf: 'one who sees without hearing, is much more perplexed, and worried, than the one who hears without seeing.' The blind ... have a more 'peaceful and calm disposition,' for it is easier to make sense of sound without sight than it is to make sense of vision without sound" (Synnott 1993:148). This particular *mɔfiala* articulated nearly the same perspective, and then proposed that going deaf actually shattered *all* one's senses, especially balance. If a person lost her sense of hearing, he indicated, it would disturb the organ in her ear related to balancing.

As was discussed in chapter 5, balancing *(agbagbaɖoɖo)* was such an important function in Anlo-land that the inability to balance signified a kind of failure to *become* or *be human* and was tantamount to the existence of wild animals or bush creatures crawling about on four legs. In a similar vein, I asked Adzoa Kokui what they called people who either did not hear well or who refused to listen well, and she offered the word *gbemelawo*—which connotes wild animals or creatures in the bush. She explained that not listening well or going deaf made you behave like *gbemelawo*—bush animals who had no family structure and ran wild through the forests and hills. Disobedience was one form of not listening well, but it seemed that losing the ability to hear was perceived as a very grave condition that disoriented a person and handicapped more general use of the various sensory functions such that it could make a person literally go wild or become insane. In the course of my fieldwork I did not meet or encounter anyone in Anlo-land who had lost their hearing or was deaf, so this account is unfortunately limited to what people thought and reported about hearing impairments. I did, however, interact with several blind people.

Ŋkuno *or Loss of Sight*

A common proverb was often cited by people as a way of capturing what they perceived of as kind of a cultural orientation toward loss of various sense modalities. The saying claimed, "If a blind man says he is going to stone you, be sure that he has his foot set on a stone" *(Ne ŋku-gbag-batɔ be yele kpe fu ge wo la, nyae be ɖee wo ɖo afɔ kpe dzi)*. This proverb seemed to suggest that sight was by no means the only sense that allowed one to actively participate in life. It implied that even if people had lost their vision, they still possessed other faculties on which they could rely (such as *touch,* in that his foot was in contact with a stone, and *hearing,* since he could detect the person's location through listening to the voice or sound of movement). Indeed, this saying seemed to sum up a fairly common attitude among many Anlo speakers toward people with altered sensory modes. When I asked what it was like to be without sight, people often pointed out that a blind person could still hear, speak, and walk. When I asked what it was like to be without sound, they often insisted that the person was still able to see. As for being lame, their logic was that one still had the ability to hear, speak, see, and use one's mind. Questions on this topic, therefore, tended toward a rather circuitous discussion or a circular form of logic, but emerging as the essence was the notion that people who had lost abilities in one sensory field were still expected to lead full and productive lives.

The cultural logic exhibited in this attitude illustrates the idea of flexibility. For instance, a blind man who lived in our village would regularly venture into the lagoon, setting out nets and capturing fish. A young woman in the community, who walked with a pronounced limp and used a cane, still balanced items on her head and was still the object of a great amount of attention from young men who flirted with her and considered her appealing and pleasant. The point is that loss of sight (or any one specific sensory function) did not equal total impairment and was not perceived as an outright handicap or an impaired state of being. Instead, dexterity was the expectation in that people were required to do what they could with the faculties they still possessed, and such differences were no reason to shun or treat people with a lack of regard.

Not long after I arrived in Anlo-land I came down with a minor medical problem that I was confident could be treated with some nonprescription drugs, and my hosts directed me to what they deemed a particularly reliable pharmacy in Anloga. When I walked in and began discussing my problem with the pharmacist, I was quite surprised to discover that the man was completely blind. After he listened to my symptoms, he turned around, walked to the glass cases lining the back wall, and silently counted shelves and jars to locate several different remedies he thought would work. He brought them over to the counter, showed me each one, and informed me of their respective merits. After this experience I asked numerous people whether they were uncomfortable having a blind man dispensing medications in their community. They usually brushed it off with a comment such as, "Oh, as for him, we've known him for so long." Or they would say, "You can trust him; he knows what he's doing." Such comments revealed more than attitudes simply toward blindness. As I explained in chapter 2, Anlo-speaking people conducted a great deal of their business among other Anlo or Ewe-speaking people, even when residing in Accra or other major cities. That is, commercial transactions occurred largely in the context of familial and language-based networks, and (more to the point) they were conducted mostly with people one knew. In comparison, the impersonal nature of many commercial transactions in other cultural settings meant that first impressions and "appearances" counted more heavily. A pharmacy with a blind man behind the counter would probably not be successful in a system where impersonal transactions were the norm. In Anlo-land, on the other hand, the pharmacist's blind condition was inconsequential since most people (most families) knew him, and they knew he kept track of the medications contained in his various vessels. Blindness in this context did not prevent individuals from contributing something to the community and from leading active lives.

Tekuno-Buno: *Lameness and the Inability to Walk*

The attractive woman with the limp, mentioned previously, moved about on public transportation (lorries, taxis, minivans) despite needing assistance for boarding and disembarking. This issue of reliance on others for assistance in basic movements raises the question of whether experiences and notions of *dependence* and *independence* are different in relatively more "sociocentric" compared with more "egocentric" societies. What specific "somatic modes of attention" are involved when there is impaired mobility or an alternative mode of movement? And what do these "culturally elaborated" forms of attention *to* and *with* the body (Csordas 1993:138) reveal about the nature and relations of *being* among Anlo-speaking people?

Blindness, deafness, or the inability to walk are rarely approached (in the scholarly literature) from a phenomenological point of view. One such piece, however, sheds light on these questions. Describing the case of an American woman with quadrilateral limb deficiency, Frank (1986:214) explains, "From the perspective of Diane's embodiment in American culture, it appears that mobility and independence of self-care are central values, ends to be striven for in themselves. Anything that gave her more mobility, more independence, was accepted and incorporated into her body scheme." Most Anlo-speaking people who engaged in alternative modes of mobility (or who possessed what Euro-Americans would call a "disability") were not experiencing this same intense striving for more and more independence. If we consider a spectrum ranging from independence to interdependence and then to dependence, I would suggest that in many Euro-

American contexts the emphasis is on the former, while Anlo-speaking people are more oriented toward and accustomed to dependence on others. The cultural meaning of disability is simply not the same.

Since balancing *(agbagbaɖoɖo)* and walking or moving *(azɔlizɔzɔ)* were such significant functions or sensory experiences for many Anlo-speaking people, how were those who had lost this sense modality treated? How was their experience different from others around them? During most of his elderly years, Mr. Kobla Ocloo had been in a wheelchair. While the topic of his disability was rarely broached, I observed a fair amount of daily interactions among members of the household. The striking thing was the ease with which Kobla's alternative mode of movement (or *azɔlizɔzɔ*) was integrated into a regular social routine typical of many Anlo-speaking households. The structure of the house included a continuous cement floor extending from the back rooms to the front sitting room and then to the outside patio covered by a canopy from a large tree. Kobla wheeled throughout these rooms, usually with the assistance of Sena or one of the younger members of the household. While their three children were grown and lived away from home (one in Accra, the other two overseas), several young nieces resided in the household under foster care. In addition, visitors came frequently and often assisted Kobla in his movements or in fetching items he wanted to use. In reflecting on these interactions, I was struck by my own hesitation in helping Mr. Ocloo move about compared to the readiness of Anlo speakers to engage with him, adjusting his wheelchair, modifying his position, and so forth. It certainly occurred to me that a sound explanation for this difference in behavior could have been that I had only known the Ocloos for a short time, while many of the other visitors were either relatives or long-standing friends and had thus accommodated themselves to this style of interaction. However, I also wondered about possible cultural differences in ways of *attending to and with the body* that might have been at play in this situation. Those of us who come from more "egocentric" societies tend to think of persons as clearly bounded and individuated selves, and these notions extend beyond personality to the level of the body. We are often reluctant to draw attention to peoples' dependencies, whereas *interdependence* and outright *dependence* (social as well as somatic) were (relatively speaking) more acceptable conditions in many Anlo-speaking contexts.

One of the points here is that among most Anlo-speaking people it would be extremely rare for a person to reside alone. This contrasts sharply with, for example, Diane's case where she had a "choice between being a *dependent person* with institutional type care or being an *independent person* with limited but attainable employment skills and capacity to take care of herself. To be 'independent' would require prosthesis use ... to 'increase her functioning,' although it was felt that Diane would always be very dependent on others" (Frank 1986:200). While I acknowledge the great discrepancies when drawing a comparison between Kobla's and Diane's situations, in part because their respective disabilities were different (hers were quadrilateral and congenital; his were acquired late in life and only affected his legs), certain cultural differences are still illustrated in the comparison. The idea that Diane would always be "very dependent on others" contained a stigma—for therapists who worked with her, for the society at large, and for Diane herself. This kind of discomfort or shame surrounding dependency did not exist among most Anlo-speaking people, thereby shifting the entire meaning of impaired or alternative mobility. Interdependence and reliance on family members were unquestioned and integral parts of life for most Anlo-speaking people, and Kobla's case was perceived and accepted as simply another facet of this mode of social interaction. While an individual could be without certain sense modalities, the *nature of being* and the *relations of being* (within Anlo-speaking contexts) already involved so much interdependence that the alternate sensory mode did not seem to engender the kind of stigma that it would in contexts where individuals were expected to be self-sufficient. This is further illustrated by the image of a buffalo and a white bird that Anlo speakers often referred to when trying to convey the interdependence on which their concept of the individual was based. They described a massive and strong animal like a buffalo tolerating or even welcoming the company of a delicate egretlike bird since the bird would pick ticks and insects from his skin. The strength and well-being of both, therefore, was dependent on their mutual support and association.

ON MADNESS, INSANITY, AND "BEING OUT OF ONE'S SENSES"

A number of *mɔfialawo* suggested that insanity was equivalent to the total loss of one's sensory and perceptory abilities. They expressed a strong preference for the loss of any one sense modality (whether it was the use of one's eyes, ears, or legs) over the debilitating state of madness. Several healers also reported that mental illness was "the most difficult sickness to cure" since these individuals could not "hear" as others around them heard, their speech did not seem to make sense, and they often "saw things" that no one else could detect or perceive. Moreover, while most people did not exhibit pity for individuals in Anlo-land who were blind, deaf, or lame (since a range of sensory faculties were still intact), a fair amount of compassion and charity was often extended to those considered "insane" or "out of their senses." A clear distinction was made, however, between people who had lost their senses due to abuse of alcohol or drugs and those who met with an accident or became insane from circumstances beyond their control. I often observed people providing "truly mentally ill" individuals with a little money or food, while they avoided, dismissed, or abused people who were habitually drunk and people who took illicit drugs.

Several Anlo-Ewe lexical terms were used to designate mental illness or insanity. They included *tagbɔgbɛgblɛtɔ, tsukunɔ,* and *efe tabgɔ flu. Tagbɔgbɛgblɛtɔ* signified "owner or master of a head or intellect which was ruined or destroyed." *Tsukunɔ* referred to "a person who was suffering from a senseless and confused disposition." *Efe tabgɔ flu* indicated that "his head or intellect was blurred." While technically correct, all these expressions were considered by a number of *mɔfialawo* to be rather harsh ways of denoting the condition of insanity, and they preferred the phrase *Mele nyuie o,* which simply meant "He is not fine" or "He is not well."

I was interested in what they believed was "not well," or more specifically if they believed it was a sickness confined to the *head,* since the phrases *tagbɔgbɛgblɛtɔ* and *efe tabgɔ flu* denoted something amiss specifically in the mind. But madness (in Anlo-speaking contexts) seemed to be perceived as more pervasive, as a disturbance throughout an individual's entire being. *Mɔfialawo* who spoke English explained that "all their faculties were disturbed" or that the deranged person was simply "out of his senses." Of the three Anlo-Ewe terms, several *mɔfialawo* definitely preferred *tsukunɔ,* which meant "a person who was suffering from (or laboring under) a senseless and confused character, nature, or disposition."

Several anecdotes about *tsukunɔ* may help to fill out the picture. One day while standing on the street in Dzelukɔfe (a borough of Keta), a man ran up to me, grabbed my elbow, and started beating me on the shoulders and chest and kicking me in the shins. Rushing to my aid, Elaine and a tailor that we had just visited pried the man away from me and pushed him down the street as he shouted obscenities. After recovering from the scare (I did not sustain any physical injury), it occurred to me that this was my first brush with insanity in Anlo-land. Or was it? He seemed psychotic to me, but what would Elaine and the tailor say? I asked, and they were quick to report that he had "ruined himself with drugs." "Well, is he mad?" I asked. "He's mean," Elaine shot back. She believed that he understood perfectly well what he was doing when he accosted me, and she pointed out that he chose me instead of her. What she meant is that his faculties were intact enough for him to see that I was not an Anlo, and he could calculate that I would not really understand what was happening, whereas he knew that she would beat him if he struck her. "And he does this because he drinks and takes drugs," she concluded.

This incident in Dzelukɔfe, in 1992, contrasted quite dramatically with an encounter I had later that summer that really did constitute my first brush with insanity in Anlo-land. Elaine and I set off one morning to take the canoe from Keta to Kedzi to visit some people in Adina and Denu. As we disembarked from the canoe and boarded a lorry in Kedzi, I noticed the tallest Ewe man I had ever seen. More striking than his physical stature, however, was his countenance and his behavior. His eyes somehow sunk deep into his face, and he seemed to look right past you when he came face to face. He was vocalizing nonstop, the pitch alternating between a whisper and a shout, and he staggered about the canoe launch. Older women placed coins in his palm as they passed by him. I asked Elaine who he was, and she furrowed her brow and shook her head, which I had come to understand as signaling she did not want to talk about it.

We made several more trips to and from Denu that summer. On a number of occasions, Elaine gave him money or food. Finally, as we were sitting on the bench one day, waiting to board the canoe for home, Elaine volunteered the following story. Years ago this tall, statuesque man was the most brilliant English teacher in all of Anlo-land. Elaine's father was a principal in one of the high schools, and she reported that he and everyone else adored this man. He was a dignified, elegant, and eloquent person who inspired his pupils by reciting long passages from Shakespeare and other great works of literature. But one day he simply snapped. She explained that he went from being the most lucid and clear person she knew to being completely out of his senses. She described him as not seeming to hear what people said to him and suggested that his eyes failed to focus on real people and things. He stared into the air, gesticulating toward invisible entities and babbling nonsensical words. Hypersensitive to touch, if you tapped him on the shoulder he jumped, startled, and lashed out. He stopped bathing. And he did not even have enough sense to beg or to eat. This was the reason people handed him money and food.

Here was a case of insanity, according to Elaine. He was not mean, as she deemed the drunken man in Dzelukɔfe, but rather this man who inhabited the Kedzi canoe launch was disturbed through and through, with each sensory field more disrupted than the next. He could not even walk in a normal fashion, indicated by the staggering and lack of motor control. As *tsukunɔ* implied, he was suffering from senselessness and confusion; there was a pervasiveness of disturbance through his body and mind. Elaine helped to translate when I had interviewed Adzoa Kokui and we had discussed how children must learn to hear things and let certain items pass right through, not affecting their *seselelame*. She agreed with Adzoa, and in a subsequent conversation between the two of us, Elaine used this man as an example of what can happen if you let things disrupt the way you feel-feel-at-flesh-inside *(seselelame)*.

In the local cultural logic about insanity, then, there seemed to be a link with sensory (as distinct from intellectual or cognitive) aspects of a person's being. Many of the Anlo speakers I consulted perceived madness as tantamount to the loss (or malfunction) of all sensorial ability, as having a nature or disposition in which the sensory functions were completely confused or amiss. From an ontological perspective, this implied that individual well-being was deeply tied to intact sensory functioning, and cases in which this was disrupted called for genuine compassion and care. Alternative modes of sensing could be sustained in one or two areas without disruption to reason, judgment, or basic knowing (as was demonstrated in the discussions of blindness, deafness, and the inability to walk). However, madness ensued when a person's entire sensorium was disturbed, which meant that people perceived the nature and grounds of knowledge to be tied to sensing. The following section will address the philosophy and methods involved in protecting this delicate balance, or keeping the sensorium and one's health and strength intact.

PERSONAL WELL-BEING AND THE VITAL ROLE OF *ДZOSASA* (TRANSFORMATIVE ARTS)

Earlier I discussed how an Anlo phenomenon called *dzosasa* (*dzo*: magic; *sasa*: tying, binding) was once interpreted as simply talismans or protective charms but that I had gradually come to understand *dzosasa* as a kind of "indigenous psychotherapy," or a way to transform psychosomatic conditions of disruption or disturbance. In addition, while *dzosasa* was considered by some as antiquated and obsolete, I found that it was used quite frequently by many Anlo-speaking people with whom I worked. Here I treat *dzosasa* as a kind of model of transformation, and

I explore some of the ways in which Anlo speakers employed *dzokawo* to safeguard and bolster their health.

Among many Anlo speakers, *dzosasa* allowed them to probe mysteries and explore relations between things, and it was ultimately aimed at directing a kind of "psychic transformation." Accomplishing psychic transformations involved manipulation of sense perceptions and somatic modes of attention. For instance, one account described the use of *dzo* in altering an onlooker's perception so that sand could seem to change into "a perfumed white powder," not through an actual material modification but by virtue of *dzo* revising the spectator's vision (Cudjoe 1971:202–203). While alterations in olfactory and visual perception are described as part of this process, questions typically raised by such an account focus on what constitutes "reality"? Phenomena like *dzosasa* are scrutinized for whether they produce "real transformations" or simply "changes in perception." From the point of view of phenomenology, this dilemma poses a false dichotomy and the transformations need not be considered any less real because they occur in the psyche instead of in the object itself.[8]

My husband and I became friendly with a young man in Anloga whom I will call Kobla. He was an enterprising and energetic entrepreneur who owned several lorries and a store carrying general goods. One evening Kobla invited us for a beer, and our conversation soon turned to the topic of dreams. I asked him what kind of dreams he had, and Kobla replied that they were "big dreams." Not understanding what he meant, I asked him to be more specific and describe one or two of his dreams. Kobla explained that his "dreams" involved becoming successful and financially powerful. Realizing that by "dreams" he seemed to mean *goals,* I was still surprised to hear Kobla relate the following (which I recorded later that evening in my fieldnotes): "I have watched women since I was young and I've seen that women will try to bring you down if you have achieved something. People here do not like to see me achieve. I work hard and I'm only thirty years old, but I have accomplished more than many older men. If you're not careful, though, and don't watch yourself, women will destroy you." If his "dreams" focused on wealth and success, these comments seemed to represent Kobla's "nightmares," or the negative counterpoint to his goals. Intrigued by this candid expression of fear concerning the power women could have over an individual, I wondered whether this was a prevalent attitude (among Anlo men) or was it just his own idiosyncratic point of view? Second, I wondered why women (rather than other men, children, or even spiritual entities) were perceived as the ones who could destroy him. And how was it that women managed to do this? Finally, how could a person protect himself from this threat (to his well-being, stability, and strength)?

Over time I found that Kobla's point of view was not particularly unique, although not everyone I consulted articulated the issue in terms quite so literal or in ways that exhibited what many Euro-Americans might interpret as a kind of paranoia. Some people (such as Kobla) perceived the threat to be from "real flesh and blood women" who could seduce men through manipulating their *seselelame*, by sweet talk (playing to their sense of hearing), and through sensual caresses (working the senses of the skin). Of seduction (and its consequent dangers), another *mɔfiala* explained that "you can hear it in women's voices [which are] soft and luring and their touch makes you melt." Both men perceived these tactics to result in sapping their energy and causing an ambitious man to become soft, lazy, unproductive, and weak. From this perspective, one's sensory and somatic modes could be manipulated such that it could render a man completely off balance (a total disruption to *agbagbaɖoɖo*). Many believed that a man relegated to this state was the victim of someone engaged in *dzosasa*.

When I consulted other *mɔfialawo* about the ideas articulated by Kobla, they interpreted his situation to be less about the dynamic that occurs between men and women and more about a conflict occurring within the young man himself. Some *mɔfialawo* suggested that the man was "putting onto women" what was going on inside of himself (a tendency he was trying to resist toward becoming soft, lazy, unproductive, and weak). Several suggested that *dzosasa* (transformative arts) could be employed in this young man's case, but the "binding" action effected by *dzosasa* would be in terms of parts of himself (the conflict between the ambitious and the weak or soft). While some Anlo speakers believed Kobla was gripped by external forces (just as Kobla thought various women were trying to sabotage his business), others understood it to be a case of workings completely inside Kobla himself. *Dzosasa* could be implicated and employed in either case, and some understood its function to be about one's own transformation, while others believed *dzosasa* could be used to change external events.[9]

As already indicated, *dzokawo* were usually considered (at least by missionaries and scholars) to be charms, amulets, talismans, fetishes, or some kind of object toward which one could direct invocations. The *bociɔ* and nail sculptures of the neighboring Fon-speaking people are counterparts of the Anlo speakers' *ʤokawo*. In these traditions, some individuals focus more on the object itself (kind of projecting their own inner conflict onto a separate person or thing), while others use the object in an effort directed at conjuring new or transformed psychosomatic states. The latter approach involves manipulation of senses and perceptions in an effort to reformulate an individual's state of being toward one of greater strength and health. In addition, I have raised the issue of "medicines" and the way a *ʤoka* usually contained a variety of ingredients (including animal, mineral, or vegetable) and could be ingested, donned, or possessed. While acknowledging that there were many charlatans and fools exploiting the use of *ʤokawo*, several *mɔfialawo* characterized *ʤosasa* as the manipulation of attitudes and behaviors, as well as reliance on pharmaceutical and material substances, to assist individuals in transformation of psychosomatic states.

A second case that illustrates the sophistication of the theory and practice of *ʤosasa* is based on a dream that Raphael reported he had in his sleep. He apologized in advance for the graphic content he felt it contained, but began by explaining that in his dream he was lying in bed and opened his eyes to see a woman descending on top of him, from no particular place. She was simply floating in the air, naked, and descended on top of him. The unidentifiable woman covered his mouth and nose with her vagina, so in his dream Raphael could not breathe. Raphael reported that he awoke the following morning with a terrible case of sinusitis, and even after going to the hospital and taking the nose drops and medication the doctor prescribed, he experienced no relief. The persistence of the sinusitis finally prompted him to consult an Afa specialist (diviner). The diviner explained that the person in the dream was "bringing witchcraft and trying to give it to him or thrust it upon him." Raphael would have to "use some herbs" and "take some steps to ward this off." He proceeded with "the steps" (which would be classified as *ʤosasa* but which he would not describe for me as he considered it secret knowledge), and Raphael's sinusitis soon cleared up.

I asked both Raphael and other *mɔfialawo* to analyze this dream and received varied and sometimes contradictory interpretations. However, the one theme that consistently emerged revolved around the notion of *ameŋumee wɔanu amɛ*, which is a phrase meant to capture or sum up ideas and experiences of how "those close to you can harm you the most." Some people's interpretations focused on the idea that his mother or wife was most certainly trying to harm Raphael, as either one of them might be jealous of his progress and achievements. Within this interpretive approach, the woman in the dream was perceived rather literally as Raphael's mother or wife. It was not clear to me why a mother or wife would try to harm rather than support and encourage him, but I was informed that she probably did not even know or realize she was causing him harm, as it was a thought or urge somewhere within the unconscious.

The second interpretive approach also drew on ideas about the unconscious but focused more on the unconscious of Raphael himself. That is, when I asked if the image of the woman in the dream was a literal manifestation of his wife or mother, some people insisted it was symbolic of a problem that Raphael was experiencing within himself, and since the conflict was within him, Raphael had the power (particularly with the assistance of *dzosasa*) to resolve it. These interpretations also stressed *ameŋumee wɔanu amɛ* (those close to you can harm you the most), but people who perceived the dream to represent an "internal battle" explained that close relatives had the greatest influence on a person and could get inside of an individual's mind and spirit and drive him mad. To my question of whether the relatives actually entered one's body or "being," people were usually amused by this simple-minded notion and explained it as a result of *influence* and workings of the unconscious or the inner person *(ameme)*. In a sense the image of the woman was considered a manifestation of psychic harm that Raphael was experiencing, based largely on the interpersonal relations and family dynamics in which he was involved.[10] This process was very similar to that described as the etiology of *enu,* or "seizing the mouth," of children (and pregnant women).

In cases such as those discussed in this chapter, *dzosasa* was often employed to bolster one's health or to strengthen *seselelame* (bodily feeling). In existential terms, while many Anlo-speaking people deeply believed that "those close to you can harm you the most" *(ameŋumee wɔanu amɛ),* the methods and mechanisms of injury were usually not obvious and were typically "invisible." Sensing was sometimes discussed as *aleke neselelame,* or "how you feel within yourself when something is done to you." Sometimes it was only through the "feeling within yourself" or through a variety of sensory channels (hearing, feeling in the skin, disruption to one's sense of balance) that a person could come to know that someone near to him was causing harm. Experiences and images that emerged from dreams were another way of acquiring such knowledge. When *social* situations and *interpersonal* interactions were perceived as dangerous or potentially harmful, herbs and sculptural objects were used to elicit *cosmological* powers in bolstering the strength and health of the self. Central to this process is the body, or how the body serves in part as a source of consciousness and information (cf. Schwartz-Salant 1995:15). *Dzosasa,* in turn, can be understood as a kind of strategy for manipulation—its practitioners dedicated to transformations of psychosomatic (including sensory) dimensions of the self. An aesthetic of the cool (letting disturbing things pass right through you) indicates a cultural value on regulation of the senses as a strategy in maintaining health.

Enu referred to the ways in which bad will and animosity among kinfolk manifested in a small child becoming deaf or mute or in a pregnant woman experiencing the ordeal of a stillbirth. In relation to such processes, one *mɔfiala* suggested a phrase directly tied to sensing: *aleke nese le lame,* or "how you feel within yourself when something is done to you" or literally, "how you feel it inside your body." The body here was clearly experienced as a source of information, not just cognitive or discursive information but visceral and intuitive messages, and such notions were what underpinned the logic of a phenomenon such as *enu.* *Dzosasa* was a practice not all Anlo-speaking people embraced, but reversing or protecting oneself from phenomena such as *enu* and preventing a *dɔtsoafe* (illness from home) from incurring *gbɔgbɔmedɔ* (a spirit in the sickness) often involved its use.

The phenomenon of *dzosasa* further underscores the idea that in many Anlo-speaking contexts there is not a rigid separation between body and mind or between the experiential and the ontological (Csordas 1994a:8). A cultural model of well-being among Anlo-speaking people necessarily draws together the personal, social, and cosmic (or spiritual) fields, and *dzosasa* demonstrates the ways these three spheres coalesce in embodied and sensate experiences, especially those associated with sickness and health.

Ethnography and the Study of Cultural Difference

CHAPTER 10

Sensory Experience and Cultural Identity

I have used four broad claims concerning sensory orders, embodiment, identity, and well-being to structure ethnographic descriptions of Anlo-Ewe sensory experiences and philosophical thought. I have argued that

1. physiological evidence suggests human bodies gain sensory information in a variety of ways;

2. a Western model of five senses is a folk model;

3. an Anlo-Ewe model is different, and it privileges balance, kinesthesia, and sound;

4. the impact of this model (or approach) can be seen in four areas, each of which affect the others:

   a. the use of language to describe the sensorium;

   b. moral values embedded in child-rearing and social development;

   c. an Anlo-Ewe model of personhood;

   d. ideas about illness and health.

In this final chapter, my goal is to develop these arguments in greater detail as a gesture toward providing an interpretive framework for the study of sensoriums and sensory experience and their place in our understandings of cultural difference.

Proposition One: Sensoriums differ as a result of cultural tradition

In contemporary Western cultures (or at least in Euro-American contexts) when we speak of "senses" we usually mean the five modalities of
sight, hearing, taste, smell, and touch. Our taxonomy of senses is organ-
based, and sensing for us corresponds to a theory of how we apprehend
stimulus from objects outside our bodies and then represent these sounds,
textures, odors, and so on in our minds and to each other. Our definition of *sensing* revolves around the idea that we have bodily structures
that receive stimulus from objects outside our bodies, and these organs
then send messages to the brain that are registered and finally interpreted
by the mind. Sensing for us is directly tied to the idea that some thing,
some object makes an impression on our sense organs, and we thereby
(somewhat passively, our ethno-theory purports) become aware or conscious of various elements in our environment.

While we may be very attached to this definition of sensing and believe that it describes a kind of anatomical reality verified by medical science and psychology, it is, as I have argued before, a folk ideology. A
burgeoning literature on the social history of the senses (e.g., Berman
1998; Classen 1993a, 1993b; Classen, Howes, and Synnott 1994; Howes
1991; Rivlin and Gravelle 1984; Stoller 1989b; Synnott 1993) demonstrates that even within Western culture there has been an evolution in
the way sensing has been defined as well as in the number of senses included in any particular taxonomy. Furthermore, sensory scientists are
in agreement that the exact nature and number of human senses is actually an open empirical question.

In the ancient world of the West, Plato's writings reveal a conflation
of sensing and feeling. Sometimes his work discusses sight, smell, and
hearing as senses, but he omits taste and touch. Instead he includes hot
and cold, along with fear, desire, pleasure, and discomfort (see Classen
1993b:1–11; Synnott 1993:128–155). This taxonomy is significant because (as we have seen) the word *feeling* plays a significant role in translating the way Anlo speakers think of sensing, along with the fact that
Plato did not confine himself to five modalities, which parallels the case
of many non-Western cultural groups. It may be Aristotle who is responsible for the taxonomy of five senses within Western culture, or it
may simply be that he reified and codified an idea that was circulating
among scholars of that time. Noteworthy is that his rationale for limiting sensing to five modalities was quite different than that used by us
today. Aristotle believed that there is an "intrinsic relationship between

the senses and the elements—earth, air, fire, water, and the quintessence" (Classen 1993b:2).[1]

During the Enlightenment there emerged a rationale for the five senses that is distinct from Aristotle's and begins to resemble our own tradition steeped in philosophical empiricism. No longer the subject of theological and allegorical interpretation, study of the senses moved into the realm of science and philosophy. Hobbes and Locke were in agreement about the senses being the foundation of thought—revealed in Hobbes's statement that "there is no conception in a man's world which has not at first, totally, or by parts, been begotten upon the organs of sense" and in Locke's declaration that "nothing can be in the intellect which was not first in the senses" (quoted in Synnott 1991:69–71). Descartes, on the other hand, was suspicious of the senses, believing that sensory experience confused logical thought since sensations were inherently deceptive. He sought to separate bodily experience from mental or intellectual judgment (Lakoff and Johnson 1999:391–414). All were in agreement, however, on the idea that sensing was a physical and natural function, a means by which information about the external world was conveyed to the mind. Locke believed this was a vital aspect of our consciousness; Descartes considered it suspiciously illusory. But during the Enlightenment, solidified were the notions of sensing as a physical function void of cultural determinants (Classen 1993b:4) and of the five-senses model representing a universal and natural account of immediate bodily experience.

Over the past century a new perspective on sensory perception has been unfolding. Efforts at replicating sight, hearing, balance, motion, and other mechanisms in robots and various space technologies have led to a deeper appreciation of the complexity of sensory systems in humans and other mammals as well as in reptiles and birds (Rivlin and Gravelle 1984). Research on artificial intelligence and virtual reality, in addition to experiences with drug-induced alternate states of consciousness, have led to questions about the potential of what the human mind can know and also about the capability for extension of our sense organs both organically and in the form of tools and machines (Rheingold 1991). By "extensions" I mean things such as remote sensing; echolocation; x-ray vision; infrared vision, or the ability to "see" heat patterns; navigational abilities (of homing pigeons as well as humans [see Baker 1981]), and so forth.[2]

In addition, medical research on the brain and technological innovations aimed at replicating human sensory systems in computers have resulted in the suggestion that we may have more sensory systems than simply five (Rivlin and Gravelle 1984:9–28). Depending upon how the

term is defined, additional human senses might include four taste receptors rather than simply one (making sweet, salty, bitter, and sour distinct
modalities); some mechanism (akin to a vomeronasal system) capable of
detecting pheromones (odorless chemicals);[3] different skin senses such
as mechanoreceptors (sensitive to pressure and indentation), thermore-
ceptors (responsive to temperature), and nociceptors (mediating pain
more severe than that handled by the other two receptors) (Barlow and
Mollon 1982:369–386); a functional pineal gland able to respond to
light (Rivlin and Gravelle 1984:16); a sensory system for apprehending
visual contour, contrast, and form that is different from that used for
color (Rivlin and Gravelle 1984:16); a magnetic sense that governs navigation or direction (Baker 1981); and so forth.

It is clear that sensing most likely involves more than five fields, and
this raises the question of how people in cultures outside of the West
have thought about this problem of *how we know what we know.* In the
accompanying scheme I graphically display what I take to be the American folk model of the general process or progression of the stages we
define as sensing, then perceiving, and then cognizing.

For example, a bodily impression that we identify as an aroma or smell
makes an impact within the realm of our nostrils. That immediate experience bridges the domain of sense and percept, while the inferences we
begin to make about such a smell ("I smell smoke") connect the arenas of
perception and cognition ("I think there is a fire"). Notice that interpretation enters into the model and the parameters of the categories. How
then do various cultural groups define the foundational category? What
are the basic bodily impressions in a given tradition that constitute something we might gloss roughly as "sensations" or "immediate experiences"?[4] How do they define the boundaries of the category? What components or what experiences do they include? And finally, what meanings
are then associated with the different components? In this book, I suggest
that culture affects not only inference and not only perception but also the
seemingly basic domain of sensation through the organization and elaboration of categories through which immediate sensations are perceived. In
this reading, culture does not only affect the mind. It changes the body.

*Proposition Two: A sensorium is embodied; sensory orientations are
acquired through processes of child socialization*

So this is a study of some of the processes by which "history is turned
into nature" (Bourdieu 1977:78). My first proposition requires that we

Sensation ——→ Perception ——→ Cognition

immediate   hearing
                             seeing
experience ——→   smelling ——→ inference ——→   thinking
                             tasting   knowing
                             feeling

excavate (so to say) cultural categories and sensory orders because immediate bodily experience is not understood or defined in any universal way. My second claim is that in a sensory order we find cultural categories for experience. We find cultural meanings that are embodied, and because they are as much a part of the body as the mind, they are considered "natural" ways of being, but in fact they are learned or acquired at an early age. In other words, a cultural group's sensory order reflects aspects of the world that are so precious to it that (although they remain largely unconscious and habitual) they are the things that children growing up in this culture developmentally come to carry in their very bodies.

This raises an important question about whether a sensorium is embodied and, hence, very dear (to members of a cultural group) or whether a sensorium and sensory orientations are so dear (i.e., they reflect values that are precious to the cultural group) that they therefore become embodied (during processes of child socialization). I want to suggest that we cannot really separate or distinguish between these two processes or even establish a definitive causal arrow. They are so intertwined in a sociohistorical sense that we are forced to use seemingly paradoxical statements to capture in words how this works. That, at any rate, is the way I have come to interpret Bourdieu's phrases aimed at summing up the habitus: "history turned into nature" or "durably installed generative principle of regulated improvisations" (cf. Csordas [1994b:278–279] on "theorizing in oxymorons"). How can something both evolve historically and be considered "of nature"? How can it be both regulated and improvisational? I would suggest that a sensorium and the process of sensing has as one of its essential qualities this very paradoxical characteristic, and that is perhaps one of the reasons it is a human function that is very difficult to study and why it has been neglected by the social sciences.[5] In this second proposition I therefore suggest a twofold (and, in my mind, noncontradictory) process: first, a sensory order is embodied, and this is one reason members of a cultural group find it precious, dear, and downright "natural"; second, a sensory order also contains cultural categories that are considered so dear (i.e., they are deemed so valuable by members of a cultural group) that they literally make these themes or these motifs into "body."

To put it another way, human beings are ushered into (or "durably installed" with) their culture's sensorium, which reflects some of the most fundamental and dear values and categories that have been reproduced in this cultural community over time. The ushering in begins symbolically in the (ritually packed) birth event itself and continues during early childhood experiences so that sensory and somatic practices become embodied. In this way, phenomena em-bodied, or made body, are "placed beyond the grasp of consciousness, and hence cannot be touched by voluntary, deliberate transformation, cannot even be made explicit" (Bourdieu 1977:94). They are some of the most "ineffable, incommunicable, and inimitable" aspects of being, and as Bourdieu suggests (1977:94), there is nothing "more precious, than the values given body, *made* body by the transubstantiation achieved by the hidden persuasion of an implicit pedagogy" embedded in cultural and socialization processes.

The idea of habitus, though first employed in anthropology by Marcel Mauss (1935), has more recently been developed and popularized by Pierre Bourdieu (1977, 1984). In Bourdieu's terms, *habitus* refers to how history is "turned into nature," with habitual practices reflecting and housing traditions and attitudes of mind passed on through symbolic systems and sociocultural processes. Likewise, *embodiment* (from the intellectual tradition of phenomenology) has been adapted to anthropology (and ethnographic endeavors) as a way of treating the body as "the existential ground of culture and self" (Csordas 1990:5). I take this to mean that existence for human beings is not separable from the body in which we experience life nor is the body removable from the process by which culture melds with the self. Rather, the body is the very medium in which this melting and welding takes place (the mind, of course, being part of the body).[6] My own study of sensing, perception, and identity, then, is part of a larger project in anthropology aimed at developing "a theory of culture and self grounded in *embodiment*" (Csordas 1994a:13, emphasis added).

By *embodiment* do I mean a theory, a methodological perspective and approach, or an actual empirical phenomenon? *Embodiment* can be used in all three ways, so let me explain. My own goals here are largely to advance our understanding of the role that sensory perception plays in the development of self, in the maintenance of psychological well-being, and in the reproduction of cultural identity. If there is a "theory of embodiment" in this inquiry, it lies in the speculation or in the hypothetical point of view that the senses are ways of embodying social categories. (This idea is very close to the notion of habitus.) Embodiment as a methodological approach has been developed most coherently by Csordas (1990, 1994a), and to a great extent I rely on and refer to his conceptions of what this means. For example, he suggests that a paradigm of textuality has dominated anthropology and cultural theory in general for some time, and he proposes not to supplant that perspective but rather to provide it with a "dialectical partner" in the form of a paradigm of embodiment (1994a:11–12). By *paradigm* he means a "consistent methodological perspective that encourages reanalyses of existing data and suggests new questions for empirical research" (Csordas 1990:5). Within this approach, Csordas distinguishes between "the 'body' as a biological, material entity and 'embodiment' as an indeterminate methodological field defined by perceptual experience and mode of presence and engagement in the world" (1994a:12). When embodiment is evoked as a methodological field (as it is in this book), that means it is an arena where a mode of inquiry or a process of doing something is carried out, and within this field or arena our locus of inquiry lies in processes of perception, experience, a person's presence, and the engagement of the self. This phenomenological approach is distinct from (but, Csordas argues, complementary to) semiotics, with its focus on language, representation, and the model of culture as a set of texts. Ultimately Csordas suggests that "semiotics and phenomenology are complementary ways to think about culture and that both can be applied to linguistic or narrative data" (1994b:xii). I highlight this effort to bridge these two methodological approaches because in a study of sensation, sensory experience, and sensory orientations, too restrictive a focus on either language or on experience would not do justice to the data, and therefore I have relied on both in my own work.

Furthermore, in empirical terms embodiment is inextricable from the habitus in that if we define *habitus* as a "durably installed generative principle of regulated improvisations" (Bourdieu 1977:78), the phrase "durably installed" is evocative of what is meant by *phenomena embodied.* That is, if an aspect of the person or self is *embodied,* this means that it is "turned into a permanent disposition." Habitus can also be explained as "an acquired system of generative schemes objectively adjusted to the particular conditions in which it is constituted ... [and it] engenders all the thoughts, all the perceptions, and all the actions consistent with those conditions, and no others" (Bourdieu 1977:78). Sensory perception is a

very significant part of the habitus since the gating aspect of sensing is acquired while at the same time is an elaborate "generative scheme" that
influences (or engenders) a person's experience and understanding of the
world. By *gating* I mean something called "sensory gating," which refers
to a feedback system between the brain and sense receptors themselves
that functions as a kind of damper or regulating mechanism on sensory
activity (Aronoff et al. 1970:347). This allows us to screen and orches-
trate stimuli from our environment; we can tone down stimulants to one
sensory field while heightening or amplifying information coming through
another channel or pathway. I would suggest that it is in sensory gating
that a certain amount of cultural variation occurs.

In turn, the sense perceptions and experiences of an individual closely
reflect the broader scheme we could call a "sensorium," or sensory order,
which can be described in terms of the historical and cultural conditions
in which it was constituted. More than one hundred years of anthropological research on perception, while being far from robust in either
amount or results, has at very least provided us with the understanding
that the senses are made to be shaped by culture. Psychologist Jerome
Bruner has long argued that the senses be treated not simply as "passive
recording devices" or receivers and that "the sensorium itself is already
a 'mind-orium.' It's not really just a sensorium as such ... there is no such
thing as the pure senses" (quoted in Shore 1997:44). In regard to the
senses as "active constructors of experience" (Shore 1997:42), a phono-
logical analogy can be drawn with the fact that humans are prewired for
the acquisition of language, but once a specific language has been learned,
it is more difficult for an individual to even hear (as in distinguish, identify, reproduce) the sounds of other human languages.[7] Phonemes are
"durably installed" or even "embodied." Hearing is not the only sense
modality that functions in this way, and it certainly does so not only in
relation to language but to a range of cultural and environmental sounds;
all of the senses are like this in that they are made to be shaped and tuned.
It is this capacity of sensing that I suggest we examine and explore, and
it is this dimension of the senses that I am arguing is a repository of cultural categories or cultural values and orientations.

*Proposition Three: Sensoriums help shape notions of the person
and ensure that persons differ culturally and yet appear natural*

We experience the world and know each other to a great extent through
our senses. I invoke this seemingly obvious point here because in com-

parative studies of concepts of the person, the cultural shaping of sensory experience and perception is often not made explicitly apparent, yet sensory orientations are an integral part of the development of self.[8]

For example, Shweder and his colleagues have advanced enormously our understanding of persons and of the ways in which culture and psyche "make each other up" (e.g. Shweder and Bourne 1991; Markus and Kitayama 1994).

> From the moment of birth (and even earlier in some cultural contexts), individuals are given meaning and engaged as persons. Through this cultural participation, they become selves. An infant's mentality or consciousness or way of being in the world is thus patterned according to the meanings and practices that characterize a given cultural community, and the communities are maintained by these mentalities. There is a continuous cycle of mutual attunement and coordination between psychological tendencies and the social realities on which these tendencies are brought to bear.... [F]eatures of the cultural system such as the characteristic ways in which one is led to focus on and attend to others can become directly incorporated into individual systems of experiencing and organizing the world. They become selfways. (Shweder et al. 1998:900)

My contribution is to insist that "attentional" or orientational processes are shaped by culture, and "selfways" therefore involve the continual cultivation of particular ways of hearing, seeing, smelling, moving one's body, and so on or of attending to the flow of life. The notion of sensory orientation is implicitly contained within the comment about "characteristic ways in which one is led to focus on and attend to others." That is to say, we not only know the environment with all its inanimate objects through our senses but we also experience our own selves and each other to a great extent through our senses. We see each other, hear each other, smell or do not smell each other, touch or do not touch each other—as the case may be from one cultural context to the next. So how one becomes socialized toward the meanings of sights, sounds, smells, tastes, and so forth, represents a critical aspect of how one acquires a mode of being-in-the-world, or an "individual system of experiencing and organizing the world."

We routinely engage in (culturally constituted) interactions or practices that are governed by the meanings assigned to (or ways of interpreting) certain smells, sounds, touches, tastes, and so forth. In turn, the orientations one develops toward smell, sight, sound, and such, are part of what shapes certain cultural practices. Sensory orientations, therefore, represent a critical dimension of how "culture and psyche make each other up" and play a critical role in a person's sensibilities around intersubjective dynamics and the boundaries between self and other. And these sensoriums may affect the very basic features of our ability to judge each other. For example, in chapter 5 I described how within Anlo cultural contexts a particular odor can mark a person as having received an improper first bath (immediately after birth) and then a more generalized improper upbringing, thereby creating a stigma for the lineage. In almost two years of living among Anlo-speaking people, I was never able to really grasp (perceive, sense, notice, attend to, comprehend) the precise odor that those around me were aware of when they decided that someone was marked by *ʤigbeʤi* (the local term used for this condition). My point here is that in specific cultural contexts persons are designated or identified as moral or immoral—as "true, beautiful, good and normal" (Shweder et al. 1998:867)—through reference to cultural categories that implicate and contain sensory phenomena. What it means to be a person and notions about the kinds of persons that exist are directly tied to the senses that a cultural group recognizes, attends to, and incorporates into their way (or ways) of being-in-the-world. So while such ways of being seem natural, sensoriums assure that notions of the person (ways of being a person) differ culturally.

Let me explain how I am using the terms *person* and *self*. My approach to these concepts has its roots largely in the work of William James (1890) and A.I. Hallowell (1955:75–110) but has more recently been elaborated in the ethnographic applications of Csordas (1994b, 1994c). What these scholars share is not only a concept of self that acknowledges the embodied dimension but, more specifically, a definite attention to or appreciation of sensory perception as a vital aspect of how people orient themselves.

James (1890:291–401) conceptualized the self as having four components: the material self, the social self, the spiritual self, and the pure ego. But here it is important to note that for James, self-awareness necessarily involved sensing and a grounding of ideas and experiences *in the body* (James 1890:296–304). Hallowell (1955) developed the concept of "behavioral environment" to attend to the relationship between culture and self and suggested that culture provides basic *orientations* that serve the self in a constitutional sense and are the basis of self-awareness. The orientations include those of self to other people, self to objects, self to space and time, self to motivations aimed at satisfying needs, and self to the normative values, ideals, and standards of the person's cultural group. The attributes of these various elements are of course symbolic, so a person develops a self-awareness and a perceptual framework in the context of what Hallowell called a "culturally constituted behavioral environment" (1955:89–109).

Both scholars were influenced by psychological and philosophical notions that stemmed from phenomenology. Building on these ideas, along with those of Bourdieu and Merleau-Ponty, Csordas has developed a working definition of the self as "neither a substance nor entity, but an indeterminate capacity to engage or become oriented in the world, and it is characterized by effort and reflexivity" (Csordas 1994c:340). My own use of *self* and *person* follows this line of thinking (from James to Hallowell to Csordas). Recognizing the indeterminacy allows us to focus on issues of *attention* and *orientation,* how these are culturally shaped, and how the senses are implicated in such attentional processes. Csordas distinguishes self and person by saying, "Self-processes are orientational processes in which aspects of the world are thematized, with the result that the self is objectified, most often as a 'person' having a cultural identity or set of identities" (Csordas 1994c:340). This way of conceptualizing *person* and *self* allows us to count the senses among various kinds of orientational processes. We can even consider various sensory fields (such as balance, kinesthesia, aurality) as "aspects of the world that become thematized" or as "somatic modes of attention" that are "phenomenon of embodied intersubjectivity ... performatively elaborated in certain societies, while ... neglected or feared as abnormal in others" (Csordas 1993:146). It is in these thematized aspects of the world (some having clear links to the sensorium) that we can make the bridge between sensing and cultural identity.

One of the central problems taken up in this book is the question of what is involved in *being a person* in particular cultural ways[9] and how comprehension of a sensorium helps us to understand issues of cultural identity. While I was in the field many Anlo speakers wanted to instruct me about stories or motifs that they deemed to be the "core" of their "traditional culture." At the time I believed (in poststructuralist fashion) that these stories and topics represented a kind of packaged or superficial rendition of their culture—a view of a kind of homogenous way of life that some subset of powerful or elite Anlo speakers had set forth as the official story about how they should be represented to the world. Gradually, however, I came to see these anecdotes and motifs as what Csordas calls aspects of the world that have become "thematized," and I began to examine the themes for what they revealed about cultural categories that were based in a sensorium. Many of these topics and themes have made up the ethnographic descriptions in this book, such as Tɔkɔ Atɔlia (the "fifth landing stage," where criminals were buried alive); Tɔg-bui Tsali, who many consider Anlo-land's greatest mystic; and the flight from Notsie over three hundred years ago. But what is important to high-light here, in theoretical terms, is the issue of "effort and reflexivity." Self processes are not automatic; we become persons in the midst of complex social relationships and interpersonal power dynamics as well as in the midst of continuous historical and cultural change. We all have individ-ual stories and narratives that reflect congruence with and disparity from others in our cultural group. The point is that self processes, including those of sensory attention and orientation, require effort or agency and intentionality, some kind of engagement with the process of life. The sen-sorium helps assure that notions of the person both differ culturally yet appear natural to those who hold them.

Proposition Four: Notions of the person and engagement with other intentional persons are central to health and well-being and so are directly tied to or based in a cultural group's sensorium

In all cultural contexts there are individuals who see, hear, and feel things differently than those around them: they see things that others consider nonexistent, they hear voices that others cannot detect, they feel sensa-tions that drive them to erratic or violent behavior. We often take for granted, I think, how well-being is based in a consensus about or a com-mon notion of sensed phenomena, sensed and perceived "realities," and interpretations and meanings ascribed to a whole host of sensibilia. This requires that people share in an understanding of what is real, perceivable, imagined, fantasized, and so forth and calls for reference to what is known in cultural psychology as "intentional worlds" (Shweder 1991:73–76).

My own use of the term *intentionality* (and the notion of agency) draws on the work of a number of different cultural theorists but at-tempts to apply the concept directly to issues of sensing, perception, iden-tity, and health. I will review some of the essential sources of my own thinking about this issue but then will bring the discussion back to the interrelatedness of well-being and the sensorium. Decades of research on perception, cognition, and personality processes has led psychologist Jerome Bruner to argue that we should not "make the organism a pas-sive recipient of anything" and (in part in response to behaviorist no-tions of stimulus control) that "a stimulus is not a stimulus is not a stim-ulus" but rather "a stimulus is something which in effect sets up processes of intentionality" (quoted in Shore 1997:52). This perspective resonates strongly with the idea of intentional worlds, which can be understood in the following way:

> Cultural psychology is premised on human existential uncertainty (the search for meaning) and on an "intentional" conception of "constituted" worlds. The principle of existential uncertainty asserts that human beings, starting at birth (and perhaps earlier), are highly motivated to seize meanings and resources out of a sociocultural environment that has been arranged to provide them with meanings and resources to seize and to use. The principle of intentional (or constituted) worlds asserts that subjects and objects, practitioners and practices, human beings and sociocultural environments, interpenetrate each other's identity and cannot be analyzed into independent and dependent variables. (Shweder 1991:74)

Inherent in this position is the premise that perception must be studied from the standpoint that it is a process or human function constituted by culture. In other words, "intentional ... things exist only in intentional worlds," or what makes the existence of "things" intentional is that they could not "exist independently of our involvements with them and reactions to them; and they exercise their influence in our lives because of our conceptions of them" or "by virtue of our mental representations of them" (Shweder 1991:74).

The first point to make about intentionality, sensing, and health, then, is that a state of well-being is dependent on a person's sensations and perceptions of "things" being congruent with the perceptions of those around him, or that a person's interpretations of various sensibilia be consonant with the mental representations that others hold about those same sources of stimulus. This implies a kind of shared sensibility. And on the other side of the spectrum, insanity involves (among other conditions) a slippage in this area: a lapse or breach in what is deemed sensible, a lack of concordance in the arena of intentional things and intentional states. That is, "intentional things have no 'natural' reality or identity separate from human understandings and activities" and "intentional worlds do not exist independently of the intentional states (beliefs, desires, emotions) directed at them and by them, by the persons who live in them" (Shweder 1991:75).

A personal anecdote might serve to illustrate the relation of sensing to intentionality that I am trying to describe. When I was in my early twenties, I had a series of experiences that seemed rather odd to me and I actually sought the counsel of a psychologist to make sure my symptoms were not somehow indicative of the onset of some kind of psychosis. The experiences are best described as premonitions and revolved around "knowing" or being aware in advance that I was going to run into a particular person that day, but the reason these experiences struck me as bizarre is that the "knowing" or awareness would first come to me in my skin. I would feel a tingling or prickly sensation throughout my skin, and only after that physical feeling passed would I be aware of a mental image of a person (always someone I knew, but different people over the course of several years) whom I was going to encounter that day. I actually changed outfits a couple times after having such a premonition in the morning—once because the premonition involved someone I had asked for a job, and I did not want her to see me in such informal attire, and another time because I had a mad crush on the person I "knew" I would be seeing. The point of this story is the following. Growing up in the cultural context of Euro-America, I had never heard of people having premonitions that occurred (at least in the first stages) in their skin. And while the psychologist I consulted helped me to understand and treat these experiences as a form of intuition that was simply embodied in an unusual way (and not symptomatic of psychosis), it was about ten years later, when I was living with Anlo-speaking people in Ghana, that I took on a whole new perspective about these experiences. Anlo speakers were trying to explain to me what something they called *seselelame* meant, and one of the consistent experiences for which they used this label concerned situations that could only be described as feeling sensations in the skin that were then linked to a premonition. A somewhat literal gloss for *seselelame* is "feeling or hearing in the flesh, the body, or the skin." In one cultural context this particular sensory orientation (this "somatic mode of attention" to the skin) is very unusual and does not fit with the profile of a psychologically sound person; in another cultural context, however, meaning and significance are readily attached to this sensory experience, such that it is labeled or identified with a specific term. In other words, this kind of attention to skin sensations and the association of it with premonition or an intuitive way of knowing are considered commonplace and perfectly healthy signs in their intentional world.

The term *intentional* seems to imply a kind of consciousness or a self-awareness about these processes. Am I suggesting, therefore, that people are continuously cognizant of processes of sensory perception (such as the one just described) and the associations or meanings they ascribe to these events and (perhaps more significantly) that health and well-being is dependent on such self-awareness? I do not mean to give this impression, so let me try to clarify. Rather than being simply a "receiv-ing function," Bruner suggests that sensing has to be considered an "out-ward seeking kind of thing" (quoted in Shore 1997:40). But by "out-ward seeking" do we mean a necessarily self-conscious process? Or can this definition include attentional processes that could be considered un-conscious? My answer to these questions can be summarized as follows: sensing, intentionality, and health coincide (shape each other) in an em-bodied field of perception and practice where the dichotomy of con-sciousness and unconsciousness is false or (more to the point) simply meaningless.[10] This point of view stems squarely from my reading of Csordas's notion of embodiment, which is a synthesis and reworking of Hallowell's perspective on the self and orientation, Merleau-Ponty's phe-nomenological theories of perception, and Bourdieu's theory of practice and the habitus. This synthesis is critical here in that it provides a foun-dation for my argument that comparative studies of personhood, iden-tity, and intentional worlds benefit from an explicit account of sensory orders and sensory engagement.[11]

Csordas acknowledges Hallowell's critical role in developing a notion of self that involves orientation (which was reviewed previously, in re-lation to proposition three), but he finds fault with Hallowell's overem-phasis on self-awareness. He suggests (Csordas 1994b:277) that making the self equivalent to a state of self-awareness involves two problems. First, it confuses *self* with *person,* or it imbues the self with a character-istic that is more accurately attributed to a person, since *persons* (in Csor-das's definition) have such objectified qualities but the self does not. His second point is related to the first: an assumption that the self has as one of its characteristics the "self-awareness" that Hallowell attributes is tan-tamount to projecting our own Western or Euro-American ethnopsy-chology into our theoretical stance. This is a significant point because we can expect that self-awareness and consciousness will vary in both quantitative and qualitative ways in different intentional worlds. Just within the United States significant variation exists in the ways different subcultural, ethnic, and class-based groups make associations between states of health/well-being and levels of awareness and consciousness (and so, for example, psychotherapy and psychoanalysis are more ef-fective at maximizing health in some cultural groups than in others). Ear-lier I recounted how awareness of sensations in my own skin and then interpretations of them as a kind of message is in the first instance not the sort of thing that the average Euro-American person tends to pay at-tention to or be aware of, and second, a consciousness of it actually runs counter to our notion of health and serves as an indication of instability or mental defect. But in contrast, awareness and consciousness of these precise sensations is a sound practice in many contexts in Anloland and contributes to health and well-being. How do other people (other cultural groups) understand this process of *becoming aware?*

My own starting point is to better understand the sensory order in which the other is functioning. Bourdieu theorizes that socialized agents possess "in their incorporated state, the instruments of an ordering of the world, a system of classifying schemes which organize all practices," with linguistic schemes being only one part of the total habitus (though it receives an undue emphasis, according to Bourdieu, in most contemporary culture theory). More extensively, Bourdieu argues that generative schemes work to bridge macro and micro levels, or to unify the sociohistorically driven traditions that constitute the objective aspects of elite culture (the kind of packaged, tourist-brochure rendition of Anlo culture that I discussed earlier) with the personal, subjective practices and experiences of daily life. And in the following extended excerpt from Bourdieu's argument (which dovetails with Csordas's concern over the problem of how self-awareness is produced), we find one of his most explicit statements on the role of "the senses."

> [T]o grasp through the constituted reality of myth the constituting moment of the mythopoeic act is not, as idealism supposes to seek in the conscious mind the universal structures of a "mythopoeic subjectivity" and the unity of a spiritual principle governing all empirically realized configurations regardless of social conditions. It is, on the contrary, to reconstruct the principle generating and unifying all practices, the system of inseparably cognitive and evaluative structures which organizes the vision of the world in accordance with the objective structures of a determinate state of the social world: this principle is nothing other than the *socially informed body,* with its tastes and distastes, its compulsions and repulsions, with, in a word, all its *senses,* that is to say, not only the traditional five senses—which never escape the structuring action of social determinisms—but also the sense of necessity and the sense of duty, the sense of direction and the sense of reality, the sense of balance and the sense of beauty, common sense and the sense of the sacred, tactical sense and the sense of responsibility, business sense and the sense of propriety, the sense of humour and the sense of absurdity, moral sense and the sense of practicality, and so on. (Bourdieu 1977:123–124)

Let me unpack a number of points Bourdieu makes in this passage. First, what is the relation between what he calls "the traditional five senses" and his list of more than sixteen additional kinds of "senses" or sensibilities? Can "sense of duty" be placed right alongside "hearing"? What is Bourdieu suggesting with this juxtaposition? On one hand we have a set of seemingly biological, anatomical functions (touch, taste, smell, hearing, and sight), and on the other hand we have what seems more like a list of functions of temperament or dispositional states, sensitivity attributes of different kinds of personalities. Why does Bourdieu want us to consider the similarities between the ability to see (can we call it a "sense of vision"?) and a sensitivity to funny things ("sense of humor") or between the function of hearing ("sense of audition"?) and a sensitivity to what is proper or an acute awareness of one's obligations (a "sense of propriety" and a "sense of duty")? While his point is not theoretically explicit nor empirically developed, what I take from this (and what I myself would argue) is that the conditioning of what and how you see, of what and how you hear, has an isomorphic relationship to the conditioning of what you consider moral, what you find funny, what is absurd, what is beautiful, and so forth. "Tastes" and desires plus compulsions and repulsions unite mind, body, behavioral practices and cultural background.

Here I return to one of the central issues of this book: my concern with the *forms of being-in-the-world* that make a person part of a cultural or ethnic group and that distinguish any given people from another (which points to issues of identity). Within my own mother tongue (English) and within my own cultural heritage (Euro-American), I find the notion of "the senses" or sensing as one of the more profoundly critical or foundational ways to get at an understanding of what constitutes the way people are orientated, their attraction or attachment to (and reproduction of) *ways of being,* or a kind of "going toward" or aversion to things (which is clearly conditioned through culture).[12] What I have tried to establish is that it is also a primary dimension of that principle on which Bourdieu focuses: the socially informed body.

Classen has written (1993b:59) that "[t]he exploration of how we grope to express sensory experience through language, and to convey non-sensory experiences through sensory metaphors, is revealing not only of how we process and organize sensory data, but also of the sensory underpinnings of our culture." In other words, to link that to Bourdieu's argument and my own: in addition to its social, political, economic, and moral dimensions, the habitus is eminently sensuous. The web of sensory experiences and sensory meanings in which everyday life takes place, in which engagements occur with other persons, other beings, inanimate objects, and landscapes (also sound-scapes, smell-scapes, touch-scapes, etc. [cf. Porteous 1990]) forms a critical foundation for conditions of interaction, well-being, and health.

Anthropologists have traditionally produced ethnographies as a way of representing some aspect of the life of a particular cultural group. When I initially began writing an account of the work I did in the early to mid 1990s in Anlo-land and of the things I learned while living with Anlo people in the homeland and in Accra, I thought of the presentation as somewhat ethnographic in nature, but I played with the term *sensography* as a kind of monograph devoted specifically to the sensate realm of a particular cultural group. As the project progressed, however, I gradually became disenchanted with this strategy. Increasingly it struck me as disingenuous since I am not an Anlo-Ewe person myself, and I have to struggle continually to grasp ever-deeper understandings of how the world is experienced and perceived by those who do identify themselves as Anlo. I can listen to their stories and I can observe my Anlo friends living their lives, but I do not feel I can claim to be able to evoke (with a text) the sensibilities that color and texture their existence. Giving up on "sensography," I had to ask myself why I resisted writing an ethnography in the first place and what it is that I hope my readers will take away from this account of culture and the senses.

   For decades now, anthropology as a scholarly discipline and ethnography as a professional practice has been under fire (from both within and without) for its history of collusion with imperialistic, colonialist, and capitalist cultures of the West. In this climate, the very act of "doing fieldwork" is politically charged, even in the most benign settings, and the production of a text representing the Other is fraught with multiple layers of complexity and harbors the potential to generate genuine offense. Desiring a way out of this quagmire is certainly behind some of the difficulty in figuring my way through crafting this account. But in the end, this text sits squarely in the middle of this problem, not producing or providing an easy way out. I say this because I cannot claim to have escaped the trappings of the bureaucratic, corporate, academic praxis that makes up the life-world of most ethnographers (cf. Rose 1990). For awhile I thought that a methodology committed to "being of two sensoria" would help me to cross over—out of my own sensibility into that of my Anlo *mɔfialawo*. That is, I adopted an approach aimed at "being able to operate with complete awareness in two perceptual systems or sensory orders simultaneously" (Howes and Classen 1991:260). And I hoped that I could perhaps transcend my own sensibility (shaped and socialized in a Euro-American, capitalist, academically anthropological habitus) and come into some semblance of the sensibilities of those in Anlo-land. All of that now sounds naive. But the relative failure of this strategy does not stop me from continuing to wonder about the same issue Dan Rose raises (1990:16) when he asks, "What relationships should ethnographers take up with people of other cultures or classes? Can we not move beyond abstract relations with them?" Rose then makes the much-needed point that despite all the recent reflexivity within anthropology, it is mainly "*the text* that has received critical attention, not *relationships* across cultural boundaries" (1990:36, emphasis added).

In Anlo-Ewe contexts if you set out to "study" something you use the term srɔ or srɔnu to talk about this practice. This same term srɔ is used for the endeavor we label in the English language as "marry."[13] They say that to marry is to study the one you have joined, and to study something is to marry it. I invoke this Ewe aphorism not simply to suggest that choosing a cultural group to study (in classic anthropological fashion) is equivalent to marriage. The lifelong commitment to a place and a people that an anthropologist is supposed to sustain is a well-established standard—although I would guess that the divorce rate is also relatively high. But my point is that there is a deeper sentiment in this aphorism that bears exploring.

Marriage in Anlo contexts is a complicated subject and does not have the same meaning, to be sure, that we attribute to "love marriages" idealized in Euro-America. But marriage is the union through which (classically speaking) procreation takes place. So to talk about the process of marriage as studying, and of studying as marriage, is to imply a deep and transformative involvement that ultimately produces fruit. What of the intimacy and physicality, or the sexual-sensual nature of marriage, when we extend the notion to studying? Studying something, truly comprehending it, involves taking it inside oneself, allowing it to change one's perspective. So the sentiment here is that to marry and to study both mean embarking on an endeavor that necessarily will alter or change a person. But nowhere in this notion is the idea that you actually "become" the other person or "become" that which you study. This harkens back to the discussion in chapter 6 about Anlo-Ewe proverbs that espouse change and mutability while at the same time encourage the maintenance of a kind of essence of who you are or the sustenance of a core identity. A black antelope can rub against an anthill and color her fur brown, but that does not change the fact the she is still a black antelope underneath

the new veneer. When you visit the village of the toads and you find them
squatting, you must squat too. But a change in body posture, to adjust
to a life among toads, does not mean you actually cross over and *become*
a toad.

This represents a knowledge about identity and difference that has cir-
culated, in the form of proverbs, in Anlo and Ewe worlds for centuries.
In this perspective is a wisdom, I believe, that has something to offer anthropologists and others outside of African worlds.[14] Claudia Strauss and
Naomi Quinn (1997:9) have bemoaned the fact that "[g]iven the importance, not just in anthropology but in the world today, of analyzing and
understanding identities, it is very unfortunate that most academic dis-
courses on identities tend to assume only two alternatives: Either identities are predetermined and fixed or identities are completely constructed
and fluid." In an Anlo-Ewe philosophy about identity we find neither of
these two poles. Instead, they espouse a way of being-in-the-world that
includes flexibility and adaptability (a "fluidity") while maintaining some
core ("fixed") sense of an identity as Anlo. Strauss and Quinn suggest
that the inadequacy of the earlier (academic-anthropological) approaches
to identity can be helped through the use of psychological models (such
as the cognitive model presented in their own work). They explain that
"identity has an implicit (normally out of awareness) component, which
is neither completely fixed nor entirely fluid. Without such psychological
models," they argue, "it is all too easy to see either fixed physical attributes or the ever-changing immediate context as more determining than
they are and to underestimate the out-of-awareness processes that shape
conscious choices" (1997:9–10). Anlo-Ewe notions of identity concur
with Strauss and Quinn's point about identity being neither completely
fixed nor entirely fluid. So, as neither fixed nor fluid, I would suggest that
the perspective on identity that we find in Anlo-Ewe contexts also fits with
Csordas's idea (discussed throughout this book) that the self is *"an indeterminate capacity* to engage or become oriented in the world"
(1994c:340, emphasis added). In the way that my *mɔfialawo* insisted I
become oriented to certain themes or motifs that they deemed critical to
an understanding of what it means to *be Anlo,* I would suggest that
we see a concurrence with Csordas's notion that "self-processes are orientational processes in which aspects of the world are thematized"
(1994c:340).

Through a dialogical process during fieldwork, these themes, or thematized aspects of the world, became the major contents of my study.
Here I am intentionally using the term *study* in an ambiguous way, to

mean the activity or work that I performed as a student of Anlo culture (i.e., attending to "homework" given to me by various *mɔfialawo*) as well as to mean the examination or analysis of a specific subject (an "ethnographic study" of sensory embodiment in Anlo-Ewe worlds). But the point is that this problem or process brings us back to the notion of *srɔnu*. To do ethnography, one must, in the end, expend a great amount of energy in the practice and activity of study. Anlo speakers would have us understand that this *nusɔsrɔ* (study or studying) is tantamount to marriage: a union that inevitably transforms those involved and that is aimed at producing offspring or fruit. The ways in which I was affected and changed by my time in Anlo-land and through my ongoing association with a wide network of Anlo and Ewe people could certainly fill a book. Perhaps some day I will write that sort of memoir or include more of that sort of information in an ethnographic text. But the "offspring" that we have here, in the form of this book, focuses more narrowly on the problem of culture and the senses. I have tried to explore that philosophical issue in a dialogical way, tacking back and forth between my concerns and information about experiences in Anlo contexts that spoke back to the "study" that my presence embodied and invoked. So the main approach taken in this work has revolved around exploration and explanation. And while I do not claim this as anything close to a definitive account of the senses in Anlo contexts or in Anlo-Ewe worlds, I hope that in the spirit of *nusɔsrɔ*, it allows Anlo-Ewe people themselves some new insight or a fresh perspective from which to explore their own history, language, and culture.

An Anlo person who herself set out to study the sensory order of her own cultural heritage, or to study experiences of sensory embodiment in Anlo-Ewe worlds, would most certainly arrive at and produce an alternate account.[15] Perhaps she would find far more congruence between the senses at play in Anlo-land and the five-senses model that I have worked to deconstruct. Or perhaps this individual would concur with Mr. Adzomada that there is nothing in their cultural heritage to suggest they have ever had a theory or philosophy of the senses. This book is meant to open the door on these issues, in both Anlo contexts and in other cultural settings. But that seemingly innocuous goal has not prevented me from worrying, each step of the way, about the possibility that this presentation simply exoticizes the life-worlds of the people who helped me to explore these questions in the first place. In the end, however, I realize that I cannot have it both ways: if I accept the reality of something I am calling "cultural difference" and I set out to explore, describe, and explain it, I cannot also end up with a book that makes Anlo-Ewe people appear as clones of my own group, Euro-Americans. So here I want to say a few words about why I am interested in "difference" and why I think the senses are one of the most significant avenues through which to understand and explain it.

In his work *On Race and Philosophy,* Lucius Outlaw argues (1996) that whether or not anthropologists accept the existence of races, the term *race* is still deeply meaningful to many African Americans. He refers to his approach as a "conservation of 'race'" and makes a case for the terms *race* and *ethnie* (or "ethnic group") as viable terms in our discourse about cultural difference. But these terms are not employed unselfconsciously. While critiquing scholarly and scientific (especially anthropological) efforts to classify and delimit human groupings, he also holds the position that there still is a reality of *difference* between groups of people and ways of life. But in relation to that phenomenon we call "difference," one of the things that concerns Outlaw (1996:138) is "how to name something that changes and by the naming provide a 'handle' for dealing with it, intellectually and practically, in a way that is more or less stable, if not permanent, over time." He then wonders, "[A]s human groups can and do change in their composition over time, whatever the rate, what is it that the name is a 'handle' on?" (Outlaw 1996:138). And he does not, in the end, arrive at a clear solution: "Racial and ethnic classification and identification, as ventures involving efforts to relate *logically* ordered classificatory terms to *historically* dynamic social realities and have the names be appropriate objectively and subjectively, are no simple tasks" (Outlaw 1996:138).

In this book I have not employed the term *race* but occasionally mentioned *ethnicity* and, more often, simply referred to the phenomenon I was invoking as *cultural difference.* But I take seriously Outlaw's point about how important it is that this "naming" be appropriate at both an objective and a subjective level. In West Africa, many of the names used to designate specific human or social groups link closely to labels for the languages that they speak. But it is never that simple, and attached to each label or name is a complex history and sociology inevitably intertwined with the nineteenth-century evolutionist-colonialist (and by implication anthropological) project of classification. In this book the name or the label "Anlo" received a fair amount of attention. I tried to show not only that there exists a grouping of people who are objectively deemed (by other West Africans and Ghanaians) as "Anlo-Ewe" and who self-monitor and subjectively identify as "Anlo-Ewe" but also that there is a "historically dynamic social reality" that we could describe as a *feeling* and a *sensibility* about *being Anlo*. That is, I have tried to take the discussion further than simply the problem of naming and probe that visceral level where we "feel" difference, or get at the place from which we "sense" cultural distinctions. And this, in the end, is where I believe a significant portion of cultural difference really lies: in the realm of the senses. I think that we can discursively portray and rationally account for only so much. In the end, there is a point of contact that involves sensory engagement. When those sensory fields are not completely in sync, we feel or detect or encounter cultural difference.[16]

Along these lines, let me quote Outlaw again, as he makes a point about the interplay between what we think of as the *social* and the *natural*.

> [H]uman groups, though historical, socially constructed realities, also have *natural* histories, and this makes for particularly thorny conceptual challenges. That is to say, humans are part of the natural world and are subject to many of the principles or laws that govern the processes that make for order in nature. To the extent that we take wisdom or true under-standing to involve systematic knowledge of the rules or principles that govern the object of inquiry, then efforts to distinguish human groups are also efforts to understand and explain varieties of human groupings as in some sense "natural": as conditioned—though by no means strictly *deter-mined*—by processes in the natural, but socially influenced world. (Outlaw 1996:138)

Here I want to highlight his statement that "humans are part of the nat-ural world," so humans, too, "are subject to many of the principles or laws that govern the processes that make for order in nature." This point takes us full circle to some of the issues I raised in chapter 1. I opened the book with the observation that the senses are often treated as defini-tively "natural"—as a psychobiological system that transcends cultural and social influence. But I went on to point out that modern sensory sci-ence may have more open questions about human sensory abilities than answers. So the line between *natural* and *sociocultural* dimensions of human sensory functioning may not be as clear or distinct as some would believe.

I have intentionally left these boundaries somewhat blurred and in-stead opted for Bourdieu's strategy of "theorizing in oxymorons" (Csor-das's [1994b:278–279] characterization). That is, I have focused in this book on neither the purely natural or purely cultural aspects of sensory experience but rather I have examined the ways in which *history is turned into nature* (Bourdieu 1977:78). I have tried to understand Anlo ways of *being-in-the-world* not as "strictly determined" but as "conditioned" (to use Outlaw's terms), or as arising from a "durably installed generative principle of regulated improvisations" (Bourdieu 1977). This approach makes room for *indeterminacy,* which I believe, in accord with Csordas, is a critical notion to grasp when studying self processes in other cultural contexts. Acknowledging the indeterminate boundaries between subjectivity and objectivity allows us to focus instead on issues of attention and orientation, thereby further breaking down the sharp nature-culture divide.

Cultural groups, despite being part of human society, are still a part of nature. And in the end, what exactly the glue is that holds human groupings together is still a mystery. Anthropology and the other social sciences have not really explained it. And while this book does not pretend to bring the curtain down on the matter, it is an attempt to bring the senses onto center stage. In returning for one last moment, then, to an Anlo-Ewe sensorium and to the thematized aspects of the world that many *mɔfialawo* asked me to present, it has become clear that they have both embodied and logical expressions and are inextricably bound up with what we might call *being a person in Anlo ways*. Many Anlo speakers migrate to other regions of Ghana, of West Africa, and throughout the world. But even when living in another geocultural setting, Anlo-speaking persons usually carry some phenomena in their *being:* they carry the sensations of *seselelame,* they carry the memory of balancing buckets of water on their heads and the model of balancing from their god Mawu-Segbo-Lisa, they carry the skill of hearing things and letting them pass right through (an "aesthetic of the cool"), and they carry a flexibility of body and mind started with the very first bath they received (from the village midwife or their grandmother) and reinforced through dance and discourse, and they carry the embodied paradox of *ŋlɔ*. These sensorially loaded aspects of the world that have become "thematized" illustrate linkages between cultural models and the social experience of the individual, for many Anlo speakers believe that maintenance of these forms (these memories, morals, logics, and sensory ways of *being-in-the-world*) are essential to their personal and their collective well-being.

Notes

CHAPTER 1

1. For discussions about why studies of so-called basic psychological processes might better be labeled as "European American ethnographies" or as "Anglo-American cultural studies" (research is typically conducted with middle-class North Americans), see Shweder (1997:155) and also Markus, Kitayama, and Heiman (1996:861).

2. Let me provide some background on why I am using the term *basic* in this statement. In an essay on culture and so-called basic psychological principles, Markus, Kitayama, and Heiman suggest that

> psychologists may be prematurely settling on one psychology, that is, on one set of assumptions about what are the relevant or most important psychological states and processes, and on one set of generalizations about their nature and function. It may be that the psychology which European and American investigators, and those trained in these contexts, have jointly elaborated in the past 50 years, is a psychology rooted in one set of largely unexamined ontological assumptions about what it means to be a person, to be a self, to be a group member and an associated set of culture-specific assumptions about the natural, the good, the worthy, the moral, the healthy, and so on. American and European researchers, guided by an epistemology tied to a particular set of philosophical orientations, have sought and found the wellsprings of behavior in systems of internal structures and tendencies, in predispositions, biases, susceptibilities, or vulnerabilities that are "inside" people. We can now ask, whether, in the course of this theoretical development, psychologists have been developing a set of universal principles about human social behavior, or whether the current view of human social behavior is at this point primarily a partial view, limited to the behavior of people within particular sociocultural and historical contexts. (1996:858)

They continue by explaining that "with the accumulation of evidence that there may be varieties of subjectivities, and that the psychological experiences of various cultural groups cannot easily be mapped onto one another, and with the realization that many of the *basic processes* as currently formulated do not seem to be equally significant across cultural contexts, we have the opportunity to re-think some of the field's 'basic' categories and their origins" (Markus, Kitayama, and Heiman 1996:860, emphasis added). I would suggest that one of the field's basic categories is the notion that sight, touch, taste, hearing, and smell repre-sent a coherent and universally equivalent domain of experience. But when it comes to sensing and perception, do psychological experiences of various cul-tural groups easily map onto one another? More fundamentally, is this domain (hearing, touch, taste, smell, and sight) even a salient category of subjectivity and experience, of perception and knowing, for various cultural groups?

3. Within the discipline of anthropology, an exception to this is Howes's dis-sertation (1992) comparing sensory orders in the West to those in Melanesia, as well as my own dissertation (Geurts 1998) describing an Anlo-Ewe sensorium in West Africa. There is a growing literature on the anthropology of the senses (described later), but few scholars have actually excavated the indigenous sen-sorium of other cultural groups (linguistically, historically, ethnographically). This means that systematic ethnographic accounts of alternate epistemologies of sensory experience are difficult to find in the literature, despite the fact that de-scriptions of subjective and sensory experiences *of* and *with* the Other have in-creased in ethnographic accounts over the past twenty-five years. Within psy-chology, Wober developed what he referred to as a "sensotype" hypothesis (1966) proposing that cultural groups would vary in terms of the typical sensory orientation most individuals would hold, but little research was subsequently carried out to test this hypothesis.

4. While my usage of the terms *sense* and *sensorium* will receive a more ex-tended treatment in subsequent chapters, let me state up front what I do and do not mean when I use these words. In general, the definition of *the senses* that was prevalent in the seventeenth and eighteenth centuries (among Enlightenment philosophers) confined the boundaries of this term to perceptual organs for ob-taining knowledge about the external world or the bodily functions that provide information about the external world. For the past one hundred and fifty years, however, with the advent of psychophysics, experimental psychology, experi-mental physiology, and so on, the senses have come to be understood in terms of bodily ways of gathering information. A contemporary text entitled *The Senses* provides a definition that appears to represent somewhat of a consensus among sensory scientists: "The senses are the bodily mechanisms for gathering up-to-date information" (Barlow and Mollon 1982:1). Taxonomies of the senses from this century (and within Western scholarship) include categories of exteroceptors, interoceptors, and proprioceptors (in various and contested configurations). I am therefore grounded in a perspective we can attribute to modern science, and I maintain that there is an empirical reality that we can refer to as *internal senses*—but that seems to be at odds with a deeply held belief that something can be con-sidered a sense if and only if it is a bodily function that provides knowledge of the external world. While the scholarly label for this perspective is "philosophi-cal empiricism," in terms of the specific application of this perspective to the senses, I will refer to this as a "Western European/Euro-American folk ideology

of the senses" since it is a notion no longer tenable in the face of more than one hundred and fifty years of experimental research in the arena of sensation and perception. For those readers desiring more information on scholarly and theoretical shifts and developments in this domain (from the mid-seventeenth to the mid-twentieth century), a good source to consult is the book *Sensation and Perception in the History of Experimental Psychology* by Edwin G. Boring (1970[1942]). As for the term *sensorium,* by that I mean the entire or whole sensory apparatus of the body. In a technical sense, I am using the term the way Laughlin, McManus, and D'Aquili define it in their book *Brain, Symbol and Experience:* "The *sensorium* is the functional space within the nervous system wherein the phenomenal aspects of the cognized environment are constituted and portrayed in moment-by-moment experience. The sensorium, a time-honored term in science and medicine (Newton used the term in the eighteenth century!), usually refers to the 'whole sensory apparatus of the body' (*Dorland's Illustrated Medical Dictionary,* 23rd ed.). *Phenomenal experience* is a construction mediated by the moment-by-moment reentrainment of perceptual and associative structures.... Phenomenal reality is thus in part an entrainment of cognitive and sensorial networks, which is designed to portray an unfolding world of experience to the organism. The functional space within which association and perception are combined into unitary phenomenal experience is the sensorium" (Laughlin, McManus, and D'Aquili 1992:106). In a less technical but more philosophical sense, I agree with what Walter S. J. Ong wrote in 1967: "[I]t is useful to think of cultures in terms of the organization of the sensorium. By the sensorium we mean here the entire sensory apparatus as an operational complex.... [D]ifferences in cultures ... can be thought of as differences in the sensorium, the organization of which is in part determined by culture while at the same time it makes culture.... Man's sensory perceptions are abundant and overwhelming. He cannot attend to them all at once. In great part a given culture teaches him one or another way of productive specialization. It brings him to organize his sensorium by attending to some types of perception more than others, by making an issue of certain ones while relatively neglecting other ones" (originally from Ong's book *The Presence of the Word,* but more recently reprinted in David Howes's *Varieties of Sensory Experience* [1991:28]).

5. I am suggesting here that on one level it is curious that we do not consider balance to be one of the senses. But on another level, our reason for this is rather obvious. A Western European/Euro-American folk ideology of the senses limits sensory modalities to bodily functions by which the mind can obtain knowledge of the external world, and balance does not yield knowledge of the existence of something outside one's body. In contrast, a phenomenon such as *intuition* (which some Americans consider a "sense of things") does provide a kind of knowing of something outside of oneself. Balance (if one agrees to consider it a sense) is one of the internal senses: it provides information about the physical state of one's own body. Or, to put it in more technical language about the role of interoceptors, it is one of the "key elements of the homeostatic mechanisms that stabilise the internal environment" (Barlow and Mollon 1982:1). I use this example about balancing, therefore, not to elicit a specific answer to the question I raise but rather to trouble the taken-for-granted notion of five senses, plus

the strict division of internal-external that we have inherited from philosophical empiricism, and to argue for the need to conduct cultural histories of the senses (Howes 1991). For example, to complicate this specific issue of what might properly be deemed a "sixth sense" (to add to a Western European/Anglo-American taxonomy), let me quote Edwin G. Boring at length as he describes a moment in our intellectual history when this precise problem was debated. In this case, it was not balance that was contemplated as a sixth sense, but rather *kinesthesia* (commonly defined as a sense located in muscles and tendons and mediated by bodily movement). Boring explains,

> The classical and most successful argument for the independent status of the muscle sense was Charles Bell's in 1826. Although the muscle spindles were not discovered until 1863, physiologists after Bell all accepted the muscle sense as a "sixth sense," arriving in the latter part of the nineteenth century at a considerable body of research on the perception of weight, effort, resistance, movement and position. It was Bastian who in 1880 pointed out that these perceptions are so complex—involving, as they do, the sensibilities of muscles, tendons, joints and skin—that it is better to refer to them as a "Sense of Movement" or *kinesthesis*. In general, the psychologists accepted this word *kinesthesis* as proper, and the term loomed large in the sensory introspections, so important in the experimental psychology of 1890 to 1920. The physiologist Sherrington, on the other hand, having contributed to Schafer's *Text-Book* in 1900 a chapter on "The Muscular Sense," invented in 1906 a new word with a physiological sound, *proprioception*. The proprioceptors, as distinguished by him from exteroceptors and interoceptors, mediate the kinesthetic sensations. It was the ultimate decline of introspective psychology and the consequent rise of physiological psychology that has today gone so far toward the replacement of Bastian's word by Sherrington's. (Boring [1970]:525)

Thus, *kinesthesis* was replaced by a more generalized term, *proprioception*.

6. There are, of course, some contexts in the United States and in the West where balance is more valued than in everyday settings. These include certain sports and physical activities, such as ice-skating, gymnastics, and ballet. Maintaining and achieving balance is also a prominent goal of many New Age rituals and practices, but I would argue that these borrow heavily from so-called traditional cultural values. The link between morality and well-being, its bodily basis and extension into English-language metaphors, is discussed at length by Lakoff and Johnson (1999:290–334).

7. In this definition I borrow some of the wording from Wober's concept of *sensotype*, which he described as a "pattern of relative importance of the different senses, by which a child learns to perceive the world and in which pattern he develops his abilities" (Wober 1966:182). But later discussions will clarify the ways in which my own notion of *sensorium* diverges from Wober's *sensotype*.

8. Sensory psychologist Conrad Mueller suggests that "we maintain an appropriate humility with respect to the ultimate correctness of the views and assumptions which we now employ in talking about sensory functioning and which we frequently accept as being obvious, self-evident, and unmodifiable" (in Tibbetts 1969:14). My point here is that we must keep in mind that, while a taxonomy of five senses (hearing, touch, taste, smell, and sight) represents the dominant way of conceptualizing perception in Western cultural traditions, it is possible that humans have additional sensory systems. The more conventional

"additional senses" include balance and proprioception (Barlow and Mollon 1982), kinesthesia (Schone 1984:292), and multiple skin receptors (making hot, cold, hard, and soft distinct sensations and defining *sense* so that pain detection is included in the way our bodies register and monitor stimulus) (Rivlin and Gravelle 1984). In addition, current research may extend our scientific sensorium to include a vomeronasal system capable of detecting odorless chemicals called pheromones (Stern and McLintock 1998), a functional pineal gland able to respond to light (Rivlin and Gravelle 1984), and even a "magnetic sense" governing navigation and direction (Baker 1981). In addition, contemporary cognitive psychologists and neurophysiologists provide a view of the brain and the human nervous system that suggests certain neural networks are "selectively stabilized" during early development (Laughlin, McManus, and D'Aquili 1990), which means that the mind is an "emergent property of the interaction of brain and organized experience" (Shore 1996:31).

9. I deliberately state that this study addresses *some* of these processes because my focus on sensing and perception marginalizes, by default, other processes by which "history is turned into nature." I want to make clear that I do not mean to discount other aspects of the equation (such as language and thought, cognition, discourse, imagination, genetics, or even Foucault's discipline, etc.) but instead mean to scrutinize the senses for the specific role they play. For instance, I see my approach as having a strong kinship with the theoretical model proposed and developed by Strauss and Quinn (1997) since we share a fundamental concern with how experience becomes internalized into fairly durable structures and identities. So while my own approach is quite distinct from their cognitive framework drawing on schemas and connectionism, this study aims to illustrate some similar processes of internalization but by focusing on the sensory and perceptory elements of the habitus.

10. These scholars have explicitly argued the same point in the cited works, but many anthropologists would agree with this statement and have written with this as an implicit and underlying notion in much of their work. While not an exhaustive list of those who pay attention to cultural difference in sensory experience, as examples see Csordas (1990, 1993, 1994b); Desjarlais (1992); Feld (1982); Feldman (1991); Hall (1959, 1966); Hallowell (1951, 1955); Hardin (1993); Houston and Taube (2000); Jackson (1989, 1996); Roseman (1991); Seeger (1981); Seremetakis (1994); Shore (1996); Taussig (1993); and so forth.

11. Identity is also a major focal point of Sandra Greene's (1996) study of ethnicity and gender in the history of the Anlo-Ewe. My work should not be seen as in any way challenging her definitions or her approach to studying issues of identity, but instead I hope that my study can complement hers. Greene's work is clearly an ethnohistory of Anlo-Ewe identity, and I see mine as a kind of "cultural psychology of identity" in a contemporary Anlo-speaking context. More specifically, her study actually addresses precisely this question that I have posed—the question of where we can look to find what it is that people share, to understand what binds them together, or to identify what links individuals to each other and allows them to adopt a label such as "Anlo" or "Anlo-Ewe"— by carefully tracing the socioeconomic circumstances that came to bear, during various phases of history, on who was considered "Anlo" and who was deemed

an "outsider." So an obvious answer to my question (though not an answer easily documented) is the historical explanation. But not many Anlo speakers actually know ("know" in a cognitive and discursive sense) the details of their own history or histories at the level of complexity covered in Greene's book. She herself occasionally uses the phrase "sense of shared identity" (e.g., 1996:138), and it is at the actual level of sensing and of embodied cultural knowledge that my study approaches this issue. So despite the common concern with identity, the methodologies as well as the contents of the two studies are quite distinct.

12. See Lucy 1992 for a detailed exploration of this aspect of Whorf's work.

13. I do not mean to discount those anthropologists who (over the course of a century) have dealt with issues of perception but rather to make the point that it is a topic that has been marginalized and neglected by the discipline of anthropology as a whole. Shore and Bruner make the point that in the early years of both modern psychology and professional anthropology, the study of the senses and perception—cross-culturally—was important, but then "that set of interests went underground in anthropology for many years and was taken up by only a few cross-cultural psychologists" (Shore 1997:37). It has been experiencing a resurgence in the late twentieth century, as is evidenced by the recent works cited throughout this book.

14. In advocating for a paradigm of embodiment, Csordas argues (1990) that we treat the body not as an object but rather as the material and existential ground for the melding of culture and self. Embodiment is a concept critical to this study and as such will be taken up at length momentarily. Furthermore, my highlighting of work situated within an anthropology of the body should not be taken as a review of this subfield. Consult Lock (1993) and also Csordas (1990:40) for overviews of work on the body.

15. Here I do not attempt to provide a comprehensive review of the anthropology of the senses but just mention a handful of significant studies to make my point. Howes (1991) and Classen (1997) are excellent sources for gaining an overview of work done in sensorial anthropology, the sociology of the senses, and cultural histories of the senses.

16. The idea that certain aspects of sensory perception are "emergent" (and dependent on culture) has been hinted at in prominent contemporary theoretical works that address the embodiment of dispositions through everyday practice (Bourdieu 1977, 1984); the cultural modeling of experience and the construction of meaning (Shore 1996); the conceptualization of self as a capacity to become *oriented* in the world, and the notion that embodiment is the existential condition of the self (Csordas 1994a); the ways in which culture and psyche make each other up (Shweder 1991); connectionist and neural network models for how cultural meanings are internalized (Strauss and Quinn 1997); the ways in which mental representations are grounded in culturally relative somatic experience (Lakoff 1987); and so forth. But while the significance of cultural factors in the shaping of sense perceptions is alluded to in all of these theoretical expositions, the problem is not explicitly or systematically addressed. My own study does not claim to advance a theory, with a capital *T,* but it does build on several of the approaches to culture theory mentioned previously and brings together a con-

ceptual framework with detailed ethnographic renderings of sensory experience and knowledge.

17. I suggest that an approach that has been absent is a developmental and psychological approach, but I acknowledge that others might call for a political-economic approach or a sociohistorical approach to understanding the role of the senses in cultural difference. A discussion of how the anthropology of the senses is neither ahistorical nor apolitical is provided by Classen (1997), who highlights the work of Bynum and Porter (1993), Corbin (1986), Feldman (1991), and Taussig (1993), among others. I would suggest that there is proba-bly more work available, to date, on the cultural history of the senses (especially in the West) than on a cultural psychology of the senses (anywhere in the world), and the dearth of material in this arena is partly what motivates me to write about it.

18. Some of the problems associated with treating the senses as a domain are taken up later in the book. How domain-centered approaches compare to structure-centered and behavior-centered approaches is addressed by Lucy in an article on linguistic relativity (1997:291–312).

19. Here we face something of a paradox or an unresolvable tension in the work. It revolves around the question of whether there is a universal notion of what the senses *are* in essence. To begin addressing this problem I refer to the object of this study in alternating ways—as "the senses" and also as "immedi-ate bodily experiences"—and raise the question of how differing cultural tradi-tions have identified such a domain. Certainly the classic five senses of hearing, touch, taste, smell, and sight are recognized universally as significant human functions, experiences, and sources of knowledge. But I want to suggest that we cannot assume that their foundational category is limited to these five fields, as different cultural traditions may have recognized more or less in their traditional accounts of the foundational bodily experiences that provide essential informa-tion. We do not yet have good cross-cultural data on this question. In addition, if we were to conduct an in-depth ethnographic study among Euro-Americans about ways in which they know things in everyday contexts and about what im-mediate bodily experiences they pay attention to, the five-senses model would probably break down. This book, then, does not provide a point-by-point com-parison between Anlo-Ewe and Euro-American understandings of the senses, but rather, the references to Euro-American modes of knowing and theories of knowledge are used primarily as a rhetorical device. The book is mainly an ex-position of Anlo-Ewe modes of experience, perception, and knowing, along with the presentation of a conceptual framework that could be used in gathering sim-ilar information in other cultural worlds.

20. I should note here that the notion of sharing this cultural stuff is not un-problematic. As Bradd Shore has pointed out (1996:45), "[T]he claim that mod-els are shared is one that deserves careful consideration. How shared must a cul-tural model be in order to qualify as a true cultural model rather than a personal construct?"

See Shore (1996) and Strauss and Quinn (1997) for contemporary theoreti-cal approaches being developed by cognitive anthropologists to address how cul-tural meanings are internalized.

21. There are, of course, different theories for how this process occurs, and the various approaches are not necessarily mutually exclusive. So while I emphasize the acquisition of sensory orientations and the development of a "sensibility," I do not consider this focus to be in conflict with propositions about cultural models and schemas (e.g., Shore 1996; Strauss and Quinn 1997), about the significance of language socialization (e.g., Miller and Hoogstra 1992), about the self as inexorably social and the "object seeking" nature of a child's early relationships (e.g., Fairbairn 1952; Greenberg and Mitchell 1983; Winnicott 1953, 1971), and so forth. They are all ultimately concerned with instantiating culture and with internalization of cultural meanings, and there undoubtedly is not a singular or monolithic explanation for how this occurs.

22. I do not wish to give the impression here that I am the first person to make this claim, and the earlier discussion about precedents in sensorial anthropology and anthropological studies of perception establish that for more than a century this idea has been of interest to a small set of anthropologists, a few psychologists, and scholars in other fields. But it seems to me that this is the starting point for an ethnography that aims to demonstrate sensory differences based on culture. That is to say, this point must be established—with ethnographic evidence—before the other propositions can be explored.

23. Competing and contrasting sensoriums can exist among people who nonetheless consider themselves to be of the same cultural group, and this proposition is aimed, in part, at addressing such complexity. Sensoriums can be gendered, age-graded, class-based, and so forth, as has been discussed by Howes and Classen (1991, esp. 272–274), Classen (1993b), and implicitly in Bourdieu's theory of class distinctions (1984).

CHAPTER 2

1. On use of the term *nation* to depict an entity called "the Ewe" through the course of the past four hundred to five hundred years, I refer to the writings of an Anlo-speaking scholar, Kofi Awoonor, who has argued:

> The highest African political unit after prehistoric times is the state, what has been erroneously called "tribe." A tribe in the original sense meant a small band bound by blood ties and hermetically sealed from all others, geographically remote and of a pre–iron age existence. The term *tribe* thus applied to African societies as original states, is both a political and an anthropological misnomer, apart from its racist connotations. It is a usage that has persisted even when the so-called African tribe consists of millions of people scattered over areas as large in size as the British Isles, and has assimilated many other people over thousands of years. Just as today you cannot talk of a Welsh or a Scottish tribe, in the same way, you cannot speak of an Ewe or a Yoruba tribe. (Awoonor 1990:11–12)

2. This section providing background on the grouping of *Anlo* and *Anlo-Ewe* should be considered a mere sketch. The extremely rich and complex history of who was "in" and who was "out of" these groupings at various points in time is the focus of Greene's (1996) historical work, which should be consulted for a much more detailed account of these categories.

3. Here I would like to add that a rather interesting debate is currently being waged among linguists concerned with the languages in southern Ghana, Togo, Benin, and Nigeria (which would, of course, include Ewe). While the problem is not particularly relevant to this study, the basic issue concerns the degree of relatedness of the languages commonly called Ewe, Gen, Aja, and Fon. For instance, Capo (1984, 1985) argues that these four languages are very close and ought to be considered a "dialect cluster," which he proposes be named "Gbe" (also see Duthie and Vlaardingerbroek 1981).

4. For a discussion of the possibility that Ewe-speaking peoples came from Ife in Nigeria, see Asamoa 1986:3–5. Asamoa thinks that the people whom he refers to as "Ewe stock" (meaning Ewe-, Aja-, and Fon-speaking peoples) were "once a minority in Yoruba-dominated Western Nigeria." He thinks it is possible that the Ewe language was that of a secret society in Ife and was carried with the members of that society as an important part of their religious system when they migrated to Oyo, then Ketu (in modern-day Benin), then Tado and Notsie (in Togo), before arriving in their present homeland.

5. Those familiar with Greene's (1996) ethnohistory will note that this is not an unproblematic comment. There is no simple correspondence between those who left Notsie in the mid-seventeenth century and those who in the 1990s were considered "Anlo people." Greene has documented the complex process, over approximately three hundred years, in which certain clans were considered "in" and others were left "out of" the grouping called *Anlo*.

6. Similar to what I indicate in the preceding note, a historically detailed rendering of this issue would present a very different picture. As Greene explains: "[T]he way in which the Anlo have defined the groups that collectively constitute their society has changed considerably over time" (1996:3–4), and oral traditions indicate that in the past people would "categorize the Anlo clans not just into one very large group of complementary units ... but rather they [would] position the various Anlo *hlowo* on a hierarchical scale that defines certain clans as ethnic insiders and others as ethnic outsiders according to their geographical origins and time of arrival in Anlo" (1996:2). The making or creation of the contemporary category of *Anlo* clearly has a very complex history in which clans play a central role, and readers should consult Greene's work for that detailed background.

7. I am grateful to Sandra Barnes for encouraging me to experiment with tenses in an effort to cope with these difficulties of representation and writing ethnography. The result is not perfect, but it approximates the notion of producing a historical document, and she was influential in my thinking along these lines.

8. More extensive discussions concerning problems of ethnographic representation can be found in Behar and Gordon (1995); Clifford and Marcus (1986); Fox (1991); Marcus (1999); and others.

9. Although I did not investigate issues around "migration out," I suspect that this gender ratio resulted from many men traveling elsewhere for work. Another cause may be the differential in education, with males usually achieving higher levels.

10. I was inspired to employ this phrase, *being a person in Anlo ways,* by E. Valentine Daniel's work on *being a person the Tamil way* (1984).

CHAPTER 3

1. Other scholars have also commented on the "lack of consensus" and the "chaos" we find in Ewe cultural patterns. See Rosenthal's enlightening discussion (1998:45–47) of this issue. I took comfort in particular with her notion of there being "a certain Ewe chaos" (Rosenthal 1998:173) that is culturally valued, utilized, and particularly characteristic of personhood.

2. Contrary to this position, most of the people with whom I worked did not consider the idea of a sensorium meaningless or irrelevant to their cultural process. They were usually quite intrigued by the research and quite in favor of it. Some stated clearly that more Anlo speakers themselves would conduct research like this if they had funding. They believed that these kinds of questions are not generally looked at by Ghanaians primarily because of financial restraints rather than due to lack of interest or intelligence.

3. "Propositional analysis" is another method that could be utilized in this kind of research. In a study describing ideas about illness among Americans, D'Andrade (1976) used sentence frames to construct a model of the way people think about and understand disease, and the same could be done for the way people think they use (or experience) various sensory modalities. Sentence frames could be used to elicit properties of the different senses, and then information about sensing could be integrated "into an organized and coherent set of propositions" (D'Andrade 1976:179). The propositions might reveal patterns of causal relationships between sensing and certain kinds of experience. This more explicit methodology might result in less idiosyncrasy than is present in the current study and in a replicable model of sensing that could be tested.

4. This limitation contrasts, for example, with some of the work that Shweder has done on the cultural psychology of emotion in South Asian contexts in that he has been able to make use of an ancient (third-century) Sanskrit text (the "Rasadhyaya" of the *Natyasastra*) (Menon and Shweder 1994:243–244). In non-Islamic African contexts we do not have such documents, so work on indigenous epistemologies is almost archaeological in that we must excavate (from habits, practices, oral narratives, lexicons, proverbs, and other nonwritten cultural forms) the shards of what is surely an indigenous structure of perception, experience, and thought.

5. The perspective captured by these initial expressions is similar to the definition for *sensing* provided in a contemporary medical text (written by a physiologist and psychologist) that indicates that senses are bodily ways of gathering up-to-date information (Barlow and Mollon 1982:1). This indicates that sensations caused by stimulus from external objects are related (epistemologically or in terms of an indigenous Anlo-Ewe theory) to sensations that stem from internal somatic modes (interoceptors governing balance, movement, etc.). That is, their way of delineating a category for immediate bodily experiences includes both exteroceptors (the external senses of sight, touch, taste, hearing, and smell) and interoceptors (internal sensations). But it should be noted that Barlow and

Mollon's definition of *sense* differs from the classic empiricist view of the senses as passive receptors of stimulus from objects outside our bodies and the notion that the domain of the senses is limited to the bodily organs that function to create representations inside of our minds. Here I do not have the space to expand on the evolution of thinking about the senses in the West, but clearly the five-senses model is not really tenable as a scientific theory. For example, see Rivlin and Gravelle's work *Deciphering the Senses: The Expanding World of Human Perception* for a synthetic account of why some sensory scientists suggest that we may have as many as seventeen senses.

6. I am grateful to Felix Ameka (personal communication, 1998) for the discussion that we had by email about these issues.

7. *Mesi* in this sentence could also be spelled *mesee*.

8. In support of this interpretation, I was struck by Judy Rosenthal's comment (1998:42) that Gorovodu (a specific Ewe medicoreligious order) "treats the whole life-text of the individual, with no teasing apart of the body from the mind or from the numerous souls that make up an individual in all his or her overlapping with totemic plants, animals, deities, and ancestors." I suspect that the category of *seselelame* is quite meaningful to the Gorovodu adepts with whom she worked, even though she does not directly address this concept or term.

9. It is possible that a more extensive language analysis will show that these associations are mainly due to what we might call technical aspects of the language and do not really represent a specific "class of words" in the strict sense of that phrase. That is, one Ewe linguist has suggested to me that in the Ewe language we get these *nu-* forms as a way of encoding situations. Whereas in English one can state, "I drank," in Ewe the same expression must contain an object—*"Meno tsi"* (I drank water) or simply *"Meno nu"* (I drank [some]thing). It is therefore through combining a verb and the *nu-* complement that we get all these nominals or terms that we can interpret as having a name. My brief examination of these terms, then, should not be taken as a final analysis of how sensing is treated in the Ewe language. A linguistic analysis of perception terms along the lines of Ameka's study "Cultural Scripting of Body Parts for Emotions" (2001a) would certainly add rich (psycholinguistic) data to our study of sensation in Anlo-Ewe worlds. At present, a linguistic study such as that does not exist, and so this passage is meant to suggest possible areas of research.

10. We limit *sensory* to things like hearing a sound, seeing a face, tasting pepper. This can be compared to experiences of some other kind, such as balancing one's body as one sits on a stool, taking strides as one moves down the road, intuiting that some event is about to happen. These do not belong in the same domain or class of experiences in our epistemological tradition, but they do seem to be categorized together by many Anlo-speaking people.

11. I am grateful to John Lucy (personal communication, 1998) for pointing out the linguistic differences between the two sets of terms and for suggesting some possible meanings for this distinction.

12. Perhaps the most well-documented aspect of the lives of Ewe people is their expressive culture, especially music, drumming, and dance. For example, in addition to Chernoff's (1979) work, which is based in part on his studies with

Ewe musicians (although it also addresses the music of the Dagomba), one can also refer to Locke (1978, 1980, 1987). Significant works also include Fiagbedzi (1966, 1977, 1985); Pantaleoni (1972a, 1972b, 1972c), Ladzekpo (1971), and their coauthored piece (1970); and Galeota (1985); and on northern Ewe music one should consult Amoaku (1975) and Agawu (1990, 1995). Ewe music and dance has also been the focus of several theses written by students in the United States from the vantage point of ethnomusicology (Conant 1985; Frischkopf 1989). Some of the earliest pieces on Ewe music include work by Cudjoe (1953), Gadzekpo (1952), and the two volumes by Jones (1959). Kofi Anyidoho (1982, 1983, 1985, 1993) and Kofi Awoonor (1974, 1975) have both written poetry and analytical pieces on ethnopoetics. Daniel Avorgbedor has written on *halo* (songs of abuse) as well as on the performance factor in *ahanonko* (drinking names) (1983, 1990–1991, 1994, 1999, 2000, 2001). This is not meant to be an exhaustive list but simply a sampling of some of the work available on Ewe expressive culture, especially as it deals with aurality and sound.

13. Technically, *le* and *me* (or *le eme*) constitute an adverbial preposition that means "within" and modifies *la,* which means "meat, flesh, or skin." But *lame* (in the skin, or in the flesh) can also be a word for the "body" proper. So one can translate *seselelame* as "hearing [with]in the body" or "hearing [with]in the flesh or skin."

14. I am grateful to Felix Ameka for his communications with me about the relation between physical movement and moral movement and for his extensive comments on some of my earlier writings about movement and walks.

15. This idea of one's character embodied in one's walk is also very alive within African-American contexts. However, I have never heard of a specific word in African-American Vernacular English that sums up morality and movement like the Ewe term *azolime.*

16. This is a distinction dancers and practitioners of yoga can often make. They are taught to differentiate between feelings in the tissue of a ligament compared to feelings in a muscle or to stimulation in bone material.

17. Rivlin and Gravelle actually argue that there are four basic skin senses, since heat sensors and cold sensors are distinct. They go on to discuss how "there are obviously more than the four kinds of tactile and thermal stimulations corresponding to the four types of skin receptors that the researchers had originally found. Besides warmth, touch, pain and cold, there are itch, tickle, different types of pain (burning/searing, stabbing/sharp, throbbing/aching, etc.), as well as sensitivity to vibration. Armed with this logic, the new wave of pain research did indeed discover that there are many more than four types of skin receptors" (Rivlin and Gravelle 1984:33). Such a proliferation of skin senses, however, is too detailed or elaborate for our purposes. The extent of our foray into this realm of the senses will be to examine the possibility of three different receptors within the skin.

18. Linguist Felix Ameka has pointed out that I should be careful not to make too much of the fact that their term for speech contains this morpheme "to strike." Along those lines, I do not know how widespread these notions are (among Anlo-Ewe people) about the power, the force, or the striking sensations that certain words or certain phrases hold. I spoke with a few people about this, but they may harbor a rather philosophical view (abstracting and playing with ideas about their

language) that most Anlo people do not hold. Notions of the power of speech are, however, often cited in the literature on West African cultural expression.

19. This is actually a quote from an unpublished paper by Judith T. Irvine. While I do not have a copy of the paper, Stoller (1984b) cites it as "Address as Magic and Rhetoric: Praise-Naming in West Africa," presented at the 79th Annual Meeting of the American Anthropological Association, 1980.

20. I am grateful to Professor G. K. Nukunya for suggesting this concept of *amɛgɔmesese*. In a letter dated August 10th, 1995, Nukunya wrote that *amɛgɔmesese* refers to understanding a person and what he stands for, what he is doing and saying, and so forth. He indicated that this is a different capacity from *nugɔmesese* which is understanding things such as words, actions, behaviors, and so forth. Nukunya also suggests that we might include these two functions as "senses." In the final passage of the book I acknowledge that Anlo people themselves may create a different model from mine of their own indigenous sensorium.

21. Other sense modalities also have a definite active and passive dimension, such as touching and being touched or seeing something happen and searching out something with the eyes. I have included a division for smell in an effort at capturing an emic, or "experience-near," perspective.

22. On pheromones, see Stern and McClintock (1998).

CHAPTER 4

1. I am grateful to Felix Ameka for reading an earlier version of this chapter and providing additional information.

2. I am grateful to Steven Feld, who, after hearing a brief presentation of this example concerning *lugulugu*, suggested that I reexamine this material in light of iconicity, reduplication, and so forth.

3. In addition, the significance of ideophones in West African languages in general has been discussed by various linguists, such as Awoyale (1978, 1989), Newman (1968), and Samarin (1967).

4. In his essay "The Power of Words in African Verbal Arts," Peek makes the point that "it should be stressed that too often we have allowed our literate analytical heritage, recording methods, and concerns about texts and contexts to obscure the primacy of the oral nature of verbal art. Verbal art forms are not merely oral 'translations' which we then 'reduce' to writing. We must continually remind ourselves of the limits of literacy and the hazards of exclusively literate scholarship. For many cultures that we seek to understand, hearing is believing" (Peek 1981:42–43). Samarin's experience of noting few ideophones in the written text but then hearing many when the performers acted the play is a good example of the difference between exploring certain characteristics of African languages in a literary venue and actually experiencing the speech itself. When one hears and experiences Anlo-Ewe speech, the significance of the sounds and tones of the language are readily apparent (as Samarin implies).

5. These terms can be found in Westermann (1930:107–109), who translated them in the following way: *zɔ bafobafo:* the walk of a small man, whose body is briskly moved when he walks; *zɔ bulabula:* to walk without looking where one is going; *zɔ kodzokodzo:* to walk with the body bent forwards stooping; and *zɔ lumɔlumɔ:* describes the hurried running of small animals, such as rats and mice.

6. I am grateful to Austin Amegashie for his observation about how people laugh, eat, and so on, and for helping me to broaden the discussion to an issue of general demeanor and overall comportment.

7. Another literary source, which is even more illustrative of the argument in this chapter, is a book called *Nya Zɔzɔ* (Know how to walk) by E. Y. Dogoe. Linguist and Ewe language specialist Felix Ameka cites this book in one of his articles on duplication (1999:104). I contacted Professor Ameka by email (February 2001) and asked if he would summarize the book for me. He responded (this is a paraphrase): *Nya Zɔzɔ* is a short fiction. It is a forty-four-page book about a beautiful girl who defied tradition and wanted to choose her own husband; she did not want an arranged marriage. She attempted a marriage but it was a flop, and then she left for Accra where she became a prostitute. In Accra she fell sick and in the end died; her body was then brought home for burial. Because she died an unnatural death (so to say), she was not brought directly into town. When she was on her deathbed, she dispensed a lot of advice for others about how to comport themselves in life. Professor Ameka then explained, "The author's desire is that it may be read by the young and the old and he hoped that the young who are about to start life would learn something from it. As he ended [the book]: 'You have heard the story of Dzanka (the principal character). Think about it and *nya zɔzɔ*.' I think its relevance is ... in the fact that such pieces are used to admonish and teach people about comportment."

8. An article that appeared recently in the *New York Times* (Pohl 2002) provides some subtle reinforcement of the central point of this chapter. It describes a study reported in the journal *Nature* that demonstrates how African women unconsciously modify their comportment when they carry loads (balanced on their heads) so as to use less energy. The shift that they make in their gait is evidently "a tiny difference that is almost invisible to the naked eye, and 'even the women don't know how they do it.'" The article touts that in this research, "African women's secret kinetic weapon is discovered." While the comment is undoubtedly meant to be facetious, the entire study about walking (conducted by physiologists and experts in biomechanics) confirms a more general point about an elaboration of and attentiveness to sensory-motor nuances in modes of walking (in Anlo-Ewe if not more widespread African contexts) that I am highlighting here.

CHAPTER 5

1. Here I have simplified some categories that are actually quite complicated and politically charged. For more information on this, see my discussion of these issues in "Childbirth and Pragmatic Midwifery in Rural Ghana" (Geurts 2001).

2. Also see Nukunya (1969b) and Fiawoo (1959a) for incidental information on stools.

3. I include taste in this sentence because if sand was tasted in the food that a person had cooked, it was a sign of low status, improper hygiene, poor character. Since a great deal of seafood is eaten in the Anlo area, washing the sand out of the fish in the process of preparation and cooking was deemed important. People would comment, however, that a person was not clean if you could detect sand in her food.

4. For an overview of similar beliefs in many African societies, see Peek (1981). Among Igbo people in Nigeria, Peek asserts (p. 22), "So important is the ability to speak well, to 'have mouth,' that it is often directly equated with intelligence and success."

5. Although the term *bush* has certain colonialist connotations, I am using it for several reasons. It was the word used by English-speaking Ghanaians to refer to wild areas of the Anlo terrain. Since those wild areas are not really forest or woods, the other terms in English that we could use (to translate *gbeme*) would be the *savanna*, the *steppe*, or simply the *wilderness*. But I think that *bush* more accurately evokes a sense of the appearance and feeling of those wild areas that are made up mostly of brushwood, grasses, and shrubs. In contrasting human and animal realms in African contexts, Jackson and Karp (1990:19) also use the word *bush*.

6. Several years after this conversation, I was fascinated to make note of people's comments in the United States when I began carrying my own baby around. Most of the time my husband or I used a front pouch, which had been given to us as a gift during my pregnancy. (Once in awhile I would try to tie her on my back, but I usually left that to one of her babysitters who was from Tanzania and had more practice than I did with *vikpakpa*.) From a very young age my daughter seemed to get a thrill out of riding face forward in a front pouch (almost contradicting the perspective of my Anlo neighbor), and when we tried to place her facing inward, she would protest and cry. As we walked through airports or through downtown Philadelphia, many people remarked that she seemed to love riding in front because it allowed her to "see everything." I found it striking that so many of the people I talked to in the United States focused solely on the visual stimulation involved in this practice, whereas in Anlo-land what the baby would be able *to see* was not emphasized at all.

7. I have borrowed the phrase *display of traditional flavor* from a preliminary program describing the events that would occur during Hogbetsotso in 1994. The document was produced by the Hogbetsotso Committee of the Anlo Traditional Council, and it was sent to me as a "Special Invitation to the Anlo Annual Hogbetsotso Festival 1994."

8. Here I want to make note that, in addition to walking, crawling is deemed a very important stage in a baby's development. Although a northern Ewe, and not an Anlo, Amoaku (1975:120) wrote, "In the past, it was customary that a child who reached the crawling stage be presented with a stool. According to traditional belief, crawling symbolized 'life'; when a child began to crawl, it meant that he had come to stay."

CHAPTER 6

1. The opening section of this chapter centers on the sound and feel of their name, Anlo, making the phonology of various terms significant to the argument. For this reason, when I am focusing attention on the phonemic qualities of the name Anlo, I spell it as Aŋlɔ—using the nasal vowel ɔ (instead of o) and the consonant ŋ (instead of n). The actual sounds of the place name Notsie and the word *meŋlɔ* (I am rolled or curled up) are also significant to my argument. Through-

out this chapter, therefore, in addition to spelling words such as *meŋlɔ* with their correct Ewe orthography, I will also spell Ŋɔtsie with special characters to place emphasis on certain sonic issues and on the alternate pronunciations. However, in passages not focused on phonology, I will continue using the conventional (Latin alphabet) spelling for the appellation Anlo.

2. Limiting this discussion to the geopolitical boundary of Ghana is somewhat artificial, as it can be argued that Anlo-Ewe and Ewe people in general are also organized and active in civic affairs in many other parts of the world. For example, the Ewe Association in Chicago alone is made up of several thousand people. But here I will confine the discussion to the role of Anlo-Ewe people in Ghana, and the diasporic ramifications of the claims I make here will be explored only briefly.

3. See Locke (1987:4) for a discussion of the influence of Ewe music on American jazz and how, through a book by Gunther Schuller called *Early Jazz,* many Euro-American jazz musicians became aware of Ewe drumming.

4. Ethnomusicologist Daniel Avorgbedor recently informed me of an Agbadza song that expresses these precise sentiments. The words are: *"Habɔ ee, Tema Habɔ ee, Habɔ yae mie ɖo, Tsie ɖe Keta, Habɔ ya mieɖo, Tsie ɖe Keta hoo,"* which means "Tema Harbor, you've arrived, / Water is taking Keta."

5. This story is also an integral part of the annual festival held in Anloga each fall called Hogbetsotso, which many people told me about prior to my participation in the event in 1994. Hogbe is another name for Ŋɔtsie. Amenumey (1986:2) lists a number of the different names used to refer to Ŋɔtsie: Glime (within the walls), Kpome (alluding to the heat), and Hahome (near the river Haho).

6. Some of the written accounts include Amenumey (1986:2–11); Fiawoo (1959a:27–38); Greene (1985:74–76,1996); Kodzo-Vordoagu (1994:1–3); and Locke (1978:7–13). Most of these written accounts simply mention the meaning of *meŋlɔ* in passing. For instance, a document by the Anlo Traditional Council (1978:12) states that "Wenya's own party hit the Ewe coast at Atiteti and then traveled east by canoe to the site of Keta where it founded that town. Going westwards again overland, Tegbi and Woe were founded. By now Wenya had grown weak and feeble and had to be carried in a hammock. At one point he decided he would go no further—that his bones had become shrunken, i.e., *"menlo"* which gave the name ANLO to the settlement that was founded there." Locke wrote (1978:11): "At Anloga, Wenya became cramped and tired, and declared that he could travel no further. Thus Anloga became the capital of the region and the people became known as the Anlo: literally, rolled up or cramped."

7. Greene (1996) documents how this story has been used by different clans at various points in history in their efforts to become "ethnic insiders," or to be included in the category of Anlo. Historically it is quite significant to note which clans actually came from Ŋɔtsie and which ones "invented" a history of tenure there, but these historical facts do not seem to affect the embodied cultural memories that I am highlighting here. This is due in part to what Greene explains about the current status of "Anlo identity" in relation to the place called Ŋɔtsie: "By the mid-twentieth century ... the factors that had generated the permeable, yet still quite limiting, boundaries between 'we' and 'they' within eighteenth- and nineteenth-century Anlo society had changed to the point where only a few groups were still defined as 'other' within this polity. The Anlo increasingly accepted as

genuine fictive kinship ties between clan ancestors and recently invented connections to Notsie" (1996:8).

8. While an oath was not sworn, there are other reasons to accept the notion of Ŋɔtsie as a place with many sacred associations for the Anlo. For instance, see Nukunya's (1969b:120–121) discussion of a powder made from the *eto* tree—a powder used to legalize marriages (in the past) and to conclude various other agreements. He explains that the original *eto* tree was at Hogbe, or Ŋɔtsie, and was associated with one of the gods in that location. Then, "on their departure from Hogbe they brought with them branches of the tree, some of which can be seen to this day." Other significant and sometimes sacred objects and traditions are clearly traced back to their time at Ŋɔtsie. So the discussion in the text—concerning sworn oaths—is not meant to detract from the religious and philosophical ties between Anlo people and Ŋɔtsie.

9. There are no precise equivalents in the English language for the Ewe phonemes ɔ and ŋ in the words *meŋlɔ* and *Aŋlɔ*, so it is difficult to get English speakers to experience the sounds and sensations involved in these speech acts. In efforts to teach the Ewe language to English speakers, the ɔ is usually likened to the sound in the words *cost* or *bought,* and the ŋ is usually described as that of the word *sing,* but there are subtle qualitative differences between how these phonemes are spoken in the two different languages. (For pronunciation guidelines for Ewe, see the preface of Westerman (1973); the *Language Guide (Ewe Version)* of the Bureau of Ghana Languages (1986:7–8); or the beginning of Warburton, Kpotufe, and Glover's (1968) *Ewe Basic Course.*)

10. Along these lines, see Amoaku's (1985:38–39) discussion of how many Ewe "names reflect tonal verbalization of the sounds they produce." He is referring mainly to a drum, *Adabatram,* and how its name means *Adabra* (insanity) + *tram* (astray), which represents the state of mind that the drumming of *Adabatram* creates. In addition, however, the sounds produced by this specific drum have a sonic similarity to the verbal utterance of *A-da-ba-tram.* I am suggesting a parallel concept for the terms *Aŋlɔ* and *"Nyeamea meŋlɔ . . . ."*

11. I have compared notes with other researchers working in Anlo contexts, and they report that people have only rarely if ever spontaneously told them this story. Why so many individuals felt compelled to relate this tale to me is rather curious, and I have tried to trace the ways in which it may have stemmed from the issues and questions I raised in conducting research. I was (in the first instance) trying to excavate their indigenous sensorium (or model of sensing), and I tried to ask questions about bodily and sensory experiences. I sometimes asked people to tell me stories or talk about proverbs that made specific reference to emotional and sensory states. But it was rarely in direct response (or as an explicit answer) to such a request that I was told this story. Instead, people often said they could not think of a story that illustrated something about the senses but that they felt I really should know their history, and then they proceeded to tell me about Ŋɔtsie and Tɔgbui Whenya. Some individuals did expressly state that they wanted me to understand "how they had suffered" (meaning their people), so it was told to me with the theme of emotion in mind. In addition, I heard the story most frequently right around the time of Hogbetsotso (their annual festival commemorating the flight from Ŋɔtsie). These dialogues occurred not

specifically in relation to my own research but rather in the course of everyday conversation during September and October (the festival is at the beginning of November), so the anticipation of Hogbetsotso would (at some level) account for the frequent telling of the tale at that time. However, in at least three instances (including the interview with the man I have called Mr. Tamakloe), the person told me the migration story somewhat out of the blue. That is to say, I had already conducted lengthy audiotaped interviews with these individuals, around numerous topics including the senses or *seselelame* (feeling in the body). Then, without reference to *seselelame* or to emotion, these three individuals (in separate situations) simply stated that I needed to know this aspect of Anlo cultural history. It did not matter to them that I had already heard the story; each person felt I should be told the story again. In retrospect, it seems they were intuiting a kind of association between *seselelame* and some of the themes of the story (including the "suffering" mentioned previously and perhaps even a kind of essence of *ŋlɔ* that some Anlo emigrants in the United States more readily discuss). It is in these ways that I have tried to trace connections between the migration story and a more pervasive Anlo sensibility, between the bodily gesture of folding into oneself and the sadness about their loss of land, and between attitudes about Anlo-Ewe people as overly powerful and their own feelings of persecution.

12. The relations between Anlo-land and its neighbors certainly needs to be scrutinized historically to appreciate this problem. Amenumey, for example, states (1968:99–100), "In the pre-colonial period Anlo had managed to make herself thoroughly hated by her immediate neighbors—some of whom were fellow Ewe people. Anlo had fought many battles with the Gen, a fellow Ewe subtribe to the east. The causes were attempts by either side to engross as much of the slave-trade as possible to the exclusion of the other, and also barefaced slave-raiding. Again there had been many conflicts between Anlo on the one hand and the people of Accra and Ada on the other. These were mostly due to a clash of economic interests, namely salt and fishing rights in the lagoon and along the river Volta." The sources of the "hate" noted by Amenumey, therefore, are complex and historically rooted. I do not mean by my description to discount the complexity of how these relations have deep historical and economic bases but rather to highlight how this aspect of their history has been "turned into nature" (to use Bourdieu's phrase).

13. *Intelligentsia* is a term I heard used by numerous people—both Ewe and non-Ewe—to describe the Anlo. When I asked one prominent Anlo-Ewe scholar about this, he stated that Ghanaians have very peculiar ideas about the Anlo, talking about them as very inward and secretive, and his final comment was that "there are even rumors about a Dzelukɔfe mafia."

14. Greene is not the only scholar to suggest that there is ethnic tension and that some of it stems from an association of Ewes and *vodu*. For instance, Locke clearly states (1978:34), "The Ewe are noted among the ethnic groups of Ghana for the number and power of magic charms, commonly referred to in broken English as juju." In addition, in a separate part of this same work, Locke (1978:23) recounts a historical anecdote about how the British could not enlist other ethnic groups to join them in attacking an Anlo camp. Locke then con-

cludes with the remark, "This episode seems to indicate the fear which other Africans had of the Anlo." Clearly, the issue of animosity along ethnic lines has a complex and deep history and cannot be summed up simply as fear of *vodu*, but this discussion is aimed at exploring certain restricted dimensions of this problem.

15. This melancholic sensibility is also described by Kofi Awoonor. See especially his discussions on pages 202–217 in *The Breast of the Earth* (1975).

16. The precise history of this story is unclear. While most people seem to think that Anlo people have been telling this story since they arrived at the area known as Keta and Anloga, it is also a story that has been used by groups to gain "insider" status (see Greene 1996).

17. While little seems to have been written about Ŋotsie, and I am not aware of archaeological excavations having been conducted there, Amenumey does mention some details in his account of Ewe precolonial history. "As late as 1927, the walls of Notsie which has [*sic*] been ravaged by centuries of exposure still measured 5 1/2 metres in thickness and 1.8 metres in height. It was estimated that originally it must have been about 5.2 metres high and 8.5 metres wide" (Amenumey 1986:4).

18. For a discussion of why the principle of the obverse is significant in phenomenology and does not represent a dichotomy, see Merleau-Ponty (1969).

19. For much more extensive discussions of the verbal arts of West Africa, see Anyidoho (1983, 1985); Awoonor (1975); Ben-Amos (1975); Finnegan (1970); Okpewho (1979); and Stoller (1997).

20. One *mɔfiala* stated that "in the olden days" *ga foɖi mawo* referred specifically to the practice of sorcery and sacrifice of a human being to acquire wealth but now includes other methods of theft such as embezzlement, plus fraudulent land sales and even prostitution.

21. Gilbert translates the term *trɔ* as "nature gods" (1982:64). Fiawoo refers to them as "nature spirits" and explains a great deal about how the *trɔwo* (plural) fit into the religious system as a whole. For background on the *trɔ*, therefore, refer to Fiawoo (1959a: 50–60, 218–240).

22. I am still unsure whether this phenomenon is referred to with the Ewe term *trɔxɔviwo* or the term *fiasiɖi*. The word *trɔxɔviwo* literally means "the *trɔ* that takes/receives/obtains your child," while the term *fiasiɖi* is translated by Westermann as "a girl or woman dedicated to a *trɔ*" (1973[1928]:49). It is my impression that they are different words referring to the same phenomenon— one being a descriptor of the cosmic spirit itself, the other being a descriptor of the human devotee. However, some *mɔfialawo* insisted that these are two very different phenomena with different procedures and rules. The basic difference was explained as follows: a *trɔxɔviwo* shrine is the holy place for the spirit to which a barren woman must appeal if she wants to have a child, and if she becomes pregnant her child must be a devotee of that *trɔ*, whereas *fiasiɖi* refers to the shrine where a family must (forever) bring a virgin girl to live as a devotee as compensation for a criminal offense committed by a family member. I am not convinced, however, that this last distinction is accurate. Clearly, the average Anlo person finds these things rather confusing, so my notes, which cover dozens of conversations on this topic, reflect some of those differences in opinion. Fia-

woo states (1959a:116) that *fiasiḍixexe* is a custom "of penal servitude by which a criminal is bonded to serve for life in a cult house in atonement for his crime" and that *trɔxɔviwo* is that "convent cult" (with the word literally referring to "cults that take in children"). His explanation supports my view of *trɔxɔviwo* as a categorical term for "spirits who obtain or take your child," and the demand can be for various reasons—atonement for a crime, payment for making the conception possible, and so on. And while I did not hear the custom or institution referred to as *fiasiḍixexe*, if the *-xexe* refers to "paying," then this also supports my view since the lineage is forever paying a *fiasiḍi* (a girl or woman dedicated to a *trɔ*) to the shrine.

23. Fiawoo states that the institution of *fiasiḍixexe*, or *trɔxɔviwo*, "as now illegally practiced, is rapidly disintegrating" and that "'trial by ordeal' no longer enjoys official recognition; nor does the custom of *fiasiḍixexe*" (Fiawoo 1959a:265, 297). However, as of the mid-1990s it had still not "disintegrated" but was indeed the topic of much controversy.

24. There is an interesting parallel here with certain aspects of African-American cultural worlds. The October 30, 1995, issue of *Newsweek* contains an article entitled "Battling for Souls" (pp. 46–47). The theme of this article is the competition in America between Christianity and Islam for the attention of Black men. The author explains that "Islam's emphasis on dignity and self-discipline appeals to many men in the inner city, where disorder prevails. Muslims are expected to pray five times a day, avoid drugs and alcohol and take care of their families. 'Even the manner of walking is different,' says Ghayth Nur Kashif, imam of a mosque in southeast Washington. When young men are first introduced to Islam, he says, many come in strutting—'swaying from side to side or walking with a little limp. In very short order the limp and swinging stops.'" In a direct parallel with Anlo culture, much about a person's moral and ethical center is embodied in his or her walk. In addition, one's way of walking used to identify the neighborhood in Philadelphia where you grew up. That is, an African-American gentleman explained to me that when he was growing up in the 1940s and 1950s, there was a general North Philadelphia walk that differed from the South Philadelphia and West Philadelphia walks. I believe this was specific to the African-American world of Philadelphia back in the 1940s and 1950s, and then within each quadrant further divisions existed in terms of neighborhood and style of walk.

CHAPTER 7

1. An example of young people not knowing their own history, language, and culture can be found in the simple word *yevu*. This is the Anlo-Ewe term used to designate "white person" or "European-American." It derives from *aye avu*, which literally means "tricky dog" and was probably coined over one hundred years ago in the context of the transatlantic slave trade. Many Anlo speakers under thirty years of age have no knowledge of the real meaning of that word and often argued with me about the etymology. We inevitably had to seek out an older person of sixty years or more to explain this word to the young Anlo

speaker. In that context I would sometimes hear the elders muttering *"Meɖu dze o"* (you did not eat salt).

2. I was told of this practice literally the day before I left Ghana, and I have not yet been able to follow up to gather more details about the symbolism of the balanced tray or what constitute the "articles of life."

3. I did not conduct research on the history or creation of Hogbetsotso, and therefore cannot explain details of its origin. I do, however, know from conversations that it is a relatively new festival, and one *mɔfiala* who was in his eighties was an active member of the original organizing committee. Furthermore, in his 1959 dissertation, Fiawoo states that there is a need for Anlo-Ewe speaking people to create a national festival like the annual Homowo event of the Ga in Accra, so we can surmise from this comment that the first Hogbetsotso event occurred after Fiawoo finished his research.

4. Initial information about Hogbetsotso can be found in Kodzo-Vordoagu (1994).

5. It seems that exceptions are sometimes made in the case of foreigners, permitting men to wear pants as long as they remove their shirts and shoes. But I do not think such concessions would be made for an Anlo person wishing to enter the grounds.

6. I am not suggesting that sensations are political phenomena in and of themselves. They have many referents. One type of sensation may be associated with a form of dress that symbolizes "colonization" or "outsiderness," while another may be associated with a form of dress that symbolizes "tradition, history, or Anlo- or African-ness."

7. Interviews with various members of the village resulted in somewhat contradictory explanations for exactly what occurred during this event. For instance, some stated that the carrier was possessed, and others said he was not; some indicated that Tɔgbui Apim directed the movements, while others stated the carrier moved volitionally. Due to these conflicting explanations, my report is rather tentative, and I am limiting a fair amount of what I say to what was simply observable to me. From my perspective (as an outsider and someone very new to this cultural context), he did appear to be possessed, but I cannot really know that he was. In future research I hope to pursue interviews with people such as this ritual specialist to get at a deeper understanding of the embodied feelings people experience during an event such as the Tɔgbui Apim rite. But this account is based on fieldnotes and interviews from my first stay in Anlo-land, and there were definite limits to how far I would push people for information or access that they did not seem to want to grant an outsider. My rapport with people in Srɔgboe and my respect for their right to keep certain things secret was more important to me at that time than was obtaining information for a book. So when people stated that they did not want to talk to me or did not want to talk about certain topics, I left that alone.

8. See Little (1965) for descriptions of voluntary associations and their significance.

9. I should make clear that I have not verified this analysis with any *mɔfialawo*, so it is offered as a tentative interpretation. While the theme of *balance* was obvious in the main activity of the carrier of Tɔgbui Apim's offering, the other displays

of *balance* that I have uncovered in the ritual's sequence are more subtle and require further investigation as to their significance and meaning.

10. This interpretation is supported by the hot and cool binary oppositions found in the pantheon of *vodu* spirits discussed by Judy Rosenthal (1998:65–70, 115–116, 217). I arrived at my own analysis of the differing personalities making up the Srɔgboe community and displayed during the Tɔgbui Apim event before I read Rosenthal's work. But upon reading her account, I was quite struck by the similarities between a kind of balancing between hot and cool that I claim for the Srɔgboe community and that which she describes for the pantheon of Gorovodu.

CHAPTER 8

1. I borrow this notion of *porosity* from a lecture Achille Mbembe delivered in the context of a graduate course at the University of Pennsylvania, The Religious Imagination (Spring 1992).

2. On religion in Anlo and in Ewe worlds, consult Avorgbedor (2000); Cudjoe (1971); Cudjoe-Calvocoressi (1974); D.K. Fiawoo (1959a, 1959b, 1968); Gaba (1968, 1969a, 1969b, 1971); Geurts (1997); Gilbert (1982); Greene (1996); Meyer (1999); Nukunya (1969a, 1969b, 1969c); Parrinder (1951); Rosenthal (1998). Also see Arkaifie (1976:64–67) for some additional sources.

3. I am deeply grateful to Tanya Luhrmann for helping me to pull out of my own material these insights about *vodu* being a *sensorium beyond the body yet continuous with it*. She made explicit for me some of the ideas that I was implicitly batting around in earlier drafts of this chapter. When other readers told me to drop this chapter from the book, Sandra Barnes encouraged me to keep working on it, and Tanya Luhrmann pushed me to bring to the surface these links between their interoceptive focus and Anlo-Ewe people's workings with *vodu* (and other metaphysical practices).

4. In my conversations with Christians I found this to be the dominant usage, and one need only glance through a copy of *Biblia* (Bible Society of Ghana 1993) to note the exclusive use of *Mawu* at the expense of incorporating the other components of *Segbo* or *Lisa*.

5. I am indebted, however, to Dzobo for the initial insight concerning the severe implications of splitting apart the masculine and feminine aspects of the Ewe concept of god.

6. *Gbo*, of course, is the same etymological *bo* as that of the Fon *bociɔ* statues (empowerment objects) that are portrayed in Blier's recent work on *vodun* (1995).

7. In a fashion very similar to this account of Mr. Adzomada's, Rosenthal reports, "Parents questioned Afa about their newborns' *dzoto* (ancestral soul), which forebear had come back, whether there was anything the dzoto itself wished them to do at the beginning of the child's life" (1998:168).

8. See Greene (1996) for extensive historical information about Nyigbla.

9. Gilbert suggests (1982:64) that Nyigbla has certain affinities to the Yoruba deity Shango, which seems to indicate Nyigbla came from the east. But Greene

establishes (1996) that Nyigbla was introduced to Anlo from Gbugbla, to the west.

10. We had a residence in Srɔgboe as well as an apartment in the Kokom-lemle section of Accra.

11. Cudjoe also discusses how Du-Legba "has no mercy with wrong-doers" (1971:200); this arbitration of life and death would presumably have been the domain of another Anlo trɔ prior to the introduction or adoption of Nyigbla in the nineteenth century.

12. For more on Nyigbla and *xexeme gbegblɛ* (ruin or destruction of the world), see Fiawoo (1959a:225).

13. For more information on Yeve, see Fiawoo (1959a:67–75), Greene (1996), and Nukunya (1969c). Fiawoo explains, "In recent years, it [Yeve] has eclipsed *Nyigbla[,]* the leading du trɔ of the whole tribe. Cutting across state boundaries, it has grown to become the largest and most famous private reli-gious cult in all Anlo" (1959a:67–68).

14. Also see Fiawoo (1959a:54) on this point.

15. This lack of self knowledge is often expressed with the phrase *Meɖu dze o,* which means "you don't eat salt," or "you're not salted," which was discussed in chapter 7.

16. Also see Fiawoo (1959a:100) on Nyigbla's role in "restoring social equi-librium."

17. In the Ewe language there exist terms that are more closely related (both morphologically and in terms of meaning) to this Fon word than is the term *legba*. These linguistically related terms include *agbonuglawo* (Fiawoo 1959a:39) or *agbonudzɔla,* which Westermann translates as "guardian at the gate" or "an idol" (1973[1928]:91). Both of these Ewe terms share the *bo/gbo* component that is in the Fon word *bociɔ* and also is the center of Mawu-Segbo-Lisa (Anlo-Ewe god concept or notion of supreme being). (This *gbo* [also *agbo*], variously means "strong, vigorous, powerful, violent; portico or gate.") However, it is my impression that in terms of physical form and in terms of function, *legbawo* are the Anlo-Ewe counterpart to these Fon "empowerment objects" *(bociɔ)* de-scribed by Blier (1995). It is interesting to note that one of the "invocative praise-names" used for Legba is *Legba agbo,* which translates as "*Legba* the gate, … a power who can both keep and break the gate" (Cudjoe-Calvocoressi 1974:62). Here the *bo/gbo* dimension (of power, vigor, gatekeeping) is simply added to Legba's proper name, further supporting the view that Anlo-Ewe *legbawo* and Fon *bociɔ* are closely related.

18. Additional explanations for the derivation of this word exist. For in-stance, one person told me that it comes from *alɛwofeagbe,* "protecting the life of the sheep" (*alɛ*: sheep; *wofe*: their; *agbe*: life). He then provided an explana-tion very similar to one given to Dzagbe Cudjoe: "In the Anlo traditional area another explanation of the origin of the Legba cult was given me. A man whose sheep were perpetually being stolen erected a clay figure of a human being at the entrance to his compound. The thieves mistook the figure for a real person and refrained from stealing the man's sheep" (Cudjoe-Calvocoressi 1974:57). In ad-dition to deceiving thieves, my *mɔfiala* stated that these scare-crow-type statues also were used to fool wild animals and keep them away from the sheep. How-

ever, this etymology for *legba* seems to be less common than "seize and collect at one place" (*le:* to seize, catch, hold, grasp; *gba:* to collect or keep at a place).

19. In fact, it was not precisely a *legba,* but rather an object called an *afeli.* They serve a similar purpose, however, because the *afeli* is a small clay figure that functions as a guardian or protector of the house. It is kind of like a mini-*legba.* I am grateful to Elvis Adikah (2001) for our correspondence on this issue.

20. Other *mɔfialawo,* however, said they do indeed use the word *seselelame* (feeling/hearing through the body, flesh, skin) when explaining symptoms to bio-medically trained doctors.

21. The same observation could probably also be made of many cultures in the West. I am thinking in particular of Erika Bourguignon's study *Possession* (1976), in which she demonstrates the abundance of representations of altered and trance states in television and film. She argues that many Westerners, too, are fascinated with the phenomenon of possession trance and that it occupies a significant place in the spectrum of our imaginings and our minor obsessions—even if we relegate it to film instead of the realm of experience and practice. I would suggest the same could probably be said of a seemingly mundane thing we refer to as *thresholds.* That is, my hypothesis is that an analysis of popular films that run in the West would probably reveal a great amount of attention paid to the potential for dangerous things to be lurking at thresholds.

22. Rosenthal's recent ethnography (1998) is an excellent source for clarification on the differences between Yeve (an older *vodu* order) and Blekete (a more recent, medicine *vodu* cult). Chapter 3 of her book provides a rich history. Greene (1996) also provides extensive information on Yeve.

23. This interpretation of *vodu* is supported by much of what Rosenthal has written. The subject of her book is Gorovodu, which she defines in general terms as an *atikevodu* (medicine *vodu* cult) and which Srɔgboe people called Blekete. But in this passage she is further clarifying what is meant by Gorovodu: "Some adepts say that they are a fusion of spirits with the plants that call them forth. The plant ingredients in the manufacture of the god-objects are said to be the most active of all the elements. While in trance, the wives or hosts of the vodus (trosis) are also called vodus or tros. They live in temporary corporal and psychic fusion with the northern spirits" (Rosenthal 1998:47–48). Here she hints at some of the sensory dimensions of *vodu* with a glimpse of potential synesthesias—a fusion of spirits with plants and the body-mind of the human host. Also see Stoller's work *Fusion of the Worlds* (1989a) for attentiveness to the sensory dimensions of spirit possession trance in West Africa.

24. The term *juju* may be of Hausa origin. See Chernoff (1979) for a discussion of this word.

25. This is not to suggest that verification of such phenomena is not important. But exploration and documentation is always framed somehow by concerns and interests, and here I am trying to argue that the *perception* of pots and pans moving is as important as the movement of the pots and pans and that they are simply two different issues and (to a certain extent) separate phenomena. While I do not want to overstate or push too far the notion that they are separate phenomena, perhaps the following will more clearly illustrate my point. A public television show (*Nova,* aired in Philadelphia the week of February 25, 1996) grap-

pled with the relatively widespread (at least in the United States) phenomenon of UFO sightings. Well-known astronomer Carl Sagan made the point that whether UFO sightings are a phenomenon of *outer space* or *inner space,* either way it is a serious and significant phenomenon for the human species. He went on to explain that within the context of his own cultural model (which we would commonly refer to as science), it is most likely a case of inner space (and still, he argued, warrants the attention of scientific researchers). But as the documentary clearly demonstrates, from the vantage point of numerous Americans who operate in the context of a different cultural model from that of Carl Sagan, UFO sightings are perceived, experienced, and explained as a phenomenon of outer space. I am not suggesting that both these cultural models are exactly equal or equally powerful, but simply that cultural models unto themselves are worthy of study—especially in relation to how they link to "the social experience of individuals."

26. Once *dzosasa* was identified, the cultural model usually indicated consultation with a specialist or diviner who would prescribe ways to transform the situation. Various types of diviners existed among Anlo-speaking people (including different types of Anlo healers: *bokɔ,* or Afa priests; *amɛgashi,* or diviners), but specifically in relation to *dzosasa* one might be inclined to consult with a *dzoḍuamɛtɔ* (*dzo:* charm, magic; *ḍu:* eat; *amɛ:* person; *tɔ:* agent): a person whose agency was dealing in (signified here as "eating") magical charms. Other terms for such a practitioner included *dzotɔ* (*dzo:* charm, magic; *tɔ:* agent) and *dzosala* (*dzo:* charm, magic; *sa:* tie, bind; *la:* agent).

CHAPTER 9

1. Here I have borrowed the phrase "the social basis of health and healing" from Steven Feierman and John Janzen's (1992) volume about Africa.

2. To conduct further research on this distinction, I think that case studies might benefit from the suggestion that we apply the categories of "intuition, imagination, perception, and sensation" (Csordas 1993:147) to try to understand the intricacies of various illnesses and how one takes the route of "sickness from home" while another is deemed a "spiritual sickness."

3. *Enu* can also result, however, from withholding things that ought to be spoken about, so it is not simply caused by the so-called striking action of the speech.

4. It may be valuable to explore this perspective on the potential power of speech to maim or kill in some African-American communities also. For instance, some aspects of *enu* seem to parallel poet Maya Angelou's story of why she stopped talking as a small child. She had been raped and was fearful that her own speech had the power to hurt those people close to her and to kill the man who had violated her. While Maya Angelou's case does not represent an exact fit with the Anlo concept of *enu,* at the root of both is the notion of the irreversibility of speech as well as "its transferential nature and its potent social and psychodynamic grounding" (Blier 1995:77).

5. Rosenthal (1998:83) mentions rules against "nursing rancor"—among the Gorovodu (an Ewe medicoreligious *[vodu]* order) adepts with whom she worked—because such bad feelings were known to cause illness.

6. There is a "mouth-opening ceremony" among Gorovodu worshipers described by Rosenthal in her marvelous ethnography of Ewe *vodu* (1998: 188–194).

7. Such isomorphic statements within cultural anthropology have often been misunderstood. For example, in a review of Gorer's famous "swaddling hypothesis" in regard to "Russian culture and character," psychological anthropologist Bock explains: "It would be a mistake to view this hypothesis as a causal argument, for it is actually a configurationalist statement of isomorphisms. Gorer does *not* claim that the practice of swaddling children causes Russians to have autocratic political institutions (Tsarism, Stalinism), nor that it produces a manic-depressive basic personality in all Russian adults. Rather, he is content to note the formal similarity among various cultural patterns, and to suggest that prolonged, tight swaddling is *one of the means* by which Russians communicate to their children that a strong external authority is necessary" (Bock 1988:85). Such a "formal similarity among various cultural patterns" is also what I am trying to point out in regard to flexibility.

8. This issue of real or unreal did not tend to be of concern to many Anlo speakers (as it might be for some Westerners who measure reality by what can be seen, which stems from an extreme emphasis on the sense of sight).

9. Rosenthal notes that in Gorovodu culture "it is not uncommon for the different components of a given individual's personhood to be at war, or at least at odds, with each other" (1998:187). So this perspective, articulated by certain Anlo-Ewe people as well, has its parallel in other Ewe contexts—and not just in Western psychotherapy.

10. It is important to note that Raphael (who had this dream) told me that most people did not want to know what their dreams meant, and they certainly did not want to analyze interpersonal and family dynamics. He said they were afraid of what they might learn about the negative influences—in spite of the fact that it was commonly understood that "those close to you can harm you the most." He asked that I not tell anyone that he seeks the counsel of diviners or Afa priests to scrutinize and interpret these phenomena, as he was fearful of what people might think of him or do to him if they learned that he utilized *dzosasa*.

CHAPTER 10

1. According to ancient and medieval philosophy, the quintessence is the fifth and highest element that permeates all nature and composes heavenly bodies. But how Aristotle linked the various senses to the various elements is not clear and shifts throughout his writings. In one instance he writes: "The eye contains water, which can absorb light; water, then, is the element of sight. The element of hearing is air, that of smell is fire, that of touch is earth. Taste is a form of touch ... and so the sum comes out even" (Vinge 1975:17). This would lead us to count the senses as four, rather than five. Then in another work he argues that "the only elements of which sense-organs are composed are air and water," which then leads to a complicated rendition of how each modality fits under those two categories (Vinge 1975:17). The point is simply that Aristotle's ra-

tionale for what constitutes a sense and how many there are was consistently connected to the elements.

2. For a provocative account of such extensions, see the February 2000 issue of *Wired* magazine. The cover is graced by cybernetics professor Kevin Warwick, whose article describes his experiences implanting chips into his own body. One of the photo captions reads: "When the new chip is in place, we will tap into my nerve fibers and try out a whole new range of senses." By "whole new range of senses" he means that "we can't normally process signals like ultraviolet, X rays, or ultrasound. Infrared detects visible heat given off by a warm body, though our eyes can't see light in this part of the spectrum. But what if we fed infrared signals into the nervous system, bypassing the eyes? Would I be able to learn to perceive them? Would I feel or even 'see' the warmth? Or would my brain simply be unable to cope? We don't have any idea—yet" (Warwick 2000:146).

3. Some argue that humans possess a vomeronasal sensory system (e.g., Rivlin and Gravelle 1984:152–156), while others state quite emphatically that we do not (Barlow and Mollon 1982:423–425). A recent study (Stern and Mc-Clintock 1998) provides definite evidence of human pheromones.

4. See Lucy 1997 for an account of how domain-centered approaches compare to structure-centered and behavior-centered approaches.

5. In Shore's interview with Bruner (1997) they discuss how the senses were studied early in this century but were then dropped as a topic or neglected as an issue for cross-cultural psychology.

6. Some maintain a view of mind that does not dichotomize between brain (bodily quality) and psyche (mental quality) but instead treats the mind as "an emergent and contingent property of social experience" (Shore 1996:32). As Shore puts it: "the active human psyche cannot be reduced to its common biological substrate, abstracted from the conditions of its development and the particular environment within which it is functioning at any given time" but rather, "while certain neurological features may be characterized as intrinsic to the normal development of any human brain, others are more flexible and inscribe in the form of particular neural networks the particular environment in which the brain has been developed" (Shore 1996:17). In certain ways this squares with the following perspective: "It is a major assumption of cultural psychology that one mind is transformed into many mentalities through the symbolic mediation of experience and that the human conceptual capacities that support culture also support language use, which is the primary means by which the symbolic and behavioral inheritances of a cultural tradition are passed on to the next generation. It is primarily by means of language that human beings negotiate divergent points of view and construct shared cultural realities" (Shweder et al. 1998:887). This is consistent with the information on the lexicon for the senses that makes up chapter 3.

7. I am grateful to John Lucy (personal communication, 1999) for suggesting this comparison.

8. In an interview with Jerome Bruner (published in *Ethos*), Bradd Shore poses the question of "whether there is a tight relationship between the way in

which knowledge is encoded sensorily and the way in which that knowledge is experienced and known. And what implications does that have for a theory of self?" (Shore 1997:44). Bruner's response to the question is, "Oh wow," and then Shore admits, "Well, it is a big question." I agree that it is a question or a problem that requires scrutiny, but it is also essentially what I am taking up here in proposition three.

9. I have borrowed this phrasing from Daniel's (1984) work *Fluid Signs: Being a Person the Tamil Way*, but I do not follow a strict semiotic approach to studying the self. And while I am in agreement with Csordas (1993:282) that an "opposition between semiotics and phenomenology is a false opposition," this debate is not something that I take up in this particular study.

10. Compare this to Csordas's point (1994b:279) about "one of the dualities challenged in the notion of habitus is that between the conscious and the unconscious." He also stresses that such dualities are really at the level of theory rather than in terms of actual "being" or existence, or they are "theoretical and not ontological distinctions" (1994b:279).

11. In chapter 1 I explained that theoretical notions from both cultural psychology and cultural phenomenology have been influential in this study. Here I would like to clarify that whereas cultural psychology seems to take "embodiment" for granted, cultural phenomenology elaborates the issue of the fundamental role of the body in development of personhood and self. As my subject matter here focuses on processes of perception and sensation, I find it necessary to make explicit how accounts of bodily experience are related to accounts of how the world is known and understood (in the African context of Anlo-Ewe worlds), rather than taking for granted that all experience is necessarily embodied.

12. Here I would like to give a little background on how the English term *sense* relates to the figurative and metaphorical kinds of senses I discussed previously. Classen (1993b:72) explains that the English term *sense* has an Indo-European root, *sent-*, which means "to go" or "to find out." In Latin, *sensus* (which derived from *sent-*) means "sense" or "feeling" and has through the ages more or less referred to "faculty of perception." But in the sixteenth century *sense* also acquired an association with "instinctive knowledge, sensation, signification, and the mental and moral faculties, often expressed as 'interior senses.' In the seventeenth century sense acquires the meaning of judgement" (Classen 1993b:72). In a similar fashion, the term *sensible* referred for a long time in the West to being "perceptible by the senses and endowed with the faculty of sensation" but then evolved (during the sixteenth to the nineteenth centuries) into a term that could also refer to "having an acute power of sensation" and "capable of delicate and tender feelings, sensitive" (Classen 1993b:72–73).

13. Linguists maintain that the *srɔ* for study and learn is expressed with a high tone, and the *srɔ* for marry is expressed with a medium tone—thereby rendering them distinct or separate words. But many average or at least nonacademic Ewe-speaking people consider the two expressions of *srɔ* to be linked, which is the basis for their philosophical musings about similarities between studying and marriage.

14. I have intentionally broadened this statement to those beyond "African worlds" rather than simply beyond Anlo and Ewe worlds because I suspect that this is a philosophy that we would find in other language groups and in other cultural settings on the African continent and in African diasporic communities.

15. When I make these observations throughout this passage, I am thinking of Dan Rose's comment about how "[c]ontradictions and collisions occur when a Western author writes about a people who can also write about themselves. If this does not pose a crisis for anthropological poetics, it certainly raises an issue of competing perspectives and sensibilities in a space of conflict between cultures" (Rose 1990:48). I am sure there will be those who object strenuously to certain portrayals or characterizations that I have put forth in this book. But I am also certain that many Anlo-Ewe people will agree with much that I have said. A point I would like to make here is something that I stress with my students, which is that to really know anything about any particular way of life they must read many different accounts. One ethnography cannot convey the entire history, sociology, philosophy, and life-world of a group of people. There is a great amount of work in print by Ewe and Anlo-Ewe authors themselves that can be read in tandem with this book (see the bibliography). And I also hope that this book will spawn additional explorations of Ewe philosophical and psychological systems and even accounts of what I think of as an Anlo-Ewe metaphysics. People who have grown up within the tradition will undoubtedly have a deeper grasp of the principles and how these are played out in daily life. I welcome the "competing perspectives" with all the "contradictions and collisions" that will arise from additional information and different interpretations.

16. Here let me make clear that the senses are not isolated from the political economy and the moral worlds in which they develop. While this book highlights child socialization practices, language, and psychosomatic orientations, this focus is not meant to detract from the importance of history, power, and materiality in the shaping of sensoriums and sensibilities.

Glossary

The words contained in this glossary are arranged according to the English alphabet rather than the Ewe alphabet. In an Ewe dictionary the nominal prefixes
(such as a-, e-, and o- do not count, so words such as amɛdzɔtɔ and amegɔmesese would be found under the letter m. In addition, words such as ŋlɔ, ŋɔli, and
ŋutɔ would not be contained in the n section but under the separate letter ŋ (pronounced ng). However, this glossary is designed for an English-speaking audience, so the alphabetical arrangement follows English rather than Ewe.

AÐIBAKU: chickenpox

AFA: a system of divination, similar to the Yoruba *Ifa*

AƒEDONU: ancestral home (AƒEDOME: in the ancestral home)

AGBAGBAÐOÐO: balancing; carrying something on the head without touching
   or supporting it; also, a vestibular sense or a sense of balance, equilibrium
   from the inner ear

AKLAMA: a personal guardian spirit

AMƐ: person or human being

AMƐDZɔTɔ: ancestral sponsor; agent of a person's birth

AMƐGɔMESESE: understanding human beings; understanding what a person
   stands for, what he is doing, etc.

AMƐGASHI: a diviner, usually female (sometimes spelled *amegasi*)

AMƐME: an inner person; a person inside of a person; the deeper, inner part of
   a human being

AMENɔ: the placenta, or the afterbirth

AMEŊUME: one who is close to you or one who is "about you"; a close relative

AMEŊUMEE WɔANU AMƐ: a phrase that means "those close to you can harm you
   the most"

AMLIMA: magical powers

ANUTIWO: oranges

ASRA: malaria

ATIKEÐUÐU: eating the medicine

ATIKEWƆLA: herbalist, or "root doctor"

ATSIBLA: a cushion women tie on their lower back

AWOAMEƑIA: Paramount Chief of Anlo-Ewe

AZƆLIME *and* AZƆLINU: style of walking; manner of life, course of life, deportment

AZƆLIZƆZƆ: walking, marching, moving, gait; also kinesthesia or a movement sense

BLEKETE: a religious sect or religious order (sometimes transliterated as Brekete)

BOKƆ: a diviner, usually male

ÐO AGBA: balance (the imperative)

DƆLELE: "catching" or "seizing" sickness; falling ill

DƆMEÐUI: stomach ache

DƆTSOAƑE: common, everyday-type sickness

ƊƵEKPLƐ: a corn meal mixed with palm oil

ƊƵIGBEÐI: literally "birth dirt"; the vernix coating on a neonate's skin

ƊƵIKUIƊƵIKUI: a condition in which the children of one woman consistently die

ƊƵITSINYA: conscience, or literally "matters spoken or voiced in one's heart"

ƊƵOÐUAMETƆ: a person whose agency is dealing in (signified here as "eating") magical charms

ƊƵOƊƵOME: the character of a person, natural qualities, or those traits that come along with the person "in birth"

ƊƵOKA: the Ewe term for *juju* or sorcery; some scholars translate *ʤoka* as "charm," but here it is glossed as "transformative arts"

EƑE TABGƆ FLU: literally "his head is blurred" but meaning that he is insane

ENU: literally "mouth" but referring to a sickness caused by animosity

ETOGATƆWO: people with magnified hearing or a large ear; people who can hear things that ordinary people cannot hear

EYE: clay or chalk formed into small oblong shapes and often ingested

FIASIÐI: according to some, a girl or woman dedicated to a *trɔ*

GA ƑOÐI MAWO: prohibitions on wealth acquired through immoral or illegal means; commandment to not steal or make "dirty money"

GBAYI: measles

GBEDALA: herbalist, or "root doctor"

GBEMELA: a wild animal or a creature from the bush

GBESASA: performing magic actions by speaking, incantations

GBƆGBƆ *(plural:* GBƆGBƆWO): spirit, breath; breathing, blowing

GBƆGBƆMEDƆ: spiritual sickness; literally means "a spirit in the sickness"

GƆMESESE: intuiting, insight, intelligence

GUDƆ: a puffiness or bloated condition associated with *enu*

HLƆWO: clan

KƆKUUU: a religious sect or religious order

KPE: cough

KPETA: dysentery

KPƆLIGA: a personal god connected with one's destiny

KPƆ NYUIE: "look well"; watch out

LAMESESE: health, strength

LEGBA: guardian of thresholds, a spirit or deity, a clay figure often placed at a threshold

LUƲO: shadow or soul

MAMAWO: grandmothers; female ancestors

MAƲU ŊKU O: "your eyes are not open"; you are being naive

MAWU-SEGBO-LISA: God; Supreme Being

MEÐU DZE O: "you don't eat salt," meaning you don't know your own language, history, and culture

MƆFIALA (plural: MƆFIALAWO): one who leads or shows the road, leader, teacher, guide; forefinger, index

ŊKUETƆTƆWO: people who can see beyond what ordinary human beings can see; people with a third eye

ŊKUGBAGBA: blindness, injuring the eye

ŊKUNO: a blind person

ŊLƆ: to fold into oneself, to curl up into a ball, to roll up

ŊƆLI (plural: ŊƆLIWO): soul, spirit of a deceased person, ghost

NU: thing, object; often used as an indefinite object or subject

NUÐƆÐƆ and NUÐƆÐƆKPƆ: terms used to describe the experience of tasting

NUÐUÐU: eating, tasting

NUFOFO: orality, vocality, and talking

NUKPƆKPƆ: seeing, visuality, sight

NULELE: a complex of tactility, contact, touch

NUNYA: knowledge, wisdom, learnedness

NUSESE: aural perception or hearing

NUSƆSRƆ: marrying; studying

ŊUTILA: human or animal body; flesh

ŊUTƆ: myself

NUƲEƲESE: smelling, olfaction

NYAIƵƆIƵƆE: truth, literally "straight word"

NYATEFE: truth, reality, in truth, indeed

NYE ŊUTƆ: I myself; the absolute form of I is nye

NYIGBLA: god of war

SA: to tie, unite, bind, join

SE: destiny, a personal spirit or god

SESELELAME: hearing or feeling in the body, flesh, or skin; a cultural category for sensation, emotion, disposition, and vocation

SIDZEDZE: recognition, noting, observing

SIDZENU: a mark, sign, symbol

SRƆ: to marry; to study

TAÐUAME: headache

TAGBƆGBEGBLƐTƆ: an insane person

TAMEBUBU: thinking, reflecting

TAMESUSU: thinking, meditation (a synonym for tamebubu)

TEKUNƆ BUNƆ: a person who is unable to walk, a lame person

TƆGBEŊƆLIWO: "souls of ancestors" or "ancestral spirits"

TƆGBUI (*plural:* TƆGBUIWO): grandfather; male ancestor; *tɔgbui* is also the term for chief

TOHEHE: literally "ear pulling" but means punishment

TOHONƆFUI: death by lightning

TƆKƆ ATƆLIA: the fifth landing stage, in Anloga, where criminals were once buried alive

TOKUNƆ: a deaf person

TOSƐSƐ: literally "hard or strong ears" but means obstinate

TRƆ *(plural:* TRƆWO*):* nature spirit, deity, sometimes called a "god"

TRƆXƆVIWO: spirits or deities that take your child; a shrine devoted to such a spirit; a form of restitution in which the lineage must provide (in perpetuity) a young girl to serve in a shrine

TRƆ ZU: to turn, to change into, to become; to shape-shift

TSUKUNƆ: a person who is senseless, confused, insane

TSYƆ: a word for exclaiming surprise, as in "Wow!"

VIXELA: midwife

VODU: a power, a philosophy or metaphysics; a power gleaned from "resting to draw the water" (sometimes translated as a "god" or a "fetish")

ʊAʊA: motion, movement

XEXEME GBEGBLE: ruin or destruction of the world

XEXEME LE NOGOO: the world, universe is cyclical

YEVE: a religious sect or religious order

YEVU: term for European or white person (formed from the contraction of *aye* and *avu* and literally meaning "tricky dog")

Bibliography

Abu-Lughod, Lila
    1991 Writing against Culture. In *Recapturing Anthropology*. R. G. Fox, ed.
    Pp. 137–162. Santa Fe, NM: School of American Research Press.

Adikah, Elvis
    2000 Personal communication, December 20.
    2001 Personal communication, March 31.

Agawu, Kofi
    1990 Variation Procedures in Northern Ewe Song. *Ethnomusicology*
    34(2):221–243.
    1995 *African Rhythm: A Northern Ewe Perspective*. New York:
    Cambridge University Press.

Alpern, Mathew, Merle Lawrence, and David Wolsk
    1967 *Sensory Processes*. Belmont, CA: Wadsworth Publishing Co.

Ameka, Felix K.
    1999 The Typology and Semantics of Complex Nominal Duplication in
    Ewe. *Anthropological Linguistics* 41(1):75–106.
    2001a Cultural Scripting of Body Parts for Emotions: On "Jealousy" and
    Related Emotions in Ewe. In "The Body in the Description of Emotions:
    Cross-Linguistic Studies." Theme issue. *Pragmatics and Cognition*.
    2001b Ideophones and the Nature of the Adjective Word Class in Ewe. In
    Ideophones. F. K. Erhard Voeltz and C. Kelan-Hatz, eds. Pp. 25–48.
    Amsterdam: John Benjamins.

Amenumey, D. E. K.
  1968 The Extension of British Rule to Anlo (South-East Ghana),
    1850–1890. *Journal of African History* 9(1):99–117.
  1986 *The Ewe in Pre-Colonial Times.* Accra: Sedco Publishing Ltd.
  1989 *The Ewe Unification Movement: A Political History.* Accra: Ghana
    Universities Press.

Amoaku, William Komla
  1975 Symbolism in Traditional Institutions and Music of the Ewe of
    Ghana. Ph.D. dissertation. University of Pittsburgh.
  1985 Toward a Definition of Traditional African Music: A Look at the
    Ewe of Ghana. In *More Than Drumming.* I. V. Jackson, ed. Pp. 31–40.
    Westport, CT: Greenwood Press.

Anlo Traditional Council
  1978 *Anlo Hogbetsotsoza Programme 1978.* Anloga, Ghana.

Ansre, Gilbert
  1963 Reduplication in Ewe. *Journal of African Languages* 2:128–132.

Anyidoho, Kofi
  1982 Kofi Awoonor and the Ewe Tradition of Songs of Abuse *(Halo).* In
    Toward Defining the African Aesthetic. Lemuel Johnson et al., eds.
    Pp. 17–29. Washington, DC: Three Continents Press.
  1983 Oral Poetics and Traditions of Verbal Art in Africa. Ph.D.
    dissertation. The University of Texas at Austin.
  1985 The Present State of African Oral Literature Studies. In *African Liter-
    ature Studies: The Present State.* S. Arnold, ed. Pp. 151–161. Washing-
    ton, DC: Three Continents Press.
  1993 *AncestralLogic and CaribbeanBlues.* Trenton, NJ: Africa World
    Press.

Appadurai, Arjun
  1981 Gastro-Politics in Hindu South Asia. *American Ethnologist*
    8:494–511.
  1991 Global Ethnoscapes: Notes and Queries for a Transnational Anthro-
    pology. In *Recapturing Anthropology.* R. G. Fox, ed. Pp. 191–210.
    Santa Fe, NM: School of American Research Press.

Arkaifie, Richard
  1976 *Bibliography of the Ewes.* Ghana: Cape Coast.

Armah, Ayi Kwei
  1978 *The Healers.* London: Heinemann Educational Books.

Armstrong, Robert Plant
  1971 *The Affecting Presence: An Essay in Humanistic Anthropology.*
    Urbana: University of Illinois Press.

1975 *Wellspring: On the Myth and Source of Culture.* Berkeley: University of California Press.

1981 *The Powers of Presence: Consciousness, Myth, and the Affecting Presence.* Philadelphia: University of Pennsylvania Press.

Arnold, Stephen, ed.

1985 *African Literature Studies: The Present State.* Washington, DC: Three Continents Press.

Aronoff, Joel, et al.

1970 *Psychology Today: An Introduction.* Del Mar, CA: CRM Books.

Asamoa, Ansa K.

1986 *The Ewe of Ghana and Togo on the Eve of Colonialism.* Accra: Ghana Publishing Corporation.

Avorgbedor, Daniel K.

1983 The Psycho-Social Dynamics of Ewe Names: The Case of Ahanonko. *Folklore Forum* 6(1):21–43.

1990–1991 Some Contributions of Halo Music to Research Theory and Pragmatics in Ghana. *Bulletin of the International Committee of Urgent Anthropological and Ethnological Research* 28–29:61–80.

1994 Freedom to Sing, License to Insult: The Influence of Halo Performance on Social Violence among the Anlo Ewe. *Oral Tradition* 9(1):83–112.

1999 The Turner-Schechner Model of Performance as Social Drama: A Re-examination in the Light of Anlo-Ewe *Halo. Research in African Literatures* 30(4):144–155.

2000 *Dee Hoo!* Sonic Articulations in Healing and Exorcism Practices of the Anlo-Ewe. *The World of Music* 42(2):9–24.

2001 "It's a Great Song!" *Halo* Performance as Literary Production. *Research in African Literatures* 32(2):17–43.

Awoonor, Kofi Nyidevu

1971 *This Earth, My Brother . . . .* London: Heinemann Educational Books.

1974 *Guardians of the Sacred Word.* New York: NOK.

1975 *The Breast of the Earth: A Survey of the History, Culture, and Literature of Africa South of the Sahara.* New York: Anchor Press/Doubleday.

1990 *Ghana: A Political History from Pre-European to Modern Times.* Accra: Sedco Publishing Ltd.

Awoyale, Yiwola

1978 On the Deep Structure of the Ideophone. *Research Papers in the Linguistic Sciences* 1(1):5–40.

1989 Reduplication and the Status of Ideophones in Yoruba. *Journal of West African Languages* 19:15–34.

Baker, R. Robin
  1981 *Human Navigation and the Sixth Sense.* London: Hodder and
    Stroughton.

Barawusu, Solomon M.K.
  n.d. *The Hogbetsotso Festival: A Comparison between the Liberation of the
    Ewes from Slavery in Notsie—Togo—under the Wicked King Agorkorli
    and the Liberation of the Israelites from Slavery in Egypt under the
    Wicked King Pharaoh.* Anloga, Ghana: Zion Secondary School.

Barlow, H.B., and J.D. Mollon, eds.
  1982 *The Senses.* Cambridge: Cambridge University Press.

Barnes, Sandra T., ed.
  1989 *Africa's Ogun: Old World and New.* Bloomington: Indiana
    University Press.

Barthes, Roland
  1989a *Empire of Signs.* New York: Noonday Press.
  1989b *The Rustle of Language.* Berkeley: University of California Press.

Bascom, William R.
  1964 Folklore Research in Africa. *Journal of American Folklore*
    77(303):12–31.
  1965 The Forms of Folklore: Prose Narratives. *Journal of American Folk-
    lore* 78(307):3–20.
  1969a *Ifa Divination: Communication between Men and Gods in West
    Africa.* Bloomington: Indiana University Press.
  1969b *The Yoruba of Southwestern Nigeria.* New York: Holt, Rinehart
    and Winston.

Bateson, Gregory, and Margaret Mead
  1942 *Balinese Character: A Photographic Analysis.* Special publication.
    New York: New York Academy of Sciences.

Behar, Ruth, and Deborah A. Gordon, eds.
  1995 *Women Writing Culture.* Berkeley: University of California Press.

Ben-amos, Dan
  1975 *Sweet Words: Storytelling Events in Benin.* Philadelphia: Institute for
    the Study of Human Issues.

Berlin, Brent, and Paul Kay
  1969 *Basic Color Terms: Their Universality and Evolution.* Berkeley: Uni-
    versity of California Press.

Berman, Morris
  1998 *Coming to Our Senses: Body and Spirit in the Hidden History of the
    West.* Seattle: Seattle Writer's Guild.

Berry, J.
   1951 *The Pronunciation of Ewe.* Cambridge: Heffer Publishers.

Bible Society of Ghana
   1993 *Biblia Alo Ɲɔŋlɔ Kɔkɔe La Le Evegbe Me.* Keta, Ghana: Bible Society of Ghana.

Blacking, John, ed.
   1977 *The Anthropology of the Body.* London: Academic Press.

Blier, Suzanne Preston
   1995 *African Vodun: Art, Psychology, and Power.* Chicago: University of Chicago Press.

Boas, Franz
   1939[1911] *The Mind of Primitive Man.* New York: Macmillan.

Bock, Philip K.
   1988 *Rethinking Psychological Anthropology: Continuity and Change in the Study of Human Action.* New York: W.H. Freeman and Company.

Boring, Edwin G.
   1970[1942] *Sensation and Perception in the History of Experimental Psychology.* New York: Irvington Publishers, Inc.

Bourdieu, Pierre
   1977 *Outline of a Theory of Practice.* Cambridge: Cambridge University Press.
   1984 *Distinction: A Social Critique of the Judgement of Taste.* Richard Nice, trans. Cambridge, MA: Harvard University Press.

Bourguignon, Erika
   1976 *Possession.* San Francisco: Chandler and Sharp.

Brown, Karen McCarthy
   1989 Systematic Remembering, Systematic Forgetting: Ogou in Haiti. In *Africa's Ogun.* S. Barnes, ed. Pp. 65–89. Bloomington: Indiana University Press.
   1991 *Mama Lola: A Vodou Priestess in Brooklyn.* Berkeley: University of California Press.

Bureau of Ghana Languages
   1986 *Language Guide (Ewe Version),* 5th imp. Accra: New Times Corporation.

Bynum, W.F., and Roy Porter, eds.
   1993 *Medicine and the Five Senses.* Cambridge: Cambridge University Press.

Capo, Hounkpati Bamikpo Christophe
   1984 Vowel Features in Gbe. *Journal of West African Languages* 15(1):19–30.

1985 Elements of Ewe-Gen-Aja-Fon Dialectology. In *Peuples du Golfe du Benin*. Pp. 167–178. Paris: Centre de Recherches Africaines.

1991 *A Comparative Phonology of Gbe*. New York: Foris Publications.

Casey, Edward S.
1987 *Remembering: A Phenomenological Study*. Bloomington and Indianapolis: Indiana University Press.

1996 How to Get from Space to Place in a Fairly Short Stretch of Time: Phenomenological Prolegomena. In *Senses of Place*. S. Feld and K.H. Basso, eds. Pp. 13–52. Santa Fe: School of American Research Press.

Chernoff, John Miller
1979 *African Rhythm and African Sensibility: Aesthetics and Social Action in African Musical Idioms*. Chicago: University of Chicago Press.

Christensen, James B.
1954 The Tigari Cult of West Africa. *Papers of the Michigan Academy of Science, Arts, and Letters* 39:389–398.

Classen, Constance
1992 The Odor of the Other: Olfactory Symbolism and Cultural Categories. *Ethos* 20(2):133–166.

1993a *Inca Cosmology and the Human Body*. Salt Lake City: University of Utah Press.

1993b *Worlds of Sense: Exploring the Senses in History and across Cultures*. London and New York: Routledge.

1997 Foundations for an Anthropology of the Senses. *International Social Science Journal* 49:401–412.

Classen, C., D. Howes, and A. Synnott
1994 *Aroma: The Cultural History of Smell*. London and New York: Routledge.

Clifford, James, and George E. Marcus, eds.
1986 *Writing Culture: The Poetics and Politics of Ethnography*. Berkeley: University of California Press.

Cole, Desmond T.
1955 *An Introduction to Tswana Grammar*. London: Longmans Green.

Comaroff, Jean
1985 *Body of Power, Spirit of Resistance: The Culture and History of a South African People*. Chicago: University of Chicago Press.

1996 The Empire's Old Clothes: Fashioning the Colonial Subject. In *Cross-Cultural Consumption: Global Markets, Local Realities*. David Howes, ed. Pp. 19–38. London and New York: Routledge.

Comaroff, Jean, and John Comaroff
1991 *Of Revelation and Revolution, Vol. 1: Christianity, Colonialism, and Consciousness in South Africa*. Chicago: University of Chicago Press.

1997 *Of Revelation and Revolution, Vol. 2: The Dialectics of Modernity on a South African Frontier.* Chicago: University of Chicago Press.

Conant, Faith
1985 The Ethnomusicology of Adzogbo. M.A. thesis. Tufts University.

Connerton, Paul
1989 *How Societies Remember.* Cambridge: Cambridge University Press.

Corbin, Alain
1986 *The Foul and the Fragrant: Odor and the French Social Imagination.* Cambridge, MA: Harvard University Press.

Csordas, Thomas J.
1990 Embodiment as a Paradigm for Anthropology. *Ethos: Journal of the Society for Psychological Anthropology* 18(1):5–47.
1993 Somatic Modes of Attention. *Cultural Anthropology* 8(2):135–156.
1994a Introduction: The Body as Representation and Being-in-the-World. In *Embodiment and Experience: The Existential Ground of Culture and Self.* T. J. Csordas, ed. Pp. 1–24. Cambridge: Cambridge University Press.
1994b *The Sacred Self: A Cultural Phenomenology of Sacred Healing.* Berkeley: University of California Press.
1994c Self and Person. In *Handbook of Psychological Anthropology.* P. K. Bock, ed. Pp. 331–350. Westport, CT: Greenwood Press.

Cudjoe, Dzagbe
1969 Ewe Sculpture in the Linden Museum. *Tribus* 18:49–71.
1971 The Du-Legba Cult among the Ewe of Ghana. *Baessler-Archiv* 19(2):187–206.

Cudjoe, Seth Dzagbe
1953 The Techniques of Ewe Drumming and the Social Importance of Music in Africa. *Phylon: The Atlanta University Review of Race and Culture* 14(3):280–291.

Cudjoe-Calvocoressi, Dzagbe
1974 A Preliminary Investigation into the Du-Legba Cult of the Volta Region Ewe. *National Museum of Ghana Occasional Papers* 8:54–63.

D'Andrade, Roy G.
1976 A Propositional Analysis of U.S. American Beliefs about Illness. In *Meaning in Anthropology.* K. Basso and H. Selby, eds. Pp. 155–180. Albuquerque: University of New Mexico Press.
1984 Cultural Meaning Systems. In *Culture Theory.* R. A. Shweder and R. A. LeVine, eds. Pp. 88–119. New York: Cambridge University Press.

Damasio, Antonio
1994 *Descartes' Error: Emotion, Reason, and the Human Brain.* New York: Avon Books.

1999 *The Feeling of What Happens: Body and Emotion in the Making of Consciousness.* San Diego: Harcourt, Inc.

Daniel, E. Valentine
1984 *Fluid Signs: Being a Person the Tamil Way.* Berkeley: University of California Press.

Davis-Floyd, Robbie E.
1992 *Birth as an American Rite of Passage.* Berkeley: University of California Press.

Desjarlais, Robert R.
1992 *Body and Emotion: The Aesthetics of Illness and Healing in the Nepal Himalayas.* Philadelphia: University of Pennsylvania Press.

Devisch, Rene
1993 *Weaving the Threads of Life: The Khita Gyn-Eco-Logical Healing Cult among the Yaka.* Chicago: University of Chicago Press.

Douglas, Mary
1970 *Natural Symbols.* New York: Vintage.

Duthie, A.S., and R.K. Vlaardingerbroek
1981 *Bibliography of Gbe (Ewe, Gen, Aja, Xwala, Fon, Gun, Etc.): Publications on and in the Language in Mitteilungen der Basler Afrika Bibliographien.* Vol. 23. Reviewed in *Journal of West African Languages* 13(1):153 (1983).

Dzobo, N.K.
1973 *African Proverbs: Guide to Conduct: The Moral Value of Ewe Proverbs.* Vol. 1. Cape Coast, Ghana: University of Cape Coast.
1975 *African Proverbs: Guide to Conduct: The Moral Value of Ewe Proverbs.* Vol. 2. Accra: Presbyterian Book Depot, Ltd., Waterville Publishing House.
1980 The Indigenous African Theory of Knowledge and Truth: Example of the Ewe and Akan of Ghana. *The Conch* 7(1–2):85–102.
1995 *Asigbe Xletigbale.* Ho, Volta Region, Ghana: n.p.

Egblewogbe, E.Y.
1975 *Games and Songs as Education Media: A Case Study among the Ewes of Ghana.* Accra-Tema: Ghana Publishing Corporation.

Evans-Pritchard, E.E.
1976[1937] *Witchcraft, Oracles, and Magic among the Azande.* Abridged. Oxford: Clarendon Press.
1962 Ideophones in Zande. *Sudan Notes and Records* 43:143–146.

Fairbairne, W.R.D.
1952 *An Object-Relations Theory of the Personality.* New York: Basic Books.

Feierman, Steven, and John Janzen, eds.
   1992 *The Social Basis of Health and Healing in Africa.* Berkeley:
   University of California Press.

Feld, Steven
   1982 *Sound and Sentiment: Birds, Weeping, Poetics, and Song in Kaluli
   Expression.* Philadelphia: University of Pennsylvania Press.
   1988 Aesthetics as Iconicity of Style, or "Lift-up-over Sounding": Getting
   into the Kaluli Groove. *Yearbook for Traditional Music.* Vol. 20, part 1.
   Pp. 74–113.
   1996 Waterfalls of Song: An Acoustemology of Place Resounding in
   Bosavi, Papua New Guinea. In *Senses of Place.* Steven Feld and Keith
   H. Basso, eds. Pp. 91–135. Santa Fe, NM: School of American Research
   Press.

Feldman, Allen
   1991 *Formations of Violence: The Narrative of the Body and Political Terror in Northern Ireland.* Chicago: University of Chicago Press.

Fernandez, James, ed.
   1991 *Beyond Metaphor: The Theory of Tropes in Anthropology.* Stanford,
   CA: Stanford University Press.

Fiagbedzi, Nissio S.
   1966 Sogbadzi Songs: A Study of Yeve Music. M.A. thesis. University of
   Ghana.
   1977 The Music of the Anlo. Ph.D. dissertation. UCLA.
   1985 On Signing and Symbolism in Music: The Evidence from among an
   African People. In *More Than Drumming.* I. V. Jackson, ed. Pp. 41–48.
   Westport, CT: Greenwood Press.

Fiawoo, Dzigbodi Kodzo
   1959a The Influence of Contemporary Social Changes on the Magico-
   Religious Concepts and Organization of the Southern Ewe-Speaking
   People of Ghana. Ph.D. dissertation. University of Edinburgh.
   1959b Urbanisation and Religion in Eastern Ghana. *The Sociological
   Review* 7(1):83–97.
   1968 From Cult to "Church": A Study of Some Aspects of Religious
   Change in Ghana. *Ghana Journal of Sociology* 4(2):72–87.

Fiawoo, F. Kwasi
   1981 *Tɔkɔ Atɔlia.* Accra: Sedco Publishing Ltd.
   1983 *The Fifth Landing Stage.* Accra: Sedco Publishing Ltd.

Finnegan, Ruth
   1969 How to Do Things with Words: Performative Utterances among the
   Limba of Sierra Leone. *Man* 4(4):537–552.
   1970 *Oral Literature in Africa.* Nairobi: Oxford University Press.

Fox, Richard G.
  1991 *Recapturing Anthropology: Working in the Present.* Santa Fe, NM: School of American Research Press.

Frank, Gelya
  1986 On Embodiment: A Case Study of Congenital Limb Deficiency in American Culture. *Culture, Medicine and Psychiatry* 10(3):189–219.

French, David
  1963 The Relationship of Anthropology to Studies in Perception and Cognition. In *Psychology: A Study of Science.* Vol. 6. S. Koch, ed. Pp. 388–428. New York: McGraw-Hill Book Company.

Friedson, Steven M.
  1996 *Dancing Prophets: Musical Experience in Tumbuku Healing.* Chicago: University of Chicago Press.

Frishkopf, Michael Aaron
  1989 *The Character of Ewe Performance.* M.A. thesis. Tufts University.

Gaba, Christian R.
  1968 Sacrifice in Anlo Religion, Part I. *The Ghana Bulletin of Theology* 3(5):13–19.
  1969a The Idea of a Supreme Being among the Anlo People of Ghana. *Journal of Religion in Africa* 2(1):64–79.
  1969b Sacrifice in Anlo Religion, Part II. *The Ghana Bulletin of Theology* 3(7):1–7.
  1971 An African People's Concept of the Soul. *The Ghana Bulletin of Theology* 3(10):1–8.

Gadzekpo, B. Sinedzi
  1952 Making Music in Eweland. *West African Review* 23.

Galeota, Joseph
  1985 *Drum Making among the Southern Ewe People of Ghana and Togo.* M.A. thesis. Wesleyan University.

Gates, Henry Louis, Jr.
  1988 *The Signifying Monkey: A Theory of African-American Literary Criticism.* New York: Oxford University Press.

Geertz, Clifford
  1973 *The Interpretation of Cultures.* New York: Basic Books.
  1983 *Local Knowledge: Further Essays in Interpretive Anthropology.* New York: Basic Books.

Geldard, Frank A.
  1972 *The Human Senses,* 2nd ed. New York: John Wiley and Sons.

Geurts, Kathryn Linn

1997 *Vodu* Metaphysics: Power Gleaned from *Resting to Draw the Water.*
African Studies Newsletter of the University of Pennsylvania
2(March/April).

1998 Sensory Perception and Embodiment in Anlo-Ewe Cultural Logic and
Symbolic Life. Ph.D. dissertation. University of Pennsylvania.

2001 Childbirth and Pragmatic Midwifery in Rural Ghana. *Medical
Anthropology* 20(2–3):379–408.

In press On Rocks, Walks, and Talks in West Africa: Cultural Categories
and an Anthropology of the Senses. *Ethos* 30(3).

Gilbert, Michelle V.

1982 Mystical Protection among the Anlo-Ewe. *African Arts*
15(4):60–66, 90.

Glover, E. Ablade

1992 Stools Symbolism. Poster documenting symbols and significance of
stools. Kumasi, Ghana: University of Science and Technology.

Greenberg, Joseph H.

1973 African Languages. In *Peoples and Cultures of Africa*. E. Skinner, ed.
Pp. 71–80. Garden City, NY: Natural History Press.

Greenberg, Jay R., and Stephen A. Mitchell

1983 *Object Relations in Psychoanalytic Theory.* Cambridge, MA:
Harvard University Press.

Greene, Sandra

1981 Land, Lineage, and Clan in Early Anlo. *Africa* 51(1):451–463.

1985 The Past and Present of an Anlo-Ewe Oral Tradition. *History in
Africa* 12:73–87.

1988 Social Change in Eighteenth-Century Anlo: The Role of Technology,
Markets, and Military Conflict. *Africa* 58(1):70–85.

1996 *Gender, Ethnicity, and Social Change on the Upper Slave Coast: A
History of the Anlo-Ewe.* Portsmouth, NH: Heinemann.

Gregersen, Edgar A.

1977 *Language in Africa: An Introductory Survey.* New York: Gordon and
Breach.

Griaule, Marcel

1965 *Conversations with Ogotemmeli: An Introduction to Dogon
Religious Ideas.* London: Oxford University Press.

Gyekye, Kwame

1987 *An Essay on African Philosophical Thought: The Akan Conceptual
Scheme.* Philadelphia: Temple University Press.

Hall, Edward T.

1959 *The Silent Language.* Garden City, NY: Doubleday.

1966 *The Hidden Dimension*. New York: Anchor Books, Doubleday.

Hallowell, A. Irving
1951 Cultural Factors in the Structuralization of Perception. In *Social Psychology at the Cross Roads*. John H. Rohrer and Muzafer Sherif, eds. Pp. 164–195. New York: Harper and Brothers Publishers.
1955 *Culture and Experience*. New York: Schocken Books.

Hardin, Kris L.
1993 *The Aesthetics of Action: Continuity and Change in a West African Town*. Washington: Smithsonian Institution Press.

Harkness, Sara, and Charles Super, eds.
1996 *Parents' Cultural Belief Systems: Their Origins, Expressions, and Consequences*. New York: Guilford Press.

Herskovits, Melville J.
1967 *Dahomey: An Ancient West African Kingdom*. Evanston: Northwestern University Press.

Hill, Polly
1986 *Talking with Ewe Seine Fishermen and Shallot Farmers*. Cambridge: African Studies Centre.

Holubar, Josef
1969 *The Sense of Time: An Electrophysiological Study of its Mechanisms in Man*. Cambridge, MA: MIT Press.

Horton, Robin
1967 African Traditional Thought and Western Science. *Africa* 37:50–71.

Houston, Stephen, and Karl Taube
2000 An Archaeology of the Senses: Perception and Cultural Expression in Ancient Mesoamerica. *Cambridge Archaeological Journal* 10(2):261–94.

Howes, David
1987a Notes on the Olfactory Classification and Treatment of Disease in Non-Western Societies. The paper is a summary of a talk given at the GIRAME meeting of February 13, 1987.
1987b Olfaction and Transition: An Essay on the Ritual Uses of Smell. *Canadian Review of Sociology and Anthropology* 24(3):398–416.
1988 On the Odour of the Soul: Spatial Representation and Olfactory Classification in Eastern Indonesia and Western Melanesia. *Bijdragen: Tot de Taal-, Land-En Volkenkunde*. Dordrecht, Holland: Foris Publications.
1989 Scent and Sensibility. *Culture, Medicine and Psychiatry* 13:89–97.
1992 The Bounds of Sense: An Inquiry into the Sensory Orders of Western and Melanesian Society. Ph.D. dissertation. University of Montreal.

Howes, David, ed.
1991 *The Varieties of Sensory Experience: A Sourcebook in the Anthropology of the Senses*. Toronto: University of Toronto Press.

Howes, David, and Constance Classen
1991 Sounding Sensory Profiles. In *The Varieties of Sensory Experience*. D. Howes, ed. Pp. 257–288. Toronto: University of Toronto Press.

Jackson, Michael
1983 Thinking Through the Body. *Social Analysis* 14:127–149.
1989 *Paths toward a Clearing: Radical Empiricism and Ethnographic Inquiry*. Bloomington: Indiana University Press.

Jackson, Michael, ed.
1996 *Things as They Are: New Directions in Phenomenological Anthropology*. Bloomington: Indiana University Press.

Jackson, Michael, and Ivan Karp, eds.
1990 *Personhood and Agency: The Experience of Self and Other in African Cultures*. Washington: Smithsonian Institution Press.

Jacobson-Widding, Anita
1990 General Editor's preface to *Personhood and Agency: The Experience of Self and Other in African Societies*. M. Jackson and I. Karp, eds. Pp. 9–13. Washington: Smithsonian Institution Press.

James, William
1890 *The Principles of Psychology*. 2 vols. New York: Dover Publications, Inc.

Johnson, Mark
1987 *The Body in the Mind: The Bodily Basis of Meaning, Imagination, and Reason*. Chicago: University of Chicago Press.

Jones, A. M.
1959 *Studies in African Music*. 2 vols. London: Oxford University Press.

Jordan, Brigitte
1976 The Cultural Production of Childbirth. In *Women and Children in Contemporary Society*. Nancy Hammond, ed. Pp. 33–43. Lansing: Michigan Women's Commission.
1980 *Birth in Four Cultures: A Crosscultural Investigation of Childbirth in Yucatan, Holland, Sweden, and the United States*. Montreal, Canada: Eden Press Women's Publications.

Jordan, J. Scott, ed.
1998 *Systems Theories and A Priori Aspects of Perception*. Amsterdam: Elsevier.

Kleinman, Arthur
  1980 *Patients and Healers in the Context of Culture: An Exploration of
  the Borderland between Anthropology, Medicine, and Psychiatry.*
  Berkeley: University of California Press.

Knapp, Mark L.
  1978 *Nonverbal Communication in Human Interaction.* New York: Holt,
  Rinehart and Winston.

Kodzo-Vordoagu, J. G.
  1994 *Anlo Hogbetsotso Festival.* Accra: Domak Press Ltd.

Kopytoff, Igor
  1981 Knowledge and Belief in Suku Thought. *Africa* 5(3):709–723.

Laderman, Carol
  1983 *Wives and Midwives: Childbirth and Nutrition in Rural Malaysia.*
  Berkeley: University of California Press.
  1987 The Ambiguity of Symbols in the Structure of Healing. *Social Science
  and Medicine* 24:293–301.
  1991 *Taming the Wind of Desire: Psychology, Medicine, and Aesthetics in
  Malay Shamanistic Performance.* Berkeley: University of California
  Press.

Ladzekpo, Kobla
  1971 The Social Mechanics of Good Music: A Description of Dance Clubs
  among the Anlo-Ewe Speaking People of Ghana. *African Music*
  5(1):6–22.

Ladzekpo, Kobla, and Hewitt Pantaleoni
  1970 Takada Drumming. *African Music* 4(4):6–31.

Lakoff, George
  1987 *Women, Fire, and Dangerous Things: What Categories Tell Us about
  the Mind.* Chicago: University of Chicago Press.

Lakoff, George, and Mark Johnson
  1980 *Metaphors We Live By.* Chicago: University of Chicago Press.
  1999 *Philosophy in the Flesh: The Embodied Mind and its Challenge to
  Western Thought.* New York: Basic Books.

Lamb, Venice
  1975 *West African Weaving.* London: Duckworth.

Laughlin, Charles, John McManus, and Eugene D'Aquili
  1990 *Brain, Symbol, and Experience: Towards a Neurophenomenology of
  Human Consciousness.* New York: Columbia University.

LeVine, Robert A.
  1973 *Culture, Behavior, and Personality.* Chicago: Aldine.

LeVine, R., S. Dixon, S. LeVine, A. Richman, P.H. Leiderman, C.H. Keefer, and T.B. Brazelton
1996 *Childcare and Culture: Lessons from Africa.* Cambridge: Cambridge University Press.

Lewis, M., and C. Saarni, eds.
1985 *The Socialization of Emotions.* New York: Plenum.

Lindenbaum, Shirley
1979 *Kuru Sorcery: Disease and Danger in the New Guinea Highlands.* Mountain View, CA: Mayfield Publishing.

Little, Kenneth
1965 *West African Urbanization: A Study of Voluntary Associations in Social Change.* Cambridge: Cambridge University Press.

Lloyd, Barbara
1972 *Perception and Cognition: A Cross-Cultural Perspective.* Hammondsworth, England: Penguin Books.

Lock, Margaret M.
1980 *East Asian Medicine in Urban Japan: Varieties of Medical Experience.* Berkeley: University of California Press.
1993 Cultivating the Body: Anthropology and Epistemologies of Bodily Practice and Knowledge. *Annual Review of Anthropology* 22:133–155.

Locke, David
1978 The Music of Atsiagbeko. Ph.D. dissertation. Wesleyan University.
1980 *A Collection of Atsiagbeko Songs.* Legon: University of Ghana Institute of African Studies.
1987 *Drum Gahu: A Systematic Method for an African Percussion Piece.* Crown Point, NJ: White Cliffs Media Company.

Lowenstein, Otto
1966 *The Senses.* Baltimore: Penguin Books.

Lucy, John A.
1992 *Language Diversity and Thought: A Reformulation of the Linguistic Relativity Hypothesis.* Cambridge: Cambridge University Press.
1997 Linguistic Relativity. *Annual Review of Anthropology* 26:291–312.

Lutz, Catherine
1988 *Unnatural Emotions: Everyday Sentiments on a Micronesian Atoll and their Challenge to Western Theory.* Chicago: University of Chicago Press.

Mach, Ernst
1959 *The Analysis of Sensations and the Relation of the Physical to the Psychical.* C.M. Williams, trans. New York: Dover Publications.

Mamattah, Charles M. K.
   1976 *The Ewes of West Africa: The Anlo-Ewes and Their Immediate Neighbors*. Keta, Ghana: Volta Research Publications.

Manoukian, Madeline
   1952 *The Ewe-Speaking People of Togoland and the Gold Coast*. London: International African Institute.

Marcus, George E., ed.
   1999 *Critical Anthropology Now: Unexpected Contexts, Shifting Consituencies, Changing Agendas*. Santa Fe, NM: School of American Research Press.

Markus, Hazel R., and Shinobu Kitayama, eds.
   1994 *Emotion and Culture: Empirical Studies of Mutual Influence*. Washington, DC: American Psychological Association Press.

Markus, Hazel R., Shinobu Kitayama, and Rachel J. Heiman
   1996 Culture and "Basic" Psychological Principles. In *Social Psychology: Handbook of Basic Principles*. E. T. Higgens and A. W. Kruglanski, eds. Pp. 857–913. New York: Guilford Press.

Mauss, Marcel
   1935 Techniques of the Body. *Economy and Society* 2(1):70–80.

McLuhan, Marshall
   1962 *The Gutenberg Galaxy*. Toronto: University of Toronto Press.

McNeill, David
   1992 *Hand and Mind: What Gestures Reveal about Thought*. Chicago: University of Chicago Press.

Menon, Usha, and Richard A. Shweder
   1994 Kali's Tongue: Cultural Psychology and the Power of Shame in Orissa, India. In *Emotion and Culture: Empirical Studies of Mutual Influence*, S. Kitayama and H. R. Markus, eds. Pp. 241–284. Washington, DC: American Psychological Association Press.

Merleau-Ponty, Maurice
   1962 *Phenomenology of Perception*. London and New York: Routledge and Kegan Paul, Ltd.
   1963 *In Praise of Philosophy and Other Essays*. Evanston, IL: Northwestern University Press.
   1969 *The Visible and the Invisible: Followed by Working Notes*. Alphonso Lingis, trans. Evanston, IL: Northwestern University Press.

Meyer, Birgit
   1999 *Translating the Devil: Religion and Modernity among the Ewe in Ghana*. Edinburgh: University of Edinburgh Press.

Miller, Peggy J., and Lisa Hoogstra
 1992 Language as Tool in the Socialization and Apprehension of Cultural Meanings. In *New Directions in Psychological Anthropology.* T. Schwartz, G. M. White, and C. Lutz, eds. Pp. 83–101. Cambridge: Cambridge University Press.

Mudimbe, V. Y.
 1988 *The Invention of Africa: Gnosis, Philosophy, and the Order of Knowledge.* Bloomington: Indiana University Press.

Mullings, Leith
 1984 *Therapy, Ideology, and Social Change: Mental Healing in Urban Ghana.* Berkeley: University of California Press.

Newman, Paul
 1968 Ideophones from a Syntactic Point of View. *Journal of West African Languages* 5(2):107–117.

Noss, Philip A.
 1986 The Ideophone in Gbaya Syntax. In *Current Approaches to African Linguistics.* Vol. 3. Gerrit J. Dimmendaal, ed. Pp. 241–255. Dordrecht, Holland: Foris Publications.

Nukunya, G. K.
 1969a Afa Divination in Anlo. *Ghana Research Review* 5(2):9–26.
 1969b *Kinship and Marriage among the Anlo Ewe.* London: Athlone Press.
 1969c The Yewe Cult among Southern Ewe-Speaking People of Ghana. *Ghana Journal of Sociology* 5(1):1–7.
 1992 *Tradition and Change in Ghana: An Introduction to Sociology.* Accra: Ghana Universities Press.

Obeyesekere, Gananath
 1981 *Medusa's Hair: An Essay on Personal Symbols and Religious Experience.* Chicago: University of Chicago Press.

Ohnuki-Tierney, Emiko
 1981a *Illness and Healing among the Sakhalin Ainu: A Symbolic Interpretation.* Cambridge: Cambridge University Press.
 1981b Phases in Human Perception/Conception/Symbolization Processes: Cognitive Anthropology and Symbolic Classification. *American Ethnologist* 8(3):451–467.

Okpewho, Isidore
 1979 *The Epic in Africa: Towards a Poetics of the Oral Performance.* New York: Columbia University Press.

Ong, Walter J.
 1967 *The Presence of the Word.* New Haven: Yale University Press.

1991 The Shifting Sensorium. In *The Varieties of Sensory Experience*. D. Howes, ed. Pp. 25–30. Toronto: University of Toronto Press.

Outlaw, Lucius T., Jr.
1996 *On Race and Philosophy*. New York and London: Routledge.

Pantaleoni, Hewitt
1972a The Rhythm of Atsia Dance Drumming among the Anlo (Ewe) of Anyako. Ph.D. dissertation. Wesleyan University.
1972b Three Principles of Timing in Anlo Dance Drumming. *African Music* 5(2):50–63.
1972c Toward Understanding the Play of Atsimevu in Atsia. *African Music* 5(2):64–84.

Parrinder, G.
1951 *West African Psychology: A Comparative Study of Psychological and Religious Thought*. London: Lutterworth Press.

Peek, Philip M.
1981 The Power of Words in African Verbal Arts. *Journal of American Folklore* 94(371):19–43.
1994 The Sounds of Silence: Cross-World Communication and the Auditory Arts in African Societies. *American Ethnologist* 21(3):474–494.

Pelton, Robert D.
1980 *The Trickster in West Africa: A Study of Mythic Irony and Sacred Delight*. Berkeley: University of California Press.

Perani, Judith, and Norma H. Wolff
1999 *Cloth, Dress, and Art Patronage in Africa*. Oxford and New York: Berg.

Pieron, Henri
1952 *The Sensations: Their Functions, Processes, and Mechanisms*. London: Frederick Muller, Ltd.

Pohl, Otto
2002 Improving the Way Humans Walk the Walk. *New York Times*, March 12: D3.

Porteous, J. Douglas
1990 *Landscapes of the Mind: Worlds of Sense and Metaphor*. Toronto: University of Toronto Press.

Posnansky, Merrick
1992 Traditional Cloth from the Ewe Heartland. In *History, Design, and Craft in West African Strip-Woven Cloth*. Papers presented at a symposium organized by the National Museum of African Art Pp. 113–132. Washington, DC: Smithsonian Institution.

Ray, Benjamin
  1973 Performative Utterances in African Rituals. *History of Religions*
  13(1):16–35.

Reid, Russell M.
  1992 Cultural and Medical Perspectives on Geophagia. *Medical
  Anthropology* 13(4):337–351.

Rheingold, Howard
  1991 *Virtual Reality.* New York: Touchstone/Simon and Schuster.

Riesman, Paul
  1992 *First Find Your Child a Good Mother: The Construction of Self in
  Two African Communities.* New Brunswick, NJ: Rutgers University
  Press.

Ritchie, Ian
  1991 Fusion of the Faculties: A Study of the Language of the Senses in
  Hausaland. In *The Varieties of Sensory Experience.* D. Howes, ed.
  Pp. 192–202. Toronto: University of Toronto Press.

Rivers, W. H. R.
  1926[1916] *Psychology and Ethnology.* New York: Harcourt and Brace.

Rivlin, Robert, and Karen Gravelle
  1984 *Deciphering the Senses: The Expanding World of Human Perception.*
  New York: Simon and Schuster.

Rose, Dan
  1990 *Living the Ethnographic Life.* Newbury Park, CA: Sage Publications.

Roseman, Marina
  1991 *Healing Sounds from the Malaysian Rainforest: Temiar Music and
  Medicine.* Berkeley: University of California Press.

Rosenthal, Judy
  1998 *Possession, Ecstasy, and Law in Ewe Voodoo.* Charlottesville:
  University Press of Virginia.

Samarin, W. J.
  1967 Determining the Meanings of Ideophones. *Journal of West African
  Languages* 4(2):35–41.

Sapir, Edward
  1921 *Language: An Introduction to the Study of Speech.* New York: Harcourt, Brace, and Co.

Scheper-Hughes, Nancy, and Margaret M. Lock
  1987 The Mindful Body: A Prolegomenon to Future Work in Medical
  Anthropology. *Medical Anthropology Quarterly* 1:6–41.

Schone, Hermann
  1984 *Spatial Orientation: The Spatial Control of Behavior in Animals and
  Man.* Princeton: Princeton University Press.

Schwartz-Salant, Nathan
  1995 *Jung on Alchemy.* Princeton: Princeton University Press.

Seeger, Anthony
  1981 *Nature and Society in Central Brazil: The Suya Indians of Mato
  Grasso.* Cambridge, MA: Harvard University Press.

Segall, M. H., D. T. Campbell, and M. J. Herskovits
  1966 *The Influence of Culture on Visual Perception.* Indianapolis: Bobbs-
  Merrill.

Sekuler, Robert, and Randolph Blake
  1994 *Perception,* 3rd ed. New York: McGraw-Hill, Inc.

Seremetakis, C. Nadia, ed.
  1994 *The Senses Still: Perception and Memory as Material Culture in
  Modernity.* Chicago: University of Chicago Press.

Shizuru, Lanette S., and Anthony J. Marsella
  1981 The Sensory Processes of Japanese-American and Caucasian-Ameri-
  can Students. *The Journal of Social Psychology* 114:147–158.

Shore, Bradd
  1996 *Culture in Mind: Cognition, Culture, and the Problem of Meaning.*
  New York: Oxford University Press.
  1997 Keeping the Conversation Going: An Interview with Jerome Bruner.
  Ethos 25(1):7–62.

Shweder, Richard A.
  1991 *Thinking through Cultures: Expeditions in Cultural Psychology.*
  Cambridge, MA: Harvard University Press.
  1993 The Cultural Psychology of the Emotions. In *Handbook of
  Emotions.* M. Lewis and J. Haviland, eds. Pp. 417–431. New York:
  Guilford Press.
  1996 True Ethnography: The Lore, the Law, the Lure. In *Ethnography and
  Human Development: Context and Meaning in Social Inquiry.*
  R. Jessor, A. Colby, R. A. Shweder, eds. Pp. 15–52. Chicago: University
  of Chicago Press.
  1997 The Surprise of Ethnography. *Ethos* 25(2):152–163.
  1999 Why Cultural Psychology? *Ethos* 27(1):62–73.

Shweder, Richard A., and Edmund J. Bourne
  1991 Does the Concept of the Person Vary Cross-Culturally? In *Thinking
  through Cultures,* R. Shweder, Pp. 113–155. Cambridge, MA: Harvard
  University Press.

Shweder, Richard A., J. Goodnow, G. Hatano, R. LeVine, H. Markus, and
P. Miller
  1998 The Cultural Psychology of Development: One Mind, Many Mentali-
  ties. In *Handbook of Child Psychology, Vol. 1: Theoretical Models of
  Human Development*. Richard M. Lerner, ed. Pp. 865–937. New York:
  John Wiley and Sons.

Stern, K., and M.K. McClintock
  1998 Regulation of Ovulation by Human Pheromones. *Nature,* March 12,
  1998: 177–179.

Stocking, George W., Jr.
  1968 *Race, Culture, and Evolution: Essays in the History of Anthropology.*
  New York: The Free Press.

Stoller, Paul
  1980 The Epistemology of Sorkotarey: Language, Metaphor, and Healing
  among the Songhay. *Ethos* 8(2):117–131.
  1984a Eye, Mind, and Word in Anthropology. *L'Homme* 24(3–4):91–114.
  1984b Sound in Songhay Cultural Experience. *American Ethnologist*
  11(3)559–570.
  1989a *Fusion of the Worlds: An Ethnography of Possession among the
  Songhay of Niger.* Chicago: University of Chicago Press.
  1989b *The Taste of Ethnographic Things: The Senses in Anthropology.*
  Philadelphia: University of Pennsylvania Press.
  1995 *Embodying Colonial Memories: Spirit Possession, Power, and the
  Hauka in West Africa.* New York: Routledge.
  1997 *Sensuous Scholarship.* Philadelphia: University of Pennsylvania Press.

Stoller, Paul, and Cheryl Olkes
  1987 *In Sorcery's Shadow.* Chicago: University of Chicago Press.

Strauss, Claudia, and Naomi Quinn
  1997 *A Cognitive Theory of Cultural Meaning.* New York: Cambridge
  University Press.

Synnott, Anthony
  1991 Puzzling over the Senses: From Plato to Marx. In *The Varieties of
  Sensory Experience.* D. Howes, ed. Pp. 61–76. Toronto: University of
  Toronto Press.
  1993 *The Body Social: Symbolism, Self, and Society.* London and New
  York: Routledge.

Taussig, Michael
  1993 *Mimesis and Alterity: A Particular History of the Senses.* London and
  New York: Routledge.

Thompson, Robert Farris
1966 An Aesthetic of the Cool: West African Dance. *African Forum* 2(2):85–102.
1974 *African Art in Motion*. Los Angeles: University of California Press.

Tibbetts, Paul, ed.
1969 *Perception: Selected Readings in Science and Phenomenology*. Chicago: Quadrangle Books.

Turner, Edith, with William Blodgett, Singleton Kahona, and Fideli Benwa
1992 *Experiencing Ritual: A New Interpretation of African Healing*. Philadelphia: University of Pennsylvania Press.

Turner, Terence S.
1980 The Social Skin. In *Not Work Alone: A Cross-Cultural View of Activities Superfluous to Survival*. Jeremy Cherfas and Roger Lewin, eds. Pp. 112–140. Beverly Hills: Sage Publications.

Turner, Victor
1967 *The Forest of Symbols*. Ithaca, NY: Cornell University Press.
1968 *The Drums of Affliction*. Oxford: Clarendon Press.
1974 *Dramas, Fields, and Metaphors*. Ithaca, NY: Cornell University Press.

Urban, Greg
1996 *Metaphysical Community: The Interplay of the Senses and the Intellect*. Austin: University of Texas Press.

Vermeer, Donald E.
1966 Geophagy among the Tiv of Nigeria. *Annals of the Association of American Geographers* 56(1):197–204.
1971 Geophagy among the Ewe of Ghana. *Ethnology* 10:56–72.

Vinge, Louise
1975 *The Five Senses: Studies in a Literary Tradition*. Lund, Sweden: Publications of the Royal Society of Letters.

von Beek, W. E. A.
1992 The Dirty Smith: Smell as a Social Frontier among the Kapsiki/Higi of North Cameroon and North-Eastern Nigeria. *Africa* 62(1):38–58.

Warburton, I., Prosper Kpotufe, and Roland Glover
1968 *Ewe Basic Course*. Bloomington: Indiana University African Studies Program.

Warwick, Kevin
2000 Cyborg 1.0: Kevin Warwick Outlines His Plan to Become One with His Computer. *Wired*, February 2000: 145–151.

Westermann, Diedrich
1930 *A Study of the Ewe Language*. A. L. Bickford-Smith, trans. London: Oxford University Press.

1973[1928] *Ewefiala or Ewe-English Dictionary.* Nendeln/Liechtenstein: Kraus-Thompson Organization, Ltd., Kraus Reprint. Original edition, Berlin: Dietrich Reimer/Ernst Vohsen.

1973[1930] *Gbesela Yeye or English-Ewe Dictionary.* Nendeln/Liechtenstein: Kraus-Thompson Organization, Ltd., Kraus Reprint. Original edition, Berlin: Dietrich Reimer/Ernst Vohsen.

Whiting, J. W. M., and I. L. Child

1953 *Child Training and Personality: A Cross-Cultural Study.* New Haven: Yale University Press.

Whorf, Benjamin Lee

1956 *Language, Thought, and Reality: Selected Writings of Benjamin Lee Whorf.* J. B. Carroll, ed. Cambridge, MA: MIT Press.

Winnicott, D. W.

1953 Transitional Objects and the Transitional Phenomena: A Study of the First Not-Me Possession. *International Journal of Psycho-Analysis* 34:89–97.

1971 *Playing and Reality.* London: Tavistock Publications.

Wober, Mallory

1966 Sensotypes. *The Journal of Social Psychology* 70:181–189.

1967 Adapting Witkin's Field Independence Theory to Accommodate New Information from Africa. *British Journal of Psychology* 58(1–2):29–38.

1975 *Psychology in Africa.* London: International African Institute.

Woolf, Henry B., ed.

1977 *Webster's New Collegiate Dictionary.* Springfield, MA: G. & C. Merriam Company.

Wudu, Frank

1989 *A Concise History of Ghana's Struggle for Independence, 1947–1957.* Accra: Catholic Press.

Yankah, Kwesi

1995 *Speaking for the Chief: Okyeame and the Politics of Akan Royal Oratory.* Bloomington: Indiana University Press.

Index

Compositor:	Impressions Book and Journal Services, Inc.
Text:	10/13 Sabon
Display:	Sabon
Printer and binder:	Malloy Lithographing, Inc.